the
ralph nader
reader

the
ralph nader
reader

foreword by
barbara
ehrenreich

SEVEN STORIES PRESS
New York · London · Sydney · Toronto

SEVEN STORIES PRESS
140 Watts Street
New York, NY 10013
www.sevenstories.com

IN CANADA
Hushion House, 36 Northline Road, Toronto, Ontario M4B 3E2

IN THE U.K.
Turnaround Publisher Services Ltd., Unit 3, Olympia Trading Estate,
Coburg Road, Wood Green, London N22 6TZ
In Australia: Tower Books, 9/19 Rodborough Road, Frenchs Forest
NSW 2086

LIBRARY OF CONGRESS CATALOGING-IN-PUBLICATION DATA
Nader, Ralph.
The Ralph Nader reader / Ralph Nader.
p.   cm.
ISBN 1-58322-046-1 — ISBN 1-58322-057-7 (pbk.)
1. Political participation—United States.   2. Public interest—United
States.   3. Consumer protection—United States.   I. Title: Reader.
II. Title.
JK1764.N33 2000
343.7307¢1¢092—dc21   00-030789

9 8 7 6 5 4 3

College professors may order examination copies of Seven Stories Press
titles for a free six-month trial period. To order, visit
www.sevenstories.com/textbook, or fax on school letterhead to (212)
226-1411

DESIGN BY POLLEN/Stewart Cauley
PRINTED IN THE U.S.A.

contents

on corporate welfare

on opposing the world trade organization (wto)

on consumer rights

on tort reform

on citizen action and social change

foreword

A S AMERICANS WE like to pride ourselves on being a culture of diversity and creativity and individualism. In fact, ours is increasingly a culture of acquiescence and obedience.

This is pretty obvious in the political part of our culture, where not only
is debate squelched within parties, but it's been almost eliminated between
the parties. Following the 2000 Republican Convention, the pundits all
agreed that it was so clever of George W. Bush to make the Republican
Party look more like the Democratic Party—you know, with all those
Latinos and black gospel choirs and talk about "compassion." Well, this was
no big trick; after all, Bill Clinton spent eight years making the Democratic
Party look more like the Republican Party—with welfare reform, Star Wars,
drug wars, and NAFTA. Naturally, the Republican Party looks like a
Democratic Party that looks like the Republican Party—what else is it going
to look like, Sharon Stone?

Leaving aside the political process (hey, everyone else does), let's look at
the media: Is there any debate and dissent in the media? FAIR (Fairness and
Accuracy in Reporting) does an excellent job of documenting the center-
right stranglehold over the media. I would just add one interesting confirmation from ABC evening news: It was around the time of the Seattle

demonstrations—a rare moment of visible dissent!—and ABC had a little teeny tiny feature on the Independent Media Center (IMC), where the ABC reporter observed in amazement that, thanks to the IMC, views could be expressed that would "never be allowed in the mainstream media." The cat was out of the bag.

Or moving along to the place where most people spend most of their time—the American workplace. Any debate or dissension allowed in the workplace? No, certainly not if you're part of the majority of workers who are not professionals or managers, but hourly workers. Some places don't allow workers to talk to each other about wages, a very subversive subject. Other places don't allow talking to other workers, period. And suppose you're fed up with wages that are, for a majority of American workers, lower now, in inflation-adjusted dollars, than they were in 1973, so you decide to take the good old American approach to self-improvement and form a union. Well, despite the very clear provisions of the National Labor Relations Act, about 10,000 workers every year get fired for doing just that.

Or look at our streets: You can get shot or beaten nearly to death for going outdoors while black. And if you're bold enough to actually protest in the streets, you can end up with a million dollar bail for committing a misdemeanor.

Now there's a sinister self-reinforcing quality to a culture of acquiescence and obedience. When you don't hear people talking back, when you don't see a lot of protest (or not enough, or what you do see doesn't make any sense when the media's done with it), you begin to believe that nothing can be done. That this is as good as it gets. Or as Margaret Thatcher once put it in the single word: T-I-N-A, Tina—There Is No Alternative. Acquiescence is infectious; conformity is contagious, and if everyone goes around saying TINA, then pretty soon TINA rules.

So we have to treasure the few notable and visible dissidents we have. It's not easy work, dissenting—you don't get much applause and certainly not much air-time, and there are always plenty of pundits around to label you a buffoon or a flake. But dissenting is what Ralph Nader has been doing full-time, year round, for roughly four decades now, without pulling a single punch. In fact, as you'll notice in these pages, he's gotten more radical over the years, not less—broader in his concerns and more holistic in his approach. He's a genuine American wonder, someone who still believes in democracy deeply enough to challenge the corporate powers that have taken it away from us. He's a role model, a pioneer, and maybe someday—if enough of us get bold enough to raise our voices in dissent—our president too.

on the presidency
and democracy

Statement of Ralph Nader, Announcing His Candidacy for the Green Party's Nomination for President

Originally delivered February 21, 2000, Washington, D.C.

TODAY I WISH to explain why, after working for years as a citizen advocate for consumers, workers, taxpayers and the environment, I am seeking the Green Party's nomination for President. A crisis of democracy in our country convinces me to take this action. Over the past twenty years, big business has increasingly dominated our political economy. This control by the corporate government over our political government is creating a widening "democracy gap." Active citizens are left shouting their concerns over a deep chasm between their government and themselves. This state of affairs is a world away from the legislative milestones in civil rights, the environment, and health and safety of workers and consumers seen in the sixties and seventies. At that time, informed and dedicated citizens powered their concerns through the channels of government to produce laws that bettered the lives of millions of Americans.

Today we face grave and growing societal problems in health care, education, labor, energy and the environment. These are problems for which active citizens have solutions, yet their voices are not carrying across the democracy gap. Citizen groups and individual thinkers have generated a tremendous capital of ideas, information, and solutions to the point of surplus, while our government has been drawn away from us by a corporate government. Our political leadership has been hijacked.

Citizen advocates have no other choice but to close the democracy gap by direct political means. Only effective national political leadership will restore the responsiveness of government to its citizenry. Truly progressive political movements do not just produce good results; they enable a flowering of progressive citizen movements to advance the quality of our neighborhoods and communities outside of politics.

I have a personal distaste for the trappings of modern politics, in which incumbents and candidates daily extol their own inflated virtues, paint complex issues with trivial brush strokes, and propose plans quickly generated by campaign consultants. But, I can no longer stomach the systemic political decay that has weakened our democracy. I can no longer watch people dedicate themselves to improving their country while their government leaders turn their backs, or worse, actively block fair treatment for citizens. It is necessary to launch a sustained effort to wrest control of our democracy from the corporate government and restore it to the political government under the control of citizens.

This campaign will challenge all Americans who are concerned with systemic imbalances of power and the undermining of our democracy, whether they consider themselves progressives, liberals, conservatives, or others. Presidential elections should be a time for deep discussions among the citizenry regarding the down-to-earth problems and injustices that are not addressed because of the gross power mismatch between the narrow vested interests and the public or common good.

The unconstrained behavior of big business is subordinating our democracy to the control of a corporate plutocracy that knows few self-imposed limits to the spread of its power to all sectors of our society. Moving on all fronts to advance narrow profit motives at the expense of civic values, large corporate lobbies and their law firms have produced a commanding, multi-faceted and powerful juggernaut. They flood public elections with cash, and they use their media conglomerates to exclude, divert, or propagandize. They brandish their willingness to close factories here and open them abroad if workers do not bend to their demands. By their control in Congress, they keep the federal cops off the corporate crime, fraud, and abuse beats. They imperiously demand and get a wide array of privileges and immunities: tax escapes, enormous corporate welfare subsidies, federal giveaways, and bailouts. They weaken the common law of torts in order to avoid their responsibility for injurious wrongdoing to innocent children, women and men.

Abuses of economic power are nothing new. Every major religion in the world has warned about societies allowing excessive influences of mercantile or commercial values. The profiteering motive is driven and single-minded. When unconstrained, it can override or erode community, health, safety, parental nurturing, due process, clean politics, and many other basic social values that hold together a society. Abraham Lincoln, Theodore Roosevelt, Franklin Roosevelt, Supreme Court Justices Louis Brandeis and William Douglas, among others, eloquently warned about what Thomas Jefferson called "the excesses of the monied interests" dominating people and their governments. The struggle between the forces of democracy and plutocracy has ebbed and flowed throughout our history. Each time the cycle of power has favored more democracy, our country has prospered ("a rising tide lifts all boats"). Each time the cycle of corporate plutocracy has lengthened, injustices and shortcomings proliferate.

In the sixties and seventies, for example, when the civil rights, consumer, environmental, and women's rights movements were in their ascendancy, there finally was a constructive responsiveness by government. Corporations, such as auto manufacturers, had to share more decision making with affected constituencies, both directly and through their public representatives and civil servants. Overall, our country has come out better, more tolerant, safer, and with greater opportunities. The earlier nineteenth century democratic struggles by abolitionists against slavery, by farmers against large oppressive railroads and banks, and later by new trade unionists against the brutal workplace conditions of the early industrial and mining era helped mightily to make America and its middle class what it is today. They demanded that economic power subside or be shared.

Democracy works, and a stronger democracy works better for reputable, competitive markets, equal opportunity and higher standards of living and justice. Generally, it brings out the best performances from people and from businesses.

A plutocracy—rule by the rich and powerful—on the other hand, obscures our historical quests for justice. Harnessing political power to corporate greed leaves us with a country that has far more problems than it deserves, while blocking ready solutions or improvements from being applied.

It is truly remarkable that for almost every widespread need or injustice in our country, there are citizens, civic groups, small and medium-sized businesses and farms that have shown how to meet these needs or end these injustices. However, all the innovative solutions in the world will accomplish little if the injustices they address or the problems they solve have been

shoved aside because plutocracy reigns and democracy wanes. For all optimistic Americans, when their issues are thus swept from the table, it
becomes civic mobilization time.

Consider the economy, which business commentators say could scarcely
be better. If, instead of corporate yardsticks, we use human yardsticks to measure the performance of the economy and go beyond the quantitative indices
of annual economic growth, structural deficiencies become readily evident.
The complete dominion of traditional yardsticks for measuring economic
prosperity masks not only these failures but also the inability of a weakened
democracy to address how and why a majority of Americans are not benefit-
ting from this prosperity in their daily lives. Despite record economic growth,
corporate profits, and stock market highs year after year, a stunning array of
deplorable conditions still prevails year after year. For example:

✣ A majority of workers are making less now, inflation adjusted, than
in 1979.

✣ Over 20% of children were growing up in poverty during the past
decade, by far the highest percentage among comparable western
countries.

✣ The minimum wage is lower today, inflation-adjusted, than
in 1979.

✣ American workers are working longer and longer hours—on average,
an additional 163 hours per year, compared to twenty years ago—with
less time for family and community.

✣ Many full-time family farms cannot make a living in a market of giant
buyer concentration and industrial agriculture.

✣ The public works (infrastructure) are crumbling, with decrepit
schools and clinics, library closings, antiquated mass transit
and more.

✣ Corporate welfare programs, paid for largely by middle-class taxpayers
and amounting to hundreds of billions of dollars per year, continue to
rise along with government giveaways of taxpayer assets such as public
forests, minerals and new medicines.

✣ Affordable housing needs are at record levels while secondary mortgage market companies show record profits.

✣ The number of Americans without health insurance grows
every year.

✢ There have been twenty-five straight years of growing foreign trade deficits ($270 billion in 1999).

✢ Consumer debt is at an all time high, totaling over $6 trillion.

✢ Personal bankruptcies are at a record level.

✢ Personal savings are dropping to record lows and personal assets are so low that Bill Gates' net worth is equal to that of the net assets of the poorest 120 million Americans combined.

✢ The tiny federal budgets for the public's health and safety continue to be grossly inadequate.

✢ Motor vehicle fuel efficiency averages are actually declining and, overall, energy conservation efforts have slowed, while renewable energy takes a back seat to fossil fuel and atomic power subsidies.

✢ Wealth inequality is greater than at any time since WWII. The top one percent of the wealthiest people have more financial wealth than the bottom 90% of Americans combined, the worst inequality among large western nations.

✢ Despite annual declines in total business liability costs, business lobbyists drive for more privileges and immunities for their wrongdoing.

It is permissible to ask, in the light of these astonishing shortcomings during a period of touted prosperity, what the state of our country would be should a recession or depression occur. One import of these contrasts is clear: economic growth has been decoupled from economic progress for many Americans. In the early 1970s, our economy split into two tiers. Whereas once economic growth broadly benefitted the majority, now the economy has become one wherein "a rising tide lifts all yachts," in the words of Jeff Gates, author of *The Ownership Solution*. Returns on capital outpaced returns on labor, and job insecurity increased for millions of seasoned workers. In the seventies, the top three hundred CEOs paid themselves forty times the entry-level wage in their companies. Now the average is over four hundred times.

This in an economy where impoverished assembly line workers suffering from carpal tunnel syndrome frantically process chickens which pass them in a continuous flow, where downsized white and blue collar employees are hired at lesser compensation, if they are lucky, where the focus of top business executives is no longer to provide a service that attracts customers, but rather to acquire customers through mergers and acquisitions. How long can the paper economy of speculation ignore its effects on the real economy of working families? Pluralistic democracy has enlarged markets and created the middle class. Yet the short-term monetized minds of the corporatists are bent on weakening, defeating, diluting, diminishing, circumventing, co-opting, or corrupting all traditional countervailing forces that have saved American corporate capitalism from itself.

Regulation of food, automobiles, banks and securities, for example, strengthened these markets along with protecting consumers and investors. Antitrust enforcement helped protect our country from monopoly capitalism and stimulated competition. Trade unions enfranchised workers and helped mightily to build the middle class for themselves, benefiting also non-union laborers. Producer and consumer cooperatives helped save the family farm, electrified rural areas, and offered another model of economic activity. Civil litigation—the right to have your day in court—helped deter producers of harmful products and brought them to some measure of justice. At the same time, the public learned about these hazards.

Public investment—from naval shipyards to Pentagon drug discoveries against infectious disease to public power authorities—provided yardsticks to measure the unwillingness of big business to change and respond to needs. Even under a rigged system, shareholder pressures on management sometimes have shaken complacency, wrongdoing, and mismanagement. Direct consumer remedies, including class actions, have given pause to crooked businesses and have stopped much of this unfair competition against honest businesses. Big business lobbies opposed all of this progress strenuously, but they lost and America gained. Ultimately, so did a chastened but myopic business community.

Now, these checkpoints face a relentless barrage from rampaging corporate titans assuming more control over elected officials, the workplace, the marketplace, technology, capital pools (including workers' pension trusts) and educational institutions. One clear sign of the reign of corporations over our government is that the key laws passed in the sixties and seventies that we use to curb corporate misbehavior would not even pass through Congressional committees today. Planning ahead, multinational corporations shaped the World Trade Organization's autocratic and secretive governing procedures so as to undermine non-trade health, safety, and other living standard laws and proposals in member countries.

Up against the corporate government, voters find themselves asked to choose between look-alike candidates from two parties vying to see who takes the marching orders from their campaign paymasters and their future employers. The money of vested interests nullifies genuine voter choice and trust. Our elections have been put out for auction to the highest bidder. Public elections must be publicly financed and it can be done with well-promoted voluntary checkoffs and free TV and radio time for ballot-qualified candidates.

Workers are disenfranchised more than any time since the 1920s. Many unions stagger under stagnant leadership and discouraged rank and file. Furthermore, weak labor laws obstruct new trade union organization and leave the economy with the lowest percentage of workers unionized in more than sixty years. Giant multinationals are pitting countries against one another and escaping national jurisdictions more and more. Under these circumstances, workers are entitled to stronger labor organizing laws and rights for their own protection in order to deal with highly organized corporations.

At a very low cost, government can help democratic solution building for a host of problems that citizens face, from consumer abuses, to environmental degradation. Government research and development generated whole new industries and company startups and created the Internet. At the least, our government can facilitate the voluntary banding together of interested citizens into democratic civic institutions, which can create more level playing fields in the banking, insurance, real estate, transportation, energy, health care, cable TV, educational, public services, and other sectors. Let's call this the flowering of a deep-rooted democratic society. A government that funnels your tax dollars to corporate welfare kings in the form of subsidies, bailouts, guarantees, and giveaways of valuable public assets can at least invest in promoting healthy democracy.

Taxpayers have little legal standing in the federal courts and little indirect voice in the assembling and disposition of taxpayer revenues. Closer scrutiny of these matters between elections is necessary. Facilities can be established to accomplish a closer oversight of taxpayer assets and how tax dollars (apart from social insurance) are allocated. This is an arena which is, at present, shaped heavily by corporations that, despite record profits, pay far less in taxes as a percent of the federal budget than in the 1950s and 60s.

The "democracy gap" in our politics and elections spells a deep sense of powerlessness by people who drop out, do not vote, or listlessly vote for the "least-worst" every four years, and then wonder why after another cycle the "least-worst" gets worse. It is time to fundamentally redress these imbalances of power. We need a deep initiatory democracy in the embrace of its citizens, a usable brace of democratic tools that brings the best out of people, highlights the humane ideas and practical ways

to raise and meet our expectations, and resolve our society's deficiencies and injustices.

A few illustrative questions can begin to raise our expectations and suggest what can be lost when the few and powerful hijack our democracy:

✴ Why can't the wealthiest nation in the world abolish the chronic
poverty of millions of working and non-working Americans, including
our children?

✴ Are we reversing the disinvestment in our distressed inner cities and
rural areas and using creatively some of the huge capital pools in the
economy to make these areas more livable, productive and safe?

✴ Are we able to end homelessness and wretched housing conditions
with modern materials, designs, and financing mechanisms, without
bank and insurance company red-lining, to meet the affordable housing needs of millions of Americans?

✴ Are we getting the best out of known ways to spread renewable, efficient energy throughout the land to save consumers money and to
head off global warming and other land-based environmental damage
from fossil fuels and atomic energy?

✴ Are we getting the best out of the many bright and public-spirited civil
servants who know how to improve governments but are rarely asked by
their politically-appointed superiors or members of Congress?

✴ Are we able to provide wide access to justice for all aggrieved people
so that we apply rigorously the admonition of Judge Learned Hand,
"If we are to keep our democracy, there must be one commandment:
Thou Shall Not Ration Justice"?

✴ Can we extend overseas the best examples of our country's democratic
processes and achievements instead of annually using billions in tax
dollars to subsidize corporate munitions exports, as Republican
Senator Mark Hatfield always used to decry?

✴ Can we stop the giveaways of our vast commonwealth assets and
become better stewards of the public lands, better investors of tril-
lions of dollars in worker pension monies, and allow broader access to
the public airwaves and other assets now owned by the people but
controlled by corporations?

✴ Can we counter the coarse and brazen commercial culture, including
television which daily highlights depravity and ignores the quiet civic

heroisms in its communities, a commercialism that insidiously exploits childhood and plasters its logos everywhere?

✦ Can we plan ahead as a society so we know our priorities and where we wish to go? Or do we continue to let global corporations remain astride the planet, corporatizing everything, from genes to education to the Internet to public institutions, in short, planning our futures in their image? If a robust civic culture does not shape the future, corporatism surely will.

To address these and other compelling challenges, we must build a powerful, self-renewing civil society that focuses on ample justice so we do not have to desperately bestow limited charity. Such a culture strengthens existing civic associations and facilitates the creation of others to watch the complexities and technologies of a new century. Building the future also means providing the youngest of citizens with citizen skills that they can use to improve their communities. This is the foundation of our campaign, to focus on active citizenship, to create fresh political movements that will displace the control of the Democratic and Republican Parties, two apparently distinct political entities that feed at the same corporate trough. They are, in fact, simply the two heads of one political duopoly: the DemRep Party. This duopoly does everything it can to obstruct the beginnings of new parties, including raising ballot access barriers, entrenching winner-take-all voting systems, and thwarting participation in debates at election times.

As befits its name, the Green Party, whose nomination I seek, stands for the regeneration of American politics. The new populism which the Green Party represents, involves motivated, informed voters who comprehend that "freedom is participation in power," to quote Cicero. When citizen participation flourishes, as this campaign will encourage it to do, human values can tame runaway commercial imperatives. The myopia of the short-term bottom line so often debases our democratic processes and our public and private domains. Putting human values first helps to make business responsible and to put government on the right track.

It is easy and true to say that this deep democracy campaign will be an uphill one. However, it is also true that widespread reform will not flourish without a fairer distribution of power for the key roles of voter, citizen, worker, taxpayer, and consumer. Comprehensive reform proposals from the corporate suites to the nation's streets, from the schools to the hospitals, from the preservation of small farm economies to the protection of privacies, from livable wages to sustainable environments, from more time for children to less time for commercialism, from waging peace and health to averting war and violence, from foreseeing and forestalling future troubles to journeying toward brighter horizons, will wither while power inequalities loom over us.

Why are campaigns just for candidates? I would like the American people to hear from individuals such as Edgar Cahn (Time Dollars for neighborhoods), Nicholas Johnson (television and telecommunications), Paul Hawken, Amory and Hunter Lovins (energy and resource conservation), Dee Hock (on chaordic organizations), James MacGregor Burns and John Gardner (on leadership), Richard Grossman (on the American history of corporate charters and personhood), Jeff Gates (on capital sharing), Robert Monks (on corporate accountability), Ray Anderson (on his company's pollution and recycling conversions), Johnnetta Cole, Troy Duster and Yolanda Moses (on race relations), Richard Duran (minority education), Lois Gibbs (on community mobilization against toxics), Robert McIntyre (on tax justice), Hazel Henderson (on redefining economic development), Barry Commoner and David Brower (on fundamental environmental regeneration), Wendell Berry (on the quality of living), Tony Mazzocchi (on a new agenda for labor), and Law Professor Richard Parker (on a constitutional popular manifesto). These individuals are a small sampling of many who have so much to say, but seldom get through the evermore entertainment-focused media. (Note: mention of these persons does not imply their support for this campaign.)

Our political campaign will highlight active and productive citizens who practice democracy often in the most difficult of situations. I intend to do this in the District of Columbia, whose citizens have no full-voting representation in Congress or other rights accorded to states. The scope of this campaign is also to engage as many volunteers as possible to help overcome ballot barriers and to get the vote out. In addition, it is designed to leave a momentum after election day for the various causes that committed people have worked so hard to further. For the Greens know that political parties need also to work between elections to make elections meaningful. The focus on fundamentals of broader distribution of power is the touchstone of this campaign. As Supreme Court Justice Louis Brandeis declared for the ages, "We can have a democratic society or we can have great concentrated wealth in the hands of a few. We cannot have both."

Thank you.

Perspective on the Presidential Race

A WAY OUT OF THE CORPORATIST GRIP

Originally appeared in The Los Angeles Times, *October 29, 1996.*

PRESIDENTIAL CAMPAIGNS occur overwhelmingly on television, in mostly empty, deceptive, 30-second advertisements that fuel public cynicism far more than they advance public enlightenment. Campaigns are now a "virtual reality" separated from real communities, real debates and real neighborhood organizing.

Predictably, this dreary daily repetition of the same slogans and buzzwords by increasingly look-alike major parties results in elections attracting a smaller percentage of voters to the polls here than any other Western country. More and more of these voters know they are choosing between the bad and the worse.

The central contention of electoral politics should be the proper distribution of power to maximize decisions on behalf of the general interest.

After a brief decade (1965–75) of consumer, environment and civil rights movements countervailing corporate power, the global companies consolidated their position and have since concentrated their influence over both political parties, our federal government, our economy and our very culture.

The reflection of this corporatist grip can be seen in what both Bill Clinton and Bob Dole, drawing on these commercial interests for cash and sustenance,

13

do not discuss or disagree on in their campaigns or their platforms. Neither has addressed pervasive corporate crime, bloated corporate welfare, genuine campaign finance reform, energy independence, universal health insurance, weakened civil liberties, collective bargaining and job safety laws for workers, the size of the military budget, housing, the corporate merger wave, GATT and NAFTA, and the nonenforcement of consumer, environmental and natural resource laws. Unfortunately, the very media that have reported frequently on these topics over the years fall right into the narrow agenda rut that has been dug by these politicians and their consultants.

Any politician who has been on the hustings knows that a unifying force among citizens of different backgrounds is their sense of having lost the ability to shape their future.

Voters find their votes being nullified by campaign money and, given the absence of a binding none-of-the-above ballot option, they cannot even register a no-confidence or protest vote.

Workers can scarcely organize trade unions, so weak are the laws, so strong the anti-union strategies of employers.

Consumers' access to the courts is being destroyed by the twin corporate-backed drives of tort reform and compulsory arbitration.

Taxpayers have virtually no legal standing in federal courts to challenge the corporate/government complex of waste, fraud and abuse of their monies. Nor do they have much influence regarding how their monies are allocated and used in the federal budget (which is why they are receptive to politicians promising tax rate deductions).

As for savers and investors, no more need be said than to mention the massive bailouts imposed on these people as taxpayers for the S&L debacle and other financial crimes and speculation.

The challenge to citizens in the polling booth is to choose leaders who will strengthen the tools of democracy for these roles that individuals play in our political economy. These tools will deconcentrate power and greatly enhance an informed community intelligence with which to solve or reduce our national problems.

Throughout our history, each time concentrated power was challenged by a strengthened democracy of citizens, America became a better, more just society. Whether by the abolitionist movement, the women's suffrage drive, the farmer populist reforms, the trade union initiatives and the more recent efforts on behalf of consumer, environmental, disabled people's and women's rights, the expansion of the power of the many vis-a-vis the domination of the few raised our society to new levels of human possibilities.

When people go to the polls next Tuesday, their vote should reach beyond helping a landslide candidate or choosing between Tweedledee-Tweedledum politics-as-usual offerings. Votes can be cast to build political futures to encourage more Americans to join progressive politics and to broaden the public agenda.

Presidential and other political campaigns should be of, by, and for the people if the resultant governance is to adhere to those same accountabilities. This means working at democracy with our time and talents long before election day.

This much is certain: If millions of Americans continue to turn off politics, politics will continue to turn on them, to the detriment of their standards of living, justice and freedom.

The Greens & the Presidency

A VOICE, NOT AN ECHO

Originally appeared in The Nation, *July 8, 1996.*

As of this writing, Ralph Nader is on the ballot as a candidate for President in Alaska, California, Colorado, Hawaii, Maine, New Mexico and Oregon. Organizers connected with "Third Parties '96" and the Greens say they are circulating petitions in at least thirty other states.

—The Nation *Editors*

THE TWO-PARTY DUOPOLY—essentially one corporate party with two heads called Republican and Democratic, each wearing different makeup—presents the citizenry every four years with a choice between the Bad and the Worse. And every four years, both the Bad and the Worse get worse because there is no counterpull to the corporate, right-wing pull. So the Bill Clintons, the Chris Dodds and the Al Froms (head of the so-called Democratic Leadership Council) are further corporatizing the Democratic Party while signaling to progressives that they have nowhere else to go.

A little over a year ago, at a television studio, Jerry Jasinowski, president of the National Association of Manufacturers, told me that the NAM liked Clinton because he fought for their issues (such as NAFTA and GATT) and did not push for organized labor's issues (such as labor-law reform).

What an understatement! Clinton's political philosophy is "protective imitation." He is determined to reduce to a minimum the ability of Dole/Gingrich to turn his right flank. This frustrates Republicans because they know that after Clinton recovered the governorship of Arkansas in 1982, he behaved as if he would never again lose an election because of principles.

On the big economic issues of fiscal policy (including public works), corporate crime, corporate welfare and corporate abuse of consumers and workers, Clinton is a RepDem hybrid. He has no consumer policy; his environmental policy is largely rhetoric and accommodation (note his obeisance to the nuclear power and timber industries, and to the auto industry on fuel economy). The federal regulatory agencies' behavior under Clinton (e.g., banking, the Federal Aviation Administration, auto safety, railroad and job safety) is either indistinguishable from their performance under his Republican predecessors or worse. About the only bright spot is the Food and Drug Administration's anti-tobacco campaign. The agency is still weak on food safety, however. Its commissioner, David Kessler, was appointed by George Bush.

Clinton's business-indentured motif went into high gear with his surrender to the Republican-fashioned telecommunications bill that so delighted the oligopolists and autocrats. To make sure that the Federal Communications Commission doesn't reverse its anticonsumer positions, Clinton undermined his own chairman, Reed Hundt, by appointing two other commissioners with pro-industry leanings, thus depriving the frustrated Hundt of a working majority. Other major Clinton nominations— to the Supreme Court, the Treasury Department and the omnipotent Federal Reserve—are all Wall Street–approved.

On foreign affairs, military budgets and policy, record tax-subsidized arms exports and serious global health issues, the President is an unwavering transition from George Bush. Like Bush, Clinton cannot make himself speak out against fast-growing brutalized child labor abroad, which GATT protects. Nor will he confront on human rights grounds global corporations that coddle dictatorships, thus encouraging the contagious corporate criminality that arises from those alliances.

The defiantly deteriorating national Democratic Party, stripped of any grass-roots engagement, obligated to corporate moneys and personnel, and chaired by the Senator from Aetna (Dodd), refuses to recognize the need for a comprehensive pro-labor agenda, leaving a supportive A.F.L.-C.I.O. as supplicant with nowhere to go.

The Democratic Party, as *Nation* readers will no doubt point out, is cling-
ing to a dwindling difference from the Republicans. But the differences in
practice are much smaller than the differences in rhetoric. The choices for
voters are exceedingly narrow and getting narrower; on the fundamental
power issue of corporate government taking over the political government,
the two parties are in a mutual kowtow. The differences are largely lodged
in the distribution of social services. But look who is defining the agenda
here and who is on the defensive to the degree that he cannot even stand
tall for children and other defenseless Americans. Didn't Clinton just
endorse Governor Tommy Thompson's welfare plan in Wisconsin, which
child-defender and former Clinton ally Marian Wright Edelman finds so
cruel to youngsters?

In no area is Clinton's protective imitation strategy more transpar-
ently expedient, given his background as a constitutional law teacher,
than in his erosions of civil liberties protections. Columnists Anthony
Lewis and Nat Hentoff have strongly criticized the President for eagerly supporting and signing Republican bills that weaken the "great writ"
of habeas corpus and seriously endanger other civil liberties of Americans
and legal residents.

When it comes to strengthening our democracy by providing organizing
and other tools for labor, consumers and shareholders, by expanding access
to justice, by protecting the health and safety rights of consumers in the
marketplace and by applying regular law and order to the rich and powerful [see Nader, "How Clinton Can Build Democracy," November 30, 1992],
Clinton has taken a pass. He has never been serious about campaign finance
reform, while sending very serious letters to the affluent, offering them a
seat at his dinner table for a $100,000 contribution. He did veto, after mad-
dening indecision, a "tort deform" bill and a securities fraud bill that would
have restricted the judicial rights of injured and defrauded people. The latter, which consumer groups called the "crooks and swindlers protection act,"
was vetoed in such a timid context that Clinton enabled his own party chairman, Senator Dodd, to lead the override of his veto.

This aversion to challenging abuses of concentrated power, coupled with
the mentality of protective imitation, made Clinton and his party very good
at electing very bad Republicans in 1994. About seventy of the cruelest
rogues who ever crawled up Capitol Hill took over the House of
Representatives for Gingrich because the well-funded Democratic Party
had no identity and progressive agenda to defeat even this extreme wing of
the opposition party.

It is one thing for progressive Democrats to be shunted aside on issue after issue by the Dodd-Clintonites; it is more deeply disturbing to realize that these corporate Democrats have lost control of Congress and their chief hope in getting it back rests on how extremist their opponents become.

Raising expectation levels to get political parties moving away from a competition between the Bad versus the Worse toward the Good versus the Better requires a civic dynamic that is incompatible with accepting the status quo. External competition is necessary to break up the two-party duopoly, either to produce really different political parties or lead to political realignments toward multiparty evolutions.

Last fall, several leading California environmentalists asked if I would agree to their placing my name on the Green Party ballot for President. Reflecting on how corporatized government is rapidly shutting out civic participation, I agreed, but said I would not accept any campaign contributions or run in a traditional manner. I've been criticized by some for choosing to go about matters in this way, but my goal is to encourage a campaign dependent on self-reliant citizen muscle at the grass roots, not some guy on a horse. This is one test, certainly for people in the Green Party and other progressives, of whether they are going to step up their mobilization. In some states, the Greens are already forming parties as a result, and they are taking a long-range view of their initiatives.

In the near term there is a need for a modest-sized party that is rooted in progressive communities, agendas and energies, and that (1) focuses on new and stronger tools of democracy for voters, workers, consumers and taxpayers; (2) breaks through the DemRep taboos against debating the supremacy of global corporations over our political, economic, educational, media and cultural institutions; and (3) brings into progressive politics a young generation of Americans.

There is no patent on these agendas; they are available to all candidates for their campaigns. Instead of telling progressives they have nowhere to go, Clinton could reduce the numbers who stay home on Election Day and open up a corporate critique of Dole. This he is unlikely to do. It is up to him. Nobody but Clinton can beat Clinton. He is too unprincipled to lose to Dole, who anyway cannot reinvent himself.

Many Americans who call themselves liberals have so lowered their expectations about what politics can mean to this nation's future that they are settling for diminishing returns. Politics has been corrupted not just by money but by being trivialized out of addressing the great, enduring issues of who controls, who decides, who owns, who pays, who has a voice and access, and why solutions available on the shelf are not applied to the existing and looming crises of our society, both local and global.

One thing politicians do understand is rejection. When voters are deciding how they wish to use their vote, they should ask themselves how best to send a clear message. The Greens and other progressives are in the early building stages of a people-first, democratic political movement for future years. They deserve our attention because they are centering on the basic issues of representative government, one of whose purposes is to strengthen the usable tools of democracy; the other, in Thomas Jefferson's prophetic words, is "to curb the excesses of the monied interests."

Democratic Revolution in an Age of Autocracy

Originally appeared in Boston Review, *March/April 1993.*

THE CLINTON ADMINISTRATION says it has big plans for "funda-mental change" in the way our government and economy work. Change was certainly the mandate of the 1992 election, and the Clinton people have already set out some ambitious plans (keeping in mind, of course, that virtually any pres-idential leadership seems bold after four years of the Bush administration).

But is fundamental change achievable?

What neither Clinton, nor his Cabinet, nor most other Democratic Party proponents of change seem to realize is that significant, enduring change will require an institutionalized shift of power from corpora-tions and government to ordinary Americans. While politicians have now made an art of populist symbolism, virtually none have a serious agenda to strengthen Americans in their key roles as voters, taxpayers, consumers, workers, and shareholders.

To deliver on his promise for change, President Clinton must adopt a more fundamental priority: the rejuvenation of the democratic culture of this nation through specific institutional reforms. It is, after all, the failure of our "civic infrastructure"—not simple fate or isolated mistakes—that is the root of many of our intractable national problems. If civic standards got the television airtime of Morris the Cat and associates, the savings and loan scandal would have never occurred: outraged citizens would have intervened long before it became a $500 billion scandal.

Thomas Jefferson said that "a little rebellion now and then" might be a good thing. He was right, and we need such a rebellion now: a democratic revolution that will reinvent and rediscover democracy. All sorts of latent energies are waiting to be tapped. But they will never be released by simple exhortations to "good citizenship," or by celebrating the values of civic engagement, praising a thousand points of light, and hosting quadrennial candidate forums.

Instead, reinventing democracy requires that we create new tools of empowerment: new mechanisms of civic communication, political organization, government assistance, and legal rights that can advance the distinct interests of citizens, taxpayers, consumers, workers and shareholders. These structural and procedural reforms will help to foster a new "fifth estate" of individual Americans, capable of acting independently from entrenched institutional—that is, chiefly corporate and governmental—power. Pursuing new forms of joint action, we can reclaim our government from the oligarchy that has made it a caricature of the Jeffersonian vision and overcome the sense of powerlessness, alienation, and fatalism that threaten to erode the commitment to democracy itself.

Here, then, is the North Star of a democratic revolution: reassert democratic principles by giving the ideal of self-government new and creative applications in everyday life. What follows are ten urgent, practical empowerment strategies that will help to advance the democratic promise by reclaiming democracy and checking corporate power.

Reclaiming Democracy

FACILITATE VOTER INITIATIVES

The 1992 campaigns dramatically illustrated the depth of voter disillusionment with politics as usual and the deep yearning of ordinary Americans to participate in the democratic process. Unfortunately, except for a few media-driven vehicles such as call-in talk shows and candidate forums (which, significantly, were convened by candidates, not by voters), citizens have few opportunities to take the initiative in bringing issues to public attention.

One of the best tools for breaking this logjam is the voter initiative—the process by which citizens may enact or reject laws directly through the voting booth rather than through elected officials. The process is simple: citizens gather a specified number of signatures on petitions. An initiative then appears on the ballot, and is enacted or rejected by popular vote. Through this initiative process citizens can propose new laws, state constitutional amendments, or city or county charter amendments.

Citizen initiatives are an important democratic remedy for unresponsive state legislators or city officials. Without initiatives, self-government all too often means only giving voters a choice of electing the lesser of two evils. With the initiative process, voters can control specific policies of government, and even change its structure. Frequently, just filing an initiative petition inspires legislators to pay attention to a citizen or community campaign. Government becomes more responsive. Political power cannot be so easily monopolized by a few influential officials. New and often crucial items can be put on the political agenda. And citizens, reacting to direct democracy, are more likely to participate in civic life.

Any politician who is serious about rejuvenating our democratic traditions must promote the use of the initiative process. Where initiatives are not now permitted—at the national level and in some states—this means changing the rules that prevent them. Congress, by majority vote of both houses, could create a non-binding national initiative process or mandate national advisory referendums on any subject at any time. This act alone would send a powerful message to the American public: that democratic principles are indeed valued; that citizen-driven participation is important in our public life; and that legislators are willing to be directly responsive to the public will.

REFORM OUR CORRUPT CAMPAIGN FINANCE SYSTEM

It is now a well-accepted fact that our system for financing presidential and congressional campaigns is fundamentally corrupt and pernicious. The only way to ensure effective and honest representation by lawmakers is through decisive campaign finance reform, with public funding of campaigns.

An important first step in the campaign to limit the impact of money in politics was taken in February. A major coalition of three hundred citizen organizations launched a massive "Clean Up Washington" campaign, announcing its own 800 number to marshal citizen support (800-847—6611). The object of the campaign is overall spending limits for congressional races, a reduction in the limits on P.A.C. and individual contributions, a ban on "soft money" contributions (which are channeled through political parties), and the elimination of special tax breaks for lobbying. By loosening the grip of entrenched interests, these reforms promise to unleash other new possibilities for the culture of citizenship.

SET TERM LIMITS FOR MEMBERS OF CONGRESS

Few issues have so galvanized spontaneous citizen action as the idea of term limits. The chief value of such limits is their ability to liberate new energy for political elections. A fresh crop of candidates can emerge—and win— and more citizens can become excited recruits to electoral campaigns. Because incumbents typically have a hammerlock on re-election, ordinary citizens who used to participate actively in campaigns have largely given up. They reasonably say, "Why bother? How could I possibly make a difference? There's no chance that a challenger-candidate could possibly unseat a well-funded lifetime politician."

Limiting terms to twelve years changes this equation. Congressional elections matter again. New blood enters the democratic process. Diversity of representation is enhanced. Legislators can be elected who have energy and determination, who are not burnt-out or bought off. Newcomers will generally be closer to their constituents than the career politicians of Washington. Their arrival can help end the reign of the ruling cliques, whose entrenched power is such a potent barrier to progressive change.

Opponents of term limitations warn that inexperienced citizen legislators will be at the mercy of special-interest lobbyists and that the voters will lose the experience and wisdom of career lawmakers. This argument is not convincing, given what the established "experience and wisdom" has accomplished in Washington. There were a lot of amateurs in Philadelphia 200 years ago; they didn't do too badly. Constitutional objections may be more formidable. Some experts argue that congressional term limits require a constitutional amendment, and not simply legislation in individual states. This was the method used to limit presidential terms in 1951. At the very least, however, it is clear that the states can limit the terms of state officials. Twenty-three states already limit the number of terms that their governors can serve.

Members of Congress are not likely to approve a constitutional amendment limiting their own terms. So attention must turn to ways to compel Congress to act. The twenty-two states with the initiative/referendum process—where voters have direct access to the ballot box—will have a head start in organizing term limit campaigns. These states account for nearly half of the House of Representatives, and forty-four of the nation's one hundred senators. A state-by-state blitz of term limitation initiatives will create tremendous national momentum to limit Congressional terms, even in the twenty-eight non-initiative states. In those states, citizens must demand that their legislators vote for term limits, or that the question be placed on the ballot for the public to make its voice heard.

EXPAND CITIZEN STANDING RIGHTS

What can be done when government itself becomes lawless, flouting the very Constitution and congressional laws that it is duty-bound to uphold? This is one of the most important yet neglected problems of self-governance of our time.

Historically, one important tool for citizens and taxpayers has been a broad right of legal standing—a right to gain access to the courts to sue the government and challenge its arbitrary and capricious actions, its failure to enforce existing laws, and its illegal behavior. The Supreme Court recognized the importance of broad taxpayer and citizen standing in a series of decisions in the 1960s and early 1970s. They upheld, for example, the standing of taxpayers to challenge expenditures of tax revenues that were alleged to violate the Establishment Clause of the First Amendment, and the standing of ordinary users of the environment to challenge the legality of environmentally harmful government regulations even though the interest of the particular plaintiffs was generalized and diffuse.

Unfortunately, since the mid-1970s the Supreme Court has reversed this tradition, and developed an increasingly restrictive law of standing. Narrowing citizen access, the Court has transformed the law of standing into a smoke screen that masks and sanctions many governmental misdeeds. The Court has refused, for example, to grant standing to taxpayers who were challenging government spending alleged to violate the Establishment Clause, or to taxpayers arguing that secret C.I.A. funding violated the Constitution's requirement of a public accounting of public expenditures. These changes in effect license government officials to violate the law whenever it is expedient for them to do so, because no one, except perhaps an attorney general, will ever be able to hold them accountable in court.

This is no way to promote official compliance with law or citizen confidence in the operation of government. If public confidence in the legitimacy of government is to be restored, Congress must immediately enact remedial legislation that gives taxpayers and citizens broad standing to sue government. Such a reform would be a virtually cost-free way to improve the quality and responsiveness of government operations. It would also send a strong message that our nation is indeed governed by law and not by the arbitrary caprice of political officials or government bureaucrats.

REGAIN CONTROL OVER "TAXPAYER ASSETS"

On behalf of the American people, the U.S. government owns and manages a wide variety of taxpayer assets: national forests, grazing lands, mineral deposits, power projects, information resources, research and development rights, broadcast frequencies, among others. The Reagan and Bush administrations boasted of their intention to run government "like a business"—before proceeding to host a massive fire sale of taxpayer assets to assorted corporate interests. Here, too, citizens and taxpayers must be empowered to stop the widespread abuses of government stewardship of publicly owned assets.

The federal government has historically funded about half of all U.S. expenditures on research and development (R&D)—some $74 billion in fiscal year 1992. Over the past twelve years, the allocation of property rights in these research projects has dramatically changed. Before Reagan/Bush, the government generally sought to have research products enter the public domain, or to patent its inventions or license them on a non-exclusive basis. Exclusive licenses were used, but only sparingly, and often for limited terms. After 1980, however, a series of statutes, rules, and policy memoranda sanctioned a broad use of exclusive licenses. In effect, taxpayers invest billions of dollars in R&D every year—and then the returns on these investments are privatized.

One of the more egregious abuses of taxpayer assets involves azidothymidine (AZT), the A.I.D.S. treatment developed chiefly through government grants. Despite the government's development funding, Burroughs Wellcome later gained monopoly rights to the drug, initially charging $10,000 ($3,000 today) to A.I.D.S. patients, many of whom have no health insurance.

This same pattern is replicated in the government's stewardship of federal information resources, many of which are available through electronic means. The U.S. Government is the largest publisher of information in the world. Yet the government has raised prices sharply for these taxpayer-sponsored information resources; has given them away to private vendors who sell the identical materials at inflated prices; and has eliminated many publications altogether, effectively barring public access to government information and policy.

One partial solution that deserves immediate congressional action is pending legislation that would require the Government Printing Office to set up a one-stop-shopping program for on-line access to hundreds of federal databases. The service would be free to 1,400 federal depository libraries, and would be available to everyone else through subscriptions priced at the relatively low "incremental cost of dissemination."

Another way to help taxpayers defend public assets against waste and abuse is to create a taxpayer watchdog group, in the form of a set-aside program, as a requirement for all uses of taxpayer assets. This money—say one or two percent of a given subsidy—would finance ongoing citizen oversight of private use of taxpayer assets. Like other accountability mechanisms, this expenditure could be one of the most cost-effective ways for the government to prevent waste and abuse of public assets.

The government does seem newly receptive to such ideas. Interior Secretary Bruce Babbitt recently announced for example, that the U.S. Government will no longer charge nominal fees for grazing rights, mineral rights and other private exploitation of federal lands. Instead, taxpayers will begin to receive market rates, and that will encourage private users to treat these resources more responsibly. Whether President Clinton will be able to overcome the cattle, farming and mining interests is, of course, another matter—which is precisely why democratic reforms are so vital.

RECLAIM THE PUBLIC AIRWAVES

The privatization of the broadcast airwaves—one of our most important taxpayer assets—has caused serious deformations of our politics and culture. The basic problem is that private broadcasters control what the public owns. In return for free licenses to use taxpayer property, broadcasters give us a steady stream of increasingly coarse, redundant, superficial programming and, of course, exclusively decide who says what on our public airwaves.

The result is that there is no place to hold a public discussion. Ordinary citizens can speak to their neighbors, but they cannot speak to millions of their fellow Americans without paying a giant toll and obtaining the permission of large corporations. The grotesque paradox is that a First Amendment originally intended to empower citizens for self-government is now being used to shield business entities, who control the major channels of communication and have little interest in using them as public fora.

To give the audience access to the airwaves that it already owns, Congress should create a new broadcast vehicle, the *Audience Network*. A national, nonprofit, nonpartisan membership organization, Audience Network would be granted one hour of prime-time television and one hour of drive-time radio on every commercial channel each day. It would function as a separate licensee, airing diverse programming shaped by the membership, which would be open to all citizens over age sixteen for a nominal fee (say, $10 annually). In addition, Audience Network would represent consumer interests before the Federal Communications Commission (FCC), Congress, and the courts. This would redress the long-standing disenfranchisement that millions of viewers and listeners have suffered under the current regulatory regime.

The Audience Network would be democratically controlled. The Network and its professional staff would be managed by persons accountable to the membership through a direct elective process. Besides membership fees, it could lease some airtime back to stations or networks. This would help assure the Network's financial security, and allow it to avoid paid advertisements. During its time slot, the Audience Network could air a variety of cultural, political, entertainment, scientific or other programs that it produced or obtained. Freed from the constraints of corporate advertisers, the Audience Network would air major abuses which are not publicized for years by the commercial media.

Over time, Audience Network would transform a powerless, voiceless audience, conditioned to a debased regime of programming, into an active audience with the ability to initiate innovative and consequential programming and reforms. Its open programming by diverse non-commercial groups would greatly invigorate the civic marketplace of ideas—a signal challenge for our times

Checking Corporate Power

CREATE SHAREHOLDER DEMOCRACY

Corporate democracy has been an illusion for nearly one hundred years—which has not of course deterred business executives and the New York Stock Exchange from annually proclaiming its vitality. What is the scope of management power and what are the checks upon it? In nearly every large American business corporation, one person or a small coterie of executives have unquestioned operational control. In theory, this small group of managers serves as an agent of the board of directors; in reality, it is just the reverse. The chief executive or executive clique chooses the board, and, with its acquiescence, controls the corporation.

The legal basis for such a consolidation of power is the proxy election—what British law professor L.C.B. Gower calls "this solemn farce." Given the nearly insuperable barriers faced by insurgents challenging management, it is no surprise that the board of directors has ceased to perform its statutory function of "managing the business and affairs of every corporation." Indeed, it is often hard to tell whether the boards of many corporations perform any independent function at all. "Directors," William O. Douglas complained as early as 1934, "do not direct." Management control has overwhelmed the rule of law.

Such autocratic corporate governance imposes serious economic and social costs—in terms of self-dealing, inefficiency, and illegality. Even Business Week now concludes, "So much of this trouble for America's corporate titans [General Motors, IBM, Westinghouse, American Express] might have been avoided had the same parochial perspectives not clouded the judgment of many outside directors. They simply failed in their duties." Many institutional shareholders such as the California State Employees Pension Fund, newly aware of the long-term economic costs of unaccountable managements, have mounted campaigns to oust lackluster management teams. This is a step in the right direction, but the impulse needs to be taken much further.

What is needed is a Corporate Democracy Act to give all stakeholders in corporate decision-making a real voice in corporate governance. Redesigning the rights and obligations of shareholders, boards of directors, and executives can make giant companies both more efficient and law-abiding. Critical to this task is installation of full-time outside directors selected by beneficial owners in elections entirely funded by the company. To short-circuit wasteful competition among states to woo corporate investment—by sanctioning unfair labor practices, pollution, and wasteful subsidies—federal chartering of corporations with minimum national standards are essential. Moreover, victims of corporate malfeasance—workers, consumers, local communities, shareholders, and small businessmen—should be accorded greater access to the court system to redress their complaints (see point 9 below for more details).

Adding together all the social costs of our baroque, ineffectual sham of corporate governance, it becomes clear that corporate autocracy is not conducive to a prudent, productive economy—nor to socially benign corporate behavior. But this will not change until corporations begin to abide by minimal national standards of business responsibility and shareholders are empowered to gain greater access to reliable corporate information, participate in fair elections for board seats, and exercise meaningful oversight of management.

ESTABLISH A NEW MODEL OF CONSUMER REPRESENTATION

Mancur Olson, in his excellent book, *The Logic of Collective Action,* asks, "Why is it that throughout history large numbers of people are preyed upon by small numbers of people? What is it about the victim class that makes it incapable of asserting itself?"

One answer is that the "victim class" has great difficulty in bringing itself together, as a group. If only because of sheer numbers, it typically lacks organizational means for asserting its collective will or developing a common identity and culture. This dynamic is played out in dozens of milieus in our political economy. For example, sellers—who are consummately capable of organizing themselves to protect their interests—develop myriad means to exploit buyers—who have preciously few means of organizing themselves. Public interest groups can help, but they often cannot provide a consistent presence that is technically competent, financially stable, and directly accountable to consumers.

The 1980s saw the emergence of a promising new solution to this classic problem. The Citizens' Utility Board, or CUB, is a model approach for bringing together large numbers of diffuse consumers into a voluntary organization, which can then pursue a common citizen/consumer agenda in banking, insurance, housing or dozens of other arenas. It is the "silicon chip" for the citizen movement because it is a low-cost, high versatility, powerfully effective device.

How does a CUB work? Typically, residential consumers lack the organization, resources, or expertise to respond to utility arguments on such matters as rate-setting and safety. CUB offers an ingenious way to provide effective citizen representation. By authority of state legislatures, a CUB is given the right to enclose notices inside certain company and state mailings to invite the public to become voluntary members of the CUB for a modest annual fee of $5 to $10. CUB pays for this enclosure. This "piggybacking" on state mailings provides a convenient, effective way for the CUB to organize a membership and to communicate with it, and a basis for self-sufficiency and financial accountability.

All members of the CUB have the right to vote in the election of the CUB Board of Directors. This process ensures that the leadership of CUB reflects the interests of the ratepayer. The Directors serve without pay and hire full-time staff of accountants, attorneys, economists, organizers, and lobbyists. The staff can intervene, for example, in rate proceedings; advocate before the legislature; research issues of concern to consumers; survey public opinion on energy and telecommunications issues; analyze the way the utilities are handling complaints; and provide information and assistance to consumers interested in conserving energy.

Illinois CUB, for example, attracts tens of thousands of members and has blocked literally billions of dollars in gratuitous rate hikes. It would be easy to apply the CUB idea to organizations like the Social Security Administration, the Veterans Administration and the U.S. Postal Service. Big mailers (magazine publishers and the direct-mail industry) routinely use lobbyists and trade associations to advance their interests in postal commission rate hearings. Don't residential mailers deserve their own independent voice?

The beauty of the CUB concept is that, as a voluntary group, it costs taxpayers virtually nothing. It is anti-bureaucratic because no new government personnel or procedures are needed. It enhances civic participation because the CUB depends for its success on the energy and vision of its members. It counters the massive inequities of power that afflicts consumers in their dealings with government and business.

PROTECT VICTIMS' RIGHTS

Another constituency of individuals that is increasingly impotent is the innocent victims of dangerous products, unsafe workplaces, toxic waste, and other hazards. In recent years, insurance companies, manufacturers, and other corporate interests have waged a massive campaign to roll back the legal rights of plaintiffs to obtain full compensation for their injuries. In one of the most unprincipled public relations scams in the history of American industry, this coalition has pursued a draconian package of changes that it calls "tort reform." Among other things, the proposals seek to place arbitrary caps on "pain and suffering" awards; eliminate punitive damage awards (often the only effective deterrent against intentionally unsafe practices); impose mandatory limits on plaintiff lawyers' contingency fees (without setting any corresponding limits on fees for defense lawyers), eliminate strict liability (one of the most effective deterrents against unsafe products and workplaces); and restrict the role of both judge and jury.

The coalition's fundamental message is that the jury system is out of control because the common law and jury awards are so unpredictable.

Claiming a ruinous "litigation explosion," insurance companies dislike the jury system because they cannot precisely budget damage awards as a cost of doing business. But this unpredictability is the very essence of deterrence—a function of the civil justice system which is just as important as compensation and which, like the system's other social benefits, cannot be precisely quantified in dollars and cents.

A citizen empowerment agenda must deal with the structural problems of the insurance industry. Congress should repeal the industry's exemption from antitrust laws, federal regulation and Federal Trade Commission scrutiny. A cycle of surge-and-decline of cash flow almost every decade has precipitated the bogus "insurance crisis." Congress should also establish a federal office of insurance to monitor the industry and establish standards for state regulators to follow. Voter Revolt, a California-based citizen group, broke important new ground by mobilizing broad-based support for Proposition 103—an initiative measure that reformed the property-casualty insurance industry in California and rolled back excessive insurance rates.

At the state level, insurance companies must be required to disclose routinely how much they take in on premiums and investment income, and how much they pay out in verdicts and settlements (plus reserves and other expenditures). State insurance departments need more authority and funding, and consumers need greater consumer representation before insurance regulatory bodies. Insurers should be required to engage in greater loss prevention efforts, and to disclose evidence of known defective products or hazardous conditions to appropriate law enforcement and regulatory authorities. And, CUB style insurance-consumer organizations should be established to enable consumers to grapple with this powerful industry.

Eroding basic victims' rights will not stop premium-gouging and policy cancellations. Only effective insurance reforms will stop the cyclical insurance crisis which leads to the volcanic eruptions of premiums and contracted coverage.

ENSURE A HOSPITABLE ENVIRONMENT FOR WHISTLE BLOWING
Alfred North Whitehead wrote, "Duty arises from our potential control over the course of events." Since the early 1970s, this insight has given rise to the ethics of whistle blowing—the lone individual of conscience within a corporate or governmental organization who sees wrong and tries to right it, often at great personal risk.

Society has an acute interest in fostering a more muscular whistle blowing ethic. Corporate and government employees are among the first to know about fraud and corruption, industrial dumping of toxics into waterways, defectively designed automobiles, or undisclosed adverse effects of prescription drugs and pesticides. They are the first to understand how to prevent existing hazards. But they are very often the last to speak out.

There is a great need now to extend the reach of this ethic into such organizations as corporate and governmental bureaucracies. But the ethic will only flourish in these settings if employees have the right to due process within their organizations, and if rights now used to protect people from state power—for example, the right to speak freely—are expanded into protections from corporations and comparable bureaucratic powers. Large corporations should have a bill of rights for their employees and a system of internal appeals to guarantee these rights. Unions and professional societies should strengthen their ethical codes. The courts, professional and citizen groups, the media, the Congress, and other sectors of society must actively work to prevent the trammeling of a fortified conscience within their midst.

If carefully defined and protected by law, whistle blowing can become another of those adaptive, self-implementing mechanisms which distinguish a free society, which empower people to govern themselves instead of being subordinated to autocratic controls.

Conclusion

The tools for democracy have fairly common characteristics. They are universally accessible; they provide instruments of self-funded voluntary community action; they can make government deliver, and have constructive effects on other areas of policy. Without a reconstruction of our democracy in order to ensure facilities for informed civic participation to all citizens, no ambitious program of political and economic change will succeed. Nor can worries about poverty, discrimination, joblessness, the troubled conditions of education, environment, street and suite crime, budget deficits, costly and inadequate health care, and energy boondoggles be addressed in a constructive and enduring way. These facilities are the magnets for the genuine exercise of rights, remedies, and responsibilities.

So it is time for a civic rebellion, Jefferson style.

Breaking Out of The Two-Party Rut

Originally appeared in The Nation, *July 20/27, 1992.*

A NTHROPOLOGISTS MIGHT call it a "cultural rut." Every four years, presidential campaigns fall into a predictable pattern of a two-party duopoly, occasionally livened by unique gaffes. The candidates select themselves, develop a fat-cat funding base, perfect a standard speech with practiced cadences and then toss their hat into the ring. Such candidate-side politics coalesce around the contenders, the handlers, the pollsters, the funders and the media reps who plunge right into the rut.

The candidates move out to formulaic meetings, audiences and photo opportunities. Except for already scheduled meetings by groups for their own purposes, the gatherings are sparse in the early months of primary season and are nothing to boast about as the primaries draw near. Candidates, by and large, engage in a parade before the people; rarely do they run with the people. Those who depart from this routine usually do so because they are way behind in the polls and in resources. These two handicaps assure that such detours receive little media attention and thereby gain little momentum.

Meanwhile, the voters' politics remain frustrated, simmering with angry alienation, painful powerlessness and cyclical cynicism. What's needed is a citizen-side politics. The civic vacuum of electoral politics comes from the people's low expectations of politicians and even lower expectations of their own role in the pre-election period. Voters are supposed to listen to the candidates' speeches, look at their TV spots, size up their personality or character on a hunch, then go to the polls and choose among candidates whom the power structure itself usually views as Tweedledee and Tweedledum.

In this year's presidential primary, no more than one out of five eligible voters (registered and unregistered) bothered to go to the polls. The vast silent majority stayed home and tuned out. Neither Jerry Brown's "We the People" campaign, with his pioneering 800 number and pledge to accept no contribution over $100, nor the increasing resort to radio and television talk-show appearances changed the democracy dropout rate. Indeed, turnouts in most states sank to record lows.

I ventured into the cultural rut in late November in New Hampshire, where I asked voters to write in my name on their ballots, not as a candidate for elective office but as an advocate for a reform agenda. To voters, who were not persuaded by any of the candidates on the ballot, the write-in campaign offered three choices other than staying home: registering a symbolic "none of the above" vote; endorsing a new democracy "tool box" called the Concord Principles, unveiled during the campaign; and supporting a citizens' movement that would campaign on the people's side of the electoral fence by denying the regular candidates their vote and affirming numerous basic reforms.

There was one additional purpose to this deployment of the primary process. Unlike the ballot candidates, who the day after the primary leave nothing behind but a closed storefront with torn posters and crumpled Coke cans on the floor, this write-in campaign was intended to leave in place a full-time citizen reform organization that would continue the drive for the Concord Principles. New Hampshirites are forming such a group now.

What ensued was a three-month pilot experiment in citizen-side politics, assisted by a small number of enthusiastic advocates and volunteers. I spent about three weeks in the state, clearly distinguishing this effort as an agenda campaign, not a campaign for elective office. Nonetheless, the audiences in November, December and January were far larger than those for the candidates on the ballot. The people who came stayed for two or three hours, leaving as much time for discussion as for speeches.

The focus of these "town meetings" was that the central purpose of electoral politics should be the proper distribution of power. The widespread recognition among Americans that there is too much power and too much of other people's money in too few unaccountable hands simply did not resonate with the major presidential candidates of both parties, except for Jerry Brown (and a few dark-horse entrants in New Hampshire). The taboo of the primary campaign was Big Business's domination of the nation's political economy from Washington to Wall Street to Main Street. The unmentionables included: corporate welfare, reckless deregulation, corporate crime, corporate buying of politicians, multinational corporate erosion of our national sovereignty, corporate munitions trade, corporatist education, corporate-dominated media and corporate environmental destruction.

The media went along with this taboo. Absorbed in calling the horse race and psychoanalyzing the candidates, the national reporters showed no interest in abuses of corporate power. Can you recall any reporter asking a candidate about his position on the contemporary corporate crime wave in America, as regularly chronicled by *The Wall Street Journal* outside its indentured editorial pages? Even their questions about health insurance avoided ever so deftly the corporate predators who have built a profitable, cost-plus, heavily tax-subsidized, over-billing industry into both a bureaucratic and fiscal nightmare.

The imbalance of power between the people and the plutocracy results in the misuse of economic resources, the curtailment of the electorate's voice, the private taking of public assets owned by taxpayers, the exploitation of consumers, the trashing of America's posterity and the reign of corporate-commercial values over our society. If a democratic society is to have any meaning, it must go beyond policies and encompass adequate instruments of civic action.

Enter the Concord Principles, which we announced on the steps of the State Capitol building in Concord, New Hampshire, on February 2. This new democracy agenda strengthens the five major roles that people play in the public arena—as voters, taxpayers, consumers, workers and shareholders. These roles are now anemic. They pit underdeveloped eighteenth- and nineteenth-century rights against near-twenty-first-century oligarchic power structures. The people need modern power tools to insure democratic procedures and results. The power tools that make up the numerous reforms embodied in the Concord Principles facilitate the acquisition of timely information, instruments for citizen-to-citizen communication and the people's ability to mobilize for democratic action. These tools would be available to all citizens, would be used voluntarily and would not cost the taxpayers any money.

Voter tools include a binding none-of-the-above option on the ballot, which would trigger a new election if it received the largest number of votes;

term limitations of twelve years; public financing of campaigns through well-publicized taxpayer checkoffs; easier voter registration and ballot-access rules; binding initiative, referendum and recall authority in all fifty states and a nonbinding national referendum procedure.

For taxpayers, a standing to sue the federal government (a right that has been nearly nullified by federal judges) is granted. A simple checkoff would appear on every 1040 tax return, inviting taxpayers to join a national action group dealing with tax reform, management of taxpayers' assets and government purchasing policies. The staff of advocates would be chosen by a board, which would itself be elected by contributing members. Such a national action group would counteract the demands of organized business groups.

For consumers, the principle of reciprocity is introduced. As long as they are confronted by legal monopolies, such as utilities, or by industries, such as banks and insurance companies, with bailout rights and other regulatory protections, they would receive notices in their bills or statements inviting them to join fully staffed advocacy groups. This is how the successful Illinois Citizen Utility Board started; it now has 150,000 dues-paying members and has saved utility consumers more than $3 billion since 1983, in addition to other results. To affirm the principle that information is the common currency of democracy, there must be a complete overhaul of consumer access to government information and databases. A new audience television and radio network, whose studios would provide one hour of prime- and drive-time programming on every licensed station, would be set up. It would be controlled by viewer and listener members in accordance with the principle that the airwaves, which we legally own together as Americans, should be more effectively controlled by and for the owners' direct benefit.

Controlling what we own means establishing effective mechanisms that enable workers to shape the investment policies for the $3 trillion in pensions they own and to insist on fundamental worker rights in the invested companies. It means giving shareholders the power to curb company executives, who now can fatten their own compensation packages while laying off employees, closing plants and destroying worker morale. It means giving depositors more control over their savings in banks that redline the very areas where these depositors live. It means giving citizens more say in the disposition of the public lands now controlled by mining, timber, energy and other corporations through their proxies in Washington. It means, in short, establishing the facilities for community intelligence needed to make democracy a daily reality.

During the Reagan-Bush years, citizen access to justice—to the courts, to government agencies and to legislatures—has been narrowing once again to the benefit of organized vested interests, who effectively use these remedies to control the government while citizens are shut out. This phenomenon needs to be reversed structurally to reduce the economic and legal barriers to entry.

Preparing the next generation of Americans to understand and use these power tools of democracy requires the introduction of an engrossing civics curriculum into the schools. If all middle school and high school students were given the opportunity to engage in practical civic experiences in their communities, the sinews of a democratic society would be strengthened. For democracy is not just a matter of rights; it is a matter of giving people the facilities, the instruments and the experience to realize these rights. Politicians, liberal as well as conservative, seriously neglect or openly reject the development and refurbishing of these instruments. Even when proposals are brought to their attention, they turn their backs. Fewer than ten of the fifty-two members of the House Banking Committee supported an amendment to the $158 billion S&L bailout legislation in 1989 that would have required sending out invitations to all bank customers to voluntarily join a self-funded, statewide consumer action group. Such staffed community-based groups would have prevented the S&L scandal at its inception.

Hearings last year on the Audience Network proposal before Representative Edward Markey's House Telecommunications and Finance Subcommittee found no consistent House champion. This June, John Dingell's House Energy and Commerce Committee voted down a proposal to require rate-gouging monopoly cable companies to carry a notice inviting subscribers to organize to represent their interests.

The Concord Principles became a litmus test of sorts for the voters, the media and the candidates. I have no doubt that the New Hampshire electorate would have voted for them in overwhelming numbers in a referendum. Indeed, my write-in votes came from a few more Republicans than Democrats, reflecting the bipartisan support for the Concord Principles and just about reflecting the turnout of the parties in the primary.

The local media found the principles interesting enough to report, despite their space and time limitations. They were more responsive to discussing the issues raised than were the national media, which focus on candidate-side politics and almost totally ignore citizen-side politics—unless citizens shout down or disrupt a candidate's speech or meeting.

As for the candidates, although the Concord Principles were sent to them through a variety of channels, only Jerry Brown and Larry Agran acknowledged receipt and endorsed them. The others—Bush, Buchanan,

Clinton, Harkin, Kerrey and Tsongas—ignored them completely, despite approaches by numerous citizens to their staffs or to some of the candidates directly on the hustings. Ross Perot, whose candidacy may yet bulldoze the cultural rut into new furrows, welcomed a copy of the principles in late May, and is reviewing them.

Brown, however, has given them the most persistent backing. In his critique of the draft Democratic Party platform in mid-June, he urged the writers to consider seriously many of the Concord proposals. However, unless there is an organized effort by the Brown delegates at the convention, the party bosses are unlikely to admit that without these and other civic tools bolstering them, the most well-intentioned politicians cannot deliver, if elected. To the politicians, "gridlock" means they do not control both branches of government. To citizens, who are worried about the nation's many problems, "gridlock" means the absence of usable tools to make the rulers serve the ruled.

In future elections, citizens must set agendas, summon the candidates to their forums and send them more than a message. We must send them a movement! In a small way, our experience in New Hampshire and later in Massachusetts confirms that a larger effort in future contests could switch the pre-election dynamic from candidate-side to citizen-side campaigns. It could end the feeble, marble-mouthed, two-party politics that have turned off so many Americans, and result in a strengthened democracy.

The Concord Principles

AN AGENDA FOR A NEW INITIATORY DEMOCRACY

February 1, 1992

WHEREAS, a selfish oligarchy has produced economic decline, the debasement of politics, and the exclusion of citizens from the strengthening of their democracy and political economy;

Whereas, this rule of the self-serving few over the Nation's business and politics has concentrated power, money, greed, and corruption far beyond the control or accountability of citizens;

Whereas, the political system, regardless of Party, has degenerated into a government of the power brokers, by the power brokers, and for the power brokers that is an arrogant and distant caricature of Jeffersonian democracy;

Whereas, Presidential campaigns have become narrow, shallow, redundant, and frantic parades and horseraces which candidates, their monetary backers, and their handlers control unilaterally, with the citizenry expected to be the bystanders and compliant voters;

Whereas, a pervading sense of powerlessness, denial, and revulsion is sweeping the Nation's citizens as they endure or suffer from growing inequities, injustice, and loss of control over their future and the future of their children; and

Whereas, we, the citizens of the United States, who are dedicated to the reassertion of fundamental democratic principles and their application to the practical, daily events in our Nation, are committed to begin the work of shaping the substance of Presidential campaigns and of engaging the candidates attention to our citizen agendas during this 1992 election year;

Now, therefore, we hereby present the ensuing *Concord Principles* to the Presidential candidates for the 1992 election and invite their written, consistent, and continual adherence to these principles during their entire campaign and in whatever public offices and responsibilities they hold or may hold upon cessation of their campaigns:

First, democracy is more than a bundle of rights on paper; democracy must also embrace usable facilities that empower all citizens
  a) to obtain timely, accurate information from their government;
  b) to communicate such information and their judgments to one another through modern technology; and
  c) to band together in civic associations as voters, taxpayers, consumers, workers, shareholders, students, and as whole human beings in pursuit of a prosperous, just and free society.

Second, the separation of *ownership* of major societal assets from their *control* permits the concentration of power over such assets in the hands of the few who control rather than in the hands of the many who own. The owners of the public lands, pension funds, savings accounts, and the public airwaves are the American people, who have essentially little or no control over their pooled assets or their commonwealth.

The American people should assume reasonable control over the assets they have legally owned for many years so that their use reflects citizen priorities for a prosperous America, mindful of the needs and rights of present *and* future generations of Americans to pursue happiness within benign environments.

Third, a growing and grave imbalance between the often converging power of Big Business, Big Government and the citizens of this country has seriously damaged our democracy and weakened our ability to correct this imbalance. We lack the mechanisms of civic power. We need a modern tool box for redeeming our democracy by strengthening our capacity for self-government and self-reliance both as individuals and as a community of citizens. Our 18th century democratic rights need re-tooling for the proper exercise of our responsibilities as citizens in the 21st century.

Fourth, the new democracy tool box contains measures for the purpose of protecting voters from having their voting powers diluted, over-run or nullified. These measures are:

    a) a binding none-of-the-above option on the ballot;

    b) term limitations—12 years and out;

    c) public financing of campaigns through well-promoted voluntary taxpayer checkoffs on tax returns;

    d) easier voter registration and ballot access rules;

    e) state-level binding initiative, referendum, and recall authority, a non-binding national referendum procedure; and

    f) a repeal of the runaway White House/Congressional Pay Raises back to 1988 levels—a necessary dose of humility to the politicians.

Fifth, the new democracy tool box strengthens taxpayers who wish to have a say in how their tax dollars are being used and how their taxpayer assets are being protected. These objectives will be advanced by according taxpayers full legal standing to challenge in the courts the waste, fraud, and abuse of tax monies and taxpayer assets. Presently, the federal judiciary places nearly insurmountable obstacles in front of taxpayers, thereby leaving the task to the unlikely prospect of government officials taking their own government to court.

Further, a facility for taxpayers banding together can be established by a simple taxpayer checkoff on the 1040 tax return, inviting taxpayers to join their national taxpayers association which would be accountable to members on a one member-one vote standard.

Finally, obscure overly complex, mystifying jargon pervading federal tax, pension, election and other laws and procedures is a barrier to taxpayer-citizen participation. The language of these laws and procedures must be simplified and clarified as a matter of national priority; otherwise, only special interests hiring decoders will be able to participate while the general public is shut out.

Sixth, the new democracy tool box strengthens consumers of both business and government services by according them:

a) computerized access in libraries and their own homes to the full range
of government information for which they have already paid but are
now unable to obtain, either inexpensively or at all;

b) facilities in the form of periodic inserts, included in the billing or
other envelopes sent to them by companies that are either legal
monopolies (for example, electric, gas, telephone utilities) or are subsidized or subsidizable by the taxpayers (for example, banks and savings and loans). These inserts invite consumers to join their own
statewide consumer action group to act as a watchdog, to negotiate
and to advocate for their interests.

A model of this facility is the Illinois Citizen Utility Board which has
saved ratepayers over $3 billion since 1983, and filled the consumer chair
before utility commissions, legislative hearings, and courtroom proceedings
on many occasions.

This type of facility costs taxpayers nothing, costs the carrying companies or government mailings nothing (the consumer group pays for the
insert and there is no extra postage) and is voluntary for consumers to join.
Had there been such bank consumer associations with full-time staff in the
1970s, there would not have been a trillion dollar bailout on the taxpayer's
back for the S&L and commercial bank crimes, speculations, and mismanagement debacles. These would have been nipped in the bud at the community level by informed, organized consumer judgement. So too would
have costly and hazardous energy projects been replaced by energy efficiency and renewable power systems; and

c) Citizen consumers are the viewers and listeners of television and
radio. Federal law says that the public owns the public airwaves which
are now leased for free by the Federal Communications Commission
to television and radio companies. The public, whose only option is to
switch dials or turn off, deserves its own Audience Network.

The Audience Network would enhance the communication and
mobilization process between people locally and nationally. The owners
of the airwaves deserve a return of their property for one hour prime
time and drive time on all licensed stations so that their professional studios, producers, and reporters can program what the audience believes
is important to them and their children. The proposal for Audience
Network, funded by dues from the audience-members and other non-

tax revenues, was the subject of a Congressional hearing in 1991, chaired by Congressman Edward Markey.

Similarly, in return for cable company monopoly and other powers, cable subscribers should be able to join their own cable viewers' group through a periodic insert in their monthly cable billing envelopes. Modern electronic communications can play a critical role in anticipating and resolving costly national problems when their owners gain regular usage, as a community intelligence, to inform, alert, and mobilize democratic citizen initiatives. Presently, these electronic broadcasting systems are overwhelmingly used for entertainment, advertising and redundant news, certainly not a fair reflection of what a serious society needs to communicate in a complex age, locally, nationally, and globally.

> d) Access to justice—to the courts, to government agencies, and to legis-
> latures—is available to organized special interests, and they widely use
> these remedies. In contrast, when consumers are defrauded, injured,
> rendered sick by wrongdoers or other perpetrators of their harm, they
> find costly dollar and legal hurdles blocking their right of access. They
> also find indentured politicians and their lobbying allies bent on clos-
> ing the doors further. Systems of justice are to be used conveniently
> and efficiently by all the people in this country, not just corporations
> and the wealthy. Otherwise, the citizen shutout worsens.

Seventh, the new democracy tool box for working people contains rights of bringing one's conscience to work without having to risk being unfairly fired or demoted. Ethical whistle-blowers have alerted Americans to numerous abuses in the workplace that damage workers health and safety, contaminate the environment, and defraud consumers, taxpayers, and shareholders. However, they often pay the penalty with loss of their jobs. The exercise of conscience needs simple, effective legal protections which will build inside the corporation, government, or other large bureaucracies the incentives for care, prudence, and accountability that foresee or forestall larger harms.

Eighth, working people, who own over $3 trillion in pension monies, need a reasonable measure of control over where these monies are invested. Presently, a handful of banks and insurance companies control and make these decisions. During the 1980s the use of pension monies for corporate mergers, acquisitions, leveraged buyouts and other empire-building maneu-vers showed what does happen when ownership is so separated from control. Control by the few often left economic wreckage behind in many communities, and such capital draining takeovers did not produce employment or new wealth.

Pension monies are gigantic capital pools that can be used productively to meet community needs, but not when their owners are excluded from any organized participation or even the right to know and review what has been decided.

Ninth, the new democracy tool box applies to recognizing shareholder democracy as well. Whether large, small or institutional shareholders (such as pension or other trust funds), the separation of ownership (of the company) from control has been documented impressively, starting with the celebrated study by Berle and Means fifty years ago. The business press is filled with reports of executives of large corporations repeatedly abusing shareholder assets and worker morale with huge salaries, bonuses, greenmail, and golden parachutes (untied to company performance), self-perpetuating boards of directors, the stifling of the proxy voting system and blocking other shareholder voting reforms such as cumulative voting powers and access to relevant shareholder lists and information. The owners of corporations should be able to prevent their hired executives from engaging in what Business Week called casino capitalism that often ends with mass layoffs, loyal shareholder losses and communities undermined.

Tenth, the new democracy tool box needs to be taught in its historic context and present relevance as part of an engrossing civic curriculum for our country's schoolchildren. Involving all students during their later elementary and secondary school education in practical civics experience so as to develop both their citizen skills and the desire to use them, under the rule of law, can enrich schools, students, and communities alike. Where teachers have made such efforts, the children have responded responsibly and excitedly to the frequent surprise and respect of their elders. Schooling for informed and experienced participation in democratic processes is a major reservoir of future democracy and a profound human resource to be nurtured.

In conclusion, these tools for democracy have fairly common characteristics. They are universally accessible, can reduce government and other deficits, and are voluntary to use or band together around. It matters not whether people are Republicans, Democrats, or Independents. It matters only that Americans desire to secure and use these facilities or tools.

Without this reconstruction of our democracy through such facilities for informed civic participation, as noted above, even the most well-intentioned politicians campaigning for your vote cannot deliver, if elected. Nor can your worries about poverty, discrimination, joblessness, the troubled condition of education, environment, street and suite crime, budget deficits, costly and inadequate health care, and energy boondoggles, to list a few, be addressed constructively and enduringly. Developing these democratic tools to strengthen citizens in their distinct roles as voters, taxpayers, consumers, workers, shareholders, and students should be very high on the list of any candidate's commitments to you. Unless, that is, they just want your vote, but would rather not have you looking over their shoulder from a position of knowledge, strength and wisdom.

Knowledge Helps Citizens,
Secrecy Helps Bureaucrats

Originally appeared in The New Statesman, *January 10, 1986.*

I F THIS YEAR marks the 75th anniversary of Britain's Official Secrets Act, which is little reason for celebrating, it is also the 20th anniversary of the Freedom of Information Act (FOIA) in the United States—and that is something to cheer.

For many years, U.S. agencies were allowed to withhold government documents from the public, if officials decided that secrecy was 'in the public interest.' That vague standard, administered as in the United Kingdom today by the bureaucracy to prevent embarrassing disclosures, cast a cloak of secrecy over many government operations.

In 1966, Congress decided to change the presumption of secrecy and to limit the agencies' discretion to withhold records. Specifically, Congress voted to make all records of federal agencies (Congress and the Judiciary are exempt) available to any person upon request, unless the documents fell within a specific exemption from disclosure (e.g., classified records, trade secrets, sensitive law enforcement records, matters invading personal privacy). This right is not only available to U.S. citizens, but to persons of any nationality.

Congress's hope that this law would usher in a new era of 'government in the open' went unrequited, however, as agencies became more creative in their efforts to evade disclosure of their records. In 1974, in the wake of the Watergate scandal and public dissatisfactions with government cover-ups, Congress amended the FOIA to deal with this problem. Specifically, it restricted the types of reference that can be automatically witheld from disclosure and it streamlined procedures which agencies must follow in processing requests for information.

These amendments were largely successful and recalcitrance by agencies in this area has generally been eroded. Despite some occasional foot dragging, agencies now recognise that the Freedom of Information Act is a fact of life and that the public is entitled to know what the Federal Government is up to. (If the government denies a FOIA request, citizens have recourse to the courts. If the denial is not justifiable, government must pay the challenger's legal fees. This encourages citizens to make use of the FOIA and diminishes the government's incentive to drag out litigation against individuals who lack resources.)

Journalists and citizens' groups routinely use the FOIA to uncover examples of government waste and abuse, as well as unsafe products which are on the market. To take but a few examples:

✢ A consumer group used the Act to uncover the evidence of serious defects in certain steel-belted radial tires. These disclosures helped prompt the U.S. Department of Transportation to recall 10 million tires.

✢ Some investigative journalists discovered that not all the billions being spent on national defense are for that purpose. Instead, they learned that the U.S. Navy was using federal funds to make admirals more comfortable on their destroyers to the tune of spending $14,000 on a sofa and $41,000 to carpet a wardroom, at a cost of $93 per square yard. These disclosures and others prompted a Senate sub-committee to investigate the matter, after which the navy spelled out critieria for furnishings and announced a settlement with the contractor regarding overcharges, which may save U.S. taxpayers as much as $170 million all told.

✢ A separate investigation by Common Cause, a citizens' group, found that the Pentagon was rubber stamping requests by military contractors to pay for the costs they incurred providing military officials and Congressional personnel with parties, shooting trips, rides on corporate jets and yachts, and free football tickets.

As the manufacturers saw it, these were simply 'costs of doing business' that had to be included in the price of missiles, tanks and other weapons they were selling to the Pentagon. They also sought to have the Defense Department pay for their costs in lobbying Congress for the orders for the weapons systems they would be granted. Following publication of a story outlining these practices, Defense Secretary Caspar Weinberger asked Pentagon officials to clamp down on this practice, a move which can save taxpayers millions of dollars in future years.

✢ The Better Government Association, another citizens' group, used the FOIA to reveal that a major meatpacking company in Colorado had violated numerous rules designed to protect beef from contamination. What made this company especially significant was that it was supplying twenty-four percent of the ground beef purchased for use in the Federal program that provides subsidized lunches to school children. After the story appeared, the Secretary of Agriculture impounded the 6.5 million pounds of ground beef in Federal warehouses and suspended the company from bidding for new school lunch contracts.

✢ Another investigation disclosed that Thomas Reed, one of President Reagan's top security advisors, had been engaging in questionable securities trading practices. Information obtained from the Securities and Exchange Commission, which regulates stock exchanges, showed that Reed had fabricated data and signed other people's names to forms required by his brokerage house to carry out 'insider trading'. Shortly after reports about his activities became public, he resigned.

✢ In 1983, the Public Citizen Health Research Group, a consumer group, used the FOIA to uncover evidence that Oraflex, a purported wonder drug for treating arthritis, had been rushed onto the U.S. market, even though the manufacturer knew that dozens of Oraflex patients had died in Britain where the drug was first licensed. Following these and other disclosures, the manufacturer withdrew the drug from the market.

These examples are just the tip of the iceberg, in the sense that disclosures prompted almost immediate reform. While not every revelation leads to change, the FOIA is used extensively by journalists and has been the basis of literally hundreds of news stories over the past decade. The value of these disclosures in terms of improved public awareness of how government is functioning is incalcuable.

One of the biggest beneficiaries of the FOIA, though, is neither the press nor the average citizen, but the corporate community. Businesses routinely make use of the FOIA to find out what the government is planning and to keep track of information that has been submitted to agencies by their competitors. At last count, more than 60 percent of all FOIA requests are made by corporations, an indication of how widespread the benefits of the Act have been.

The success of the FOIA inevitably raises the question of whether the Act can be exported to other countries. The answer is 'yes'. Recently, Canada adopted its own version of the Freedom of Information Act that covers Cabinet departments. While journalists and historians in Canada have complained that too much information is still 'off limits', the Canadian law is still a first step in the right direction—and provides powerful support for adoption of a similar law in the United Kingdom.

One of the principal arguments made against adopting a FOIA in Canada was that it would not work because the United States has a clear division between Congress and the Executive Branch of government, whereas the distinctions are not as clear in a Parliamentary system. The Canadian experience should help to dispel that myth. While it is true that Canadian law is overly deferential to the bureaucracy, it does suggest that such a system could be successfully employed in Britain.

Such a reform ought to commend itself to the present British government—though there seems little prospect of that. Although many of the FOIA's initial supporters in Congress were political liberals, the Act can be viewed ideologically as a 'Tory reform.' Political conservatives in both Britain and the United States claim that they are mistrustful of centralized national government and support efforts to limit its scope and power.

What they fail to realize, however, is that *knowledge* is power and that secrecy is one of the principal tools which an unresponsive bureacracy can use to perpetuate its existence and its way of doing business, regardless of what reforms are being demanded by the public and elected officials.

A Freedom of Information Act helps to expose more clearly what government is doing on a day-to-day basis, thus promoting public understanding of what programs are and are not working, what abuses are taking place, and what changes are needed.

One of the strengths of a democracy is that it trusts its citizens to make intelligent choices about how they should live and be governed. But knowledge is necessary in order to make such intelligent choices and openness in government helps to achieve that end. Information is the currency of democracy.

For most of this century, Britain has lived with an Official Secrets Act, which gives the national government the power to punish the disclosure of information which it regards as damaging. But the presumption needs to be reversed. Instead of an Official Secrets Act, is it not now the time for an Official Disclosure Act?

on the corporate state
and the corporatizing
of america

Why Microsoft Must Be Stopped

BY RALPH NADER AND JAMES LOVE

Originally appeared in ComputerWorld *magazine, November 9, 1998.*

E VERYONE WHO USES a computer or depends on computers has an interest in seeing Microsoft's anticompetitive and anticonsumer practices curtailed by antitrust authorities. Microsoft's claim that it's defending its right to innovate is a cruel joke in an industry that sees its best innovators attacked by the company's anticompetitive actions. Microsoft's agenda isn't innovation, it's imitation, as well as the imposition of suffocating control over user choices and an ever-widening monopoly.

If the government can't curtail Microsoft's anticompetitive conduct in the browser market, the company gets the green light to become even bolder elsewhere. And for Microsoft, elsewhere is just about everywhere. It isn't only the browser market, it's virtually any mass-market software application, all server products, programming languages and the growing fields of electronic commerce, multimedia publishing and Internet navigation.

Companies spend enormous resources anticipating and responding to Microsoft's use of restrictive contracts, strategically shifting standards, manipulation of product compatibility and other forms of monopolistic warfare. That detracts from efforts to innovate or improve existing products. The victims of Microsoft's monopolistic activities aren't just the companies that go belly-up; they are the consumers who pay high prices to use mediocre and unreliable products.

Microsoft's public relations machine has tried to paint the antitrust laws as outdated and irrelevant in the fast-paced computer industry. But antitrust laws were created in response to the new technologies of the industrial revolution, and they have been a factor in each new wave of technology. We still embrace the Bill of Rights, which is much older than the antitrust laws. What's critical for antitrust enforcement is to find remedies that address the sources of anticompetitive conduct and are appropriate for an industry with short product cycles, changing product definitions and production innovations.

If there are criticisms of the legal case against Microsoft, they are that it was initially too narrow and that the government has been slow to suggest remedies for Microsoft's conduct. In the 1995 agreement between the Justice Department and Microsoft, the government settled for minimalist and ineffective remedies that didn't address major sources of Microsoft's power. Fortunately, antitrust authorities can avail themselves of a plethora of remedies for Microsoft's anticompetitive conduct. Even in the area of anticompetitive conduct, Microsoft is mainly an imitator.

Drawing from past antitrust actions in the computer, software and other industries, the government could require Microsoft to make the following concessions to fair business: divestitures; nondiscriminatory sharing of APIs and other technical information, such as data file formats; "Chinese walls" between the developers of operating systems and applications; nondiscriminatory licensing; and required support for or noninterference with nonproprietary Internet protocols. Ultimately, the industry will benefit from more diversity and less monopoly.

We need to build on the lessons from the Internet and stop Microsoft's efforts to transform the Internet into a private network dominated by a single, ruthless company.

U.S. Companies Should Pledge Allegiance

Originally appeared in The Washington Times, *Tuesday, June 4, 1996.*

THIS IS THE TIME for annual shareholder meetings for many of the nation's largest corporations. This is the time when the owner-shareholders, who attend these meetings to ask questions, see once again how shabbily they are treated by the CEOs and presidents of these companies and their rubber-stamp boards of directors sitting stiffly nearby.

Around the country, though, there is increasing criticism of these global companies, criticism centering on their abandoning America and jettisoning any allegiance to the country where they are chartered and got their start and made their billions in profits. Indeed, these business giants prefer to be "anational"—that is, from *no* country, instead transversing the planet and nations seeking maximum profits with minimum labor and other costs.

This "anational" status is a practice of daily corporate behavior. But, legally, the parent corporations are still chartered in a single country. For example, ITT, GM and Citicorp are all chartered in the permissive state of Delaware. In the United States, state governments grant most of the corporate charters that give the companies their legal existence and the privileges and immunities they are accumulating out of those artificial legal entities.

The question that needs to be given prominence, in these times of exporting plants overseas and outsourcing blue and white collar work to people earning serf-wages that keep them in poverty in places like Indonesia, China or India, is this: Do these U.S. corporations have any allegiance to the United States and the communities that labored and nurtured these companies?

Certainly, our local, state and national governments have displayed, with your tax dollars, a great deal of allegiance to these large companies over the years. Our soldiers and sailors have protected these corporate investments with their lives for a century—from defending the United Fruit corporation in Central America to the oil companies in the Persian Gulf. A famous Marine commander pithily pointed out over forty years ago how his Marines were ordered to make sure the flag followed the companies.

The commercial attachés of American Embassies have as their purpose the safeguarding and promotion of U.S. corporations. This has frequently meant the U.S. government both supporting and subsidizing brutal dictatorships that open the doors to raw materials and other markets for these firms. Your tax dollars go to finance these unholy alliances.

When the investment environment in Mexico got shaky for U.S. companies recently, due to heavy market speculation and corruption of the Mexican plutocracy, President Clinton fashioned a $50 billion bailout package for the dictatorial Mexican regime without congressional approval. You, the taxpayers, will bear the largest share of this bailout both directly and indirectly.

Maybe you didn't realize that the tax code subsidizes foreign investment by U.S. corporations, that the Export-Import Bank provides subsidies as loan guarantees for U.S. multinationals operating abroad and that a federal agency, called OPIC, insures these companies against political risks.

Through these supports and numerous other measures, the U.S. government and the American taxpayers supply the dollars and bear the risks for these giant corporate welfare programs.

So what kind of allegiance do these companies give back to the country where they started and where they are chartered? In the past, the lack of allegiance has been shockingly callous. DuPont and General Motors worked with fascist Germany and its companies openly before World War II and did not entirely sever all dealings when hostilities began. Congressional investigations showed that what the arms merchants did during World War I was considered treasonous by some close observers of their machinations.

There needs to be a crisp and public display of allegiance demanded of these U.S. multinational corporations. The best place for this to happen is at their annual shareholder meetings, with the press and nominal owners present. These companies, with the officers and the directors standing at attention, should pledge allegiance to our country.

The phrasing is obvious: "The General Motors [or Exxon or Citicorp or DuPont] corporation pledges allegiance to the Flag of the United States of America, and the Republic for which it stands, one Nation under God, indivisible, with liberty and justice for all."

Bank Mergers Skip Along, Right Past the Customers

Originally appeared in The New York Times, *Sunday, November 12, 1995.*

THE UNITED STATES banking landscape is changing as rapidly as lawyers can prepare merger papers. By the end of the century, most of the nation's banking resources may well be concentrated among a mere handful of huge institutions with offices stretching across the country.

Even before the new mergers, just one hundred banking organizations—slightly more than 1 percent—controlled more than 70 percent of the nation's banking assets.

The consequences of the new consolidations will be immense as marketplace choices diminish, particularly for consumers, small businesses and underserved low- and moderate-income and minority neighborhoods. A tightly concentrated industry also poses significant new challenges and risks for federal and state regulatory agencies and a poorly capitalized taxpayer-backed deposit insurance fund.

So where is official Washington? Largely on the sidelines, uninterested, it appears, in the impact on many of its constituents of giant mergers like the $300 billion marriage of Chase Manhattan and Chemical Bank in New York that will create the nation's new banking leader.

Even that deal may be eclipsed if rumors become reality about a merger of the Bank of America and Nationsbank, which would create a $429 billion institution with a massive network of offices throughout the Middle Atlantic States, the Southeast, the Southwest and the West Coast. The friendly bid announced last week for First Interstate Bancorp of Los Angeles by First Bank System of Minneapolis, to thwart Wells Fargo's hostile overture, would create a $92 billion institution.

Overshadowed by these headliners is the rapidly expanding merger activity under way in every region of the nation among many large and medium-sized institutions.

This rush to consolidate has been accompanied by a blizzard of public relations handouts that speak, invariably, in glowing terms about efficiency and benefits for bank consumers. But the hard, cold truth is that there are no such identifiable benefits.

As Federal Reserve Governor Janet Yellen acknowledged in recent testimony before the House Banking Committee, studies have found that banks in relatively concentrated markets "tend to charge higher rates for certain types of loans, particularly small business loans, and tend to offer lower interest rates on certain types of deposits than do banks in less concentrated markets."

This same trend will translate into new and higher fees for basic services, particularly for low- and moderate-balance customers. Access to credit will be more difficult as consumer and neighborhood concerns are filtered and muted through longer and more distant lines of managerial control.

Thousands of bank workers will be declared surplus as the merged corporations padlock neighborhood branches in an effort to insure the sharchold-ers' gain from the consolidations. A big accounting firm, Deloitte & Touche, predicts that as many as 450,000 bank jobs will be swept away in the next decade. The Chemical-Chase merger alone is expected to eliminate 12,000 jobs over the next three years—about 4,000 in New York City alone.

And those are just estimates. Reality can prove much worse. When Chemical acquired Manufacturers Hanover in 1992, the bank promised that only eighty branches would be closed; in the end, 177 were eliminated.

This time, Chase and Chemical have promised to increase lending in underserved areas. Such a pledge is unenforceable, but it does provide cover for regulators eager to rubber stamp the mergers.

The economic and political power wielded by these financial giants will be awesome, particularly if Congress goes ahead with plans to authorize banks, insurance companies and securities firms to affiliate under a single holding company. It's easy to envision a Chase-Chemical combination becoming a trillion-dollar conglomerate controlling significant areas of finance nationwide.

Much of the debate about concentration of economic power has been obscured by the exaggerated claims that efficiency and savings result when big banks become bigger through mergers. But Stephen A. Rhoades, an economist with the Fed, examined thirty-nine studies conducted between 1980 and 1993 on the efficiencies produced by bank mergers. He found "little support" for such conclusions.

His finding reinforces that of two experts at the Federal Reserve Bank of Minneapolis, John H. Boyd, senior research officer, and Stanley L. Graham, an economist. Four years ago, they found that most research suggested that economies of scale are exhausted "below the relatively modest size of $100 million in deposits." Consolidation "is not all it seems," the authors concluded.

At a minimum, the mergers are creating a new class of "too big to fail" institutions—banks that must be bailed out, various Presidents will inevitably tell us, to prevent a "domino" economic effect. These institutions will then enjoy what is tantamount to a taxpayer guarantee of all their liabilities (not just the customers' deposits).

Before all the merger horses are out of the barn, the Clinton Administration and Congress must make a full examination of the economic impact of bank concentration. There is an immediate need to modernize and toughen the Bank Merger Act by placing greater emphasis on determining the "public interest" in these massive mergers.

For its part, the Justice Department should adopt stronger, more realistic guidelines than those of the Reagan-Bush era for measuring bank competition. And it is imperative that the Administration move now to restructure the regulatory machinery by creating an independent consolidated agency from the three Federal banking agencies with the sole function of regulation. Nothing less will be able to cope with these giants.

The banking industry is setting new speed records in its rush to consolidate. The Clinton Administration should show the same urgency in putting public interest protections in place.

How Clinton Can Build Democracy

Originally appeared in The Nation, *November 30, 1992.*

BILL CLINTON will be receiving much advice in the coming weeks about the direction his Administration should take on the economy, health insurance, education, environmental and consumer protection, labor rights, the cities, housing, the poor, foreign trade agreements and on and on. But he probably won't be hearing or seeking proposals about where he is going to get the power to do the right things for the American people.

Presidents have overdeveloped powers to advance corporate interests, owing to the relentless shaping of government by these lobbies over the decades. In contrast, their powers to advance the citizens' interests are woefully underdeveloped. Held hostage by (and responsible for) an economy that is overwhelmingly private and corporate, Presidents cater to the expectations of major corporations, whose demands are transmitted in hundreds of ways from near and far to the White House, the Cabinet, the agencies, the Federal Reserve, Congress and the courts.

Presidents find plenty of corporate power to shape the tax system so that liquor and tobacco entertainment expenses are deductible, as are interest payments on loans for mergers, acquisitions and leveraged buyouts. What they lack is the citizen power essential to help them enact legislation to replace these wasteful deductions with, for example, deductions for college tuition payments.

Presidents find ample business backing for giving away to corporations publicly owned assets such as the minerals on federal lands, the medical innovations of the National Institutes of Health and the public airwaves. Where is the power to reverse *these* policies?

Corporate power turns Washington into a bazaar of accounts receivable, replete with business subsidies, bailouts, giveaways, grants, inflated contracts and other aids to dependent corporations. Where is the President going to get the political power to represent the small taxpayers and the consumers, who end up paying all the bills? In the late 1970s, consumers were denied even a tiny advocacy agency that could fit in a small corner of the Department of Commerce, whose main mission is to promote business profits.

There are boundless absurdities in this imbalance of power between the corporate government's domination of the presidency and the weakened tools the people have to control that government. Taxpayers now pay, through the Pentagon budget, for the criminal fines that other agencies impose on defense contractors for toxic contamination. Taxpayers also pay to promote Big Macs and tobacco overseas. Yet they are not even permitted to have a checkoff on their tax return so they can form a taxpayers' advocacy association to protect their tax dollars from legal and illegal looting.

Clinton wants to give health insurance coverage to more Americans. How? He has only the power to do what is acceptable to the insurance, hospital, drug and doctor lobbies. These power brokers, not the patients or consumers, have the veto.

Notice Clinton's economic policies. They consist largely of providing incentives (read corporate welfare payments) to the business community directly or indirectly. His Putting People First agenda flies in the face of reality because the citizenry has no power to make him put people before corporations when the two interests conflict. Sensitive to who wields daily power, Clinton declined to make a major campaign issue of law and order against widespread corporate crime, fraud and abuse (abetted or permitted under three Republican terms).

Unless Presidents deliberately set out to place more democratic tools in the hands of citizens, the White House will simply consolidate the corporate agenda and send the bill to the people. The S&L crimes and debacles illustrate the servile quality of Presidents and Congresses, who view themselves primarily as agents of business, serving up a costly feast of corporate socialism for which powerless taxpayers get the check.

Clinton believes that enterprise zones are a major answer to the economic problems of the inner cities. Puerto Rico has been one large enterprise zone for many years and has lavished "business incentive" after business incentive on corporations. Yet the unemployment rate and poverty in that commonwealth are staggering. What poor people need is more functioning democracy with which to mobilize communities into action against exploiters and redliners. Absent this, the parameters of Clinton's urban-policy powers will be largely set by the banking, real estate and insurance lobbies.

Nothing illustrates better how presidential power is structurally tilted to favor the powerful corporate interests over the rest of America than the system of ownership without control. The people legally own major national assets: $3 *trillion* in pension funds, more than $2 trillion in savings deposits, hundreds of billions more in insurance company equity, federal lands (one-third of America), large blocs of shares of companies on the stock exchanges, as well as the airwaves. Although the people own these assets, they do not *control* any of them. Corporations do. Presidents have ample backup power to preserve this split between ownership and control, but they and Congress have little backup power to make such ownership *mean* control.

If Clinton is serious about putting people first, he must pursue a two-track presidency. The first track, which is supposed to focus on problems and help the country solve them, cannot deliver very much, for the reasons described. Clinton should apply his and his Vice President's energies to a second track, one that builds democracy. Democracies do not thrive untended. They are diminished by plutocracy and oligarchy, by political betrayals that feed public frustration and lead to resignation and then fatalism. Democracies need nourishment at the local, state and national levels, wherever raw power is hurled against vulnerable citizens. Democracies need updating, remodeling and, above all, they need tools that citizens can use individually and together.

Compared with the hundreds of billions of dollars Clinton will spend perpetuating corporate welfare, guarantees and promotional programs, building democracy is cheap. It can be done by voluntary checkoffs on tax returns to enable citizens to fund political campaigns instead of the Fortune 500. It can be done by requiring all legal monopolies—electric, gas, telephone and water companies—to include inserts in their bills inviting customers to form their own consumer protection associations. Companies, such as banks, receiving any of the myriad government bailouts and subsidies should be required to do the same thing as a matter of reciprocity. Such mechanisms for communities of people to band together and fund their full-time specialists and advocates cost the taxpayer little or nothing, are universally accessible, and may be joined or not.

The three elements of democratic activity—timely information, the technology to communicate with one another, and then mobilization for action and results—could also be served by an Audience Network established by Congressional charter. Voluntary dues-paying members of the Audience Network would support local and national television and radio studios, with producers and reporters programming daily one-hour prime-time shows on the public's airwaves. Moreover, the government itself, through Social Security envelopes, postal service deliveries and many other forms of communication, could provide notices making it easier, state by state, for people to band together in nonprofit citizen-action groups.

Washington is a federal forum whose operating slogan has been, "Billions for corporations, bills for the people." Without a second-track presidency to build democracy, the first track cannot produce fair solutions. It does not have the necessary civic backbone to overcome the concentrations and abuses of power that breed the many problems that roll so easily off the tongues of politicians at election time.

Societies rot from the top down. They reconstruct from the bottom up. Democracies are not just good for the economy. They are good for peace and tranquillity, for character and local initiative, for justice and the pursuit of happiness. So, if you ever meet Bill Clinton, ask not only what he wants to do for his country. Ask what tools he wants to provide his fellow citizens to help him do it.

Run the Government Like the Best
American Corporations

Originally appeared in the Harvard Business Review, *November/December 1988.*

TIME AND AGAIN, corporate executives have told me that government would function better "if it were run more like a business." I've never found this sentiment very persuasive. As one U.S. industry after another fails to meet foreign competition or legitimate consumer standards, can business in general offer itself as a model of sound management? But our best corporations do provide some relevant principles that can be adapted toward making government more efficient, more responsive, more creative, and more humane. The next president can learn from these principles.

1. *The best companies understand that people drive organizational innovation; human resources matter more than money or machines. The next president should adopt policies that will unleash the productivity, morale, and initiative of the federal work force.*

For more than a decade, politicians have run for national office by campaigning against the federal government. They have denigrated the role of the civil servant, thereby discouraging an entire generation of young Americans from public service careers and reducing the quality and integrity of the government.

The next president can take concrete steps to motivate civil servants, increase their sense of worth, and liberate their minds from bureaucracy-induced inhibitions. He should break through the legendary Oval Office cocoon to communicate regularly and directly with federal workers. He should visit major departments, mix it up with the employees, listen to their ideas, stimulate their thinking, and remind them of the importance of their mission. Of course, a president struggles under enormous time pressures. But these give-and-take sessions would make modest demands on his schedule—and they would have an electric and repercussive impact on employee productivity.

In 1978, when Paul Oreffice became chief executive officer of Dow Chemical, he promised to meet in small groups with at least 5,000 workers a year. He told me he reached or exceeded that goal throughout his nine-year tenure. Oreffice found the meetings extremely valuable. He believes they gave him a gut-level feel for the company's mood, allowed him to articulate his goals directly, provided feedback he could not get from his immediate staff, and encouraged a climate of openness at all management levels.

The president should also instruct his cabinet secretaries to test aggressively alternatives to standard government procedures. New thinking among civil servants requires creative management policies; those policies start in the Oval Office. More and more companies are using job rotation, skunk works, self-managed teams, and other techniques to fight bureaucratic lethargy. The federal bureaucracy desperately needs such experimentation. One small but powerful idea is for agencies to open "invented here" offices to evaluate and diffuse throughout the government better ways of doing the public's work.

Finally, the president can ensure that government celebrates rather than punishes civil servants who do their jobs. He can give concrete meaning to the still-inadequate protections afforded ethical whistle-blowers by not only providing a climate of reform and respect, but by also rewarding them for taking personal risks on behalf of the public interest. He can demand vigorous implementation of the Freedom of Information Act, which, by exposing government practices to outside scrutiny, helps check management abuses and indifference. And he can end interference by the Office of Management and Budget in the government rule-making process. Under President Reagan, OMB's unprecedented reach of power to obstruct proposed health and safety regulations has deeply demoralized the dedicated and expert staffs in such agencies as the Environmental Protection Agency, the National Highway Traffic Safety Administration, and the Occupational Safety and Health Administration.

2. *Some companies are becoming tougher and more intelligent customers. Similarly, the next president should leverage federal buying power to improve product quality and promote innovation.*

John Nevin, CEO of Firestone, told me what it's like to be a supplier to the automobile industry these days. The car companies not only expect better quality and on-time delivery, but they also influence how Firestone itself operates. His major customers inspect Firestone's plants and evaluate its investments in manufacturing equipment. If they are not satisfied with Firestone's tires, they can effectively shut down its production lines. These manufacturers understand their power as large buyers, and are using it to win better supplier performance.

What a contrast with government procurement! The federal government acquires about $200 billion worth of goods and services each year. It buys almost everything that individual consumers buy: food, clothing, pharmaceuticals, motor vehicles, fuel, utility services, health care, you name it. Yet government seldom wields its marketplace power to win better deals for itself or indirectly for consumers.

Most federal procurement is motivated by a narrow accounting mindset: buy goods and services at the lowest acquisition price. Needless to say, government often fails to achieve even this modest goal, witness the recurring scandals over weapons and computer systems. The Office of Federal Procurement Policy, which Congress created in 1974 to straighten out the buying mess, has been dormant for the last eight years.

So government should buy more efficiently, keeping product life-cycle costs in mind. But its greatest impact would come from buying more creatively—that is, promoting practical but little-used innovations and advancing already-authorized national missions like safety and energy conservation. This important leveraging of the taxpayer dollar should be a top priority of the next president.

Federal agencies, for example, can use their purchasing power to negotiate model contracts for telephone service and health care, and then publicize the terms to show what individuals and businesses should try to achieve. The agencies can also be a vast and reliable source of comparative product information. Every day, government purchasing agents make buying decisions based on product evaluations: who makes the best light bulbs, who makes the best photocopiers, who makes the best wool socks. The government could publish a monthly bulletin of its purchases and explain why it selected specific products, with any proper qualifiers. Consumers could use such bulletins to inform their purchases. Companies who want to sell to the government would have fresh public performance standards to exceed.

Most importantly, government can leverage its buying power to create markets for important and beneficial technologies that might otherwise languish. Government contracts are often so large that the prospect of winning one convinces a company to make a product it wouldn't otherwise be willing to make. The initial government purchase can stimulate subsequent sales in the civilian market.

Military hospitals pioneered the use of generic drugs. Pharmaceutical companies were not enthusiastic about supplying generics, but large institutions like Walter Reed Army Medical Center had the market power to demand them. The Carter administration began a Buy Quiet project to stimulate the design of less-noisy machines and office equipment.

The most dramatic example of the stimulation effect, though, is the automotive air bag. Apart from a few thousand cars in the early 1970s, U.S. auto companies refused to offer air-bag protection, despite twenty years of legislative and regulatory pressures. Then, in 1985, the General Services Administration issued a request for proposals to add 5,000 air-bag equipped cars to the government fleet. The order was large enough to interest Ford Motor Company, which won the contract. Soon thereafter, several insurance companies that had long supported air bags followed the government's lead and ordered their own air-bag equipped cars.

The auto industry got the message. Ford began offering air bags as an option on two models. Last May, Chrysler announced it would install driver-side air bags as standard equipment on all 1990 cars. Virtually all manufacturers are now phasing in this key safety device. The leverage of a large government contract (combined with prodding safety laws) created a marketplace dynamic that overcame two decades of industry recalcitrance.

Many other socially constructive processes and products could benefit from creative government procurement. Federal policy has long encouraged the use of recycled materials. Why not announce that government agencies will meet 25 percent of their annual paper needs with recycled stock? This would create economies of scale for producers—and thus bring down unit costs, lower prices for civilian buyers, and encourage supplier competition. The same goes for solar energy. If the Defense Department used photovoltaic units to generate electricity in remote and other adaptable installations, it could save years of building efficient scale in the civilian market—and lower solar energy prices dramatically.

3. *Just as the best executives build customer-driven companies, the next president should pro-mote citizen-driven government.*

A basic function of the presidency in a democracy is to enhance, not ham-per, the ability of citizens to find out what public officials are doing, to express their voice, to gain a role in the policy-making process, to challenge waste and corruption, to discipline government insensitivity. Virtually every president comes to office promising greater citizen access to and influence over the workings of the federal government. Few ever deliver.

Some of the problems boil down to government agencies ignoring the needs of their citizen-customers. In February, the General Accounting Office reported that IRS personnel were giving incorrect advice to 39 per-cent of the taxpayers who telephoned with questions. The Postal Service has scaled back door-to-door delivery to new homes, stopped Sunday mail col-lections, and raised postage prices faster than inflation. Government forms remain maddeningly and unnecessarily complex.

One immediate way to improve government responsiveness is for the president to put his personal prestige on the line. He should make specific and public commitments to better service. The president might guarantee that taxpayers will receive refund checks within a fixed number of weeks after filing their returns. He would then report to the country on the IRS's success in meeting the pledge. Whatever the service areas, the important point is that the president makes commitments—and holds his cabinet sec-retaries and agency heads accountable for them.

The president should also expand feedback mechanisms within federal agencies. Government offices make remarkably limited use of toll-free com-plaint hotlines, surveys, and other familiar information-gathering tools that companies use to monitor product quality and customer satisfaction. The creation of thorough and sophisticated complaint data bases would allow officials to distinguish between episodic service problems and systemic inef-ficiencies. The necessary communications and data processing technologies have existed for years. All that's missing is leadership from the top.

A more far-reaching initiative is to build a citizen empowerment infra-structure that campaigns *on its own* for more effective government. Corporate customers routinely band together to influence suppliers. Computer buyers, for example, form user groups that meet with vendors, evaluate new prod-ucts, and make complaints. Individuals often lack the resources and ease of communications to organize themselves. Government can help create vol-untary associations, open to all interested people, to represent citizens.

This concept has proved successful on a state level. Several years ago, Wisconsin and Illinois created independent Citizen Utility Boards (CUBs) to represent ratepayers. On a regular basis, utilities (which are government-sanctioned monopolies) were required to include literature in their monthly bills explaining CUB's mission, structure, and how to join. The groups quickly attracted tens of thousands of members and became skilled intervenors in rate hearings, administrative proceedings, and the courts. Most utilities are no longer required to distribute CUB literature, but the groups are functioning well after their modest government-facilitated launch.

It would be easy to apply the CUB idea to organizations like the Postal Service, the Social Security Administration, and the Veterans Administration. Take the postal case. Big mailers (magazine publishers and the direct-mail industry) use lobbyists and trade associations to advance their interests in postal commission rate hearings and to monitor legislation that affects service. Don't residential mailers deserve their own independent voice? The next president could urge that once or twice a year, the Postal Service distribute literature to all households bearing a message something like this: "We are always trying to improve our service. But we know we don't have all the willpower and ideas to make our service as good as it can be. We think you should have an opportunity, in an organized fashion, to be part of a voluntary association that deals with complaints, postal policies, and postage rates, and that regularly convenes with postal managers to evaluate service quality. If you're interested, send an annual membership fee of $10. You will then have an opportunity to elect a board of directors that will establish an office, hire staff, and set the policies of your organization."

The empowerment approach brings many important advantages. It costs taxpayers virtually nothing; the groups are funded by voluntary contributions. It is anti-bureaucratic; government is not creating another layer of personnel or a new set of procedures. And it enhances civic participation; such independent organizations depend for success on the energy and vision of their members.

4. *Aggressive CEOs put corporate assets to their highest use for the best return. The next president must exercise more effective control of the country's vast public assets.*

Public assets are tangible or intangible items of value owned by the public and managed by the federal government for social, economic, historical, or security reasons. They fall into three categories: natural resources such as public lands, mineral rights, air rights, and broadcast rights; physical assets such as roads, laboratories, defense factories, and power stations; intangible assets such as government-sponsored research and development, patents on government inventions, and government-collected information and statistics.

The next president doesn't need another blue-ribbon commission to investigate asset-management practices. Decades of congressional hearings, GAO investigations, and federal task forces have documented a pattern of gross neglect. If the U.S. government, with its vast mismanaged assets, were a public corporation, Carl Icahn would have launched a hostile tender offer years ago. Here are just a few of the many opportunities for more aggressive asset management.

The government owns and administers 760 million acres of land, roughly one-third of the entire United States. This acreage contains huge stores of valuable minerals: 30 percent of the country's coal reserves, 35 percent of its uranium, 80 percent of its oil shale. Counting offshore areas, government holdings also contain 40 percent of the country's natural gas reserves and 85 percent of its oil. But the Interior Department is a notoriously careless landlord. It has failed to collect adequate royalties on government-owned logging, grazing, mineral, and oil and gas resources. With many leases, it doesn't even require competitive bidding. The cumulative lost revenues amount to billions of dollars.

The Federal Communications Commission *gives away* the licenses that authorize radio and television broadcasters to use the public airwaves. Meanwhile, local television stations change hands for hundreds of millions of dollars—and a huge percentage of any station's value is the government-assigned broadcast license. Shouldn't the FCC, as a representative of landlords (the people), charge rent to these broadcast tenants for the privilege of profiting from the public airwaves?

Government agencies underwrite or directly conduct huge amounts of research and development, but they often let the financial rewards accrue solely to the private sector. The National Institutes of Health hand over many valuable research findings to pharmaceutical companies, which patent new drugs and profitably enjoy a 17-year monopoly on their production. Shouldn't NIH collect a royalty on revenues from these patents?

Perhaps the most widely abused federal asset is government's unique power to grant subsidies, preferences, guarantees, and exemptions: tax breaks to oil and gas producers, maritime subsidies, low-interest export financing, bailouts of mismanaged companies, and the list goes on. These direct and indirect subsidies to business cost about $100 billion a year. Yet federal authorities demand next to nothing with respect to corporate performance. Would a well-run company finance R&D by a supplier or provide low-cost financing to a customer and ask for nothing in return?

The next president should implement a workfare system for this aid to dependent corporations. Some politicians are insisting that welfare recipients work for their financial assistance. We should ask no less of multibillion dollar corporations. The central concept is quid pro quo—if government writes a check to business, government has the right to set performance standards in terms of job creation, environmental practices, and other criteria. Failure to meet these targets should result in penalties or the return or withdrawal of the subsidy. Under such conditions, perhaps there would be fewer subsidies.

5. *Strategic planning at the best companies looks beyond tomorrow's results and identifies long-term challenges and market opportunities. The next president must expand the government's planning horizon to address problems whose impacts extend beyond his term.*

Critics decry the short-range mentality of corporate managers who respond to Wall Street pressures by focusing on quarterly results at the expense of long-term corporate growth. Presidents are not very different. They usually govern as if the future of the United States ends when their term expires.

This short-term orientation reached new heights under Ronald Reagan, whose administration has demonstrated an outright aversion to addressing the long-term problems it helped create (i.e., huge budget and trade deficits) or problems it inherited such as acid rain, the greenhouse effect and ozone depletion, and toxic-waste cleanup. Political realities encourage short-term thinking in the White House. So a president must work hard to overcome these forces—or, at the very least, to provide a functioning legacy that helps future administrations face these woes.

One approach is to assemble a series of planning task forces on long-range environmental, economic, health, and social problems. The key to success with these planning groups is appointing members who genuinely want to solve the problem—which means appointing members who are directly affected by the problem. A task force on radioactive waste disposal should include not only nuclear scientists and geologists, but also citizens who live near atomic plants or in communities designated as possible waste sites. A task force on ocean pollution should include not only marine biologists and chemists, but also fishermen and residents of beachfront communities.

I do not want to push the government-as-business metaphor too far. After all, the government of the United States is *not* a business. It delivers unique services and bears special legal responsibilities—curbing marketplace abuse, promoting world peace, fighting disease, meeting the needs of the disadvantaged—that have no direct corollaries in the private sector, except perhaps as a moral imperative of corporate citizenship.

The next president faces a whole set of challenges that speak to these broader duties. It is hard to imagine a more basic domestic function of government than protecting and advancing the health and safety of the American people. The next president must make up for eight years of neglect in promoting clean air, clean water, safe foods, drugs, cars, and workplaces. The same is true of government's role in curbing marketplace abuse. The next president must breathe new life into the antitrust laws to reverse the growing concentration of corporate power, protect the increasingly endangered legal rights of injured people, and crack down on military procurement fraud, toxic-waste dumping, and other business crimes documented regularly in the newspapers.

Finally, the next president faces a challenge that goes to the heart of our independence as a nation. I have always decried the excessive influence of U.S. multinational corporations over the economies of other countries. Never did I imagine that the United States itself would confront the hazards of such widening absentee ownership.

The next president cannot afford to ignore the growing foreign economic presence in the United States. Absentee ownership, heavily fueled by a depressed dollar, compromises political sovereignty, reduces our freedom of judgment as a nation, and increases our dependence on foreign banks and corporations in ways that have nothing to do with the proper exploitation of comparative advantage. There is no pretense of reciprocity in this foreign invasion. Does anyone seriously believe that the Japanese government would permit Firestone to buy Bridgestone or CBS to buy a major division of Sony?

I'm not proposing a ban on foreign acquisitions, although the federal government has a legitimate role in scrutinizing and approving them. The most effective way to reduce absentee ownership is to reduce the budget deficit.

The deficit should be reduced through three steps. Deep reductions (say, 50 percent) in our expenditures for military forces in Western Europe could save at least $50 billion. It is absurd that British and German companies swallow our industry and real estate while we have absorbed so much of their countries' defense expenditures.

Tougher asset management and steep reductions in the corporate welfare budget could generate an additional $50 billion. The next president should slash government payments to large agribusinesses and eliminate subsidies for nuclear power. He should collect higher royalties on timber, oil, natural gas, and hard minerals on federal lands.

Finally, further reform of the corporate and personal income tax—specifically, eliminating business loopholes left open in 1986 and modestly increasing tax rates for the richest Americans—could generate another $50 billion. These three steps alone would reduce the federal deficit by $150 billion and help reassert U.S. economic stability and stature.

By empowering the citizenry with information, access, and participation rights, and by applying the best of appropriate business principles to our federal government's distinctive roles, the next president can preside over a problem-solving present and bequeath a comprehensive legacy upon which his successors and the American people can build.

Corporations Are Not Persons

BY RALPH NADER AND CARL J. MAYER

Originally appeared in The New York Times, *April 9, 1988.*

O UR CONSTITUTIONAL RIGHTS were intended for real persons, not artificial creations. The Framers certainly knew about corporations but chose not to mention these contrived entities in the Constitution. For them, the document shielded living beings from arbitrary government and endowed them with the right to speak, assemble and petition.

Today, however, corporations enjoy virtually the same umbrella of constitutional protections as individuals do. They have become, in effect, artificial persons with infinitely greater power than humans. This constitutional equivalence must end.

Consider a few noxious developments during the last ten years. A group of large Boston companies invoked the First Amendment in order to spend lavishly and thus successfully defeat a referendum that would have permitted the legislature to enact a progressive income tax that had no direct effect on the property and business of these companies. An Idaho electrical and plumbing corporation cited the Fourth Amendment and deterred a health and safety investigation. A textile supply company used Fifth Amendment protections and barred retrial in a criminal antitrust case in Texas.

The idea that the Constitution should apply to corporations as it applies to humans had its dubious origins in 1886. The Supreme Court said it did "not wish to hear argument" on whether corporations were "persons" protected by the Fourteenth Amendment, a civil rights amendment designed to safeguard newly emancipated blacks from unfair government treatment. It simply decreed that corporations were persons.

Now that is judicial activism. A string of later dissents, by Justices Hugo Black and William O. Douglas, demonstrated that neither the history nor the language of the Fourteenth Amendment was meant to protect corporations. But it was too late. The genie was out of the bottle and the corporate evolution into personhood was under way.

It was not until the 1970s that corporations began to throw their constitutional weight around. Recent court decisions suggest that the future may hold even more dramatic extensions of corporate protections.

In 1986, Dow Chemical, arguing before the Supreme Court, suggested that the Fourth Amendment's prohibition against unreasonable searches and seizures should prohibit the Environmental Protection Agency from flying planes over Dow's manufacturing facilities to monitor compliance with environmental laws. Although the Court permitted the flights on technical grounds, it appeared to endorse Dow's expansive view of the Constitution.

That year, corporations received the most sweeping enlargement of their free speech rights to date. In a 5-3 decision, the Court invalidated a California regulation ordering a public utility monopoly to enclose in its billing envelopes a communication from a nonprofit rate-payer advocacy group that financed the insert. The purpose of the regulation was to assist the Public Utility Commission in achieving its authorized goal of reasonable rates. Even so, the Court held that the enclosures violated a new corporate First Amendment right "not to speak." Associate Justice William H. Rehnquist wrote in a pro-consumer dissent that to "ascribe to such artificial entities an 'intellect' or 'mind' [for constitutional purposes] is to confuse metaphor with reality."

Today, corporations remain unsatisfied with their ascendant constitutional status. They want much more. At a 1987 judicial conference in Pennsylvania, lawyers counseled that corporations use the First Amendment to invalidate a range of Federal regulations, including Securities and Exchange Commission disclosure requirements that govern corporate takeovers, and rules affecting stock offerings.

Businesses angry at Congressional attempts to ban cigarette advertising—by that, we mean commercial carcinogenic speech—are alleging First Amendment violations.

The corporate drive for constitutional parity with real humans comes at a time when legislatures are awarding these artificial persons superhuman privileges. Besides perpetual life, corporations enjoy limited liability for industrial accidents such as nuclear power disasters. They also use voluntary bankruptcy and other disappearing acts to dodge financial obligations while remaining in business.

The legal system is thus creating unaccountable Frankensteins that have human powers but are nonetheless constitutionally shielded from much actual and potential law enforcement as well as from accountability to real persons such as workers, consumers and taxpayers.

Of course, individuals in these companies can always exercise their personal constitutional rights, but the drive for corporate rights is dangerously out of control.

Too frequently the extension of corporate constitutional rights is a zero-sum game that diminishes the rights and powers of real individuals. The corporate exercise of First Amendment rights frustrates the individual's right to participate more equally in democratic elections, to pay reasonable utility rates and to live in a toxin-free environment. Fourth Amendment rights applied to the corporation diminish the individual's right to live in an unpolluted world and to enjoy privacy.

Equality of constitutional rights plus an inequality of legislated and de facto powers leads inevitably to the supremacy of artificial over real persons. And now the ultimate irony: Corporate entities have the constitutional right, says the Supreme Court, to patent living beings such as genetically engineered cattle, pigs, chickens and, perhaps someday, humanoids.

This is not to say that corporations should have only the legal rights emanating from state charters that create them. What is required, however, is a constitutional presumption favoring the individual over the corporation.

To establish this presumption, we need a constitutional amendment that declares that corporations are not persons and that they are only entitled to statutory protections conferred by legislatures and through referendums. Only then will the Constitution become the exclusive preserve of those whom the Framers sought to protect: real people.

The Megacorporate World of Ronald Reagan

Originally presented at The National Press Club, *Washington D.C., June 6, 1984.*

MANY YEARS AGO, when some of our nation's political leaders were wise, Thomas Jefferson said that the purpose of representative government was to curb "the excesses of the monied interests." Many decades later, in 1936, Franklin D. Roosevelt, one of the last presidents to hold corporations accountable for the state of the economy, promised that while "the malefactors of great wealth" had met their match in the previous four years, they would meet their master in the following four years.

Ronald Reagan has the opposite plan in mind. During Mr. Reagan's first term, "the malefactors of great wealth," now described as big business or multinational corporations, have regularly met their obedient servant in the white house. The power of "the monied interests" has become ever more focused on turning representative government into a versatile accounts receivable for too many mismanaged, speculating, negligent, avaricious, unsafe or downright criminal companies. This Reagan-corporatist revolution, whereby business regulates government in pursuit of private profit at the expense of the legitimate interests of Americans as taxpayers, consumers and citizens, has little to do with being conservative. It has everything to do with building a government of the Exxons, by the General Motors, and for the DuPonts.

So systematic, recurrent and widespread are these retrograde policies against basic, historic American values, as shall be noted shortly, that political commentators have wondered aloud how Mr. Reagan can still be so much in the running for re-election. The implication in their observations is proper: Presidents should be judged for what they do, not for what they say, or what they say they do. These commentators still expect a framework of accountability around the White House that includes the departments and agencies of the Executive Branch directed largely by presidential appointees or Schedule C personnel.

"The Teflon President"—one of those very apt descriptions by Democrats that ironically serve to encourage their discouragement about November— has a strategy for irresponsible power that invites closer scrutiny.

Rule One is never get openly involved in the details. He who rises by details falls by details could be his motto. Stay abstract, using heroic phrases of reassurance and national pride.

Rule Two is amiability—especially in 'Aw shucks' demeanor with lots of even-toned voice, pendant smiles and head shrugs. Remember Reagan in China. When asked by American reporters what he thought of Peking censoring his remarks on Chinese television, he replied with a slight smile: "You fellows do it all the time." Imagine how Nixon would have been treated had he tried that one.

Rule Three is insulate the President from impromptu media exposure. His aides even joke about it, as Lyn Nofziger did on the campaign trail in 1980 when he told reporters, "I've got Ronnie under house arrest from you guys."

Rule Four is induce condescension. If people think they are so much smarter than you, they don't expect much and they forgive more.

Rule Five is create a banality of wrongdoing, of cruelty, of hypocrisy, of selling the country short. Banality avoids the constant search for novelty by the media and helps opposing politicians throw up their hands in despair. Any President whose administration can incite the response of the jaded— "So what else is new"—is already almost out of the woods. Banality is nourished by a numbing frequency of abuses whose very quantity depreciate their provocative impact.

Rule Six is seize the semantics and wrap the national symbols around one's own political ideology.

Rule Seven is be blessed by an opposition party that has largely surrendered the basic contention of its politics—namely that of challenging the mal-distribution of power between the haves and have nots. The formula which used to win again and again for the Democrats—that they were the party of the people and the Republicans were the party of the rich—is no longer used. It fails because these are times of massive campaign finance beggary and a giant corporate lock on an economy increasingly within corporate prerogative to transfer operations overseas or close down plant by plant. People see this overlap by the two parties in currying the favor of business interests. Deprived of distinct political choice, citizens begin to doubt the credibiliy of the party out of office when it claims it will be different. The candidates who can convince us that there will be a difference on concrete policy after concrete policy will move people's minds.

The radical regime of Ronald Reagan does provide a background against which there indeed can be significant choices affecting the perceived needs and rights of citizens. Here are some of the directions pursued by the Reagan-Big Business axis:

I.

The concentration of power within government and business has increased in both political and economic manifestations. The corporate merger movement, given the green light by Reagan, is moving from rabid to frenzied. Nine of the ten largest mergers in U.S. history have occurred under the permissive reign of Reagan. It is difficult to know what limits Reagan would put on mergers, most of which promise no greater efficiencies, no economies of scale, no market discipline of bad management (without golden parachutes) and no new jobs. His former Justice Department antitrust chief, William Baxter, said: "There is nothing written in the sky that says the world would not be a perfectly satisfactory place if there were only one hundred companies, provided each had one percent of every product and service market." Nothing written in the sky, but there is much written in the anti-monopoly laws, their legislative history and judicial decisions that would give pause to such a concentrated political economy. Corporate bigness makes its demands on small business and the consumer in prices, in political manipulation, and in being too big to fail without a bailout. The loss of the family farm in the tens of thousands each year to agribusiness and banks receives no attention from this former rural Illinois native who extolls this way of life when he wants votes and forgets it after the election.

Over at the Federal Communications Commission, with Mr. Reagan's full support, his appointees, led by Chairman Mark Fowler, want to eliminate the few viewer's rights under the Fairness and Equal Time Doctrines. They want to repeal 7-7-7 limitation (7 am, 7 fm and 7 tv) stations which can be under a single owner and allow a vastly greater concentration of electronic media ownership.

Within the Federal Government there is greater concentration of power from many agencies to one—the White House Office of Management and Budget. The OMB makes political judgements, invites back door "ex parte" meetings with business lobbyists, excludes the public from its right to know and respond under the Administrative Procedures Act, and generally translates unilateral white house dictates. OMB does this in violation of fair play, and by some expert opinion, in violation of administrative laws as well. The Reagan Government also shuts Americans out of its decision-making processes by ending legal aid for poorer petitioners before regulatory agencies such as the Federal Trade Commission. They do so by using every technical objection to deny citizens legal standing to challenge their government, and by giving early preferential notice of proposals to their industrial and commercial friends. If there is any company on the fortune 100 list that objects to these anti-democratic powerplays, it has kept a very low visibility.

2.

There is a wholesale repudiation of the historic role of the American Government's duty to protect or expand the public's health and safety. Health and safety laws go unenforced or underenforced below even laggard levels of the past. The Food and Drug Administration's enforcement level is down about 50 percent, as are the enforcement actions against dirty meat and poultry plants and violators of motor vehicle regulations. The enforcement record at OSHA—the job safety agency—is a disgrace made worse by Reaganite reductions in serious inspections and redrawing what constitutes sanctionable violations. Since taking office, Reagan has not issued a single new worker health standard to limit any chemical or gas, though dozens in January 1981 were nearly ready to be issued to reduce cancer, emphysema, and other diseases and injuries in the workplace. These diseases claim about 100,000 American lives a year. Only one motor vehicle standard has emerged—that dealing with rear mounted lights on automobiles, while several critical lifesavers were revoked or shunted aside. The list can go on and on to demonstrate that Mr. Reagan has little interest in saving American lives when it inconveniences his corporate masters.

With the stroke of Transportation Secretary Drew Lewis' pen, a lifesaving, crash protection standard was illegally repealed (according to a 9-0 decision by the U.S. Supreme Court). Thousands of Americans are now dying or being seriously injured every year in frontal collisions by their non-

crashworthy cars. Mr. Reagan campaigned against this humane and economical engineering system right along with General Motors which pressed
upon him this macabre position. The pattern recurs in one industry after
another. What do the pesticide companies want? Just follow the Reagan
trail of waivers and exceptions for dangerous pesticides, the absence of regulatory action against suspected farm chemicals, the virtual cessation of testing foods for pesticide residues and the reduction of research for non-toxic
ways of controlling pests.

The sordid behavior of Reagan's Environmental Protection Agency in
bowing to corporate polluters on demand has been reported many times. But
Mr. Reagan's responsibility needs to be made clearer. EPA Chief Ann Gorsuch
did the president's bidding. It was the Reagan White House that stopped the
new EPA Chief William Ruckelshaus from doing anything to reduce the
sources of acid rain. It is Mr. Reagan and the corporate polluters who oppose
overdue implementation of stricter safety standards for America's drinking
water—now contaminated with heavy metals and cancer-causing chemicals.
The corporate polluters want the air and water polluton laws severely weakened. Many polls conclude that the overwhelming majority of people want
them strengthened. Ronald Reagan joins with his corporate patrons on these
issues as well. Even in the field of toxic waste dumps, scarring and poisoning
the America that he professes to revere, Mr. Reagan exerts no leadership. For
the Great Communicator, there is no time for compassionate recognition of
victims of corporate abuses, corporate cancer and other forms of industrial
violence. It is as if there needed to be proof that the contamination of
America's air and water were the products of an International Communist
Conspiracy before Mr. Reagan would leap into action. Alas, for those sick or
dying under Reagan—"The Real King of The Special Interests," as a *Washington
Post* headline put it—there is no such relief ahead.

Mr. Reagan's insensitivity seems at times to go beyond taking orders from
business. It reaches to uncharted realms of indifference and irresponsibility that congeal to form a type of intellectual incontinence. Some view his
hard line determination against law and order for corporations and his soft-
ness on corporate crime as the result of an ideologically indentured mind.
It is perfectly attuned to his political creators—the multimillionaires of the
Southern California kitchen cabinet who, like they'd acquired a sure winner horse, selected, groomed, trained and financed him for Sacramento, and
finally for Washington. It is all that but more.

How else can anyone explain why Mr. Reagan would so mistreat the
most vulnerable in our society when he could so easily defend their right

to live in health, safety, and dignity? Infants and children surely cannot be expected "to vote with their feet," Mr. Reagan. Yet, in 1981, he pushed to drop requirements that gasoline refiners reduce the amount of lead in gasoline. Too many little children in this country already have the devastating symptoms of lead poisoning; more lead violence cannot be allowed in their bodies. What of asbestos in thousands of school buildings? Despite visible protests from concerned parents, Mr. Reagan and Mr. Stockman refused to ask Congress to appropriate any money to help seal or remove exposed asbestos surfaces spinning off deadly microscopic particles into those young lungs. This Commander-in-Chief, who has never met a weapons system he didn't like, wanted to abolish the Consumer Product Safety Commission—a tiny agency with a major mission of protecting children from household and other product hazards. With an annual budget worth less than two hours of pentagon expenditures, the CPSC did not fit within Mr. Reagan's defintion of defense in depth. Fortunately, Congress disagreed, so just the budget was cut. There is more. After mothers of brain-damaged infants lobbied through Congress a bill to have the Food and Drug Administration establish quality control standards for commercial infant formula, Mr. Reagan's White House delayed the issuance of these regulations for eighteen months. Without press exposure, the delay may have been longer. Because of the lack of care and compassion so characteristic of this Administration, three million additional cans of deficient formula were sold to unsuspecting parents.

Two years ago, health officials at the Food and Drug Administration wanted to require aspirin makers to place a label on their product warning about Reye's Syndrome, a disease causing convulsions and sometimes death in some children who take aspirin when they have chicken pox or the flu. The White House OMB intervened on behalf of aspirin manufacturers and blocked both the move and distribution through supermarkets of a half million copies of pamphlets cautioning parents. Again there was wide publicity of this intra-government struggle but Mr. Reagan let the aspirin industry prevail.

It was said about Woodrow Wilson that he disliked individuals but loved humanity. The reverse seems to apply to Mr. Reagan, with the qualification that the individuals are those friends who share his dogmas or who are politically useful symbols during photo opportunities. He brought back, with calculated media exposure, two Korean children who needed medical operations. Would that he wield his great powers as President on behalf of America's infants and children instead of reducing special nutrition programs for impoverished pregnant women, mothers and their newly born.

He must know by now that polls consistently are showing sizeable majorities of people dislike his policies though they think he is a nice fellow. As long as that anomaly continues, he has little incentive to sensitize himself by meeting with active-victim groups such as the disabled. He has little incentive to ask his speech writers for genuine declarations of his compassionate recognition of their plight and determination to alleviate pain and prevent further trauma and disease.

Recently a young pediatrician took a long unpaid leave of absence from his California practice to crusade for reinstatement of the Crash Protection Standard (commonly called the Airbag Rule). He has received some mass media coverage of his efforts. He held a well-prepared vigil of physicians at Lafayette Park one Saturday afternoon and delivered a "visual letter" on video tape to the President. The White House, I subsequently learned, did not even bother to do the routine thing and forward it to the Secretary of Transportation. The doctor wondered why he and his fellow physicians could not see the President on a matter that public health specialists have called "the single most effective domestic life saving decision that the administration is in a position to make this year and perhaps for many years." I could have told the physician, recalling the list of past visitors to the President, that he did not qualify for a meeting since he had not won a boxing championship, performed a decisive slamdunk or won an Emmy.

Mr. Reagan is consistent with his pitiless deregulatory generalities. Had Congress not stopped him, he would have abolished crucial health and safety requirements imposed on the heavily tax-supported nursing home industry. Instead of firmer enforcement efforts and more adequate standards, he was content to leave defenseless the more than one million elderly in nursing homes.

3.

So extreme is the President's corporatism that he is finding more genuine conservative groups taking sharp issue with his policies. In a little reported evolution that may change the future complexion of American politics, organizations who call themselves conservative populists are teaming up with their progressive counterparts to oppose corporate bailouts. Last year this coalition defeated the breeder reactor boondoggle—a high Reagan priority. In 1981, it nearly defeated the legislation regarding the Alaska gas pipeline that would coerce consumers into paying for the pipeline even if the project isn't completed and consumers did not receive any natural gas. The synfuel industry's welfare project is under similar pressure, though its predicted mismanagement and awful economics appear to be self-dismantling. This new coalition put up a strong fight against the Reaganite bailout of the big U.S. banks that made such imprudent loans at skyhigh interest rates to foreign countries. Reagan, who spent years lecturing around the country for General Electric on the virtues of sink or swim free enterprise, has become the most prominent advocate of big business bailouts in American history.

If this all goes against his philosophic grain, it demonstrates the contrary power of giant business over his government. His formerly strong belief in states' rights is surrendered when companies want his backing for a weaker federal law replacing the adaptable common law in the fifty states that gives people injured by dangerous products rights to sue and recover compensation from manufacturers. It is surrendered when the banks demand that his agencies preempt stronger state regulations designed to protect depositors and borrowers. It is surrendered again when the nuclear industry wants him to strip state and local governments of their police power over the transportation of radioactive materials through their communities. Corporatizing the ex-conservative Ronald Reagan is a routine matter these days, even when Wall Street's economic and tax policy demands result in placing Main Street, with its small businesses, at a comparative disadvantage.

4.

The simplest of international decencies are rejected by the Reagan administration in obeisance to the multinationals. Mr. Carter's executive order requiring notification to foreign governments was revoked early in this republican administration. The order had been intended to restrain the export from this country of hazardous products illegal for domestic sale but not for export (e.g., certain drugs, pesticides) or to stop outright illegal exports. Now, with Mr. Reagan's knowledge and support, a clutch of global corporations, State and Commerce Department officials, and this government's United Nations' mission is working to stop the United Nations' draft guidelines on consumer protection. These principles of consumer safety and economic rights (the freedom to form consumer associations and the like) are drawn heavily from U.S. law and practice. They are just principles, having no force of authority but meant to have a moral impact on many countries and companies. Apparently, however, suggesting that the world has something to learn from U.S. consumer protection achievements over the past century is too provocative for the corporate statists in the Reagan camp. They seem unmindful of the disasters that have occurred in Third World countries, not a few generated by Western corporations taking advantage of the absence of indigenous consumer safeguards.

Such unmindfulness has become a habit. The Reagan government is the only member of the United Nations to vote against a U.N. resolution seeking to deter the kind of dumping of hazardous materials as occurred with the export of tris-treated (a carcinogen) children's pajamas from the U.S. All our allies voted the other way. The World Health Organization, with just one dissent, that of Ronald Reagan, approved a code for better marketing practices for infant formula promotion. This code was stimulated by the death of millions of Third World babies during the seventies linked to over-promotion of infant formula through scare techniques and other deceptions in conjunction with unsanitary village water sources. This tragedy has been reported in the context of the Nestlé boycott that was recently settled with international children's defense groups after Nestlé agreed to modify its actions.

5.

Every president has a unique mission of trust imposed upon him by certain conservation laws, some of them enacted by Republican-dominated congresses and presidents early in this century. I refer to the federal lands onshore and offshore with those glorious wildernesses and natural resources for present and future generations of Americans to enjoy and preserve. These lands comprise one-third of our nation from the pristine wilds of Alaska to the barren deserts of Arizona (a prime solar energy region someday). Does Mr. Reagan use his communications skills to graphically etch in the minds of more Americans the grandeur and permanence of his public trust? No, although he no longer talks about his support of the Sagebrushers who want the states to have these lands on their way to private ownership and exploitation.

Instead, he launched, through his agent James Watt, the biggest natural resource giveaway program to corporations in modern American History. The Reagan-Watt team wanted to lease billions of acres of offshore lands so fast that the oil company beneficiaries-to-be had to say, "Whoa, we can't absorb that rapid a transfer." So they settled for merely massive leaseholds on public lands whose oil and gas potential the government could not independently verify. In a glutted market of declining prices, Reagan-Watt proposed to lease as much coal in fifteen months as eleven administrations have done in the sixty-three years since the government began to lease its coal-bearing lands. These men knew that the coal and oil companies already were sitting on existing federal coal leases without producing any coal. What these companies want is not to produce but to control huge reserves of the people's resources at giveaway prices obtained in a depressed market. Reagan was all too eager to deliver, until organized civic opposition retired Watt and cooled off an election-sensitive President.

One would at the very least expect Mr. Reagan to want to give taxpayers (that majority of the taxpayers who will pay more in total taxes in 1984 than in 1980) value for what they paid government contractors to develop. Not at all. By presidential directive, agencies are urged to turn over to companies exclusive patent rights to government-financed discoveries to the fullest extent permissible. This is one of many areas of corporate privilege to which the Reaganites neglect to apply their cost-benefit formula. But the formula is so often rigged to cater to corporations, one shouldn't be surprised when it is not applied at all.

6.

The curtain around Reagan's corporate state is one of intense secrecy whose function of excluding the public's participation and monitoring is nourished by a rising base of zero data. This administration does not want to know what corporations do; it has stopped collecting much data about the large oil companies. It has stopped collecting data about line of business reporting by conglomerates. Referring to across-the-board cuts in federal statistical gathering services, University of Chicago Dean William Kruskal wrote: "When a vessel is in stormy seas, it is foolhardy to cut corners on radar, navigational equipment, good maps, and ample, well-trained crews." Coupled with not wanting to know, the government has defined as trade secrets whatever information companies want withheld from the public, even though it is supplied to the government for particular proceedings affecting the public.

The price of government reports and pamphlets has skyrocketed to levels reachable only by the affluent or desperate. Look at the government printing office's price list and you will see pamplets of only a few pages selling for over two dollars each. Price hikes have driven the number of publications requested from the government's consumer information center in fiscal year 1984 to half of what they were in fiscal 1982. Many publications, such as the popular *Car Book,* have been discontinued. Citizens wanting to be placed on mailing lists of the FCC or the ICC for agency press releases are referred to private contractors who will sell you this service. The principle of the broadest possible distribution of information about what the government is doing and deciding has been destroyed. The pretext is that the user should pay and as printing volume declines the prices go up in a vicious circle of exclusion. The government pays almost $100 million a year for marching bands. (That's twice as much as the cost of administering the Freedom of Information Act and there are no viewer fees charged there.)

To top off Reagan's Darkness at Noon, the basic research and development which elevates awareness of hazards to be averted and opportunities to be developed have been severely weakened due to industry demands. Thus, the experimental Safety Vehicle Program and the Fuel Economy Research Program have been closed. Sharply reduced are research undertakings in energy conservation, cancer prevention, drug safety, toxic chemicals and consumer product safety. Such inquiries could lead to stronger future safety standards—a prospect companies usually like to cut off at the pass. What is so deplorable about Mr. Reagan is that his supine relations with business brings out the worst in corporate behavior. Executives see that they do not have to do safety research or be concerned about compliance with laws that are about to be enforced. General Motors' Chairman, Roger Smith, disbanded the company's crack air-bag technology development section unit in April 1981, after learning that Transportation Secretary Drew Lewis was going to scrap the Automatic Crash Protection Regulation. Companies that stretch to advance the cause of safety, as have State Farm and Allstate, receive no plaudits, no medals, no encouragement from the man in the White House. If anything, these firms think they may be inviting resentment for their efforts.

All in all, the Reagan government is the consummate promoter of the rich and powerful when the latter are arrayed against the interests of the rest of America. We must not forget that it is not just Reagan who occupies that eminent political office. It is the network of collegial business interests who have learned so well that the essence of privilege in America's marketplace today requires control over the government's powers and its public wealth. Subsidies, monopolistic licenses, protectionism, selective enforcement, lucrative contracts, loan guarantees, bailouts, and the free results of expensive research and development are among the dispensations of modern Uncle Sugar in Washington, D.C. Together these goodies make a bustling bazaar of corporate welfare and largess that requires nurturing and enlargement. Toward this objective it helps to have your own business agent in the White House. It helps to have someone who does not raise American's expectation levels.

Americans have every right to some solutions to their everyday afflictions, some value for their everyday tax dollars and some voice for their everyday concerns, some remedies for their everyday injustices, and some civic mechanisms for building their futures.

The empowerment and widespread exercise of citizenship is a prerequisite for a sound, democratic society. Leadership that empowers more people, that reduces the severe concentration of power and information, and that lifts a nation into missions of accomplishment which will increase justice, happiness and opportunity—that is the leadership citizens must demand by involving themselves in a national political campaign. So too, the media should rise to their higher responsibility to report the White House and not just mimeograph its rhetoric.

Our history has demonstrated that the well-being of society springs from the growth of daily, active citizenship that provides an enabling environment for good leaders to come forth. Every significant social movement in this century has sprung from active citizens fighting for their cause—women's suffrage, workers' rights, civil rights, environmental and consumer protection, peace. Put in today's terms, citizens in our country need to spend more time being citizens. That is the real bottom line.

Reforming Corporate Governance

Originally appeared in California Management Review Vol. XXVI, No. 4, Summer 1984.

OVER THE PAST one hundred years, the impact and range of the modern corporation over the world, its peoples and future generations, have been vastly extended. Large concentrations of capital, new technologies, and the accumulated experience of using power have been major factors in the dominance of the multinational corporation. Yet the board of directors, the corporation's governing institution, has changed far less than that which it is directing. Between the company and its board, there is an evolutionary mismatch, if the standard of board responsibility is applied to the legitimate demands which today can be made upon the directors.

To say that corporations are spreading their wings compared to the early 20th century Ajax company producing widgets is to frame the arena for any discussion of corporate ethics. Presently, companies are interacting with a variety of constituencies in ways that raise questions of corporate criminality, negligence, fraud, and other forms of illicit or coercive behavior. Shareholders, workers, consumers, the communities where plants are located, taxpayers, political institutions such as Congress, universities, local school systems, suppliers, the unborn, foreign nations, the environment, outer space—all these subjects of corporate impacts have experienced with varying frequencies wrongful corporate behavior.

While there is not enough space here to present the evidence of corporate abuses in much detail, it is appropriate to list some of the reporting from the *Wall Street Journal* over the years, to wit: looting of shareholders, worker health and safety hazards, seriously mistreating consumers, contaminating community water and air, demanding preferential subsidies which unfairly burden smaller taxpayers, lobbying for direct preferential tax treatment, and pouring money into Congressional campaigns tailored to specific members and committees in order to gain influence not based on the merits. Other reports have documented firms that distort university research and pressure educational institutions to propagandize corporate views with corporate-supplied materials, higher education grants, contracts, and moonlighting invitations. Other studies have shown how companies pollute the genetic inheritance, help to overthrow foreign governments or destabilize them, and move to privatize more of outer space and oceanic exploitation.[1]

In recent years, the very concept of limited liability is being expanded beyond applying to shareholders to applying to the corporation itself. The nuclear industry has its Price-Anderson limited liability law and comfortably solvent companies such as Johns-Manville are using the bankruptcy petition to escape judicial claims by their workers or repudiate collective bargaining agreements.

Probably nothing has highlighted the board of directors incapacity more than the bribery scandals of the seventies and the collapse of companies such as the Penn-Central. In these cases, the board of directors was severely humiliated because the mismanagement and crimes were known and often condoned at the highest executive levels of the companies over a period of time. Yet the boards either did not know, did not want to know, or did not want to do anything about what they knew. Inescapably, the spotlight was on the board and the manner of its non-function.

The appointment of audit committees, the expansion of insurance coverage for directors' liability and the arrival of more outside directors were the major enduring legacies flowing from the decade of corporate troubles during the seventies and late sixties. The general routine of directors' meetings, their level of attentiveness and the information that they are supplied with by corporate executives may have changed a little but not very much from the satiric treatment they received in Robert Townsend's *Up the Organization*.[2] Notwithstanding all the trouble involving Citicorp over the past fifteen years, the bank's board of directors remains cast in the mold and image of CEO Walter Wriston.

In viewing the potential for boards to be forces behind corporate ethics, one can start with the perception of the board by rank and file within the company. Of all the workers—blue collar and white collar—who have come to us over the years with complaints about hazardous products, worker diseases, financial corruption, or invasion of privacy, none perceived their board of directors as an avenue for their appeal or communication. When, on occasion, we ask them to explain why they did not go to the board, their response is one of disbelief. It had never occurred to them, an absence of expectation that normally does not prevail in the area of political hierarchy, judging by the extra-jurisdictional complaints which are appealed to other elected officials in the political arena.

The board is not viewed, it is fair to say, as a place to take one's discoveries or one's conscience by people within the corporation. Nor do members of external groups have different expectations. Whether in Dupont's Delaware or General Motors' Detroit, community efforts may reach out to GM's President or Chairman but very rarely, if ever, to the board. It may be said that such a view is a shrewd judgment about the irrelevance or powerlessness of the corporate board. Boards have done little to disabuse this view, remaining quite remote, aloof and well camouflaged by company executives. But appeals are made to pretense as well as reality and boards possess a great deal of pretense which they could be held to by aggrieved parties inside and outside the company.

During the seventies, there were proposals to increase the independence, assertiveness, and diversity of large corporate boards. Former Chairman of the Securities and Exchange Commission Harold Williams was a strong proponent of more outside directors; others pushed for more women and minorities. Many companies responded affirmatively to these urgings. But the board's norms, its indentured environment selected and shaped by top corporate management, has overcome these changes. Little, indeed, has changed, except the enhanced recognition of the board's acculturating influence over nearly all newcomers to its rolls, regardless of their background. Anyone who has studied the little difference that co-determination has made for the boards of large European corporations, as in West Germany, would not be surprised with the above observation. When black residents of Poletown in Detroit were being dispossessed by the city's takeover of their area for resale to General Motors, under heavy subsidy terms, their written appeal and telephone calls to Leon Sullivan, the only black member on GM's board, brought no assistance nor even any response. No doubt, Mr. Sullivan could have explained the boundaries which limited his engagement with the issue—not unlike the boundaries that GM Chairman Roger Smith would have elaborated as well on Mr. Sullivan's behalf.

There are directors who have serious misgivings about one or more doings in their company. Their course of action is usually to resign from the board rather than stay and conduct the good fight. Exit rather than challenge is the cultural norm. For a significant number of large- and medium-sized companies, a little-publicized clearance of members of the board is in place. The Department of Defense performs these reviews as a precondition to awarding contracts of a given classification to the contractor or subcontractor. This oversight is but part of a selection pattern that assures little prospect of there being a 'minority of one' on most corporate boards of any size.

What changes could help the board do its job of holding the CEO accountable and exercising its governing responsibilities to foresee crises or respond to them appropriately? Here are some suggestions. First, board members might commit more time to their duties. The idea that boards can govern corporations the size of Exxon, Lockheed, or Sears by flying to the scene for a few hours of meetings is anachronistic. A stronger case can be made for full-time outside board members than can be made for the present symbolic visits that are supposed to congeal two dozen or so people coming from all points of the compass into an informed body that directs companies or conglomerates of extensive complexity. Some of these people hold down full-time careers and positions on three, six or more boards of directors.

Second, why shouldn't the board have its own small staff that can develop or obtain critical information about what is going on inside the company that the CEO and his/her president are reluctant to share in a full and timely fashion with the board? Such a staff can also do some full-time thinking so that the board can bring to its company matters of a broader horizon than can be expected of day-to-day top managers. A staff would also make possible a more arm's length relationship to operating management than is presently the case. Sometimes the care and feeding of a rubber-stamping board that the CEO selects is carried to extremes.

My third suggestion relates to specialized duties attached to individual members of the board in addition to their current general obligations. There is a propensity for conventional corporatists to misunderstand this proposal.

In our past writings on this subject,[3] we proposed that specific dimensions of large corporate activity (consumers, workers, environment, research marketing, finance, compliance, etc.) be assigned to different members of the board. Shareholders would elect the board from candidates running for these various designations. Cumulative voting rights would encourage both diversity of representation and a heightened public sense of candidates standing for specific assignments in addition to their general duties. A little specialization within the board would bring improved focus internally and a more visible expectation of oversight externally. In short, there will be a special member of the board with knowledge about his or her area of specific responsibility from which to communicate information, complaints, and proposals.

Apart from the personalities of members and the structure of the board itself, what other factors could impel the board to advance the level of ethical awareness and application within the company? First and most obvious are the twin impositions of legal duty and legal risk. Corporation law prescribes various duties for board members and establishes boundaries and sanctions for their breach. Some of the liability risk is attenuated by insurance coverage, but there are risks to position and reputation which are not responsive to insurance. Moreover, there is the slim risk of criminal prosecution. Just as slim a risk is their removal from the board by shareholders. Without cumulative voting, without a more selective voting interest by large institutional shareholder blocs, and without bringing greater choice and democracy to the corporate electoral process, the quality of board performance will not be accountable to the company's owners. There has been extensive documentation of conventional and outrageous mismanagement of large corporations in America. While occasionally the chairman and president are replaced, the board escapes the reach of either internal or external corporate accountability mechanisms, short of involuntary bankruptcy.

Where the courts impose sanctions—fines, incarceration, probation, damage awards—the impact is almost always either on the corporation or, more rarely, on the managers. Such defendants buffer board members from legal exposure and sanction. The public's low expectation level has translated itself into the law's operational avoidance of imposing sanctions on board members, notwithstanding the board's legal duties as an internal auditor of the corporation, responsible for constraining executive management from violations of law, breach of trust, and major error. Certainly corporate disclosure through the media, as in the Firestone radial tire case, provides incentives for more diligent board performance, if only to replace executives. More systematic corporate disclosure at public offices around the country or by computerized retrieval systems can create a climate around the board that breeds alertness. Less prevalent would be the syndrome verbalized by the line: "We don't want to know, because the more we know the more we may be liable."

It is tempting to give significance to market sanctions—the kind that flow from a defective product's or service's declining sales. But for the larger companies, it is remarkable how little effect such sales drops have on changing board behavior, procedure or composition. The more conglomeratized large companies become, the less impact on the board there is from one of the divisions' or subsidiaries' sales loss. The insulating effect from the board's aloof factor is more pronounced in such sprawling structures.

In discussing corporate reform proposals, attention is properly directed toward stimuli proceedings from regulatory, market and information disclosure impacts. But there is a potential area of voluntary discretion and wisdom which boards can avail themselves of to great effect. Who the board selects as chairman and president of its company may well be the most important decision shaping the firm's "corporate character." Much has been made of the company's technocrats or the company bureaucracy's hold over the firm or, at least, its ability to keep anyone at the top from really running the store. Again and again, however, the display of corporate ethical behavior at its heights reflects the guiding hand of the people at the top who set the tone and the direction. State Farm and Allstate have been leaders in supporting the federal motor vehicle crash protection standard #208 because of the personal commitment of CEO Edward Rust and CEO Arch Boe respectively. General Motors boosted air bags between 1970 and 1974 because of GM President Edward Cole; after Cole's retirement, CEO Richard Gerstenberg and his successors reversed policy completely and continued with active opposition.

It is not a little significant that Cole was an engineer and his successors were financial executives. Abstraction from empirical data and experience can be a useful intellectual tool, but excessive abstraction leads to remoteness from reality. Detachment from the highway anguish of motorists in crashes can anesthetize the moral or ethical impulses of persons who spend all their working hours high up in executive suites. Sensitizing the better impulses within executives becomes more likely when they climb down their abstraction ladder and observe other peoples' lives once in a while. In an interview with Paul Austin, CEO of the Coca Cola Company, a few years ago, I found him not reluctant to say that his visit to observe migrant worker conditions in the company's Florida orange groves shook him visibly and led him to resolve to improve their plight. I was once told by a member of the board of directors of a steel company about the day his chairman convened them and said: "Why don't we do something different for once; let's go down to a coal mine." They went down, down, down into the coal mine and spent 30 minutes, cramped and cold, chatting with the miners. They could not wait to re-emerge. He told me that he will never again say that coal miners are overpaid. A less traumatic mode of feedback would be for the board to hold periodic hearings for employees and for outsiders it believes worth hearing. Even some autocratic kings of the past would have public sessions with their aggrieved subjects. There are also emergencies affecting companies which invite the need for such hands-on involvement by the board. The mere likelihood of such hearings would help keep top executives on their toes.

These suggestions no doubt will raise the question of the absence of board independence to accomplish these tasks. One can scarcely imagine even an overwhelmingly favorably disposed Citicorp Board weighing in against CEO Walter Wriston on such an expansion of Board oversight and knowledge. The insufficiency of board independence to act is a most basic problem that must be addressed in any consideration of ways to preserve and extend corporate ethical behavior. Such a subject is beyond the ken of this presentation; however, two internal changes can help the board exercise more necessary functions and understandings. One is to establish a company ombudsman out of the line of hierarchy who can receive complaints from employees and can decide when it is appropriate to contact the board on some serious matter being ignored by the CEO or president or because the issue is clearly within the formal purview of the board's obligations. The ombudsman should have direct access to board members. In the late sixties, the *Harvard Business Review* published an article by Professor I. Silver on the advisability of the corporate ombudsman and how such an office would be structured and empowered. It deserves reading today.

The other change would be to explicitly accord employees of business corporations "whistleblower rights" on matters of conscience such as free speech, safety, and health, and provide employees reasonable due process for handling conflict with management. In books and articles by David Ewing, an editor of the *Harvard Business Review,* this area of employee rights in the context of the Bill of Rights has been given extensive treatment. His most recent book, *Do It My Way Or You're Fired!,*[4] presents case studies about what happens to people who refuse to heed the company line when they observe or experience sexual harassment, malfeasance, fraud, safety violations, and unethical practices. His purpose is to illuminate the obligations of the whistle-blower and the ways management can work to the advantage of the organization as well as the individual in nourishing dissent and dignity.

It is abundantly apparent that boards of directors can no longer operate with the slogan of "confidence in management" unless there are mechanisms and information flows that give such confidence empirical foundations. Without a willingness to commit the time and resources, the board will continue to be a social gathering where people largely of means and other elitist positions get together regularly to place *pro forma* imprints on management decisions that would never pass muster under a monocle's worth of a real board's scrutiny.

References

1. For more information and case studies, see *Power, Inc.* by Martin Mintz and Jerry Cohen (New York, NY: Viking Press, 1976) and *The Big Business Reader* edited by Mark Green (New York, NY: The Pilgrim Press, 1983).

2. Robert Townsend, *Up the Organization*, (New York, NY: Alfred Knopf, Inc., 1970). Also see Townsend's Further Up the Organization (New York, NY: Alfred Knopf, Inc., 1984).

3. Ralph Nader, Mark Green, and Joel Seligman, *Taming the Giant Corporation* (New York, NY: W. W. Norton, 1976).

4. David Ewing, *Do It My Way or You're Fired!* (New York, NY: John Wiley & Sons, 1983).

Corporate Power In America

Originally appeared in The Nation, *March 29, 1980.*

WRITING IN THE LATE 1950S, William Gossett, the vice president of Ford Motor Company, described the corporation as the dominant institution of American society. His candor troubled some of his business colleagues who liked to diminish the impression that corporations have the power to control or condition so much behavior in this country. What Mr. Gossett said over twenty years ago is even more accurate today.

The mercantile values of the modern giant corporations shape more than market forces in their image. They pervade government, politics, law, taxation, environment, education, communications, foundations, athletics and even institutions formerly believed to be outside their influence, such as the family or organized religion. The calculated penetration of children's minds by exploitative advertisements on children's television illustrates how the mercantile thrust can undermine parental authority, as well as proper diet. Indeed, both in space and time, the large corporation is expanding its impact, as multinational activity and chemical and other technological burdens on future generations increase. Many multinational corporations' general revenues today dwarf the GNPs of dozens of foreign nations. General Motors, Exxon and ITT together took in more dollars last year than the Pentagon—which has the largest military budget in the world.

A corporate economy, a corporate society, a corporate state were not always part of the American ethos. Jefferson viewed the new representative government as curbing the excesses of "the monied interests." The pre-Civil War period reflected an established belief in the merits of a decentralized economy based on farmers and small businessmen, which culminated in the Homestead Act under President Lincoln's Administration. There was suspicion widespread during the first half of the nineteenth century about letting "legal fictions" called corporations, with limited liability to their investors, engage in production without legal constraints. Advocate Daniel Webster could thunder in court about a corporation having "no soul." Legislatures were very restrictive in their chartering of corporations.

The post-Civil War period of that century witnessed what some historians describe as a major and dramatic change in the economy and in the prevailing ethos. The Industrial Revolution was underway with large corporate capital gobbling up small competitors. The oil, steel, tobacco, sugar and other "trusts" ushered in the first wave of corporate concentration. The Horatio Alger ideology with its mercantile definition of success insinuated itself deeply in the psychology of the culture. At the same time, the restrictions on corporate chartering loosened. State legislatures delegated the functions to state agencies, and they in turn delegated more discretion about what economic pursuits corporations could follow and what were the responsibilities of company officers and boards of directors. Late in the nineteenth century, states, led by New Jersey, began to turn corporate chartering into a competitive race for state revenues by enacting more permissive chartering laws. This "race to the bottom," in Professor William Cary's words, was won by Delaware in the early 1900s, and that state remains the domicile of many of the world's largest corporations.

The Delaware corporation syndrome, which pulled other states toward a lower common denominator for chartering, represented a major victory for corporate power in America. No longer would the corporate charter constitute even a pretense of being a corporate governance mechanism providing accountability to shareholders and other affected corporate constituencies. Instead, the state-granted charters devolved with each succeeding weakening of the Delaware corporate law over the next eight decades. By conscious lobbying, corporations turned restrictive charter laws into instruments for further concentration of power in the hands of management. A constitutional structure for accountability rights by people inside as well as outside the corporate structure passed into history.

By contrast, the growth of various forms of corporate management power over shareholders, workers, consumers, community residents, taxpayers and governments proceeded apace—through the "Robber Barons" period into World War I (wars always increase a lasting kind of corporate entrenchment), the "business of America is business" 1920s, the "New Deal" 1930s, World War II and the massive acceleration of influence and impact during the past generation. Greater aggregations of natural resources, capital, labor and technology under more centralized management also daunted the ability of entrepreneurs, inventors and small businesses to challenge this megacorporate hegemony. Small business instead survived increasingly by becoming an appendage, a franchise to corporate headquarters, economically and politically.

Yet monopolies, oligopolies and giant business generally did not expand without challenge. A series of these challenges began in the 1880s with the farmers' revolt out of Texas and Oklahoma, so well chronicled by Lawrence Goodwyn's *The Populist Moment: A Short History of Agrarian Revolts in America*. The banks and railroads were the focus of this fundamental power struggle which, in weakened form, led to the populist progressive movement a few years later. The first regulatory agencies, price supports, public enterprises (grain elevators), producer cooperatives and direct democracy instruments (initiative, referendum and recall) emerged from this agrarian political and economic mobilization. This reform movement was probably the most basic and deeply rooted in our country's history. For all its continuing legacies, however, it failed to stem the tide of Big Business. Four other challenges during this century have had some intermittent success in curbing some of the more egregious excesses of these large industrial and financial companies—the labor, consumer, civil rights and environmental movements.

There is a uniquely consistent pattern to the strategy of response by companies once they decide that they cannot totally defeat the reform drive. Where regulations or standards are issued by an agency for health and safety, a deliberate process of delay, attrition and political influence is initiated. That is why statutes read more promisingly than the regulations and the latter read more promisingly than the reality in the marketplace, workplace and environment. Wherever the political government is empowered to protect the interests of labor, consumer or other constituencies, the corporate government increases its financing of political elections. Where the law requires a redirection of investment to reduce the costs of pollution or consumer injury, companies find ways to transfer these costs to the victims themselves, through tax preferences or administered pricing; they often avoid internalizing these proper costs to compete against other internal cost decisions (safety versus style in cars). And because of the inordinate secrecy permitted these multinational companies, management can wildly exaggerate the costs of compliance to prod public resistance to health and safety standards while at the same time keeping secret the evidence of hazards (chemical waste dumps, automobile defects, food contamination and drug risks).

There is always a lag between the actual adverse impacts of large corporations and public knowledge of them. This is true of almost every industrial danger exposed during the past thirty years, from pesticides to nuclear power to occupational disease. There is also a great lag from corporate diagnosis to public prescription. The public consequences of these dual lags for people, nation and world are becoming more ominous with the advent of highly perilous technology in the hands of country-hopping multinational corporations. Fifty years ago an imperious utility might have cost consumers a few exorbitant dollars a year on their electric bills. Today that same utility is building or operating a nuclear plant in their community. Fifty years ago, the petrochemical industry was in its infancy; today it is flooding the human environment with carcinogens and a wide variety of other toxic chemicals. Love Canal-type dumps are being discovered all over America the Poisoned. Wherever Love Canals are revealed there are no conservatives and there are no liberals; there are only victims becoming angrier.

The contemporary challenge to giant business is quite modest compared to historical movements in our past. There is no strong demand for basic ownership changes. The furthest the contemporary critique goes is to offer alternatives such as greater self-reliance, more consumer cooperatives and a little public enterprise involving, for example, energy extraction and production on federal lands to compete with the big companies. The principal call is almost primitive in its simplicity. It is a call for corporations to stop stealing, stop deceiving, stop corrupting politicians with money, stop monopolizing, stop poisoning the earth, air and water, stop selling dangerous products, stop exposing workers to cruel hazards, stop tyrannizing people of conscience within the company and start respecting long-range survival needs and rights of present and future generations.

Is Bigness Bad for Business?

BY RALPH NADER AND MARK GREEN

Originally appeared in Business and Society Review, *Summer 1979.*

Is BIGNESS BADNESS?

Ask businessmen about bigness and *business,* and the answer is reflexively "no." Absolute size is absolutely irrelevant, it is said. Yet ask businessmen about bigness and *government,* the answer, just as routinely, is "of course." Big government is wasteful, unresponsive, bureaucratically bogged down in red tape. But business advocates can't have it both ways—especially now, as conglomerate mergers grow more frequent and big business grows yet bigger.

Indeed, as one studies the empirical record of our large multinational conglomerates, there are substantial economic and social costs inflicted by their giant size, without offsetting benefits. So let us ask the ritual question once more—and, like the citizen who saw the emperor naked, actually look at the answer rather than assume it. Is bigness badness? Yes, for ten reasons:

I. DEEP POCKET

In the words of economist Corwin Edwards, "The big company can outbid, outspend, or outlose the small one." Or, as Professor Walter Adams once put it, "Pretending that a firm with ITT's absolute size and aggregate power is a run-of-the-mill newcomer to the grass seed business is not unlike the suggestion that injecting Kareem Abdul Jabbar into a grade school basketball game would have no impact on the . . . probable outcome of the contest." Clorox, for example, was the leading firm in the bleach industry, but when Procter & Gamble acquired it in 1957, the firm became the unassailably dominant leader in the industry. As the Supreme Court said in 1967, smaller competitors and potential competitors, appreciating P&G's financial ability to underwrite huge advertising campaigns or cross-subsidize its subsidiary if necessary, "would become more cautious in competing due to their fear of retaliation by Procter."

2. POTENTIAL COMPETITION

Since LTV, for example, might have entered the steel industry via internal expansion or the acquisition of a small steel firm, there was a loss of potential competition when it took over Jones & Laughlin, the sixth largest steel company. Indeed, the threat of potential entry by a major firm outside an industry can discourage the dominant firms in that industry from raising prices.

3. RECIPROCITY

When subsidiaries within a large conglomerate or between large conglomerates say you-buy-from-me-and-I'll-buy-from-you, competitors can be locked out of markets not because of a superior product, but because of a network of quid pro quos. Cities Service in 1962 was frustrated when it attempted to enter the rubber-oil market, because major tire companies had pervasive reciprocal arrangements with the large petroleum companies. ITT-Sheraton bought Philco-Ford TV sets in exchange for that company's use of Sheraton hotel rooms. "The U.S. economy might end up," *Fortune* magazine once worried, "completely dominated by conglomerates happily trading with each other in a new kind of cartel system."

4. MUTUAL FORBEARANCE

In 1923, a DuPont executive described his company's policy to Imperial Chemical Industries of Great Britain, number two in the world to DuPont. "It is not good business sense to attempt an expansion in certain directions if such an act is bound to result [in] a boomerang of retaliation." Four decades later, when Continental Foods slashed prices at its Chicago stores, the National Tea Corp., its competitor and a buyer of some Continental items, threatened to drop Continental lines from its shelves. Continental then ended its price-cutting campaign. As conglomerate size and diversification increase, argues economist Willard Mueller, who has developed the "mutual forbearance" theory, "the number of contacts shared with competitors, suppliers and customers [increases], thereby increasing the mutual awareness of common interests among firms." As a result, companies pull their punches in the competitive arena.

5. DISECONOMIES OF SIZE

Conglomerate mergers are usually justified by the magic of synergy, that 2 + 2 = 5. To be sure, economies of scale require that firms be large enough to be efficient. But firms can also be *too* large to be efficient (or 2 + 2 = 3). Studies by the Federal Trade Commission and House Antitrust Subcommittee in the late 1960s could not detect any efficiencies as a result of large conglomerate mergers. Which should not be surprising. All chairmen and vice-presidents have the same twenty-four-hour day as the rest of us, and if they try to manage one hundred subsidiaries rather than two, there will be too little time to make quality judgments about the numerous issues that fly across their desks. The bigger a firm, the bigger the costs of bureaucracy: excessive paper work; committees reviewing committees; undetected sloth; institutional caution and delay; and Parkinson's law that superiors like to proliferate subordinates. "There is no obvious association between firm size and such dimensions of managerial quality as dynamism, intelligence, awareness, and skill in interpersonal relations," said Frederick Scherer after eighty-six interviews with business managers. "I am inclined toward the view that the unit costs of management, including the hidden losses due to delayed or faulty decisions and weakened or distorted incentives . . . do tend to rise with the organizational size."

In the ultimate perversion of the marketplace, our dinosaur firms may grow so large that, whatever their inefficiencies, the government cannot afford to let them fail. But if the marketplace is no longer allowed to "penalize" poor managerial decisions, then business has less discipline or incentive to make good decisions and revise bad ones. No wonder, then, that entrepreneurs prefer big to small: It is the ultimate insurance policy. John Cobbs in *Business Week* a few years ago understood this dilemma:

In the years before World War I, Germany invested so heavily in battleships that, when the war came, it did not dare let them fight. As the U.S. economy slides deeper into recession, the federal government finds itself in a similar position. The huge U.S. corporations have become such important centers of jobs and incomes that it dare not let one of them shut down or go out of business. It is compelled, therefore, to shape national policy in terms of protecting the great corporations instead of letting the economy make deflationary adjustments.

6. INNOVATION

It is often argued, from an a priori basis, that companies have to be very large in order to afford the risk of large investments in research and development. But facts contradict this abstraction. Having examined many R&D expenditure analyses, Leonard Weiss concluded, "Most studies show that within their range of observation, size adds little to research intensity and may actually detract from it in some industries." Scherer, based on his own compilation of studies correlating firm size and innovation, observed that there were economies of scale for innovation for firms up to 5,000 employees (*Fortune*'s 500th firm in 1974 had 6,450 employees), but no advantage beyond that. The famous Jewkes study of invention showed that of sixty-one basic inventions examined, only sixteen resulted from organizational research by large companies. For example, the ballpoint pen was invented by a sculptor, the dial telephone by an undertaker. The firms which introduced stainless steel razor blades (Wilkinson), transistor radios (Sony), photocopying machines (Xerox), and the "instant" photograph (Polaroid) were all small and little known when they made their momentous breakthroughs.

It appears that the best innovation usually emerges from solo inventors or small- and medium-sized firms—not our giant corporations. The latter may be able to *afford* it, but do they *desire* it? If you already dominate an industry, where is the incentive to take a chance on a new and costly approach? We don't associate inventiveness with the centralized planning of socialist economies, even though the planners have substantial R&D resources under their control. The reason is that they, like big businessmen, are not eager to give the green light to new ways which threaten their investment in the old ways.

7. JOBS AND UNIONS

Conglomerate mergers mean plants are bought, not built. Wealth and jobs are transferred, not created. Antitrust Division Chief John Shenefield has estimated that more than one-fifth of the growth of large firms has been due to acquisition, not internal growth. Or as Thomas Murphy, the chairman of General Motors, said in 1977, "One reason, in my opinion, that the long-predicted capital spending boom never seems to get off the ground is these acquisitions. Money that would normally go into plant and equipment at this stage of a recovery is being siphoned off by acquisitions."

Workers are also affected, for conglomerate acquisitions upset the power balance between management and labor. Suppose a union represents a small minority of all the workers of a far-flung conglomerate. Then why bother striking the Pittsburgh subsidiary when it accounts for only 5 percent of company production, and production can simply be transferred to the union-free plant in Spain? This evolution can annul the right to strike, which is labor's only power vis-à-vis management.

8. COMMUNITY EFFECT

Absentee corporations can have a profound impact on the local communities of companies they purchase. They can decide not merely that a plant is not making money, but that it is not making *as much money* as some other profit center in the worldwide enterprise. Hence an executive in New York City or Brussels might decide to pull the plug on a facility in Youngstown, Ohio, in a way that local ownership would never do.

A study by Jon Udell of the University of Wisconsin indicated that firms acquiring Wisconsin companies tended to use fewer professional services in local communities after a merger. "Most of the acquired firms covered in the survey now use the financial institutions, legal services, and accounting services of parent companies." So after the Chase Manhattan Bank extended a line of credit to Gulf & Western to make acquisitions, G&W reciprocated by moving the acquirees' financial services from local banks to Chase. Following a West German firm's take-over of a Detroit chemical company, the late Senator Philip Hart (D-Mich.) asked, "To what extent will a firm whose headquarters are in another state or another country be disposed to play a significant role on something like the New Detroit Committee?" This erosion of community by absentee business control especially worried former Supreme Court Justice William Douglas. In 1949, he wrote:

"Local leadership is diluted. He who was a leader in the village becomes dependent on outsiders for his action and policy. Clerks responsible to a superior in a distant place take the place of resident proprietors beholden to no one. These are the prices which the nation pays for the almost ceaseless growth in bigness on the part of industry."

9. POLITICAL IMPACT

Our democracy assumes, in Judge Learned Hand's phrase, a "multiplicity of tongues" competing in the political marketplace. But as large conglomerates grow larger, there are fewer decision-makers deciding who gets business campaign contributions and who doesn't, what advocacy advertisements run, what bills get their decisive support. Montgomery Ward was a strong supporter of a Consumer Protection Agency a few years ago, but it became an inactive supporter after its acquisition by Mobil Oil. Of course, small producers organized into trade groups can have significant political impact, but a giant conglomerate still has privileged political status, as Senator Philip Hart recognized: "When a major corporation from a state wants to discuss something with its political representatives, you can be sure it will be heard. When that same company operates in thirty states, it will be heard by thirty times as many representatives." A study by political scientists Lester Solomon and John Siegfried in 1975 tried to document this shadowy relationship using the petroleum industry as an example. Their conclusion:

Particularly striking was (1) the discovery of a negative relationship between firm size and effective corporate income tax rates; (2) empirical evidence systematically linking the relative dominance of large firms in the refining industry in each state to the level of state motor vehicle fuel excise tax rates; and (3) a pattern of regulatory policies with substantial economic payoffs for the industry.

10. SECRECY

Single-line firms have to disclose publicly their profits and losses for their product. But as a conglomerate acquires additional firms, its consolidated income statement describes the firm's overall health but not the profit or loss per product line. So small businesses have to make greater disclosures than their larger, more diversified competitors. And investors and government agencies cannot easily evaluate whether some divisions are earning monopoly returns, or are being subsidized. As conglomerates acquire smaller firms, there is, in an FTC phrase, "information loss."

Some mergers, of course, can lead to genuine economies of scale or can be pro-competitive, as when an outside company acquires a non-leading firm ("toehold acquisition") in an industry in need of competitive stimulation. Too frequently, however, in the words of Henry Simons, a founding father of the Chicago School of Economics, the existence of giant conglomerates "is to be explained in terms of opportunities for promotion profits, personal ambitions of industrial and financial Napoleons, and advantages of monopoly power."

Our public policy goal should be to encourage competition. The sentiment and speeches behind the 1890 and 1950 antitrust acts reflect Judge Learned Hand's view that "great industrial consolidations are inherently undesirable, regardless of their economic results." But the language of the law does not reflect this view. It's time to rewrite the law to make it coextensive with the problem.

A two-stage bill could accomplish this goal. First, huge conglomerate mergers—e.g., where each entity had over $100 million in annual sales or assets and the resulting firm was worth more than $2 billion in annual sales or assets—would be flatly prohibited unless the partners could prove that "significant economies of scale" or "significant competitive benefits" would result. Second, no firm with over $500 million in annual sales or assets could acquire any of the four leading firms in concentrated markets, and to the extent that the large firm made any acquisitions it would have to spin off a comparable amount of assets. This approach would leave it to private firms to decide what assets were truly economical to maintain and which to drop. Mergers would be spurred by efficiencies, not the ambitions of "financial Napoleons."

This legislation is socially desirable, economically workable, and politically viable. Indeed, its prospects have never been better. The public is understandably dismayed at the unresponsiveness of big institutions. For the first time in memory, there is a chairman of the Senate Judiciary Committee, a chairman of the Senate Antitrust Subcommittee, an Attorney General, an Antitrust Division chief, and chairman of the FTC who publicly concurred that unchecked conglomerate mergers are deleterious. At the same time, a renewed merger wave makes reform urgent.

How to Recognize Capitalists and Corporatists

Originally appeared in The Washington Star, *January 14, 1978.*

JIMMY CARTER should meet Freddie Laker. The jolly chairman of Laker Airways could regale him with stories about the differences between capitalists and corporatists. As a British capitalist, Mr. Laker is making heaps of money these days by transporting people back and forth between New York and London at less than half the price the regular airlines charge.

Freddie Laker's determined drive of the past six years, culminating in his September 1977 low fare breakthrough, is weakening the international airline cartel called IATA (International Air Transport Association) and is bringing some price competition back into the business. He believes in strict government safety standards but wide-open price competition in the marketplace.

Corporatists, on the other hand, reject Laker's quaint beliefs. They want price security and if government protections can assure price-setting cartels, all the better. They want subsidies, tax benefits, free research and development, non-competitive government contracts, import quotas and other federal and state welfare supports as "incentives" to make profits. What government guarantees they lack, they try and obtain by collusive or anti-competitive practices such as price or product-fixing. Some call this welfare mentality of giant corporations in concentrated industries "corporate social-ism" and its practitioners "corporatists!"

Corporatist ideology has increasingly shaped the White House's eco-nomic policies. The President is supposed to stay out of the corporate econ-omy but be responsible for its failings. His role is to provide "incentives" (read taxpayer money) and "guarantees" (read taxpayer credit). Dozens of major corporate subsidy programs and over $200 billion worth of loan guarantees outstanding attest to the power of the corporatists' "business confidence" test that is imposed on recent Presidents. Wall Street expects Uncle Sam to stay out of its hair but line its pockets.

Major industries in this country, from steel to oil, have become masters at placing the blame on Presidents for the consequences of their misman-agement, non-competitiveness or greed. Although the nation's economic machine is still overwhelmingly in private corporate hands, the barons of industry and commerce make sure that governments coerce the small tax-payer and the consumer to bail them out.

President Carter has not escaped this corporate strategy whose code word is "business confidence." His State of the Union message will recognize many of the same economic policies that a Ford administration would have urged.

PLAYING CATCH-UP with the powerful Business Roundtable mentality will never produce much more than costly palliatives and a demeaned pres-idential leadership. What Jimmy Carter needs to tell the corporate sector is to stop whining and start competing, stop milking the taxpayer and start serving the consumer, cease wallowing in waste and commence innovating for the real needs of people.

There was a glimpse of such thinking in the otherwise fawning remarks of President Carter on December 14 before the Business Council—a group of influential corporate executives. "I see the major redressing of our prob-lem with unemployment being in your hands; in the private business sec-tor. The major means of redressing the permanent underlying inflation rate lies in your hands," Carter told them.

These words could signal a fresh approach to government economic pol-icy. Some things the government has to do directly for the economic well being of Americans. But propping up a corporate welfare system constantly cloying at Washington is not the way to any economic solutions, whether intermediate or long range.

The absurdity of such cloying was reflected recently in a *Wall Street Journal* editorial railing against "Mr. Carter's determination to attack the 'three martini lunch' and business-related entertainment." The *Journal* observed that "keeping this drop of malice in the bill will not improve the condifence of business in future economic policy." Since when should the taxpayer in this country be required to subsidize a wholly non-meritorious technique for selling goods and services. Should "martinis" be encouraged by a tax subsidy to become a competitive factor in winning a sale, not to mention their shoring up business confidence?

Mr. Carter's Council of Economic Advisers needs to be provoked with a sense of fundamentals about the economic structure of this country and about the dislocating influence of concentrated industries. Trying to recommend policy based on corporate-defined indicators does little to advance equity, quality or productivity in our economy. However, it does serve further to encourage unjust corporate demands on Washington.

My father once told me that the more political power corporations possess, the less economically efficient and creative they become. Freddie Laker, the challenger of government-supported corporate cartels, would go along with that observation.

Who Rules the Giant Corporation?

BY RALPH NADER, MARK GREEN, AND JOEL SELIGMAN

Originally appeared in Business and Society Review, *Summer 1976.*

ALL MODERN STATE corporation statutes describe a common image of corporate governance, an image pyramidal in form. At the base of the pyramid are the shareholders or owners of the corporation. Their ownership gives them the right to elect representatives to direct the corporation and to approve fundamental corporate actions such as mergers or bylaw amendments. The intermediate level is held by the board of directors, who are required by a provision common to nearly every state corporation law "to manage the business and affairs of the corporation." On behalf of the shareholders, the directors are expected to select and dismiss corporate officers; to approve important financial decisions; to distribute profits; and to see that accurate periodic reports are forwarded to the shareholders. Finally, at the apex of the pyramid are the corporate officers. In the eyes of the law, the officers are the employees of the shareholder owners. Their authority is limited to those responsibilities which the directors delegate to them.

In reality, this legal image is a myth. In nearly every large American business corporation, there exists a management autocracy. One man—variously titled the President, or the Chairman of the Board, or the Chief Executive Officer—or a small coterie of men rule the corporation. Far from being chosen by the directors to run the corporation, this chief executive or executive clique chooses the board of directors and, with the acquiescence of the board, controls the corporation.

In its most consolidated form, corporate autocracy assumes the character of a corporation like ITT. Here is the ninth largest industrial corporation in the United States, with annual sales over $11 billion; 200,000 shareholders; over 400,000 employees; operations in ninety separate nations; administered through some 265 subsidiary corporations. Yet for over a decade ITT management has been constructed around a single domineering executive, Mr. Harold S. Geneen. . . .

A basic defect with corporate autocracy, at ITT and elsewhere, is its inefficiency. As corporate operations have grown more complex and technologies more sophisticated, checks upon senior management have all but disappeared. The result has often been irrational decisions, hurried decisions, decisions based upon inadequate factual analysis or executive self-favoritism. Surveying a decade that had seen the wreck of the Penn Central, cost-overrun catastrophes at both Lockheed and Douglas Aircraft, the slow, resistible decline of A & P, and a host of conglomerate stock collapses, J. Irwin Miller, president of Cummings Engine, concluded, "I think we've just gone through a decade of rather surprisingly bad decisions by businessmen worldwide. Some of them so bad that nobody would have guessed it." . . .

The common theme of these many instances of mismanagement is a failure to restrain the power of senior executives. A corporate chief executive's decisions to expand, merge, or even violate the law can often be made without accountability to outside scrutiny. Consider, for example, the detailed disclosures of the recent bribery cases. Not only do these reports suggest how widespread corporate foreign and domestic criminality has become; they also provide a unique study in the pathology of American corporate management.

At Gulf Corporation, three successive chief executive officers were able to pay out over $12.6 million in foreign and domestic bribes over a fifteen-year period without the knowledge of others on the board of directors or of senior executives. To do so, chairman William K. Whitehead transferred an Assistant Comptroller to a Bahamian subsidy in 1959 to launder Gulf monies and hide transactions "off-the-books." Whitehead also hired Claude Wild to serve as Gulf's Washington lobbyist, and empowered Wild personally or through nineteen other executives to make illegal political contributions to politicians ranging from such national figures as Senator Lyndon Johnson, Senator Hugh Scott, Senator Henry Jackson, and Congressman Wilbur Mills to such local figures as utility commissioners in Pennsylvania. Although the actions of Whitehead and his successors as chairmen were found by the McCloy Committee to be "shot through with illegality," these executives were able to involve as many as forty Gulf executives in fraudulent accounting or delivery of pay-offs, and banish at least one squeamish vice president all without public disclosure or effective internal challenge.

At Northrop, chairman Thomas V. Jones and vice president James Allen were able to create and fund the Economic and Development Corporation, a separate Swiss company, and pay $750,000 to Dr. Hubert Weisbrod, a Swiss attorney, to stimulate West German jet sales without the knowledge of the board or, apparently, other senior executives.

The legal basis for such a consolidation of power in the hands of the corporation's chief executive is the proxy election. Annually the shareholders of each publicly held corporation are given the opportunity of either attending a meeting to nominate and elect directors or returning proxy cards to management or its challengers signing over their right to vote. Few shareholders personally attend meetings. Sylvan Silver, a Reuters correspondent who covers over one hundred Wilmington annual meetings each year, described representative 1974 meetings in an interview: At Cities Service Company, the 77th largest industrial corporation with some 135,000 shareholders, 25 shareholders actually attended the meeting; El Paso Natural Gas with 125,000 shareholders had fifty shareholders; at Coca-Cola, the 69th largest corporation with 70,000 shareholders, twenty-five shareholders attended the annual meeting; at Bristol Meyers, with 60,000 shareholders, a like twenty-five shareholders appeared. Even "Campaign GM," the most publicized shareholder challenge of the past two decades, attracted no more than 3,000 of General Motors' 1,400,000 shareholders, or roughly two-tenths of one percent.

Thus, corporate directors are almost invariably chosen by written proxies. Yet management so totally dominates the proxy machinery that corporate elections have come to resemble the Soviet Union's euphemistic "Communist ballot"—that is, a ballot which lists only one slate of candidates. Although federal and state laws require the annual performance of an elaborate series of rituals pretending there is "corporate democracy," in 1973, 99.7 percent of the directorial elections in our largest corporations were uncontested.

Of the 6,744 corporations required to file data with the Securities and Exchange Commission, incumbent management retained control in at least 6,734 companies, or 99.9 percent. In the 500 largest industrial corporations—corporations which account for some 66 percent of the sales of all industrial corporations in the United States—no incumbent management was even challenged in 1973. . . .

What Money Can Buy

The key to management's hegemony is money. Effectively, only incumbent management can nominate directors—because it has a nearly unlimited power to use corporate funds to win board elections while opponents must prepare separate proxies and campaign literature entirely at their own expense.

There is first management's power to print and post written communications to shareholders. In a typical proxy contest, management will follow up its initial proxy solicitation with a bombardment of five to ten subsequent mailings. As attorneys Edward Aranow and Herb Einhorn explain in their treatise, *Proxy Contests for Corporate Control:*

> Perhaps the most important aspect of the follow-up letter is its role in the all-important efforts of a soliciting group to secure the *latest-dated* proxy from a stockholder. It is characteristic of every proxy contest that a large number of stockholders will sign and return proxies to one faction and then change their minds and want to have their stock used for the opposing faction.

The techniques of the Northern States Power Company in 1973 are illustrative. At that time, Northern States Power Company voluntarily employed cumulative voting, which meant that only 7.2 percent of outstanding shares was necessary to elect one director to Northern's 14-person board. Troubled by Northern's record on environmental and consumer issues, a broadly based coalition of public interest groups called the Citizens' Advocate for Public Utility Responsibility (CAPUR) nominated Ms. Alpha Snaby, a former Minnesota state legislator, to run for director. These groups then successfully solicited the votes of over 14 percent of all shareholders, or more than twice the votes necessary to elect her to the board.

Northern States then bought back the election. By soliciting proxies a second, and then a third time, the Power Company was able to persuade (or confuse) the shareholders of 71 percent of the 2.8 million shares cast for Ms. Snaby to change their votes.

Larger, more experienced corporations are usually heavy-handed. Typically, they will begin a proxy campaign with a series of "build-up" letters preliminary to the first proxy solicitation. In Campaign GM, General Motors elevated this strategy to a new plateau by encasing the Project on Corporate Responsibility's single 100-word proxy solicitation within a 21-page booklet specifically rebutting each of the Project's charges. The Project, of course, could never afford to respond to GM's campaign. The postage costs alone of soliciting GM's 1,400,000 shareholders would have exceeded $100,000. The cost of printing a document comparable to GM's 21-page booklet and mailing it—accompanied by a proxy statement, a proxy card, and a stamped return envelope—to each shareholder might have run as high as $500,000.

Nor is it likely that the project or any other outside shareholder could match GM's ability to hire professional proxy solicitors such as Georgeson & Company, which can deploy up to 100 solicitors throughout the country to personally contact shareholders, give them a campaign speech, and urge them to return their proxies. By daily tabulation of returned proxies, professional solicitors are able to identify on a day-by-day basis the largest blocks of stock outstanding which have yet to return a favorable vote.

Management's "army" in a proxy contest will also include attorneys to prepare necessary documents for the SEC and distract the opposition with costly litigation, accounts and statisticians to prepare the most self-serving financial analysis allowable, and public relations advisors to prepare advertisements for trade journals and the financial section of major newspapers. In the past twenty-five years there have been no more than a dozen instances in which insurgents have been able to match management expenses in a major proxy fight. Over the past decade, only the MGM proxy contest of 1967 has seen insurgents match management expenses in a large corporation's proxy contest for control.

A second advantage—and one that no outsider can match—is management's ability to use corporate personnel on its own behalf. Clerical help and clerical facilities including printing presses, photocopying machines, and addressing machines are invariably employed. Salespersons skilled in talking to customers are frequently assigned to the telephones to answer inquiries and to supplement the professional proxy solicitors by making direct calls to shareholders. Moreover, senior executives can be assigned to telephone particularly important shareholders who may be impressed by the personal call of a top executive.

State corporation law has done nothing to correct this inequality of corporate resources. Although leading cases in Delaware and New York have engaged in much gnashing of teeth about limiting management expenditures to: (a) proxy contests involving a "policy" issue, (b) expenditures necessary to inform shareholders about the "policy" issue, and/or (c) "reasonable" expenses—no decision since 1907 in either jurisdiction has denied management the power to expend corporate funds or use corporate personnel exactly as management chooses. Even such seemingly "unreasonable" expenditures as public relations counsel, "entertainments," chartered airlines, limousines, and the indirect cost to the corporation of using officers and employees on behalf of an incumbent director slate, have survived judicial scrutiny. By contrast, state courts have firmly established the rule that insurgents, unlike management, are not entitled to reimbursement of any campaign expenses as a matter of right. Challengers must defray all their own expenses, with the single slim hope of later being reimbursed *if* they are successful and the stockholders approve.

Management Control of Information

Management's grip on corporate power is tightened by its authority to print and distribute annual, quarterly, and other reports to shareholders. Besides the formal proxy statement, these reports usually embody the only detailed information shareholders receive about their corporation.

Neither state nor federal law places any meaningful restrictions on the amount of money management may spend reporting to shareholders. SEC Proxy Rules *do* require certification of financial statements. The report, however, "may be in any form deemed suitable by the management" and is not subject to the same standards of truthfulness that the text of a proxy solicitation is subjected to. Consequently, though every word of an insurgent shareholder's communications with other shareholders may be challenged if it is arguably "false or misleading," most management reports are subject to no textual regulation whatever.

Unfortunately, management reports are frequently "false and misleading." They are often written in an upbeat public relations jargon which emphasizes "positive" aspects of the past business year while rationalizing or ignoring management mistakes, financial losses, corporate or executive criminal violations, or civil actions successfully prosecuted against the corporation. Frequently, as much as half of the text of an annual report is represented by oversized charts, colored illustrations, and kindred public relations gimmickry.

There is often little difference between the text of a failing corporation's annual report and a healthy corporation's report. For example, although subsequent congressional testimony made clear that Lockheed would have gone bankrupt unless it received an emergency loan guarantee from the federal government, Lockheed's 1969 annual report managed to ignore the prominent debate in Congress over whether the federal government should "bail out" the firm. . . . It was only *after* the Senate voted an Emergency Loan Guarantee by the razor-thin margin of 49-48 in August 1971 that Lockheed reported to its shareholders that without this congressional subsidy the corporation would have collapsed.

A similar lack of veracity appeared in the 1973 Annual Report of the Franklin New York Corporation, whose principal subsidiary was the Franklin National Bank, the largest state bank ever to fail in the United States. Just a few months before the Comptroller declared the Franklin National Bank insolvent, the corporation's management reported to its shareholders, "In 1973, Franklin crossed an important threshold so that it is now in a position to move forward in establishing itself as a major worldwide financial institution and a leading money center banking operation."

Nor can insurgent shareholders obtain much additional information from their own corporation when they prepare for a proxy challenge. They lack the legal tools to gain access to live interviews with corporate executives, board meetings, or memoranda which could document internal debate, management error, derogations of law, sloppy execution of policy, or even the content of management's policy formulations.

All of which is a bizarre commentary on the Securities and Exchange Commission. The federal securities laws emphasize disclosure. The Commission has claimed that its Proxy Rules "represent an effective contribution to corporate democracy" because disclosure enables individual investors to exercise some measure of control over the management of their corporation. Although the Securities Exchange Act of 1934 authorizes the SEC to require annual and quarterly reports, including the authority to prescribe "the items or details to be shown in the balance sheet and the earnings statement . . . ," shareholders cannot compel their corporation to give a product line or division accounting so as to uncover unprofitable operations. Specific management mistakes may thus be submerged in consolidated financial reports. Shareholders may wish to know whether executives are using expense accounts improperly or are being indemnified for certain civil or criminal liabilities. They cannot find out. They may wish to read minutes of the meetings of corporate directors—whom they elect—or reports of decisions by executives respecting corporate property—which shareholders own. Under federal securities laws, they have no legal rights to do so.

Under state stautory law shareholders technically have broad rights to examine corporate records. State statutes typically authorize inspection of shareholder lists—without which a shareholder could not even begin a proxy solicitation—and "other books and records." But this access is circumscribed by legal requirements of "good faith," "proper purpose," and minimum share ownership, as well as ample opportunities for management to delay compliance with legitimate shareholder demands by forcing expensive court tests.

Almost invariably shareholders prevail in court battles to secure a shareholder list, for, as a leading Pennsylvania decision put it, ". . . the right to examine the stockholders' list is a basic privilege of every stockholder of a corporation and should be given the widest recognition as fundamental to corporate democracy." But the courts are reluctant to enforce shareholder demands for other information. Doctrinally, this has been rationalized as deterring excessive "stockholder agitation." The Supreme Court of Minnesota rather melodramatically explained why in the leading case of *State ex rel. Pillsbury v. Honeywell:*

> In terms of the corporate norm, inspection is merely the act of the concerned owner checking on what is in part his property. In the context of the large firm, inspection can be more akin to a weapon in corporate warfare. The effectiveness of the weapon is considerable: "considering the huge size of many modern corporations and the necessarily complicated nature of their bookkeeping, it is plain that to permit thousands of shareholders to roam at will through their records will render impossible not only any attempt to keep their records efficiently, but the proper carrying on of their business . . ." Because the power to inspect may be the power to destroy, it is important that only those with a bona fide interest in the corporation enjoy the power. . . .

Alarming as the specter of "thousands of shareholders roaming at will" through once-efficient corporations may be, it can only be conjured up by courts so cunning as to overlook their inherent judicial power to restrict any shareholder access to corporate data to reasonable numbers of shareholders at reasonable times and reasonable places.

Management Control of the Law

Management power is further entrenched by three significant legal advantages.

First, in approximately 90 percent of all large industrial corporations, cumulative voting is not required. In these corporations, a minority of shareholders—even a minority as substantial as 49.9 percent—may be precluded from electing even one director to the Board.

Under cumulative voting, each shareholder is entitled to votes equal to the number of his or her shares multiplied by the number of directors to be elected. The shareholder may cast all his or her votes for a single candidate or distribute them among two or more candidates as he or she sees fit. Cumulative voting, therefore, helps to protect the *financial* interest of minority shareholders by assuring them voice on the board of directors. And it protects the *political* interest of minority shareholders. For without cumulative voting, the tendency of large industrial corporations to perpetuate one-party rule is powerfully enhanced. As professor Charles M. Williams demonstrated after analyzing proxy contests for the years 1943–1948, corporations with cumulative voting were more than twice as likely to have proxy contests as those without.

Because of these benefits, cumulative voting has enjoyed considerable popularity. From 1870, when Illinois became the first state to require cumulative voting, until 1955, twenty-three states had established absolute requirements of cumulative voting. Additionally, federal law requires cumulative voting for over 5,000 banks subject to the Federal Banking Act of 1933 (although the intent of this law has often been frustrated by bank holding company structures); and the Securities and Exchange Commission has consistently required cumulative voting for corporations subject to the Public Utility Holding Act of 1935 and corporations undergoing reorganization under Chapter X of the Bankruptcy Act. As an attorney snapped in 1950 in frustration at Wisconsin's refusal to enact cumulative voting, "Cumulative voting is so obviously in accord with our basic political philosophy of group representation and the party system that it is difficult to understand the legislature's repeated rejection of it, except in terms of a response to the pressure of corporate management's interest."

Unfortunately, "the pressure of corporate management's interest" often does prevail in state corporation law. Between 1955 and 1972, five states dropped mandatory cumulative voting. In 1973, Michigan changed from mandatory to permissive cumulative voting; in 1974 both California and Ohio considered—but did not enact—similar legislation. Today, in Delaware, as well as thirty-two other states, cumulative voting is not required. True, in most of these states, cumulative voting is permissive. In practice, however, permissive cumulative voting offers little but an illusory right.

Even in those few corporations which voluntarily institute cumulative voting, most states provide ample devices to subvert it. Although cumulative voting aims to prevent a simple majority from maintaining absolute corporate control, Delaware permits a simple majority to amend the corporate charter to repeal cumulative voting. And Delaware and some forty-two other jurisdictions allow the "classification" of the board of directors. This device reduces to one-third or one-half the number of directors required to stand for election annually and thus increases the minimum vote necessary to elect a director.

Management's second legal edge is its power to issue nonvoting stock or classes of stock with unequal voting rights. For example, prior to December 1, 1955, there were three classes of stock in Ford Motor Company: common, Class A, and Class B. Only the Class B shares (4.94 percent of total equity), all of which were owned by Ford family interests, were entitled to vote.

Only Illinois and a few other states forbid the issuance of classes or series of stock without voting rights. But the refusal of both the New York Stock Exchange and the American Stock Exchange to list corporations with non-voting stock has substantially reduced the number of corporations which may totally eviscerate shareholder suffrage, although neither exchange actively enforces equal voting rights.

The third statutory device for impairing shareholder suffrage rights is a provision common to the law of Delaware and apparently every other jurisdiction requiring the submission of proxy materials only to *shareholders of record*. This innocent-sounding requirement effectively disenfranchises approximately 50 percent of the beneficial owners of corporate stock in the largest industrial corporations. For approximately 50 percent of the stock in the 1,800 companies traded on the New York Stock Exchange is held by mutual funds, life insurance or property and casualty insurance companies, private pension funds (usually administered through commercial bank trust departments), state and local pension funds, foundations, university endowment funds or other institutional investors. The result is a mockery of shareholder democracy: *Approximately 50 percent of the votes in our largest industrial corporations are cast by financial intermediaries—not the real owners.*

These institutional shareholders provide virtually no check to corporate management. Most financial institutions, according to the SEC's 1971 *Institutional Investor Study*, follow what is known as "The Wall Street Rule": An investment in a business corporation is considered an investment in that corporation's management; if the financial institution ceases to like what management is doing, the institution sells the stock. By examining the voting practices of 215 large institutions between January 1, 1967 and September 30, 1969, the SEC determined that approximately 30 percent of these institutions *always* voted for management (in elections other than votes for directors). For the remaining institutions, both voting against management and abstention were found "to be a relatively infrequent phenomenon." For example, in only twenty-six instances did any of the 215 institutions vote against an acquisition favored by management, "a miniscule fraction of such transactions."

Historically, shareholders controlled the business corporation not only through the election of directors but also through shareholders' power to initiate and vote upon all fundamental changes in the character of the corporation. Management's ability to initiate change was carefully circumscribed by requiring two-thirds or three-fourths affirmative votes for charter amendments, bylaw changes, mergers, sales of assets, stock issuance, recapitalization, or dissolution and was further limited by shareholder appraisal and preemptive rights.

Under Delaware's General Corporation Law, shareholders have lost nearly all power to initiate corporate change. Only the board of directors may propose charter amendments, a merger, or a sale of assets. The SEC Proxy Rules complement Delaware's corporation law by denying shareholders opportunity to communicate opposition to management proposals or to suggest modifications in their formal proxy proposals.

This route has been substantially replicated in all other leading chartering states. Indeed, the trend of recent revisions to state corporation law has been to attempt to deny the shareholder any vote at all! Modern corporate draftsmen invariably write short, purely formal certificates of incorporation and then place most of a corporation's actual governing rules in its bylaws, which the certificate establishes can be revised by the corporation's directors without any shareholder vote. For example, when ITT reincorporated in Delaware in 1967, it did so by creating a Delaware corporation called the "DeLitt Corporation" and by then merging ITT, previously a Maryland corporation, into DeLitt. The certificate of incorporation of DeLitt was only 1 1/2 pages long. It reads in toto:

Certificate of Incorporation of Delitt Corporation

ARTICLE I

The name of the corporation is DeLitt Corporation (hereinafter called the "Corporation"). The name and mailing address of its incorporators are as follows:

Name   Mailing Address

John J. Navin   320 Park Avenue, New York, N.Y. 10022

William J. Donovan   320 Park Avenue, New York, N.Y. 10022

DeForest Billyou 320 Park Avenue, New York, N.Y. 10022

ARTICLE 2

The address of the registered office of the Corporation in the State of Delaware is No. 100 West Tenth Street, in the City of Wilmington, County of New Castle. The name of its registered agent at such address is The Corporation Trust Company.

ARTICLE 3

The purpose of the Corporation is to engage in any lawful act or activity for which corporations may be organized under the General Corporation Law of Delaware.

ARTICLE 4

The total number of shares of stock which the Corporation has authority to issue is 100 shares of capital stock of the par value of $100 per share.

ARTICLE 5

Whenever the vote of stockholders at a meeting thereof is required or permitted to be taken for or in connection with any corporate action by any provision of the General Corporation Law of Delaware, the meeting and vote of stockholders may be dispensed with if the holders of stock having not less than the minimum percentage of the vote required by statute for the proposed corporate action shall consent in writing to such corporate action being taken, provided that prompt notice must be given to all stockholders of the taking of such corporate action without a meeting and by less than unanimous written consent.

ARTICLE 6

In furtherance and not in limitation of the powers conferred by law, the Board of Directors is expressly authorized:

(a) To make, alter, amend or repeal the By-Laws of the Corporation.

(b) To direct and determine the use and disposition of any annual net profits or net assets in excess of capital; to set apart out of any of the funds of the Corporation available for dividends a reserve or reserves for any proper purpose; and to abolish any such reserve in the manner in which it was created.

(c) To establish bonus, profit-sharing, stock option, retirement or other types of incentive or compensation plans for the employees (including officers and directors) of the Corporation and to fix the amount of the profits to be distributed or shared and to determine the persons to participate in any such plans and the amounts of their respective participations.

(d) From time to time to determine whether and to what extent, and at what time and places and under what conditions and regulations, the accounts and books of the Corporation (other than the stock ledger), or any of them, shall be open to the inspection of the stockholders; and no stockholder shall have any right to inspect any account or book or document of the Corporation, except as conferred by statute or authorized by the Board of Directors or by a resolution of the stockholders.

(e) To authorize, and cause to be executed, mortgages and liens upon the real and personal property of the Corporation.

ARTICLE 7

The Corporation reserves the right to amend, alter, change or repeal any provision contained in this Certificate of Incorporation, in the manner now or hereafter prescribed by statute, and all rights conferred upon stockholders herein are granted subject to this reservation.

The key sentence is contained in Article 6: "In furtherance and not in limitation of the powers conferred by law, the Board of Directors is expressly authorized: (a) To make, alter, amend or repeal the By-Laws of the corporation..." What ITT tried to do, as so many other giant Delaware corporations have tried to do, was to totally shut shareholders out of the governing process except in those rare instances in which the Delaware General Corporation Law explicitly requires a shareholder vote, which is not very often.

True, technically, Section 251(c) of Delaware's General Corporation Law grants shareholders a vote on management merger proposals. But this, in fact, is a mere snare for the dim-witted. Only a small minority of corporate fusions actually trigger this shareholder vote. The overwhelming majority employ one of three conventional loopholes.

Similarly, section 271 limits shareholder suffrage in a sale, lease, or exchange of assets to transactions involving "all or substantially all" of a corporation's property and assets. Since most large industrial corporations are highly diversified, this provision effectively insures that their shareholders will never vote. For example, General Motors could sell an automobile division such as Pontiac, or Cadillac and not require a vote.

Moreover, section 271 is the only Delaware statute concerning corporate divisions. A Delaware corporation may create and fund new subsidiary corporations, regardless of size; liquidate these subsidiaries or comparable divisions and distribute assets to shareholders; or spin-off new corporations altogether without any shareholder vote. As business corporations have evolved these new forms, Delaware and other principal chartering states have deliberately not kept pace.

Introduction to *The Company State*

Originally appeared in The Company State *by James Phelan & Robert Pozen, 1973.*

E. I. DU PONT DE NEMOURS & COMPANY began in Delaware in 1802 with a little gunpowder plant on the Brandywine River and spread, after many corporate acquisitions, throughout the United States and many foreign countries. It is now the world's largest chemical company. But its headquarters and its "political economy" remain rooted in Delaware.

DuPont dominates Delaware as does no single company in any other state. The scope and mechanisms of its influence are studied and assessed in this report. Virtually every major aspect of Delaware life—industry, commerce, finance, government, politics, education, health, transportation, media, charitable institutions, environment, land, recreation, public works, community improvement groups, and taxation—is pervasively and decisively affected by the DuPont Company, the DuPont family, or their agents.

The wealth and power of this family dynasty have not escaped wide public notice, but they have escaped detailed public study. This report is concerned only with DuPont in Delaware, not with DuPont outside Delaware or with DuPont's consumer products. There were a number of cogent reasons for selecting DuPont and for concentrating the efforts of the study group in Delaware.

First, DuPont is a mammoth enterprise and has many of its activities in a compact geographical area. These characteristics permitted a gathering of facts that would not have been possible with a more dispersed, less visible company.

Second, DuPont was no stranger to many issues now enveloped in the concept of "corporate responsibility." It has substantially controlled Delaware for decades and it received a sustained public relations setback in the thirties because of congressional investigations into its munitions sales and profiteering during World War I. For these reasons, DuPont has prob-ably thought more about its role in the community, its public image, and its relations with other institutions than most giant corporations. Consequently, the study group could observe a historical process in ascer-taining what standards of performance could be applied to DuPont policies and practices as they affect Delaware.

Third, DuPont's techniques in using its power are, by and large, not as crude or roughshod as is so often the case in textile, paper, or coal company towns. DuPont's deployment of direct and derivative power in the state is complex, subtle, far-reaching. It is festooned with the symbols of respectability, stolidity, charity, and recognition. But, like bad medicine that goes down sweetly, the effects of the company on the community too often include damage across a score of areas, as detailed in the following pages.

Fourth, there is little hesitation or doubt in DuPont's corporate view about community involvement. A decade ago, the company plunged into community activities directly and through a variety of official and charita-ble institutions. Its employees, liberally released for part-time or full-time civic duties, proliferate throughout the state's institutional structure. The family's ownership of the two major daily newspapers is not concealed, nor are the obvious consequences. The same can be said of the DuPont com-plex's legal control over two of the state's largest banks; and the list goes on, as the report details. With such a high intensity of involvement, the idea that DuPont is to be judged solely on the basis of its profit (and it is a very prof-itable company) or the wages it pays is rejected by a long line of company executives, including Lammot du Pont Copeland, recently retired as DuPont's board chairman, who said:

> Business is a means to an end for society and not an end in itself, and therefore business must act in concert with a broad public interest and serve the objectives of mankind and society or it will not survive.

This attitude explains in part DuPont's intense interest, as distinguished from concern, in this report. For even if DuPont Company executives and family members have convinced themselves of the rightness of their paternalism and charitable giving toward the community, there still remains the nagging realization that something is wrong in the state of DuPont. That something includes poverty, racism, urban dislocation, discriminatory highway monuments to DuPont's corporate needs, gross underpayment of income and property taxes by the DuPonts and the other rich, manipulated legislators and public officials, a business-coddling judiciary, a disgraceful state of health and education for all but the well-to-do, and the brooding inhibitions on dissent and diversity of community initiatives which sometimes come from the omnipresent DuPont complex.*

The relatively small city of Wilmington (pop. 80,000) displays great contrasts between the businessmen, who profit by day and scurry to the suburbs by night, and the poor and blue-collar people, who suffer a deteriorating city whose principal forms of renewal are malls near DuPont buildings and highways to get the suburbanites in and out quickly. The company and the extended DuPont family structure loom so large in the wealth of Delaware that they bring up the averages to levels which belie the plight of many Delawareans. The per capita income in Delaware for 1970 was $4,324, compared with the national average of $3,921. Given these conditions, and many others analyzed in this study, it must have occurred to some of the more thoughtful DuPonters that much more can be done to make a big company do better by a small state. For a giant corporation, owned by one of the world's wealthiest families, consistently profitable, and with substantial operations in a small state like Delaware (pop. 550,000), the potential of becoming a relatively model corporate citizen is very real.

For such a process to emerge, the DuPonts will have to be challenged before they respond. Their pattern of response will itself make a revealing chapter in the growing chronicle of corporate behavior in this country. Will they realize that they can give more to the community by relinquishing some of their power instead of accruing more? Will they recognize that by fully paying their fair share of state income, property, and estate taxes, they would be contributing far more to the state than by their charitable contributions in both dollars and achievement? These are only two of many questions that are considered in this report. But the most important immediate impact, one hopes, will be to generate a greater and more detailed awareness in Delawareans of how, when, and where DuPont power works and to encour-

---

* Typical of the far-reaching penumbra of DuPont's deterrence is a clause in its pension plan that provides for cancelation of a retired employee's rights to receive benefits if he has involved himself in "any activity harmful to the interest of the company."

age a greater examination by DuPont leaders of the company role and the family role in the future of the state.

One of the first steps in such a self-examination by the DuPont Company is for management to ponder why it must conceal so much that should be public information. The study group came up against this systematic secrecy right from the beginning. There were roadblocks at every turn. The company tried to prohibit interviews with employees on their own time. Procedures for interviewing employees at work required the presence of a company lawyer, a public relations man, and a tape recorder. The lawyer decided what questions should not be answered. The employee could hardly help being affected by such conditions. True to its concern for appearances, the company offered cooperation in theory but withheld it in practice. Questions submitted in writing about matters not remotely connected with trade secrets were frequently unanswered or labeled "confidential" when the information would be at all significant. Tours of some company plants were allowed, but workers could not be spoken with, even in the lunchroom. Because of such restrictions on freedom of speech, many employees and residents spoke with the study group anonymously.

This is not to say that DuPont responded harshly, petulantly, or with totally closed doors. But more openness might have been expected of a company whose written claims about its public pride and civic responsiveness are so grandiose. In addition, DuPont officials apparently prejudged this report from the beginning. But the researchers who produced this report were as fascinated by the prospect of finding models of progressive change within and around the DuPont complex as they were concerned that the contrary might often be the case. They conducted approximately five hundred interviews with Delawareans in all walks of life, including company employees and directors, DuPont family members, lawyers, leaders of the black community, representatives of white ethnic groups, physicians, city and state politicians, bankers, real estate agents, educators, clergymen, newspaper reporters, architects, scientists, engineers, blue-collar workers, union officials, and social workers. They read countless newspaper files, reports, studies, and public relations releases. They lived in the city of Wilmington but traveled throughout the state, from chateau country to Dover to Seaford. Two members of the group even found themselves invited to the sanctum of sanctums—the Wilmington Club. And they thought long about the issues and the problems surrounding the DuPont Company and the DuPont family.

But the corporate impact on ever-widening communities is by no means restricted to situations similar to DuPont and Delaware. The spread of corporate power into control of public government and allocation of public resources; the growth of hazards to people and environments from the uncontrolled effects of widening technologies; the increasingly determined management of larger social systems by giant, multinational corporations—these and many other problems created by the corporate Leviathan demand intensive citizen scrutiny.

Washington, D.C.

November, 1971

Taming the Corporate Tiger

Originally delivered before the National Press Club Washington, D.C., December 21, 1966.

T HE MODERN BUSINESS CORPORATION has come a long way since the early days of the Republic when its ancestor served primarily as a legal instrument to limit the liability of investors. In 1957, the general counsel and vice-president of Ford Motor Company, William T. Gossett, offered this description:

> The modern stock corporation is a social and economic institution that touches every aspect of our lives; in many ways it is an institutionalized expression of our way of life. During the past 50 years, industry in corporate form has moved from the periphery to the very center of our social and economic existence. Indeed, it is not inaccurate to say that we live in a corporate society.

Eleven years earlier, in 1946, Peter Drucker, fresh from a study of General Motors, was even more expansive:

> What we look for in analyzing American society is therefore the institution which sets the standard for the way of life and the mode of living of our citizens; which leads, molds, and directs; which determines our perspective on our own society; around which crystallize our social

problems and to which we look for their solution. . . . And this, in our society today, is the large corporation.

These observations by Drucker and Gossett are receiving increasingly impressive confirmation with every passing year. The size and concentration of these corporate units intensify relentlessly. "Some of these corporations," says Adolf Berle, "are units which can be thought of only in somewhat the way we have heretofore thought of nations." The merger tide, unless abated, will leave us by 1975 with two hundred corporations holding 75 percent of all manufacturing assets. The largest of them all, General Motors, last year grossed more than the entire GNP of Brazil, more than the gross receipts of any foreign government, except the U.S.S.R. and Great Britain. General Motors took in, on the average, $2.3 million an hour, twenty-four hours a day, 365 days a year. Twenty-five percent of business profits in the U.S. are produced by seven companies.

Less recognized than size and concentration trends, but certainly of comparable importance, are the new dimensions of corporate activity brought about by new technology and a massive capability to undertake larger missions. General Electric announces its intention to construct a series of new cities. More companies and joint ventures are plunging into education and welfare enterprises. Others are pushing for the development and marketing of elaborate artificial limbs and human organs such as hearts and kidneys. "Big Biology" may be a growth industry by the seventies. The pervasive genetic impact of the drug industry transcends the more publicly debated engineering products such as birth control pills. Looming on the horizon is the commercial exploitation resulting from research and development in molecular biology. The beginning is just beginning. (It is not inconceivable that the year 2000 will witness an announcement by DuPont that it can now produce a prototype man as part of its 'progress through chemistry.' And General Electric may declare that it at last can abolish night, an environmental enlightenment whose adoption is urged in order to reduce crime and traffic accidents.)

The point about these new dimensions of corporate activity is that they are inherently and immediately clothed with the public interest. Such activities require more insistent prophylactic structures of planning and responsibility than, say, the production of widgets. Who gets artificial hearts? When? Under what conditions and warranties? At what price? Who, indeed, participates in controlling the rate of engineering innovation and the publicizing of technical information? The discipline of the market becomes a somewhat more detached force in such contexts. Other socio-political mechanisms require establishment and refinement.

It is not necessary to reach into the future to raise concerns about the adequacy of the corporate institution to perform in the public interest. There are more than enough problems today. The forces streaming out of our large corporations are changing the nature of the economy, altering the man-made environment to the point of mass crises, and transforming our system of government.

The traditional characteristics of a capitalistic economy seem like relics of a bygone age. Consider one of the more publicized cases of closed enter-prise—the electrical price fixing conspiracy which went on undetected for years at very high executive levels. After convictions were obtained by the Justice Department, President Mark Cresap of Westinghouse developed a compliance system to avoid future violations with these words: "We have to build into the organization an understanding of what competition is and how to be competitive in a profitable way. We must change executive think-ing from the old idea that the only way to protect profits is through keep-ing prices up . . . We're going to try for an understanding of the positive forces of competition, getting into new products and new markets." Shortly after the system was underway, Mr. Cresap gave an illustration of how it presumably worked: "A competitor recently called up one of our men to ask when we were going to raise prices. He also requested that no certificate be filed on the call. Our man hung up and immediately reported the conver-sation to the head of Westinghouse's antitrust enforcement section."

It sure is tough to buck a way of life, and many other industries and sub-industries aren't even making the effort. Many expressions of free market atrophy are brought about by concentrated corporate collectivism: economic power without property (the separation of ownership and control); the prevalence of oligopoly in industry after industry; price fixing (or its alter-native—identical pricing); "administered pricing"; and the "protective imi-tation" of product design determined by the dominant firm.

There are some observers who view this concentration as desirable and who urge that relics be recognized for what they are—phenomena which have outlived their usefulness in a complex society. Their argument is that such giant corporate organization and power are necessary to marshall the skills and programs for the ever more intricate products and processes demanded by a national, even international, marketplace.

This is not the time to denote the truths and fallacies in this viewpoint and to illustrate that diminishing returns can set in rather promptly, particularly in the area of innovation, under the grip of bureaucratic rigidities. Set aside from the alleged benefits of such concentrations of corporate power: What about the social costs of private closed enterprise in such a monolithic framework? What avenues for reform, for the reduction of these costs, are available to the citizenry when the diversity of competing, countervailing or penalizing centers of economic power is over-ridden?

These are very real questions. For what we do about corporate air and water pollution, corporate soil and food contamination, corporate-bred trauma on our highways, corporate lack of innovation or suppression of innovation, corporate misallocation of resources, corporate inflationary pricing, corporate dominance over local, state and federal agencies, and corporate distortions of political campaigning—to suggest a few issues—will decide our quality of life. There are many other illustrations and those given can be elaborated by anyone familiar with the news of the day.

Take just one area, surface transportation—a standing insult to a rational society. There are hours during the day in downtown Washington when it is unfair to compare vehicular travel speed with that of the old horse and buggy. Congestion, inefficiency, pollution, overcapacity, an epidemic of death and injury in an era when science-technology can make transportation a spectacular service instead of a dismal chore, if only the vested interests would unvest. Devoting, as we do, one out of every five retail dollars to getting around on the ground should be a source of deep concern, not unthinking pride.

There should be few dissenters from the proposition that an affluent society with the capacity to literally invent the technological future should not have to tolerate such costs, or to put it in more human terms, such collective cruelties, as preconditions of "progress." But it has and it is. Profound neglect, however, tends to generate observable disasters such as seem imminent in air pollution. But many disasters are not observable in terms of the contributing factors. Thousands of people die every week from "cancer,"— a strictly terminal designation which some day may be much more traceable to industry's products and pollutants than presently is determined. The same holds true for respiratory diseases, circulatory ailments and mental afflictions. The many stresses on the New York City taxi driver, for example, will be considered an inhuman exposure by the hopefully more humane society of the future.

So much of what we do for and to ourselves is done through the large corporate institution directly and indirectly acting on other derivative institutions. The challenge is how to bring corporate powers, privileges and de facto immunities into greater conformance with the public interest. The large corporate has far outstripped the restraining embrace of its charter and laws designed for a former generation.

The double standard, one for corporate behavior and the other for individual behavior outside a corporate framework, is becoming more severe. A study of the decline of statutory penalties dealing with corporate behavior and their infrequent enforcement would point this out in instructive detail. Individual embezzlement, theft of industrial secrets, stealing a horse, or negligent homicide on the highway can and do bring jail terms up to several decades duration. Large corporations, on the other hand, have deliberately kept secret or falsified results for drugs, deliberately refused to notify owners of defective vehicles, deliberately bilked the government of millions in inflated cost submissions under government contracts, negligently wasted millions of public funds in wasteful or promotional endeavors. These acts often do not even result in sanctions and almost never in criminal penalties on the culpable officers. Statutory penalties, take the drug laws for example, are utterly trivial. And in the new auto safety law, the industry managed to delete a criminal penalty for wilful and knowing violation of the law in such a manner as to threaten or take human life. Attorneys for the industry argued that it would be punitive to have a criminal fine and one or two year maximum imprisonment provision. Note carefully their argument—that it would be punitive to subject corporate officials to such penalties even if it was proved that they wilfully and knowingly violated the law. Their argument prevailed. It is time to recognize that any society which exempts corporate action in whole or in part from legal sanctions should know what it is doing and the consequences thereof. The weaker the sanction, the stronger must be efforts at prevention of the anti-social behavior.

Here too, the breakdown is evident. Galbraith's theory of countervailing power, published in his "American Capitalism" fourteen years ago, was criticized at the time for being over-simplified. Now, it reads like a quaint economic fable, however appealing the underlying idea may be. The effective life cycle of countervailing forces—such as expressed by unions, government, different industries, big buyers, etc.—is notoriously short. It is terminated by an even stronger force called 'accommodation.' Few countervailing forces can stand the creative tension of their condition, once their own parochial and symbolic interests are recognized. Devolution sets in, and the system is praised as being "pluralistic," as if that description suffices to set our minds at rest.

Anyone who has studied the tortuous workings of most of the federal regulatory or subsidy agencies can be forgiven for viewing these assertions of pluralism with cynical skepticism. The regulatees have largely insulated these agencies from attention to their first constituency—the general public—and narrowed their concern to the special interests that are the subject of their supposed expertise. Those who are concerned with 'government in business' might turn some attention to 'business in government.' They may learn, in the process, what Frankensteins the marriage of the two are spawning.

The problem of corporate power comes in three expressions—misfeasance (the improper use of proper power), malfeasance (the use of improper power) and non-feasance (the non-use of proper power).

Suppose in the next few weeks you were to pick up the newspaper and read the following announcements:

1. "Tonight on Town Meeting of the Air, the head of Standard Oil of New Hersey, Michael L. Haidar, will debate with Martin Luther King the following proposition: 'Resolved, that the oil and gas depletion allowance should not be repealed in order to devote the resultant tax receipts to the War on Poverty and double the current budget in this area.' Needless to say, Mr. Haidar will argue for the affirmative."

2. "The casualty insurance industry, through their three trade associations, jointly released a statement today sharply criticizing the automobile industry for laggard and unsafe product design leading to avoidable casualties and high repair bills. Spokesmen for the insurance industry acknowledged that its action was in its own economic interest, because claims would be reduced, but they maintained that safer design was also in the public interest."

3. "The National Association of Securities Dealers passed a resolution at their annual convention objecting to the SEC's circulation, in draft form, of the mutual fund report to representatives of the mutual fund industry. NASD stated that any pre-release of a government report in the making to a special interest group amounts to an invitation to censorship pressures without any opportunity for other interests to rebut."

4. "In a free-wheeling press conference, several executives of General Dynamics criticized the Pentagon and the State Department for pursuing a policy in southern Atlantis contrary to the national interest. When a reporter politely reminded the executives that their company was under a hundred million dollar contract to pro-

duce weapons for operations in southern Atlantis, one executive flushed and retorted—"We're for free speech in the 'military industrial complex.' "

5. "General Motors announced today that it had contracted with William F. Buckley, Jr. to write a personal, in-depth biography of the company. It will be called "God and Man at General Motors." Mr. Buckley is to have complete access to personnel, memoranda, and other company records, subject only to the requirement that he will not be shown anything not known by Ford Motor Company. An impartial arbiter will make any determination when conflict arises, but informed sources say that the Ford qualification will insure the opening of most files. A General Motors spokesman added that this contract was in the public interest. He concluded that "GM had nothing to lose but its shame and nothing to gain but its pride."

"In a related development, the company announced that car buyers would be told that the fully tinted windshields they are paying more for actually result in their seeing less, especially at night, when seeing has even more relevance to good driving. "The customer has a right to be warned," said a GM official, "so that he can know how to choose recklessly." The same official notified reporters that a press conference would be called next week to reveal the results of a new consumer poll on the question: "Would you prefer hood and radiator ornaments and other sharp edges to be retained on next year's models in order to protect your cars from pedestrians or would you desire the elimination of these ornaments and edges in order to protect pedestrians from cars?"

6. "The American Tobacco Company reported its annual profits today and coupled it with a historic disclosure. The large and rapidly diversifying tobacco concern is discontinuing the manufacture of Lucky Strike by the end of the year and other brands by the end of next year. Delays in ceasing other brands was attributed to the need for additional time to train and relocate displaced workers. When asked to justify this drastic cutback, an ATC spokesman referred all questions to the U.S. Surgeon General."

7. "The North American Philips Company has completed a survey of diagnostic X-ray machines in hospitals and offices of physicians and dentists. A spokesman described the results as "shocking," and

indicated that unsuspecting patients were receiving radiation doses far in excess of what is necessary to obtain clear X-ray pictures. He attributed this hazard to obsolete machines, poorly maintained machines and inadequately trained operators. Under questioning, he did not hesitate to disclose details, citing one Connecticut report condemning forty local dental X-ray machines as exposing patients' sex glands to radiation. He added that his company was embarking on a widespread educational campaign about diagnostic radiation over-dosage and preparing to market a broad series of new X-ray machinery that will tremendously reduce the hazards. One reporter accused his company of profiteering. The spokesman drew taut his facial muscles and politely murmured: 'If THIS be profiteering, my good fellow, let's have more of it.' "

8. "Ford Motor Company announced the implementation of a professional bill of rights for employees whose expertise is commonly recognized as being of a professional character. Mr. Ford explained the new program by saying: 'Its about time our most skilled people received rights within our company comparable to those long held by our stalwart assembly-line workers who are members of the UAW.' The company statement began by drawing an analogy between professional employees in a corporate democracy and citizens in a political democracy. It stressed that democracy in the latter context does not assure democracy in the former, or corporate, context. A long list of specific rights were listed. Among these were included the right to invoke a professional committee of peers to resolve disputes between the scientist, engineer or other professional employee and management over:

   (a) the safety of the product or process

   (b) conduct leading to dismissal by superiors

   (c) the right to publish technical papers or reports,

as well as rights prohibiting blanket waiver of patent rights as a precondition to employment and affording realistic rewards for relevant inventions. Professional employees were given liberal guidelines encouraging their independent participation in professional societies and recognizing the need for expert testimony before courts, government agencies and other public bodies. It was explicitly stated that the company understands that professional ethics may result in employees taking stands before these forums contrary to company policy or performance. It pledged no overt or covert pressure to penalize such expressions, except those inspired by fraud, deceit or economic conflict of interests. The statement recognized that a professional must be able to pursue an independent life of his own within his profession and pursuant to its mandates."

9. "Warner-Lambert Pharmaceutical Company announced a fundamental corporate reorganization for the purpose of sharply allocating various responsibilities of the company to specific personnel. A top executive explained in a background briefing the motivation for this shakeup: 'Drug manufacturers have a special responsibility to the public,' he said. 'Drugs afford great benefits, but their hazards, where they exist, are latent and often very long-term in their debilitating effect. This is one reason for the government having an intricate set of laws and a large agency to administer these laws. We found that laxness, carelessness and actual coverups are more likely to occur when responsibility is diffused throughout the company and no one is really accountable for the net results. Our executive council decided that regardless of what the rest of the industry fails to do, we are going to designate the responsibilities imposed upon us by statute to specific officials. So if there are any violations these officials are the responsible persons. There has been too much buck passing for our taste. The history of drug violations indicates that top company officials claim in their defense that they didn't know what was going on, and lower company personnel claim that they were just executing orders. Well, we're going to put an end to that. From now on, a specific man will be ultimately responsible for company compliance with various sections of the law. These may be hot seats,' he concluded, 'but the sitters will be well paid and full of incentive to avoid any easy indulgence in petite-Eichmannism.'"

I WISH TO EMPHASIZE that these are hypothetical situations. Any resemblance to actual occurrences is coincidental and highly unlikely. But the principles involved point to directions in corporate behavior which should absorb much more public discussion in the near future.

There is need to establish a national commission on corporate reform to collect hitherto inaccessible or ignored information. This commission would be composed of free minds who would bring to bear on this information relevant experience, skills and values. The commission's output should be fearless reports that contribute to public understanding of both the existing performance and promise of corporate institutions. The commission would make explicit recommendations for private and public policymaking. For the burdens of reform rest not only on the law but also on newly felt awarenesses by corporate leaders and by other groups from Universities to Churches to professional societies whose critical oversight functions are so much needed.

I would single out five major problem areas in corporate behavior which such a commission should treat:

A. What new disclosure criteria should be imposed on corporations so that the public's right to know, on which effective citizenship and deterrents are based, is given due recognition? The federal government has developed its most intricate disclosure requirements for corporations in the field of investor protection. But corporate information in the area of safety (such as product performance or a company's quantitative contribution to air or water pollution) or merchandising fairness or innovation needs searching public scrutiny as well. Systematic disclosure produces self-correcting policies and provokes planning for prevention. It can minimize more coercive measures by government in the regulator form of control by detailed prescription, which leads, as in the past, to that dreaded merger of government and business which is euphemistically labeled the "partnership."

B. What new dimensions of due process are required for furthering the internal democracy of a corporation? These private governments reveal bureaucratic and political tyrannies that are a disgrace to our nation's commitment to freedom of expression and individualism. We are losing priceless contributions to our well-being because stifled men are walking around corporate halls in invisible chains. The cry is for corporate constitutionalism.

C. Under what conditions should products be proscribed or phased out because of their menace to humans and the readiness of new technology to perform similar or greater benefits with far fewer social costs? It seems obvious that we cannot rely on the market as the sole discipline to rid ourselves of these products. Indeed, we never have, as drug, food and narcotic laws show. But as our technological capability becomes more and more programmable, there is a need to intensify the application of reasoned intelligence to rid the society of grossly hazardous products and processes. What, for instance, is so eternal about the internal combustion engine? It gets us around but it is making each breath more difficult. Its inefficiency is costing drivers hundreds of millions annually. Must we continue to swallow the disingenuous outpourings of the auto companies? After finally becoming sensitive to certain outside companies' research and development, these companies admitted recently that an electric car was a possibility but certainly not one that can begin until 1975 or later.

D. What should be our expectations as far as corporate citizenship between corporations and industries are concerned? Just consider what an immense contribution the insurance industry could have made if it pursued a vigorous citizenship role for safer automobiles—by its informing the public of the vehicle's role in collisions and casualties, by engaging in research and development, by responsibly criticizing the auto industry, and by adapting part of its rating policies to the realities of vehicle performance, instead of making the driver bear the entire brunt.

E. What kind of effective sanctions for corporate misbehavior should be devised and implemented? The issue of sanctions is inescapably coupled with the mechanism of adequate and prompt enforcement. The issue of sanctions is a more subtle one than the simple insertion of civil and criminal fines and imprisonment clauses in statutes. Take the per se violation of price fixing. There are criminal penalties for such violations. Against the spectrum of the rampant price-fixing that has existed and does exist, such monetary penalties are rarely imposed, and imprisonment for wilful and knowing violations is almost unknown. One of the reasons for the absence of an effective legal deterrent is the trivial resources at the command of the two agencies given the job of enforcing the antitrust laws. The combined, total annual budget of the Antitrust Division of the Justice Department and the Federal Trade Commission is less than half a day's gross revenue of General Motors. (The FTC has many other laws to enforce as well.) These two agencies are confronted with a physically impossible task of policing just the most clearcut violations, not to mention the more

difficult transgressions, which are usually the most important
cases, that merit attention. What sanctions should apply only to
the corporation and what sanctions should pierce the corporate
veil and attach to individuals? What kinds of behavior either singly
or spread over time should serve to disentitle a corporation from
its claim on immortality and require its dissolution? Answers to
these questions—effective answers—are central to the establishment of adequate social control over our corporate behemoths.

UNLESS THE CHALLENGE of corporate reform is undertaken, this country will be heading toward a choice between a corporate state or a socialist
state. Present indications are that the winner will be the corporate state.
But the spirit of a meticulously evolving democracy demands a reach away
from both these alternatives and toward a higher aspiration which permits
a diversity of initiatives under due process and prevents the deadening conformity of monopolistic power centers—be they private or governmental.

A comprehensive federal corporation law is needed with the dual characteristics of all great law—the just capacity to restrain from decadence and
liberate for greatness. The old dialectics of economic ideologies are dead.
But other obstacles remain. It will take stamina to cast away the remaining
totems and tabus. It will take statesmanship for corporate leaders to eschew
the subtle repressions and permit this open criticism and free debate on the
part of those who feel a responsibility to do so.

With the indulgence of America's 200 largest corporations, may we proceed.

on corporate welfare

Cutting Corporate Welfare

From Cutting Corporate Welfare *(New York: Seven Stories Press, 2000).*

CORPORATE WELFARE—the enormous and myriad subsidies, bailouts, giveaways, tax loopholes, debt revocations, loan guarantees, discounted insurance and other benefits conferred by government on business—is a function of political corruption. Corporate welfare programs siphon funds from appropriate public investments, subsidize companies ripping minerals from federal lands, enable pharmaceutical companies to gouge consumers, perpetuate anti-competitive oligopolistic markets, injure our national security, and weaken our democracy.

At a time when the national GDP is soaring but one in five children live in deep poverty, one might expect that a public effort to curtail welfare would focus on big handouts for rich corporations, not small supports for poor individuals. But somehow the invocations of the need for stand-on-your-own-two-feet responsibility do not apply to large corporations.

While President Clinton and the Congress have gutted the welfare system for poor people—fulfilling a pledge to "end welfare as we know it," no such top-down agenda has emerged for corporate welfare recipients. The savage demagoguery directed against imaginary "welfare queens" has never been matched with parallel denunciations of gluttonous corporate welfare kings—the DuPonts, General Motors and Bristol-Myers-Squibbs that embellish their palaces with riches taken from the public purse.

At a time when even growing federal budget surpluses do not persuade our nation's political leaders to devote public resources to repairing and enhancing the built elements of our commonwealth—such as the nation's schools, bridges, clinics, roads, drinking water systems, courthouses, public transportation systems and water treatment facilities—one might expect to see calls to divert taxpayer monies from flowing into private corporate hands and instead direct them to crying public needs. But somehow the cramped federal budget—as well as similarly situated state and local budgets—always has room for another corporate welfare program.

The Political Origins of Corporate Welfare

It is raw political power that creates and perpetuates most corporate welfare programs. There is no serious public policy argument for why television broadcasters should be given control of the digital television spectrum—a $70 billion asset—for free. The endless tax loopholes that riddle the tax code—such as an accelerated depreciation schedule that's worth billions to oil companies—cannot be explained by any exotic theory of fair taxation. Local taxpayers rather than billionaire team owners pay for the new sports stadiums and arenas that dot the American landscape because of the political leverage sports teams and their allies gain through corporate cash and the threat to move elsewhere.

An examination of corporate welfare is, therefore, at one important level, an examination of the state of our political democracy. Unfortunately, the burgeoning corporate welfare state does not speak well for the state of democratic affairs. The following examples illustrate how political payoffs — what former Member of Congress Cecil Heftel, D-Hawaii, calls "legalized bribery"—distort decision-making so that the public commonwealth is corporatized to enrich the already-rich:

THE SAVINGS AND LOAN DEBACLE

Perhaps still the largest corporate welfare expenditure of all time — ultimately set to cost taxpayers $500 billion in principal and interest — the S&L bailout is in large part a story of political corruption, the handiwork of the industry's legion of lobbyists and political payoffs to campaign contributors. The well-connected S&L industry successfully lobbied Congress for a deregulatory bill in the early 1980s which freed the industry from historic constraints and paved the way for the speculative and corrupt failures that came soon after. Then more industry campaign contributions and lobbying led the Congress to delay addressing the problem—resulting in more S&L failures and skyrocketing costs for corrective measures. When the Congress finally did address the problem, it put the bailout burden—totaling hundreds of billions of dollars—on the backs of taxpayers, rather than on the financial industry.

Of the many contributing factors to the S&L debacle, which festered throughout the 1980s and into the early 1990s, none was more important than industry lobbying money and campaign cash. "Leaving aside the financial and economic complexities," writes economics commentator William Greider, "the savings and loan bailout is most disturbing as a story of politics—a grotesque case study of how representative democracy has been deformed."

"At every turn, any effort to rein in the thrifts' powers and accountability has been shackled," Representative Jim Leach, R-Iowa, then a House Banking Committee member and now the Committee chair, told the Los Angeles Times in 1989. "If there ever has been a case for campaign finance reform, this is it."

THE GIVEAWAY OF THE DIGITAL TELEVISION SPECTRUM

In 1996, Congress quietly handed over to existing broadcasters the rights to broadcast digital television on the public airwaves—a conveyance worth $70 billion—in exchange for... nothing.

Although the public owns the airwaves, the broadcasters have never paid for the rights to use them. New digital technologies now make possible the broadcast of digital television programming (the equivalent of the switch from analog records to digitalized compact disks), and the broadcasters sought rights to new portions of the airwaves. In recent years, the Federal Communications Commission has, properly, begun to recognize the large monetary value of the licenses it conveys to use the public airwaves—including for cell phones, beepers and similar uses—and typically auctions licenses. The 1996 Telecommunications Act, however, prohibited such an auction for distribution of digital television licenses, the most valuable of public airwave properties, and mandated that they be given to existing broadcasters.

How to explain this giveaway, especially when other industries, such as data transmission companies, were eager to bid for the right to use the spectrum?

Look no further than the National Association of Broadcasters (NAB).

The broadcasters are huge political donors, donating about $3 million in the 1995-1996 election cycle. They have close ties to key political figures, notably Senate Majority Leader Trent Lott, R-Mississippi; NAB head Eddie Fritts is Lott's college friend. Lott took good care of his buddy, threatening the FCC in no uncertain terms if it failed to promptly oversee the transfer of the licenses to the broadcasters.

Above all, the broadcasters are able to leverage their control over the most important media into influence over politicians. Not surprisingly, the nightly news was silent on this giant giveaway. Few if any Members of Congress were willing to challenge the giveaway. Most feared that bucking the industry would result in slanted news coverage in the next election. Those few who feel secure in their position figure it is not worth taking on the broadcasters—given the fealty of their fellow Members to the industry; they conclude, why bother?

THE 1872 MINING ACT

This nearly 130-year-old relic of efforts to settle the West allows mining companies to claim federal lands for $5 an acre or less and then take gold, silver, lead or other hard-rock minerals with no royalty payments to the public treasury. Thanks to the anachronistic 1872 Mining Act, mining companies—including foreign companies—extract billions of dollars worth of minerals a year from federal lands, royalty free.

From 1987 to 1994, the mining companies gave $17 million in campaign contributions to congressional candidates—a small price to pay to preserve their right to extract $26 billion worth of minerals, royalty free, during the same period. More recently, in the 1997-1998 election cycle, the industry— led by the National Mining Association, Cyprus Amax Minerals, Drummond, Phelps Dodge and Peabody Coal—rained more than $2 million in contributions on congressional candidates.

Those campaign donations are concentrated on a relatively small number of key members who go to bat for the industry—including Senators Larry Craig, R-Idaho, and Pete Domenici, R-New Mexico, and Representatives J.D. Hayworth, R-Arizona, and Don Young, D-Alaska. Because of the way the Congress, especially the Senate, functions, it is much easier to block changes in the status quo than to enact changes. The industry's focused contributions ensure it has enough heavyweights and devotees on call in the Congress to block the perennial efforts to reform the 1872 Mining Act.

TAX LOOPHOLES AND SUBSIDIES

If anyone needs convincing about the need for campaign finance and political reform, they need look no further than the Internal Revenue Code.

The Code is riddled with calculated loopholes, exemptions, credits, accelerated depreciation schedules, deductions and targeted exceptions — many of unfathomable consequence even to trained experts — that are carefully crafted to benefit one or a handful of companies and exist solely because well-paid lobbyists representing fat cat campaign contributors managed to convince a legislator to insert a special provision in long, complicated tax bills.

To take one recent egregious example, in July 1997, the House and Senate Republican leadership, with the apparent awareness of the Clinton White House, slipped a one-sentence provision into the tax bill that would have saved the tobacco industry $50 billion on the money it was expected to pay as part of a federally approved settlement of the state's lawsuits against the industry. Once the provision was publicly disclosed, many Members of Congress claimed not to have known it was included in the complicated tax bill. Revealed in the light of day, this massive tax favor for an industry falling rapidly out of political favor quickly withered. Both Congressional chambers soon voted to repeal the tobacco industry tax credit—a sign that, despite the fundamental flaws in the political system, news coverage and public outrage can still thwart corporate efforts to loot the treasury.

HIJACKING LOCAL DEMOCRACY

Perhaps nothing illustrates the ruthlessness and shameless power plays of the corporate welfare kings than their extortionate demands for state and local subsidies on threat of picking up and moving elsewhere.

And no case illustrates the hijacking of democratic procedures more clearly than billionaire Paul Allen's buying of an especially-made-for-Allen Washington state referendum to approve $300 million in public subsidies to build a football stadium for his Seattle Seahawks. Mega-billionaire Allen, co-founder of Microsoft with Bill Gates and one of the richest men in the world, bought the referendum both literally and figuratively.

In a stunningly brazen maneuver, he paid the state of Washington for the costs of running the special referendum election in June 1997.

Having paid for the issue to get on the ballot, Allen then waged a $6.3 million campaign—the most expensive in Washington state history—to convince voters to support the $300 million public subsidy to the stadium. He devoted $2.3 million to radio and TV ads. In total, Allen outspent opponents of the referendum by a 42-to-1 margin.

Allen's investment proved just enough: Washington voters, initially opposed by overwhelming numbers to the idea of public funding for the stadium approved the referendum with a 51 percent majority.

A New Framework for Analyzing Corporate Welfare

It is time to break through the corporate welfare mentality and propose new approaches for thinking about corporate welfare.

Rejecting corporate-welfare-think, citizens should ask probing question of government subsidy programs for big business:

+ What rationales do private interests use to secure subsidies from the government, and then to shield them from challenge, from either the legislative and judicial branches?

+ How do corporate welfare programs become entrenched and immune to cessation or reform?

+ To what extent do foreign corporations benefit from the expenditure of U.S. taxpayer dollars on corporate welfare?

+ How can fair pricing mechanisms be used to allow beneficial programs to be preserved, while eliminating welfare subsidy components?

+ What criteria should be used to determine when corporate welfare programs should simply be cancelled, and when they should be restructured to extract public benefits, pay-backs or investment returns from the government-supported enterprise?

+ What administrative due process should apply to corporate welfare? How can taxpayers be given standing and procedural rights under the Administrative Procedures Act and other relevant statutes to challenge arbitrary agency action in the corporate welfare area?

ON CORPORATE WELFARE   153

✛ How do economic subsidies disadvantage non-subsidized competing businesses, who pay their dues, and foster undesirable market
outcomes?

It's Time To End Corporate Welfare As We Know It

Originally appeared in Earth Island Journal, *Fall 1996.*

THE ISSUE OF CONCENTRATION of power and the growing conflict between the civil society and the corporate society is not a conflict that you read about or see on television. So unfortunately, most of us grow up corporate; we don't grow up civic.

If I utter the following words, what images come to mind: crime, violence, welfare and addictors? What comes to mind is street crime; people lining up to get their welfare checks; violence in the streets; and drug dealers—the addictors.

And yet, by any yardstick, there is far more crime, and far more violence, and far more welfare disbursement (and there are far more addictors) in the corporate world than in the impoverished street arena. The federal government's corporate welfare programs number over 120. They are so varied and embedded that we actually grow up thinking that the government interferes with the free enterprise system, rather than subsidizing it.

It's hard to find a major industry today whose principal investments were not first made by the government—in aerospace, telecommunications, biotechnology and agribusiness. Government research and development money funds the drug and pharmaceutical industry. Government research and development funds are given freely to corporations, but they don't announce it in ads the next day.

Corporate welfare has never been viewed as debilitating. Nobody talks about imposing workfare requirements on corporate welfare recipients or putting them on a program of "two years and you're out." Nobody talks about aid to dependent corporations. It's all talked about in terms of "incentives."

At the local community level, in cities that can't even refurbish their crumbling schools—where children are without enough desks or books—local governments are anteing up three, four, five hundred million dollars to lure very profitable baseball, football and basketball sports moguls who don't want to share the profits. Corporate sports are being subsidized by cities.

Corporations have perfected socializing their losses while they capitalize on their profits. There was the savings-and-loan debacle—and you'll be paying for that until the year 2020. In terms of principal and interest, it was a half-trillion-dollar bailout of 1,000 savings-and-loans banks. Their executives looted, speculated and defrauded people of their savings—and then turned to Washington for a bailout.

Foreign and domestic corporations can go on our land out West. If they discover gold, they can buy the acreage over the gold for no more than $5 an acre. That's been the going rate since the Mining Act of 1872 was enacted. That is taking inflation fighting too far.

There's a new drug called Taxol to fight ovarian cancer. That drug was produced by a grant of $31 million of taxpayer money through the National Institutes of Health, right through the clinical testing process. The formula was then given away to the Bristol-Myers Squibb company. No royalties were paid to the taxpayer. There was no restraint on the price. Charges now run $10,000 to $15,000 per patient for a series of treatments. If the patients can't pay, they go on Medicaid, and the taxpayer pays at the other end of the cycle, too.

Yet what is the big issue in this country and in Washington when the word "welfare" is spoken? It is the $300 monthly check given a welfare mother, most of which is spent immediately in the consumer economy. But federal corporate welfare is far bigger in dollars. At the federal, state and local levels there is no comparison between the corporate welfare and poverty welfare programs.

We have 179 law schools and probably only fifteen of them (and only recently) offer a single course or seminar on corporate crime. You think that's an accident? Law school curricula are pretty much shaped by the job market, and if the job market has slots in commercial law, bankruptcy law, securities and exchange law, tax law or estate planning law, the law schools will oblige with courses and seminars.

One professor studying corporate crime believes that it costs the country $200 billion a year. And yet you don't see many congressional hearings on corporate crime. You see very few newspapers focusing on corporate crime. Yet 50,000 lives a year are lost due to air pollution, 100,000 are lost due to toxics and trauma in the workplace, and 420,000 lives are lost due to tobacco smoking. The corporate addictor has an important role here, since it has been shown in recent months that the tobacco companies try to hook youngsters into a lifetime of smoking from age 10 to 15.

When you grow up corporate, you don't learn about the reality of corporate welfare. The programs that shovel huge amounts of taxpayer dollars to corporations through inflated government contracts via the Pentagon, or through subsidies, loan guarantees, giveaways and a variety of clever transfers of taxpayer assets get very little attention.

Knowing What's Ours

We grow up never learning what we own together, as a commonwealth. If somebody asks you what you and your parents own, you'd say: homes, cars and artifacts. Most of you would not say that you are owners of the one-third of America that is public land or that you are part owners of the public airwaves.

When you ask students today who owns the public airwaves you get the same reply—"the networks," or maybe "the government." We own the public airwaves and the Federal Communications Commission is our real estate agent. The radio and TV stations are the tenants who are given licenses to dominate their part of the spectrum 24 hours a day, and for four hours a day they decide who says what.

You pay more for your auto license than the biggest TV station pays for its broadcast license. But if you, the landlord, want in on its property, the radio and TV stations say, "Sorry, you're not going to come in." These companies say they've got to air trash TV—sensual TV, home shopping and rerun movies.

We have the greatest communications system in the world and we have the most demeaning subject matter and the most curtailed airing of public voices (known in the trade as the "sound bite"). The sound bite is down to about five seconds now.

You and your parents also may be part owners of $4 trillion in pension funds invested in corporations. The reason this doesn't get much attention is that although we own it, corporations control it. Corporations, banks and insurance companies invest our pension money. Workers have no voting mechanism regarding this money. If they did, they'd have a tremendous influence over corporations that have major pension trust investments.

Not controlling what we own should be a public issue, because if we begin to develop control of what we own, we will marshal vast existing assets that are legally ours for the betterment of our society. That will not happen unless we talk about why people don't control what they own.

All of the reforms require a rearrangement of how we spend our time. The women who launched the women's right-to-vote movement decided to spend time—in the face of incredible opposition. The people who fought to abolish slavery also decided to spend time. The workers who formed trade unions gave time.

The Power of Civic Action

Historically, how have we curbed corporate power? By child labor prohibition, by occupational health and safety rules, by motor vehicle standards and food and drug safety standards. But the regulatory agencies in these areas are now on their knees. Their budgets are very small—far less than 1 percent of the federal budget.

Their job is to put the federal cop on the corporate beat against the illegal dumping of toxics. But these laws do not get high compliance by corporations, and the application of regulatory law and order against corporate crime, fraud, abuse and violence is at its lowest ebb. I've never seen some of these agencies as weak as they are now. President Ronald Reagan started it and President George Bush extended it. And now we have "George Ronald Clinton" making the transition very easy.

The dismantling of democracy is perhaps now the most urgent aspect of the corporatization of our society. And notice, if you will, two pillars of our legal system—tort law and contract law.

The principle of tort law is that if you are wrongfully injured, you have a remedy against the perpetrator. That's well over two hundred years old. And now, in state legislatures and in Congress, laws have been passed, or are about to be passed, that protect the perpetrators, the harm-doers, that immunize them from their liability.

When the physicians at the Harvard School of Public Health testify that about 50,000 people die in hospitals every year from medical malpractice— a total larger than the combined fatalities in motor vehicle accidents, homicides and death by fire each year in the US—it raises the issue of why our elected representatives are vigorously trying to make it more difficult for victims of medical malpractice to have their day in court. [Note: President Clinton vetoed one such far-reaching tort reform bill.]

As in the Middle Ages, 1 percent of the richest people in this country own 90 percent of the wealth. The unemployment rate doesn't take into account the people who looked for a job for six months and gave up, and it doesn't take into account the underemployed who work twenty hours a week. Part of growing up corporate is that we let corporations develop the yardsticks by which we measure the economy's progress.

Democracy is the best mechanism ever devised to solve problems. That means the more we refine it—the more people practice it, the more people use its tools—the more likely it is we will not only solve our problems or at least diminish them, we also will foresee and forestall risk levels. When you see corporations dismantling democracy, you have to take it very seriously and turn it into a public political issue.

Among the five roles that we play, one is voter-citizen, another is taxpayer, another is worker, another is consumer and another is shareholder through worker pension trusts. These are critical roles in our political economy. Yet they have become weaker and weaker as the concentration of corporate power over our political and cultural and economic institutions has increased year by year.

We're supposed to have a government of, by and for the people. Instead we have a government of the Exxons, by the General Motors and for the DuPonts. We have a government that recognizes the rights and liabilities and privileges of corporations, which are artificial entities created by state charters, against the rights and privileges of ordinary people.

Jefferson warned us that the purpose of representative government is to counteract "the excesses of the monied interests"—then the merchant class; now the corporations. Beware of the government that doesn't do that.

Looting the Medicine Chest:
How Bristol-Myers Squibb Made Off
with the Public's Cancer Research

BY RALPH NADER AND JAMES LOVE

Originally appeared in The Progressive, *February 1993.*

TAXOL, A DRUG MADE from the bark of the Pacific yew tree, may be the most important cancer medicine yet. The news media have served up a feast of articles on Taxol, including several sensationalizing a highly misleading conflict between the welfare of cancer patients and the fate of the spotted owl. But very little has turned up in print about how one firm, Bristol-Myers Squibb, gained its monopoly over this drug.

At present, the only approved source for Taxol is the Pacific yew, a rare and slowly maturing tree found mostly on Federal lands. The discovery of Taxol and its cancer-fighting properties was made possible by decades of taxpayer-funded research, which has been widely published and is now in the public domain.

The Federal Government played an extensive and undisputed role in Taxol research. A recent article in the *Journal of the National Cancer Institute* lists 138 published citations of Taxol research, including reports on studies by the NCI dating to the late 1960s. Early (Phase I) studies of the effect of Taxol on cancer patients were carried out on Government grants at Johns Hopkins Oncology Center, Albert Einstein College of Medicine, Memorial Sloan-Kettering Cancer Center, the University of Texas, Mount Sinai School of Medicine, and the University of Wisconsin.

According to Dr. Samuel Broder, director of NCI, his Federal agency was "totally responsible" for the development of Taxol, including:

✠ collection of the bark;

✠ all biological screening in both cell cultures and animal-tumor systems;

✠ chemical purification, isolation, and identification;

✠ large-scale production;

✠ preclinical toxicology;

✠ filing of an Investigative New Drug Application (INDA) with the Food and Drug Administration, along with all required documentation;

✠ sponsorship of all clinical trials.

Because research on Taxol, including its effectiveness in treating cancer, has been publicly reported in professional journals, neither the drug nor the idea of using it on cancer patients can be patented, even by the Federal Government.

Nonetheless, Bristol-Myers Squibb has secured a monopoly on the drug despite the fact that it was in the public domain and is produced from trees found on public lands. How? It happened through a series of unusual contracts. The Bush administration gave the company exclusive rights to harvest the Pacific yew trees that grow on Federal lands and exclusive rights to use the millions of dollars' worth of Federal research on Taxol.

One contract gives Bristol-Myers Squibb the rights to Pacific yews growing on lands managed by the U.S. Forest Service, at no charge. A second agreement gives it the rights to Pacific yews growing on lands controlled by the Bureau of Land Management—in this case, at token prices of five to twenty cents per pound for the scarce bark. (Less than forty pounds of bark is needed to produce enough Taxol for a complete *course* of treatment for ovarian cancer, so the cost to the company per completed patient treatment tops out at $2 to $8.)

By virtue of a remarkable "Cooperative Research and Development Agreement," NCI has agreed to make historical research findings completed before the company entered the Taxol picture, as well as "new studies and raw data" from NCI-funded Taxol research, "available exclusively to Bristol-Myers Squibb," so long as the company is "engaged in the commercial development and marketing of Taxol."

What are these "raw data"? Most important are the medical histories of sick persons who turn to Government-funded programs to receive experimental drugs. Information about whether these people live or die, or how they suffer, has become, under this agreement, the exclusive commercial property of Bristol-Myers Squibb. Given this monopoly on the Pacific yew bark and the Government's research data, this one company is the only party now holding FDA approval to sell Taxol.

UNDER THE TERMS of the agreement, Bristol-Myers Squibb asked the FDA to approve Taxol for the treatment of ovarian cancer, anticipating that the firm would receive exclusive marketing protection under the Federal Government's poorly drafted and much-abused Orphan Drug Act. When this law was enacted a decade ago, its purpose was to promote the development of drugs for rare diseases. Drugs were considered "orphans" when no company found them profitable enough to market. The Orphan Drug Act has since been amended several times, and each time the definition of an "orphan disease" has expanded until, today, ailments such as asthma, AIDS, lung cancer, and chronic pain qualify. Many highly profitable drugs, such as AZT, ddl, and human growth hormone now receive monopoly marketing rights under the Act.

The market for Taxol will be highly profitable. In late December, the FDA approved Taxol for the treatment of ovarian cancer, which has a client population of 160,000 women, after a speedy process taking only five months instead of the average twenty it takes the agency to act.

Taxol also shows promise in treating other forms of cancer. NCI's Broder estimates the taxpayers will spend about $35 million in past and future Taxol research, including clinical trials on thirty types of cancer.

The success of the Government's continuing research on Taxol has added a new twist. NCI-funded trials now show the drug to be an effective treatment for breast cancer, a disease which afflicts 1.6 million women—a client population so large that it doesn't qualify as an "orphan" disease. As a result, Bristol-Myers Squibb has abandoned its request for orphan-drug marketing protections. However, the Government agreements which give the company exclusive rights to the Pacific yew and to all government-funded research on Taxol have created large barriers to market entry which no other firm can easily overcome.

If the company pays a trivial sum for the Pacific yew trees harvested on public lands and doesn't pay the government anything for its exclusive rights to Federally funded research information, what do the taxpayers get in return?

Not much.

The Federal Government will not get any royalties on Bristol-Myers

Squibb's sales of Taxol. We get only the company's "best efforts" to commercialize Taxol.

Such a deal! The taxpayers pay for the invention of a promising treatment for cancer and then give a marketing monopoly to one company, complete with a free or nearly free supply of the primary ingredient. And the company's role is to agree to sell it back to us.

The National Cancer Institute says the agreements with Bristol-Myers Squibb were necessary, since firms won't develop new drugs without the prospect of a marketing monopoly.

Moreover, government officials are quick to point out that new sources for Taxol may lead to future competition in the Taxol market; therefore, Bristol-Myers Squibb is actually facing large risks which need to be rewarded.

Indeed, progress is being made on the development of new sources for Taxol, and several companies are spending millions of dollars to find ways to enter the market. For example, Rhone-Poulenc Barr is testing Taxotere, a synthesized product obtained from the leaves of the European yew tree, to treat ovarian, breast, and lung cancer.

But the fact that other firms are spending millions of dollars hoping to find some way to compete against Bristol-Myers Squibb is compelling evidence that NCI did not need to create a monopoly in the first place. NCI and Bristol-Myers Squibb also assert that the exclusive contract will speed up the development of Taxol. However, consider a different view: Bristol-Myers Squibb was shielded from the possibility that other companies would have obtained Taxol or used the Government's own clinical data on Taxol trials to file an earlier FDA application—a particularly important issue when it was thought Taxol would be protected under the Orphan Drug Act.

In fact, NCI never gave any serious consideration to a nonexclusive development plan, though several companies expressed interest in marketing Taxol. As things stand now, Bristol-Myers Squibb's monopoly will substantially reduce competition for Taxol or Taxol analogues for several years.

EVEN IF THE EXCLUSIVE agreement had been necessary, couldn't the Government have driven a harder bargain? After all, the Government discovered Taxol in the first place and did all the early development work. What important ingredient does Bristol-Myers Squibb bring to the table?

According to NCI officials, Bristol-Myers Squibb's main asset is its marketing expertise; it already sells more cancer drugs in the United States than any other firm. But this oncology empire is built on a number of other drugs that were also invented through taxpayer-funded research, including cis-platin, carboplatin, carmustine, and lomustine, to mention a few.

"Marketing expertise" seems like a slender reed to justify this deal, since a promising new drug does not exactly require a hard sell, like a new brand of perfume. Before Bristol-Myers Squibb entered the picture, the government was able to manufacture Taxol for about 60 cents per milligram, or $1,000 for an entire *course* of treatment, and this cost should have fallen with larger-scale production. But Bristol-Myers Squibb prepared the public to pay more.

In a March 1992 interview on *The MacNeil/Lehrer NewsHour,* Bristol-Myers Squibb's Dr. Zola Horovitz said the company had made a "huge" investment, and that "Taxol will probably cost more than any other oncology product that's ever been developed." What does it mean to say that Taxol will "cost more"? More than Pentostatin, sold by Warner-Lambert for more than $10,000 to some cancer patients? More than Roferon A, which costs some more than $50,000?

When questioned later, Dr. Horovitz said he did not mean to imply that Taxol would be the highest-priced cancer drug, but rather that it was the most costly to develop. How can this be? The government invented the drug, developed the manufacturing process, and funded extensive clinical trials.

Bristol-Myers Squibb refuses to say how much it spent to bring the drug to market. According to Dr. Horovitz, the "huge" investments he was referring to were primarily related to the development of new sources for Taxol, including synthetic analogues. The company also hopes to gain ownership or control of the patents for developing these "new sources."

Bristol-Myers Squibb wants to apply the profits from Taxol to its research-and-development budget for new drugs. Does this make sense? No. Consumers of Taxol should pay only for Bristol-Myers Squibb's costs of testing, manufacturing, and marketing Taxol. If the company wants to make investments in the development of new Taxol analogues, it should get the money from investors just as others drug companies do.

Cancer patients have already financed the invention of Taxol once as tax-payers. Why should they be forced to pay Bristol-Myers Squibb a second time, as consumers?

Can NCI stop Bristol-Myers Squibb from gouging the public?

In fact, the agreement between NCI and Bristol-Myers Squibb includes a so-called "fair pricing" clause, which appears to deal with this problem. But it is so weakly worded and lacking in enforcement measures that it may only serve the public-relations interests of the company.

The National Cancer Institute has waived its right to set Taxol prices, and it doesn't even require disclosure of Bristol-Myers Squibb's cost of development.

Rather than focus on the company's actual costs, NIH officials reportedly told the firm that it expects the drug to be priced similarly to other cancer drugs. Given a list of the monthly wholesale prices of fifteen drugs, Bristol-Myers Squibb was asked to price Taxol at no more than the median for the group. In essence, NIH has told the company that it could price Taxol, a government-funded invention, the same as other cancer drugs regardless of who paid for the drug's development.

The median cost of the drugs on the list is reportedly more than $1,700 for a month of treatment. In December, when the FDA approved the marketing of Taxol, Bristol-Myers Squibb announced it would price the drug at $986 per three-week treatment cycle. This figure was based upon a dose of 202.5 milligrams at $4.87 apiece—more than eight times the Government's manufacturing cost of sixty cents.

According to NCI officials, the actual amount of Taxol used in cancer therapy will be considerably higher than the amount cited by Bristol-Myers Squibb in its press releases. Patients in clinical trials currently receive from 210 to more than 300 milligrams of Taxol per dose. A patient who receives 240, a common dose, will pay $1,169. A patient who responds favorably to treatment receives up to eight cycles of Taxol injections, for a total treatment cost of $9,350. The government's manufacturing cost for this much Taxol was $1,152.

Representative Ron Wyden, an Oregon Democrat and critic of the government's Taxol agreements with Bristol-Myers Squibb, has scheduled hearings on the pricing of Taxol and other government-developed drugs for late January.

While it is important to encourage the development of new drug discoveries, it is also important to protect the interests of the millions of Americans who bear the increasing burden of health-care costs. Price gouging on government-developed drugs is a costly abuse of ailing patients.

Rip-off, Inc.

Originally appeared in Mother Jones, *May/June 1991.*

A CARDINAL PRECEPT OF capitalism is that if you pay for an asset, you own it. But a fundamental tenet of *corporatism* is that if taxpayers pay for an asset, corporations should own or control it. Corporatism is winning the day.

Mining Our Pockets

Start with the Mining Act of 1872. At any time, any U.S. or even Japanese corporation can go prospecting on more than 300 million acres of federal land. If they strike gold, silver, copper, molybdenum, or other "hard-rock" minerals, they have the right to buy the land for between $2.50 and $5.00 an acre—the going rate in 1872—and extract and sell these minerals free of charge by the government. Since 1872, a Connecticut-sized chunk of land owned by the American people and managed with our tax monies has passed into private ownership. Some of this land has become ski areas, private homes, even a Phoenix golf course. All this is legal. Once the mining companies simply prove their discovery, they can turn around and sell the land for huge profits, as did the Stocks Mill and Supply Company, which in 1981 bought two sand-and-gravel areas near Las Vegas for $1,124 under the Act's provisions. Soon thereafter, the land was appraised at more than $2 million. Every year, over $4 billion worth of minerals are hauled out of the ground under the 1872 Act; taxpayers get not a cent in royalties.

Taxpayer Chain-Saw Massacre

Timber from the 191 million acres of public-owned national forests is often sold at prices that do not even pay the Forest Service's costs of cutting roads for the loggers' trucks. In the Tongass National Forest in Alaska, your government takes in $10 for every $100 it spends, and timber companies pay less than $4 for a 120-foot spruce tree. Overall, the Forest Service spent 71 cents on timber expenses (as in preparing roads) for every dollar it received in 1989. Seventy-three out of 122 national forests lost money. If taxpayers don't benefit, who does? Corporations, including, in many cases, large Tokyo trading companies: Much of the timber that we subsidize is shipped directly to Japan.

R&D for Free

In 1989, the federal government spent over $60 million on research and development, which was nearly half of all R&D money spent in the United States. Profitable inventions flowing from government-funded research range from satellites to medicine to energy technology. Until the 1980s, Senator Russell Long used his power to attach amendments to taxpayer-financed R&D, which preserved most patents in the government's name. Federal agencies such as NASA or the Department of Defense could license the patents to companies on an exclusive or nonexclusive basis in return for royalties, and retain some say in how the new technology might be used.

No more. Thanks largely to the Reagan "revolution," universities and companies can, under their exclusive control, patent federally funded inventions for industrial and consumer markets. While this giveaway rampages, consumers are often forced to pay a gain for an innovation that they've already bankrolled as taxpayers.

Info-Robbery

The United States government is the most prolific source of legal, scientific, economic, technical, and statistical information in the world. Information is power. And it is the currency of democracy. If information is too costly or hard to access for most citizens, but not for companies and other special-interest groups, democracy suffers and the powerful become more so. That's exactly what's happening.

Government libraries, fed via federal agencies' powerful computers, are ever more specialized and critical to decision-making. But Reagan succeeded in privatizing many such data bases. Key data on oil companies or occupational hazards were suppressed or no longer collected. Until this year, the Securities and Exchange Commission's document room was run by Bechtel.

Meanwhile, McGraw-Hill, Dialog, West Publishing, Ziff-Davis, Cambridge Scientific Abstracts, and hundreds of other firms offer "products" that consist of government records and data. They often try to convert a right to sell uncopyrighted information into a proprietary interest by lobbying to keep the government from disseminating the information. By doing this, corporate data vendors can charge their customers exorbitant prices for information that was assembled by the government and already paid for by taxpayers.

Once these vendors get hold of a data base, they turn around and argue to Congress or the Office of Management and Budget that the agency that collected the information should not be allowed to compete with private business. And they win. Today, for example, if you want on-line access to Federal Maritime Commission ocean-tariff data bases, you have to pay Knight-Ridder or other data vendors a high price. The same holds true if you wish to receive regularly the notices and press releases of the Federal Communications Commission or the Interstate Commerce Commission. You'll have to pay private firms hundreds of dollars per year for the agency information that your taxes already bought.

The federal courts, increasingly dominated by Reagan-Bush judges, are making it nearly impossible for taxpayers to have "legal standing" to sue agencies that recklessly mismanage or give away public assets. Imagine where the labor, environmental, consumer, or civil-rights movements would be now if their advocates could not even get through the federal courthouse doors to plead their cases. Moreover, when federal agencies make decisions about how to manage or sell taxpayer assets, most frequently, there are no public proceedings and appeals at all. To complete the insulation from democratic participation, often even the Freedom of Information Act isn't enough to overcome agencies' secrecy about what they are doing with the public's land, trees, research, and information.

How to Put the Punch Back in Politics

Originally appeared in Mother Jones, *July/August 1990.*

WILLIAM GOSSETT, former vice-president of Ford Motor Company, said it over thirty years ago: the corporation is the "dominant institution" in our society. Today that institution is busily expanding its privilege and power through the use of computers, satellites, video imagery, "psychographic" profiling of consumers, and state-of-the-art advertising, public relations, and political influence.

The future has not arrived, however, for activists who would try to balance that corporate power and let citizens have a more democratic role in society. While corporations master the tools of the twenty-first century, their opponents are stuck with the political equivalent of picks and hoes, nineteenth-century tools that are becoming more rusty and antiquated as the nineties rev up.

There's no trouble finding a *need* for a new politics. The needs have been cited so often as to constitute a litany: growing poverty, layoffs and cutbacks, business crime and fraud, crumbling infrastructure, homelessness, child exploitation, stagnant wages and family income, drugs and crime, adult illiteracy, schools in chaos, taxpayer bailouts of corporate crooks, triple deficits, falling behind foreign competitors, environmental pollution, health-care costs, consumer abuse, land erosion, discrimination against color, gender, and age, inequitable taxation, government waste, fraud, and abuse, and everywhere bureaucratic rigidity. Not many people would deny that these problems are widespread. Yet not a single mass movement worthy of the name exists to address the concentration of power that breeds these injustices.

There's no difficulty in seeing the *potential strength* arising out of such frustration—one can find it in, of all places, Eastern Europe. While some on the Left worry that those revolts might have been in favor of "consumerism" rather than some supposedly purer goal, such motivation should be a source of inspiration. Eastern Europeans were protesting that their governments were not delivering the goods, services, and opportunities that their monopoly of power had been promising all these years. They were fighting for what is an American ideal, if not a reality. They wanted the consumer, not the producer, to be king.

Here in the United States, the nineties promise to be a time of pent-up consumer and citizen frustration, which, if joined to a new, modernized assortment of political tools, could fuel a new political movement for real democracy. How do we get from here to there? To answer that, we need first of all to revisit the nineteenth century.

We Own It; They Control It

Citizen revolt these days amounts to occasional marches where people come to voice their anger and leave litter and little other impact behind. There is nothing to compare to the farmers' drive in Texas during the late 1880s, which signed up 250,000 farmers and led to the early stage of the thirty-year progressive revolt—still the country's most fundamental political and economic reform movement since the Constitution was ratified. And these farmers did it largely on foot and with pamphlets.

How, without today's communications and transportation facilities, did the farmers manage to cover so much ground, create so many lasting institutions, and elect so many state legislators, governors, members of Congress, and almost the president of the United States? Because they owned what they controlled—the land. And they controlled what they owned—the land. And they aggregated their vote around specific agendas designed to limit the power of the railroads, banks, and absentee "Eastern" financial moguls.

The defense of the family farm bought time, staving off the giant "trusts" while industrial labor and the regulatory state took hold as countervailing forces to tame some excesses of these corporations. Farmers established their own credit institutions, built producer cooperatives, enacted direct democracy reforms like the referendum process, and strengthened the laws against monopoly and marketplace fraud.

However, for stamina and singleness of purpose, there has been no match in U.S. society for the modern corporation as apolitical, economic, and cultural force. The capacity to co-opt, absorb, or intimidate its adversaries has become ever more refined and successful in the past half century, especially since the onset of the Nixon years. Few would deny the decline in the strength of organized labor and most federal regulatory agencies to check these companies, for it is dramatic indeed.

The clearest manifestation today is the growing corporate control over other people's property. In the next decade, we risk the increasingly rapid separation of real asset ownership from real asset control. Consider that:

The public *owns* one third of the United States—the federal lands largely out west and in Alaska—and companies, mostly multinationals, *control* these rich resources of timber, oil, gas, copper, iron, zinc, etc., through leaseholds. And taxpayers put up the money to make private profit possible. The cost to taxpayers to facilitate private cutting of virgin timberlands, for example, is more than ten times what they get back in royalties—mills pay a few dollars for a five-hundred-year-old tree, while taxpayers foot the bill for roads that make cutting possible. Under the Mining Law of 1872, companies are still able to take control of hard-rock mining resources discovered on federal lands and keep the entire profits. Third World nations demand tougher royalty agreements from U.S. oil companies than our own government does.

The public *owns* the government's research findings that taxpayers fund, but corporations *control* the patents and profits emerging from such research. The National Cancer Institute, which developed the application of the drug AZT against AIDS, allowed Burroughs Wellcome Company to obtain an exclusive patent to market the medicine without any price restraints or royalties. A year's treatment with AZT costs $2,800 and recently ran as high as $8,000. Under Medicaid, the taxpayers are paying twice for a drug their taxes developed.

The public, say Congress and the Supreme Court, *owns* the airwaves; but the broadcasters *control* them. Workers *own* over $1.7 trillion worth of pension monies; banks and insurance companies *control* their investment policies. Depositors and mutual-assurance policyholders *own* hundreds of billions of dollars in savings and insurance; management of these mutuals *controls* their disposition. It is obvious that the brokers of wealth scarcely care who owns the wealth, so long as they can get rich by controlling such assets. Meanwhile . . .

Citizens' hands are slipping off the levers of control over government. Voter turnout has been in a free-fall for twenty-five years, and most races aren't really races. In most congressional districts, incumbents run against little or no opposition at all. Taxpayers may revolt against tax rates every now and then, but they have virtually no say in how tax revenues are spent, wasted, or given away.

Indeed, politicians see their role as friends of sellers rather than consumers. They leap to help when faced with a case of a mismanaged or corrupt industry in need of aid, but rarely identify with the citizen who must pay. Meanwhile, the lion's share of campaign contributions comes from business, and their influence has become the stuff of legend on Capitol Hill and in state legislatures. In the name of helping "troubled industry," politicians have created a huge corporate welfare system composed of hundreds of billions of dollars in tax abatements, tax preferences, grants, inflated contracts, and a long menu of subsidies to industry and commerce. Bailouts, as in the up-to-$500-billion program for the savings-and-loan wreckage, may devour any "peace dividend."

Citizens are losing their influence in the marketplace. Parents, perhaps more than anyone, are acutely aware that they are losing control to the legal and illegal marketplace. Companies and other marketers of addictions have far more control over the time, values, and behavior of youngsters than parents do. Preteens and teenagers have become marketing mechanisms for sellers of tobacco, alcohol, drugs, clothing, medications, diets, mind-blowing music, war toys, junk food, cosmetics, and other absorptions.

This is a young generation that has spent less time with adults, including their often absentee parents, than any generation in our history. It is also true that no generation has spent more time, through television, video games, and products, with the offerings of promoters. From infant formulas to teenage fashions, corporations are raising our children. From Kinder Care to McDonald's to HBO, the values desired by marketers are taking hold.

The boosters dismiss such criticism. What matters, they say, is economic growth and jobs; the American business economy has been a job machine. And hasn't the inflation-adjusted GNP almost doubled per capita since 1960? That question begs a more profound one: how many Americans can say that their standard of living has doubled since 1960? In many important respects—the crime rate, education, health costs, real wages, public services—living standards for many citizens have fallen or stagnated.

This decline in the actual standard of living corresponds to the dramatic loss of control by citizens in their roles as voters, taxpayers, consumers, parents and co-owners of property. It is conventional to describe this loss of control as inconsequential (the ruling stewards are doing all right), oppressive (the ruling oligarchies have taken away these participatory rights), or even consensual (people are not bothered delegating these powers to representatives, trustees, surrogates).

Changing the Debate

All these explanations, however, ignore the average American's natural inclination to want more democracy, not less, and to instinctively distrust power that is concentrated in a few hands. In order for a new politics to speak to these basics, we will have to change the terms of the current debate.

In the eighties, conservatives and all too many liberals arrived at a consensus that production is the engine of consumption (supply-side thinking). Moreover, they accepted that production should *lead* and *shape* consumption. Both conservatives and liberals make the unexamined assumption that production is king; production puts people to work so they can be more-liquid consumers. Therefore, the pre-eminent yardstick of a "healthy" economy—the gross national product—counts money but does not describe quality of life.

Here is the flaw in such thinking: it is the number of cars and drugs sold that is the measure, not what the auto and drug industries add and subtract from the transportation usage and health of people.

The present seller-sovereign economy is quite different from the classical market model, where consumer sovereignty is supposed to reign supreme. A seller-sovereign economy includes monopolistic or oligopolistic sellers who are not confronted by consumers organized in monopolistic or oligopolistic modes. It is an economy where sellers work overtime to control their customers through unrebutted advertising, using sensual images or contrived complexity, rather than providing reliable, comparable information that nourishes rational choice. If consumer were really king, would there be shortages for millions of Americans in housing, food, and health care, while there are ample supplies of cosmetics, video games, soft drinks, and entertainment? Dependence, not critical capability, is what firms seek from consumers.

Government regulation, the liberal answer, is not enough of a solution to foster a consumer-sovereign economy. When it comes to regulating oligopolies, government invariably adopts the seller-sovereign priorities. Take the energy industry. If the consumer were valued, there would be much more pressure for energy efficiency—renewable, self-reliant, safer, and competitively priced energy. More highly valuing the energy seller encourages what we have today: more centralized energy, supplied by often interlocked sellers whose technologies create waste, pollution, disease, and political corruption. Exxon makes money when gas-guzzling motor vehicles are sold— and the consumer loses money. Energy waste for the consumer equals energy profit for Exxon. If in the last fifty years the consumer value had the power to prevail, our nation would be humming along on one-third of the energy now used, with highly advanced passive and active solar energy.

How, apart from election day and its narrow choices, can the citizen balance the scales? There has been little in the regulatory laws to give consumers the power to initiate or challenge any of numerous economic and safety rules regarding food, drugs, transportation, communications, housing, banking, insurance, energy, health, and other services. Consequently, the administration of these laws ebbs and flows according to who is in office, which breeds poor agency morale and public cynicism.

A new politics, a populism for the nineties, could break out of the current producer-versus-government debate by identifying a new target: the corporate state's "transfer economy." Aided by the government, companies transfer their risks, failures, waste, and corruption onto the consumer with increasing ease. Where this is recognized, it often drives conservative and liberal groups into active alliances, crossing race and class lines. Such coalitions came forth in struggles against the Alaska gas pipeline, the breeder-reactor subsidy, and, most recently, California's insurance-industry rip-off. In the new decade, more liberals and perhaps more conservatives will begin to view the megacorporations as principal subverters of the market-enterprise system.

Getting Control Back

The right to vote, the right to speak, the right to homestead 160 acres of farmland, the right to collective bargaining and social security, the right of judicial redress by consumers, have all expanded the frontiers of justice, opportunity, and well-being. Yet these rights need to be kept up-to-date. The right of freedom of speech has to be more elaborate in an age where the decibel imbalance is huge between a person on a soapbox and a broadcast commentator over television. The right to petition one's government must be modernized to give consumers better leverage with utility companies, banks and insurance firms, cable companies, and pension trusts.

In short, it is time to bring the citizens' agenda into the twenty-first century, so that it can keep pace with the corporate agenda. We must create new democratic mechanisms by which citizens can make their will felt, and regain control of what they already own. Some new tools to fashion and fight for:

Let taxpayers sue. Today, the federal courts rarely grant taxpayers "standing to sue" so that they can plead their cases against corporate subsidies, loan guarantees, or giveaways. For example, why can't you, who foot the bill, bring suits challenging the endemic Pentagon procurement fraud, since Congress clearly is not willing or able to step up to the job?

Claim the airwaves. Although there is an abundance of available communications technologies, it will take a public-access drive to make them usable by the nation's people. For starters, Congress should establish an "audience network." Since public airwaves belong to the public, Congress would charter a nonprofit viewer and listener group and revert back to this organization (open to membership for five dollars a year) one hour of prime or drive time each day on each television and radio station. The audience network would use that time locally and nationally for a vast variety of consumer-informing subjects that are largely ignored by today's advertising-driven or corporate-sponsored media monopolies.

Self-power consumer groups. An idea called the "consumer checkoff" can revolutionize the consumer movement into voluntary, mass-based policy organizations with professional staff backed at the grass roots by active members. Periodically, citizens of Illinois find that a small, postage-paid envelope comes inside mailings from their state government. The envelope contains a stimulating headline and several paragraphs explaining why consumers should band together as part of the Citizens Utility Board. By joining the CUB, they can represent themselves with technical skills, public information, and political power, before all branches of government, on electric, gas, and telephone matters affecting them. Minimum dues are five dollars a year, and over 150,000 residential customers have chosen to join. Pressure from the Illinois CUB has helped pass utility-reform packages and save ratepayers $3 billion. More important over the long term, the group's meetings and activism are increasing knowledge and self-confidence among Illinois consumers.

The structure is in place for this form of advocacy in many areas. Legislatures can give consumer groups the right to insert their solicitation message in the billing envelopes or printed contracts of utilities, banks, insurance companies, auto companies, etc. The postal service could be required to deliver, free of charge, two envelopes a year inviting residential postal users to join their own advocacy group. National-park rangers could hand visitors environmental consumer-group solicitations at the entrance kiosk.

Giving Americans more democratic muscle is not on the agenda of elected officials. Although these proposals cost taxpayers little or nothing to enact and implement—since they are facilities open to voluntary membership and are self-financing—they test well the depth of indenture into which legislators have fallen on behalf of their powerful patrons.

During the House banking committee's markup of the then $150 billion S&L bailout last year, we suggested to the members that they require the S&Ls to regularly insert a solicitation in their monthly deposit statement, inviting customers to join a congressionally chartered, nonprofit depositors' consumer group in each state. It was suggested that the least Congress could do was to empower these fully staffed action groups, funded by voluntary membership dues and controlled by depositors who join, so that this huge debacle will not recur. It would be no burden on the taxpayer, voluntary to join, and self-governing, yet the proposal introduced by Congressman Charles Schumer (D-NY) never even got out of committee.

The bailout bill passed both houses and was signed by President Bush as the first step in charging taxpayers, who had nothing to do with the S&L crimes and did not benefit from them, at least $3,200 each.

While it may not be surprising that elected and appointed officials show little interest in the consumer-power agenda, it is astonishing how little attention is paid by the citizens' groups themselves. So absorbed are they in dealing with daily unjust incursions that they end up bringing obsolete hoes and picks to the fray. Working to update the tools of democracy does not naturally inspire the emotional fervor that specific, substantive conflicts, from students' rights to flag burning, possess. Yet without acquiring these tools, people can have the soundest grounds for demanding changes, but their voices will neither be heard nor heeded.

Over the next year, in a regular column for *Mother Jones,* I will lay out the design for these and other such tools in more detail, and describe how and where they are already being used successfully. These will not be opinion pieces; they will be action guides. Each one will include information about how you can directly participate in the most important modernization program of all—bringing citizen democracy into the next century.

✦ Of America's 250 most profitable corporations in 1988, 45 reduced their tax liability to less than 10%, 6 received refunds.

✦ Between 1981 and 1987, the Justice Department received 10,723 merger notifications, and challenged only 26.

✦ The Alyeska corporate consortium has extracted $45 billion in net profit from its low-cost leases on Alaska's North Slope since 1970, but has spent almost no money to prevent or respond to a major oil spill there. Despite the "hardship" of the Valdez spill, Exxon's profits for 1989 exceeded $3.8 billion.

✦ The average American's health-insurance costs have risen nearly 300% since 1980; more than 38 million Americans still lack adequate health care.

✦ The savings-and-loan bailout, estimated at $325 billion, could provide free catastrophic health care to all Medicare recipients for the next 29 years.

✦ A common pharmaceutical-industry justification for increasing prices is the huge amount of money needed for R&D. But between 1982 and 1986, price increases for existing drugs generated additional revenues of $4.7 billion for 25 companies—which spent only $1.6 billion on R&D during that period.

✦ Since 1981, when the Clean Air Act became due for reauthorization, GM has spent over $1.8 million fighting clean-air legislation.

✦ A Federal Reserve study found that banks make an average profit of 27% on checking and other non-interest-bearing accounts. Nevertheless, almost all banks charge a service fee to cover the "cost" of handling checking accounts.

✦ 40% of the research money spent at large corporations in 1987 came out of taxpayers' pockets.

✦ Nuclear-industry R&D, infrastructure, and waste disposal are almost completely government subsidized. The nuclear industry now owes the government $9.6 billion for uranium enrichment. An industry-backed bailout, already Senate approved, would be second in size only to the S&L one.

✦ Tobacco companies spent $3.25 billion on advertising in 1988, several hundred million of which was taxpayer subsidized.

✦ MCA, Inc., which owns all concession rights in Yosemite National Park, had $78 million in sales and paid taxpayers 0.75% of that in 1988. All park maintenance is done by the National Park Service, whose budget is the same today as ten years ago; visitor attendance, meanwhile, has jumped 29%.

Corporate Welfare State Is On a Roll

Originally appeared in The Los Angeles Times, *March 5, 1990.*

RAIDING TAXPAYER ASSETS is the big game in Washington, but not everyone can play. From bailouts to outright giveaways and from military procurement fraud to bloated subsidies, our national government has become a golden accounts receivable for hordes of organized, corporate claimants who lobby daily to get something for nothing or a lot for a little.

Taxpayers and their lobbying groups focus on tax rates and loopholes, paying insufficient attention to misappropriation of their dollars by corporate welfarists. One reason for this inattention is that the laws shut taxpayers out—they may not petition the offending agencies and departments or take them to court for the arbitrary and capricious transfer of taxpayer assets to corporate use and control. The stakes are enormous for both present and future generations of Americans.

Four areas of abuse are booming:

BAILOUTS

The prominent bailouts of the 1970s—the $250-million Lockheed loan guarantee and the $1.5-billion Chrysler loan guarantee—were legislated after public hearings and now look like small change. The taxpayer bailout of the wreckage caused by fraud and speculation in the savings and loan industry will reach at least $300 billion before the dust settles. Estimates of cleanup costs for U.S. nuclear weapons plants, managed by private firms such as DuPont and North American Rockwell, range from $50 billion to $150 billion.

Bailouts are increasingly being shaped and decided with fewer and fewer congressional standards. In December, 1988, in a secret frenzy of round-the-clock giveaways, the Federal Home Loan Bank Board unloaded the assets of dozens of S&Ls into the laps of financiers who had to invest comparatively tiny amounts of their own capital, while the board assumed open-ended liability for these failing institutions. The board obligated the taxpayers for more than $40 billion in this feeding frenzy, without any congressional authorization. Congress turned down efforts to reopen these deals (whose full texts are still secret) and instead retroactively ratified the board's wildcat indebtedness.

To illustrate the lucrativeness of these back-room bonanzas: One financier, Ronald Perelman, recouped 80% on his investment in a Texas S&L in just the first ninety days after concluding his deal with the board.

It is not corporate taxpayers who must endure the bailout burden of these corporate scandals; it is primarily the small taxpayer, who neither caused nor benefited from the scandals.

RESOURCE DEPLETION

Public lands make up one third of the United States. The laws declare them to be commonwealth: They are owned by the people in trust for posterity and managed largely by the Departments of the Interior and Agriculture. For a century, in a trend that accelerated under the Ronald Reagan-James Watt regime, rich mineral rights, timberland and other wealth have been taken from the commonwealth and leased at bargain-basement prices to corporations. The cost to taxpayers to facilitate private cutting of virgin timber lands is more than 10 times what they get back in royalties. One Alaskan pulp mill paid $2.12 for a 100-foot-high spruce, while taxpayers footed the bill for roads to make the cutting possible. Third World nations demand tougher royalty agreements from U.S. oil companies than our own government does. The under-reporting and under-payment of royalties, and the longer-range depletion and destruction of public natural resources, erode these taxpayer assets.

TAXPAYER-FUNDED RESEARCH AND DEVELOPMENT

This giveaway also expanded rapidly under the Reagan Administration. The prevailing practice is to give exclusive patents on government-financed inventions to private contractors. Even inventions generated by government laboratories are being given over to private business. The National Cancer Institute, which developed the application of the drug AZT against AIDS, allowed Burroughs Wellcome, Inc. to obtain an exclusive patent to market the medicine without any price restraints or royalties. A year's treatment with AZT costs from $6,000 to $10,000. Under Medicaid, the taxpayers are paying twice for a drug their taxes developed for clinical use. Total federal and state purchases of AZT from Burroughs Wellcome between 1982 and 1987 are estimated at $2.4 billion.

The federal government funds nearly half of the nation's R&D. Taxpayers, who provide the roots for this work, are denied the fruits, which mostly flow into corporate coffers.

SUBSIDIES TO PROFIT-MAKING BUSINESSES

Perhaps the most grotesque example of corporate welfare is the millions of dollars in Urban Development Action Grants and other subsidies given to General Motors in 1981 to build an automated Cadillac plant in Detroit. There are many examples of UDAG grants going to profitable companies, along with a large menu of other direct grant and subsidy programs. There are even subsidies for exporting nuclear power plants and tobacco. The overall value of these corporate welfare payments is easily more than $100 billion a year.

There are simply no open administrative procedures, as there are with environmental and consumer regulations, for taxpayer participation in the use and disposition of such public wealth. The Supreme Court has ruled that federal taxpayers cannot appeal to the courts to stop waste, fraud and unlawful conversion of taxpayer assets because they have "no standing to sue." The usual argument by the court is that a taxpayer's interest is shared with millions of others and is comparatively minute and indeterminable. When Richard Nixon's White House aides were openly using their time and government facilities to advance his reelection campaign in 1972, a federal court refused to admit a taxpayer's suit to enjoin such unlawful behavior because of the standing issue. Even 50 million taxpayers in a class action would not have made a difference to the court.

Many states give taxpayers standing to sue state government. Some explicitly authorize taxpayers to sue as private attorneys general to uphold the laws that officials are ignoring. If President Bush and Congress really are serious about preventing taxpayer assets from being looted, mismanaged or converted to private parties, legislation is needed to protect the public's property from giveaways, as in the patent area; to establish procedures that will assure more open and accountable government policy-making regarding taxpayer assets, and give taxpayers standing, under what constitutional lawyers call a "participant-review provision," to defend their interests in federal courts.

Hundreds of billions of dollars in tax-payer assets have been squandered. It is time to give taxpayers the means to correct these injustices. After all, they pay the bills.

No More Bailouts!

Originally appeared in Mother Jones, *Sept/Oct 1990.*

"JAIL THE CROOKS," "Seize their wealth." "Throw the bums out of Washington." On one radio talk show after another, the callers are raging at the makers of the savings-and-loan scandal, a disaster that will cost each American an average of at least $2,000 (one estimate put it at $5,000 over forty years). But it's not enough to demand retribution. We need to look ahead, and develop a strategy that shifts power fast from the perpetrators to the public. That's the only way to forestall coming financial calamities in commercial banking, insurance, and pension depletions. The lessons of the S&L system breakdown are clear: At each *cause-point,* an opportunity for greed and thievery to develop, and at each *checkpoint,* a safeguard that would have stopped the nation's biggest bank robbery, the people were betrayed.

CAUSE-POINT. For some forty years, the S&Ls were nearly all mutuals—legally owned by their depositors and prevented from "playing" in money markets. In the seventies, federal banking agencies succumbed to industry demands for easier conversion from mutuals to stock corporations, which then could raise more capital from the money markets. These conversions

opened the door to risk-taking high rollers.
There was no organized opposition by depositors to this conversion movement.

CAUSE-POINT. In 1980, legislators well connected to banking lobbies pushed through Congress a $100,000-per-bank-account insurance guarantee. In 1982, Reagan got Congress to enact a deregulation bill that allowed the S&Ls to invest these growing pools of Uncle Sam—insured money in junk bonds, risky real estate, etc. This trail led many S&Ls down the path to bankruptcy.
There was no organized opposition to these actions by bank consumers.

CAUSE-POINT. In late 1988, with Reagan's blessing, secret deals were cut between megamillionaires like William Simon and Ron Perelman and the Federal Home Loan Bank. These agreements allowed rich men to assume ownership of billions of dollars of S&L assets in return for their investing less than three cents on the asset dollar—while Washington assumed all the liabilities. Taxpayers, who bore the brunt of the giant giveaways, have never been allowed to see the full text of these agreements.
There was no organized opposition by the consumer-taxpayers.

CAUSE-POINT. In mid-1989, Congress curtsied to George Bush's demands and millions of S&L-PAC dollars by passing the first-stage $157 billion S&L bailout bill. No special tax on banks and other corporations was considered.
Apart from a few scattered consumer groups, there was no organized opposition.

CHECKPOINT. Throughout the Reagan eighties, the president insisted on deregulation. This meant abandoning historic bank safeguards—bank examiners learned that the best way to lose their job was to do their job.
There was no organized citizen group to watch these "sentinels."

CHECKPOINT. Outside accounting firms passed hundreds of S&L financial statements that glared with phoniness. Hundreds of appraisers inflated real-estate values in order to remain in favor with banking clients.
There was no organized depositor group with a skilled staff to blow the whistle on professionals who lucratively slept at the switch.

CHECKPOINT. Outside directors of the S&Ls were handpicked for their sycophancy, or they were rife with conflicts of interest, speculative lending, or insider transactions, à la Neil Bush.
There was no organized group representing small shareholders and homeowners.

CHECKPOINT. Time and time again, Congress and state regulatory agencies, as in California and Texas, saw the dark clouds approaching—yet abdicated by further weakening the bank regulations. Even now, the large accounting-firm lobby and its corporate allies are pushing Congress to severely weaken the civil RICO law—a major tool to bring these S&L culprits and their cover-up advisers to justice. *There was no organized grass-roots group to expose this mockery of representative government.*

CLEARLY, WE NEED a new breed of citizen watchdog groups, and there is a simple, proven way to launch them. S&Ls, utility monopolies, commercial banks, insurance companies, and other financial institutions should be required to carry, in their regular statement or billing envelopes, a printed insert inviting their customers to join financial consumer organizations. These watchdogs, with their own organizers, canvassers, lawyers, and economists, would be chartered as nonprofit advocacy and educational groups by Congress and controlled and funded by an electorate of dues-paying members. Through these groups, bank consumers would have a say in future decisions about the S&L bailout, and similar crises.

This very reform proposal was placed last year before the Senate and House banking committees during their deliberations over the $157 billion S&L bailout bill. Senate committee members did not even consider the idea as they war whooped the bill to Senate passage in just one week. The House committee produced only six supporters, who were jeered down by a voice vote. To these members of Congress, it is fine for the U.S. League of Savings Institutions to finance its lobbying with depositors' money, but outlandish to help depositors band together in their own interest.

Yet the idea works. Illinois, Wisconsin, and the San Diego area have adopted proposals requiring utilities to allow inserts in their mailings. The resulting Citizen Utility Boards (CUBs) flourished—until February 1986, when the Supreme Court ruled five to three that the First Amendment right of a monopoly utility was violated by the polemical tone of the insert. (It is quite constitutional for a utility monopoly to speak and oppose ratepayer interests through its attorneys, accountants, and PR agents before the public and government, and then send the bill to consumers.) It is believed that a less polemical insert written by the state or federal regulatory agency, inviting consumers to join such groups, would not be prohibited by the Court's decision.

Not to be deterred, the Illinois CUB successfully pressed for a state law allowing its insert to be placed in any Illinois *government* mailing to 50,000 or more Illinois citizens. With some 200,000 dues-paying members, Illinois' CUB has saved ratepayers about $3 billion since 1983. If we'd had similar "Citizen S&L Boards" in all fifty states, they could have saved you $5,000 and all of us as much as $1.4 trillion.

Remarks before the Conference
on Property Tax Reform

Originally delivered before the Conference on Property Tax Reform,
Washington, D.C., December 12, 1970.

Introduction

OF ALL THE TAXES levied by governments upon their citizens, the property tax is one of the oldest, it is probably the most controversial, and it is clearly one of the most important. It has been and is still the financial life-blood of local city and county governments. Revenues collected from the property tax have grown sevenfold since 1945, and now amount to over $33 billion a year. This represents close to 80 percent of all local revenues. City, county and some state services are financed almost entirely through ad valorum taxes. Fire protection, police protection, water and sewage services, maintenance of streets and parks are all services financed in part or in their entirety through the property tax. The local educational systems in our country are almost universally financed through levies upon property.

Despite its importance, the quality of the administration of the property tax is notoriously poor. The results are clear. Financially starved cities are losing billions of dollars a year. Taxes on residential property are increasing to a point where the average citizen can no longer afford to own a home, especially in the cities. Entire school systems are considering closing down because of the unwillingness of overburdened property owners to subject themselves to even higher taxes. Senior citizens are being forced out of their homes. Many of these elderly citizens are now paying taxes on their homes that are higher than the monthly payments they made to purchase them. Land use patterns throughout the country are being disturbed and having an adverse effect on the environment and ecology of many areas.

There are, of course, other factors that contribute to these problems. The costs of city services are increasing rapidly, but these costs are being borne disproportionately by the homeowner and small businessman because of the inequalities in the administration of the tax system. If all taxpayers were to bear their proper share of the property tax burden, taxes on residential and small business property could be decreased as much as 25 percent while increasing revenues for the local governments.

There is nothing new in saying that there are gross inequalities in the administration of the property tax. Inequality has been an issue in property taxation for over one hundred years and citizens have been calling for an end to discriminatory administration for equally as long. E. R. A. Seligman in the late 1800s described a property tax that must have been much the same as the one known by most citizens today. He said:

> ... the general property tax as actually administered is beyond all doubt one of the worst taxes known in the civilized world. ... It puts a premium on dishonesty and debauches the public conscience; it reduces deception to a system, and makes a science of knavery; it presses hardest on those least able to pay; it imposes double taxation on one man and grants immunity to the next. In short, the general property tax is so flagrantly inequitable, that its retention can be explained only through ignorance or inertia. It is the cause of such crying injustice that its alteration or its abolition must become the battle cry of every statesman and reformer.

(Essays on Taxation, 10th Ed., 1928, p. 62).

Seligman's call to battle against inequities in the property tax has largely been ignored. The fact is that up until recently little or nothing had been done to correct inequitable administration. Effective action to end abuses can be accomplished only if there is a clear and accurate understanding on the part of all citizens of the source and cause of inequitable administration as well as the means by which they may obtain reform. A clear understanding of these factors has been hidden by a brace of myths that have developed and which need to be replaced with facts.

Myths about Who is Undertaxed

There is a belief that is widely held among those who deal with property taxation that underassessment and undertaxation apply equally to all types of property and in equal amounts. Many of these people insist that if any property is overtaxed it is commercial and industrial property. The logic of their argument is that since large industrial and commercial property is easy for the assessor to spot and since the owner is a non-voting corporate entity, there is a tendency to assess or tax them more than other property in the jurisdiction.

Not only is the belief that commercial, industrial and mineral property is overtaxed a myth, it verges on being hyperbolically ridiculous. There are a number of factors that have led to this belief, but whatever the basis for this widespread myth, it is, with perhaps a few exceptions, factually just plain wrong. Underevaluation, underassessment, and consequently undertaxation of large commercial, industrial and mineral property is of epidemic proportions across the entire country. Studies conducted by my staff, by interested citizens, and by professional organizations have documented case after case of undertaxation of these large economic interests. A few examples may be cited: In Chicago, a city not known for a lack of official abuses, nearly every major building in the city is grossly underassessed. The twin Marina Towers, the Merchandise Mart, the John Hancock Building, all multi-million dollar structures, are undertaxed by as much as 50 percent. Ah, but the critics reply, you can't count Chicago, we all know that Cook County is the exception. Look, then, at Houston, Texas. A recent study done by law students revealed that commercial property was being assessed at a rate that is approximately one-half that used for residential property.

If these two cities are not sufficiently probative, then look at Allegheny County, Pennsylvania or Gary, Indiana or Anmoore, West Virginia. In each of these locations, some of the industrial giants of our country devote a substantial amount of time and resources to deliberately avoid the payment of property taxes. United States Steel, for example, refuses to open its records to city or county officials in order to facilitate an accurate appraisal of their property. They even defy the law by refusing to take out building permits whenever they construct additional facilities on their property. The results of these tactics are easy to see. In Pennsylvania, one of U.S. Steel's plants is underassessed by at least $100 million. Over a five-year period, the company added over $350 million in capital improvements, while their property tax assessment increased only $3 million. In Gary, Indiana, U.S. Steel's taxes went down this year while the taxes for all other taxpayers increased.

Another example is the Union Camp Company in Savannah, Georgia. Union Camp is the largest manufacturer of bags and cartons in the country. Yet they have a special tax rate that is less than one-half the tax rate which other taxpayers must pay. In addition to avoiding taxes on their plant property, Union Camp held property that was assessed at $10 to $15 per acre but which they sold for over $2,000 per acre. Still another example is Union Carbide, whose plant and facilities in Anmoore, West Virginia is assessed at 20 percent below residential property.*

Undertaxation of mineral and timber property is equally as widespread. Oil properties in east and west Texas, the largest oil-producing state in the nation, were shown in two recent studies to be underassessed by more than 50 percent when compared to assessments on residential property. In a ten-county area in east Texas, the same study showed that over $600,000 a year in tax revenues were lost due to undertaxation of timberlands. Coal properties in Kentucky, West Virginia and other Appalachian states escape taxation almost completely.

Railroads, which are now before Congress asking for special legislation to protect them from alleged overtaxation, also receive fantastic tax breaks. An example is the B.& O. Railroad in Maryland. In Baltimore city, they pay $50,000 in lieu of taxes on over 640 acres of prime land. Moreover, they also receive a special tax rate on their intangible property—a reduction of 75 percent in their rate compared to that of other public utility property.

Commercial and industrial property are not the only types that receive special tax breaks. The homes and playgrounds of the wealthy who control these large economic and corporate interests also receive favorable tax treatment. A study done this summer of country clubs in the Virginia and Maryland suburbs of Washington, D.C. showed that because of special legislation and some double accounting, country clubs are undertaxed. It was determined, in fact, that the average homeowner in these areas subsidizes these clubs to the tune of 25 to 45 dollars per member, members such as Vice President Agnew and General Westmoreland.

It is these examples, and others, that demonstrate a clear trend that is in no way related to the common belief, the myth, that all property is

---

* In tiny Anmoore, West Virginia (population 960), the town council last week repealed a loophole in a local ordinance which allowed the mighty Union Carbide Corporation to pay sales taxes at one-fifth the rate paid by Anmoore's small businesses. The new influx of revenue will allow the town to pave its streets, install a sewage system for the first time, build parks and recreational facilities—in short, to escape the syndrome of bleak Appalachian poverty which Union Carbide's colonial rule has inflicted upon them. The dollar amount involved was small—a few hundred thousand dollars in the next three years—but the implications are far-reaching.

equally underassessed and that commercial, industrial and mineral property is overtaxed.

Myths of Why There are Inequities

The myth of commercial and industrial overtaxation is a result of even more myths about the reasons for inequitable taxation.

Myth #1. Large economic interests are overtaxed because they are easy targets for the assessor because they don't have the "vote".

Fact: This assertion demonstrates a profound naivete. Economic power and therefore political power is far more important within community power structures in determining who is to receive favorable tax treatment than the possession of one or even one hundred votes. On a political system that depends on expensive media coverage for successful campaigning, the winner is the candidate with the best source of funds. In Chicago, for example, to receive favorable tax treatment one must contribute to the local political machine, to the campaign of the assessor, or purchase land in certain development companies. It is the offer of campaign funds that is the quid pro quo for lower property tax assessments.

Economic strength is perhaps the most important factor in achieving favorable tax treatment. Industrial units with a national financial base are totally insensitive to the financial needs of the communities in which they are located. They are constantly threatening the city with: "If you raise our taxes, we will move." It is simply another example of irresponsible use of corporate economic power and demonstrates a total disregard for the responsibilities of industrial citizenship. Too often, moreover, companies in company towns drain the area of tax revenues and then contribute a fraction of their windfall toward some charitable activity to further their hold on the community.

Myth #2. Another myth contributing to the under-assessment of large commercial and industrial property is the belief that it is impossible to accurately appraise industrial property. The extremely difficult job of industrial assessment is used as an excuse to justify a negotiated settlement between the local government and the industry.

Fact: The facts, however, are that there are generally accepted methods of industrial appraisal that if competently used provide defensible figures for assessment of the industrial plant. There are a large number of professional appraisers who could be hired by a community if in-house appraisal expertise is missing. The extra expenses involved in hiring an outside appraiser will be more than offset by the additional revenue received from the industrial and commercial giants.

The appraisal of industrial property is by no means precise. There are a myriad of factors that must be considered. But the basics of the appraisal process are well known and there are generally accepted principles that can be applied. Appraisal of any property involves applying three methods of assessment to determine a rational fair market value from the basis of the figures arrived at from each method. The first method is the use of values from sales of the same or similar property. The second method is to determine the reproduction cost of the plants and then subtract depreciation. The third method is what is called the capitalized income approach. Under this method, the projected income from the plant is determined and discounted to present value.

For the purpose of appraising industrial property, the sales method is usually inadequate because of the lack of relevant sales data. The other two methods, however, can be used with a fairly high degree of exactness. The problem has not been with inexactness of the procedures for appraisal, but with the recalcitrant corporation that refuses to cooperate with the local taxing authority. U.S. Steel, is a leading example. The corporation's management refuses to divulge any cost information from which the assessor as an independent appraiser could determine the reproduction cost of the plant. Similarly, U.S. Steel as well as other companies such as Union Carbide refuse to divulge income information in order to facilitate an appraisal by the income approach.

Myth #3. That tax shelters must be offered to industry in order to attract them. Opposition to industrial tax-shelters is "anti-industrial."

Facts: There is simply no evidence that the existence of a property tax shelter is a decisive or significant factor in the process involved in deciding where to relocate a major plant. Other factors of production, labor, entrepreneurship, capital, and transportation are all far more important to an industry in determining where to locate than property taxes.

The existence of these shelters cause more difficulties than they can possibly be worth. This is especially true where suburban communities provide tax sheltered greenbelts for the purpose of attracting industry out of large urban centers. At the same time, these communities restrict through zoning laws the living space within the communities so that the workers still live within the city. The result is an enhancement of the power of an already powerful industry. They now have the leverage, which they use to threaten urban centers with relocation if their taxes are not lowered. Suburban industrial park tax shelters tend to bring the level of taxation of industry within the entire area down to that level. It is an endless cycle enuring only to the benefit of the industry at the expense of the community and the schools.

There is another fallacy involved in the tax shelter. It is implicit when a tax shelter is offered that the citizens of the community believe that the industry will impose less costs on the community than other property owners. But this is simply not true. No doubt, additional employment is created when a new plant is built. At the same time, the community costs for schools, roads and the like increase. Moreover, the industry poses a serious pollution threat. A relevant example is Augusta, Georgia. An illegal tax shelter was offered to a plant that was involved in reprocessing paper for pulp. The plant moved to Augusta and within a short period of time ruined a new sewage system with its waste products. This was a 14 million dollar sewage system that the citizens had just bought through their property taxes. The industry did not help pay for it—nor will it pay for the repair because of its tax shelter.

Myths about What Can Be Done

There is no doubt that the inequities in the property tax are outrageous and that they are caused in large part by political and economic power of large economic interests. The real issue is what can be done to bring about reform of the system. Here again, a number of myths have developed that act as deterrents to positive action for reform.

Myth #1: Many respected authorities on state and local finance claim that it is impossible to have a well administered property tax and therefore efforts toward reform should be aimed in other directions.

Fact: High quality administration is in fact possible if certain basic reforms are instituted. Most of these reforms will require basic legislative reform in most states. The efficacy of political and economic influence can be substantially reduced if the assessment positions are taken out of the political spectrum. A majority of the assessing officials in this country today are either elected officials or are political appointees. As a result, assessing officials are frequently not qualified. They are also willing to bend to the influence of the politically and economically powerful in order to assure their continuance in office.

The assessor himself is not the only one to be blamed. He is perhaps the most underpaid of all public officials. In many states the assessor is a part time position and salaries range as low as $1800. It is foolish to expect any sort of quality from this type of administration but it doesn't mean that there cannot be improvement. Appointed fulltime assessors that are paid salaries commensurate with their educational requirements would be a significant step toward preventing inequitable assessments.

Professional assessors, who are adequately paid in an office equipped with the latest in data processing equipment, would comprise significant steps towards eliminating inequalities. There are additional specific reforms that can be taken by the state legislatures and other legislative bodies that will also avoid many of the inequities in administration. These reforms have been called for as far back as 1963 by the ACIR, and as recently as last May by a panel of forty experts in the assessment field. Both groups claimed that the property tax system can be made to work within reasonably acceptable cost-benefit limitations and in an equitable manner.

Myth #2. You can't fight city hall. The old adage that the average citizen is helpless to work against entrenched political and economic power is perhaps the most frequent reason given for why definite reforms have not been adopted.

Fact: There is concrete evidence that hard and courageous work on the part of the average citizen can result in dramatic improvements within a community. In Annmore, West Virginia the city council, led by Mayor Buck Gladden, a $3.00 an hour laborer, voted to increase the taxes on a Union Carbide plant that had not paid its fair share of the property tax for over 20 years. That increase amounted to over 400%.

What Annmore has demonstrated, and what is going on in other communities around the country, is that effective action can be taken by organized citizen efforts with the help and backing of a national organization. This conference, the Property Tax Newsletter, and technical aid and support from our Public Interest Research Group, combined with citizens who are determined and who have the courage to stand up to the frequently abusive tactics of those receiving favorable tax treatment can achieve positive results.

Anyone working for reform within his community should in fact be prepared for the worst. The tactics that special economic interests will resort to are virtually unlimited. There are cases where business and personal affairs of those working towards reform have been severely damaged. In Augusta, Georgia, for example, a group of forty citizens, including an employee of the assessors office, began a campaign to eliminate illegal tax breaks offered under the auspices of a "Committee of 100". Within a period of a year the size of the group had been effectively whittled down to 6 and the employee in the assessors office had been stripped of all official duties.

The group finally prevailed. Their perseverence resulted in a court action that barred the illegal activity. Yet even to achieve this small victory the group had to go to another county to find a judge willing to hear the case. This phenomenon is commonplace: Attorneys are unwilling to represent taxpayers for fear that their reputation or financial interests within the community will be hampered; judges are unwilling to hear cases, or offer outrageous excuses for finding against taxpayers.

Clearly it is not an easy road, but Annmore, West Virginia is a shining example of what can be achieved. If citizens organize, what happened in Annmore will happen in every city and every county in the country. It is time that the myth of corporate responsibility be exposed and that the facts of corporate irresponsibility be acknowledged. The double ethical standards that have been applied to corporations and to individuals should be remedied at once. Union Carbide, U.S. Steel, Union Camp, General Motors, and all the other corporate giants, as well as the large economic interests within the communities are citizens and must exercise the responsibilities of citizenship that are expected of all citizens.

Conclusion

Some problems cannot be solved by citizen action in only one jurisdiction. The movement of industry from one state or city cannot be prevented by its citizens when another state or city offers outrageous tax shelters. Inequities in administration are so widespread that, like pollution, which is simply another manifestation of the corporate abuse of power, the problem is national as well as local.

The combined force of courageous citizens in every locality, together with efforts by national organizations and authorities, will rapidly lead to a much more equitable property tax system with all that means for city and county services, education, small property holders, land use, the elderly and a more honest political structure.

It can be expected that this Conference, with its sincere and knowledgeable participants and speakers, will launch to a new stage of action the quest for tax justice and corporate responsibility.

Thank you.

on opposing the world trade organization (WTO)

Reject This Flawed Treaty

Originally appeared in USA Today, *November 22, 1994.*

HOW IRONIC: *USA Today*'s editorial supports the General Agreement on Tariffs and Trade–World Trade Organization, but *USA Today*'s reporters would be prohibited from covering any of WTO's secret tribunals.

These closed courts would be deciding whether U.S. laws challenged by other countries would have to be repealed, or if you, the taxpayer, would have to pay fines to the winning foreign nation.

You, the readers, would be barred from observing, participating in or appealing any of these tribunals' decisions affecting your health, safety and workplace conditions.

Fifty-one leaders of the media, led by John Seigenthaler of the Freedom Forum First Amendment Center, protested this shutout in a letter to President Clinton in September, but to no avail.

Should you try to improve conditions by amending our country's laws, the State Department would inform you if it considers your consumer, environmental or labor proposals to be trade-restrictive and thereby illegal under GATT-WTO.

This chilling effect from Geneva, where WTO technocrats and global corporate lobbyists will gather together, is made colder by WTO's twin mandates:

198 THE RALPH NADER READER

✤ One is the supremacy of foreign trade over non-trade practices such as food safety, pollution control, occupational health and tax policies. Trade agreements should stick to trade.

✤ The second is the international harmonization of standards.

This would often mean harmonization downward for our generally higher safety conditions.

Currently, for example, under a similar North American Free Trade Agreement mandate, U.S. and Mexican officials are meeting secretly in Acapulco to harmonize truck-weight standards which in the United States cannot exceed 80,000 pounds. Since the U.S. trucking lobby likes the bigger Mexican rigs that have a 175,000-pound ceiling, which image do you think your rear-view mirror will reflect in a few years?

As a governing regime, the WTO's 123 member-nations are each given one vote. Two dictatorships can outvote the United States, which has no veto. This is why the Bush administration itself opposed this WTO idea before leaving office in December 1992.

Remarkably, countries that mistreat their workers, consumers and environment (including condoning brutalized child labor) do not violate the GATT-WTO. But our country, with more humane standards than many other countries, can be charged at those secret tribunals with restricting trade.

That is why the proposed WTO is a "pull-down," not a "pull-up," trade agreement.

Fifteen years ago, when the prior revision of GATT called the Tokyo round was completed, Washington made similarly inflated promises of more jobs for the United States.

Since then, our country has suffered from even larger annual trade deficits, including a deficit in manufactured goods.

Even with a cheap dollar, this year's deficit will exceed $150 billion. That is exporting lots of American jobs from a nation experiencing falling real wages for the past two decades.

Congress should defeat the GATT-WTO and return it to Geneva for renegotiation under democratic processes and "pull-up" standards of prosperity.

This would also avoid busting the federal budget and overcentralizing unaccountable power in Geneva, and it will prevent the foreign regulation of America.

This lame-duck Congress, with more than ninety defeated or retiring job-seekers, needs to hear by next Tuesday from concerned Americans, who may call their senators and representatives at 202-224-3121.

Trade in Secrets

Originally appeared in The Washington Post, *October 6, 1994.*

THERE IS SOMETHING about foreign trade agreements, such as the Uruguay Round of the General Agreement on Tariffs and Trade (GATT), that removes them from broad public discourse and examination. This phenomenon is pronounced when the business/government axis that drafts these agreements in exclusionary surroundings connects the thought-stopping label "free trade" with a congressional fast-track, no-amendment procedure that makes inquiry into details futile.

People in positions of influence, who should know better, suspend their usual dedication to seeing such trade proposals as propositions to be evaluated and instead view them as articles of faith to be intoned.

The proposed GATT agreement establishes an international system of governance known as the World Trade Organization (WTO). With an electorate of more than 120 nations—each with an equal vote and none with veto power—the WTO has expandable legislative, executive and judicial authority over both trade and non-trade laws and practices. More than an economic framework, the WTO is a major international political regime.

Yet neither the relevant congressional committees nor the national political columnists are intrigued enough to explore how this WTO would affect our democracy. They remained unperturbed after fifty-one leaders of major news organizations and journalism groups sent a letter to President Clinton last month, protesting the exclusion of both the public and the press from WTO deliberations and urging "democratic openness to this crucial process," for "to do otherwise would break a sacred pact with the American people." This remarkable letter received almost no media coverage.

The press also ignored public letters sent to a concurring Sen. Robert Byrd and an unreceptive President Clinton by constitutional scholar and Harvard law professor Laurence Tribe. He asserted that the "shift of sovereignty from state and local governments to the proposed World Trade Organization" was so substantial "that the agreement requires Senate ratification as a treaty," requiring the approval of two-thirds of the Senate. Instead, President Clinton rushed the massive trade legislation to Congress in its final pre-adjournment days, seeking a simple majority vote in each House.

The same editorial writers who objected strenuously to a recently announced judge's ban on television cameras in federal courtrooms find the secret WTO tribunals, which exclude all media and citizens and which lack public transcripts or independent appeals, insufficiently provocative of their due-process sensitivities.

With few exceptions, congressional human rights advocates remained dormant when they learned that this "free trade" agreement prohibits linking trade to human rights improvements and disallows bans on products made by brutalized child labor. This will be a relief to the governments of China and India.

Those countries that treat their workers, consumers and environment too harshly can also be relieved. Official cruelties, apart from prison labor, do not violate GATT's so-called "non-tariff trade barrier" provisions. Only nations, including the United States, with more humane laws protecting human health and safety are vulnerable to being taken by another nation before the secret WTO tribunals in Geneva and facing charges that such standards are WTO-illegal because they hamper foreign trade.

Whenever the United States loses these cases (and the burden of proof is on the defendant), it has to either repeal the offending federal, state or local law or pay perpetual trade sanctions to the winning nations. Recent reports by the European Union, Japan and Canada already list many U.S. laws that they deem WTO-illegal.

If the WTO is established, some corporate law firms will match up domestic companies that don't like our safety laws with companies abroad in order to persuade a foreign government to challenge the United States before these tribunals. The same domestic-foreign alliance will also press legislatures to repeal WTO-invalidated laws rather than pay the tribute to keep them.

The widening shift in power that stems from the WTO's mandate of trade *uber alles* can overcome the supporters of consumer, environmental and worker protection laws and severely chill any future proposals to strengthen them.

President Clinton, who would not seek a special session of Congress after the November elections to consider reforms of health insurance, labor laws or campaign finance, secured a special session of the Senate to vote on the Uruguay Round of GATT. Apparently, only the Business Roundtable can turn this cautious president into a fighting tiger.

Trade agreements bring out the worst in official policy journalism. Proponents, whether in the congressional or executive branches, are given voice. Opponents to the GATT, or the timing of its vote, as expressed in letters to Clinton by twenty senators and fifty-five representatives, including six committee chairs, are ignored. So are numerous critical reports on the GATT by reputable civic and academic sources.

All the national environmental groups, including those that supported NAFTA, oppose GATT. And all the trade unions, blue and white collar, and almost all national and local consumer groups oppose GATT.

But because House majority leader Richard Gephardt is not challenging the White House this time, the growing grass-roots coalition against GATT has rarely been seen as newsworthy.

Reporters are missing a deepening political skepticism in the country that has led Sen. Fritz Hollings and Sen. Robert Dole to raise serious questions about the broad domestic consequences of this business agreement.

The public concern over GATT's effect on jobs, sustainable economic growth and on not losing control to unaccountable trade bureaucrats in Geneva should not be casually dismissed. Nor will this pursuit of autocracy over democracy, of trade over living standards, be casually forgotten.

WTO Means Rule by Unaccountable Tribunals

Originally appeared in The Wall Street Journal, *August 17, 1994.*

MOST MEMBERS OF Congress and the American people know little about the proposed agreement to establish the World Trade Organization and the damage it would inflict on this country's democratic ways and standards of justice. Nonetheless, very shortly, the Clinton administration intends to send it to Capitol Hill for quick approval under a no-amendment, fast-track procedure.

While U.S. Trade Representative Mickey Kantor eagerly highlights the pact's hypothetical economic benefits, President Clinton has regularly ignored the autocratic structure of this new system of global governance with its expected membership of more than 120 nations.

The WTO's mandate is based on the supremacy of trade matters over consumer, worker and environmental safeguards, even including existing environmental treaties. The agreement's controlling provision is that any domestic law that affects trade in any way must be the 'least trade restrictive' possible.

Thus, countries could not violate the WTO's rules by treating their workers, consumers or the environment too harshly. Ironically, countries with more advanced protections in these areas are the vulnerable ones. This bias makes the proposed GATT and its WTO a 'pull down,' not a 'pull up,' agreement.

Under the WTO, member nations can challenge each other's health and safety laws before trade tribunals in Geneva, charging that these laws are 'WTO-illegal' because their effect is to restrict trade. Since our country has numerous laws that are more protective of its citizens than those of other nations, the U.S. would be a frequent defendant. If these unaccountable tribunals decide that our laws—for example, limiting the use of exported nuclear materials; advancing food, air and water safety and recycling; protecting dolphins; and required labeling—are 'non-tariff trade barriers,' we would be obligated to repeal them or pay perpetual fines.

The foregoing illustrations are not merely hypothetical. These laws are among many U.S. federal and state statutes and rules marked for challenge in recent reports by the European Union, Japan and Canada.

Foreign businesses, as well as U.S.-based multinationals, that object to our laws, even if, like motor-vehicle safety laws, they are not discriminatory, will have strong motivation to see that such challenges are made. Given the wide array of member nations in the WTO, the temptation for companies, unable to prevail in the U.S., to 'rent a government' and go to the Geneva tribunals would be strong.

These tribunals could declare a domestic law 'WTO-illegal' if its purpose is not achieved in the 'least trade restrictive' manner. For example, under the existing GATT, the European Union has challenged the U.S. fuel efficiency law and gas guzzler tax, arguing that gasoline consumption should be curtailed not by minimum automobile miles-per-gallon standards, as is now required, but by a carbon tax. Under similar logic, the Europeans view our new mandatory nutrition labeling law as 'not least trade restrictive,' because its goals could be accomplished, for example, by signs in supermarkets, not disclosure on the products themselves. Such 'process' arguments could not be made in our courts.

Under the existing GATT, the U.S. can simply refuse to comply with tribunal recommendations. However, under the proposed governing framework, which becomes federal law if approved, the U.S. could not disregard the ruling; it must obey or pay. Moreover, the WTO's 'trade uber alles' regime adds another layer of unaccountable bureaucracy to chill future proposals by civic groups to advance health and safety standards in the U.S. and abroad.

The tribunals would be a staggering rejection of our due process and democratic procedures. They would be staffed by three trade experts, who may pursue simultaneous business careers and who would not have to adhere to conflict-of-interest rules. The tribunals would operate in closed-door secrecy, banning the press and prohibiting citizen groups from either participating or even attending. Also, there would be no required disclosure of the contending governments' briefs and other evidence, no public transcripts and even no independent appeal.

Only national governments would have standing; even a state's attorney general or governor would have no right to participate in the defense of state laws before the WTO tribunals.

This autocratic overlay on our nation's federal system has provoked forty-two state attorneys general, thirty state treasurers, the National Association of Counties and many other state and local associations, to raise serious concerns about the trade deal's effect on state-federal relations. By far the most important of their demands—that there be specific congressional authorization for any federal pre-emption of state and local laws declared illegal by a WTO tribunal—was not accepted by Mr. Kantor.

Harvard Prof. Laurence Tribe, one of the nation's pre-eminent constitutional law scholars, shares the concerns of the attorneys general. On July 19, he wrote to Sen. Robert Byrd that the WTO's legal regime 'represents a structural rearrangement of state-federal relations of the sort that requires ratification by two-thirds of the Senate as a Treaty.' Not so, says the Clinton administration, which designates this regime as a trade agreement requiring only a majority vote in both Houses.

The new GATT-WTO treaty constitutes quite a legislative brew for citizens to swallow. President Clinton should give the American people and Congress a decent interval to absorb and assess such serious consequences for society, and wait until next year to send the WTO proposal to Congress, when lawmakers will have a less congested legislative calendar. Since all prospective WTO members have until July 1995 to approve or disapprove, why should the Congress or the president rush to judgment?

A Pull-down Trade Agreement

GLOBAL CORPORATIONS PUSH WTO
DECLARATION OF DEPENDENCE

Originally appeared in The Charleston Gazette, *July 18, 1994.*

THE WTO AGREEMENT subordinates non-commercial issues like health and safety standards to the supremacy of foreign trade imperatives. IN JUST ONE DAY of their coverage, the television networks have paid more attention to Michael Jackson, Lorena Bobbitt, Tonya Harding and O.J. Simpson than they have to the proposed World Trade Organization.

The WTO, you ask? What's that? Oh, "that" is a big, boring international trade and investment agreement between over one hundred countries that may affect whether or not you keep or get a job. "That" is a complex, legalistic system of international governance, to be headquartered in Geneva, that can chill your citizen campaigns in the environmental, consumer and worker justice areas.

"The media is not interested in the WTO," declared President Clinton's trade representative, Mickey Kantor, who wants to whisk this agreement through Congress later this summer as fast as possible. The proposed World Trade Organization, with its secret tribunals, harmonization committees and one-nation, one-vote, no-veto procedures, is the darling of the global corporations. They played a large role in drafting its terms and structure so as to give the auto, drug, food, chemical and other Goliaths advantages over workers, children, small farmers, sick people and the environment. For example, there are no protections for children who are exploited for seventy hours a week in some countries to produce goods for export to the United States and other nations. Child labor is not a violation of the WTO agreement.

The price of medicines in poorer countries will increase because the WTO deal virtually provides for member nations to grant a 20-year monopoly drug patents instead of a system of compulsory licensing that stimulates competition.

The WTO is a pull-down trade agreement. Nations do not violate its terms by treating consumers, workers and the environment badly. Member nations violate its terms by having health, safety or workplace standards that other nations can convince secret tribunals to find to be too advanced or protective. Since America has more advanced standards than many countries in these areas, our country is vulnerable to such tribunal decisions, if these standards are seen as designed to keep out imports, such as food with impermissible residues of pesticides.

You may ask, how can this be happening? Because the WTO agreement subordinates non-commercial issues like health and safety standards to the supremacy of foreign trade imperatives. It does not require trade to bend beneath health and safety standards. In the arcane tunnel vision of international commerce, global corporate lobbyists and government bureaucrats have had an extended immunity from citizen scrutiny and public attention. Under WTO, auto safety, recycling, food safety, chemical controls, and any number of proposals to improve our society's health and safety, can be construed as impairing or blocking certain exports. If the tribunals rule against America, we would have to repeal laws or pay perpetual trade penalties.

Is all this just theoretical? Well, in the past few months, Japan, Canada and the European Community issued reports naming the very U.S. federal laws and state laws they intend to take to Geneva as being illegal under the WTO.

Already under the weaker trade agreement that the WTO would replace, Mercedes, through the European Community, is challenging our fuel efficiency and gas guzzler laws.

Communicate with your senators and ask them how they intend to vote when President Clinton sends this WTO proposal to Congress for approval. Your senators and representatives have already tied their own hands by prohibiting any amendments. The vote will be up or down without changes on this Declaration of Dependence. You will either find out about the WTO before it is voted on, or you will surely feel the boomerangs afterward, should it be approved.

on consumer rights

Unsafe at Any Altitude

Originally appeared in The Conde Nast Traveler, *September 1999.*

I AM OFTEN ASKED about what rights air travelers have. Unfortunately, the short answer is few to none. Indeed, most laws and regulations labeled "consumer rights" are in fact airline policies or government guidelines aimed at curbing common-law protections.

One of the only ways passengers have obtained any justice at all is by consumers or flight crews saying "enough" and following through. In 1968, I was bumped from an Allegheny Airlines (now US Airways) flight. The rule at the time was "too bad." However, I decided to sue the carrier for breach of contract since I had paid for a reserved seat. After the U.S. Supreme Court decided that the suit was valid and could not be dismissed because of the lack of a government rule, the airlines proposed a settlement which allowed them to continue to overbook but gave displaced passengers compensation and required carriers to first ask for volunteers to give up their seats. This settlement became the bumping rule that we have today.

The past forty years have brought the speed and convenience of jet travel to nearly all Americans, as well as to most of the world. But something is wrong. Comfort has been sharply diminished, U.S. safety standards are being degraded as never before, and many airlines are raising prices to the point of gouging. What's more, the federal government has been consistently unwilling to set or enforce rules governing fair competition, consumer protection, service, or even basic health and hygiene, to say nothing of establishing higher safety standards for commercial aviation.

The 1978 deregulation of airlines was supposed to remedy all of that with reduced fares, increased choice, and improved service. But the results are mixed at best. As reported in the September 1998 issue of this magazine ["Low prices! Better service! More choices!"], Alfred Khan, the father of deregulation, is disillusioned with his own idea. He calculates that the average airfare has gone up 39 percent, after adjusting for inflation, and that unrestricted fares have shot up 70 percent or more.

This year alone, the six major U.S. carriers—American, Continental, Delta, Northwest, United, and US Airways—have raised domestic fares in both coach and business class four times, for a total increase of 8 to 14 percent, depending on the carrier. Many domestic business fares have increased by more than 15 percent since 1998 and have more than doubled over the past ten years. Meanwhile, in 1998 the U.S. airline industry as a whole reported its third year in a row of record profits.

Raising prices at four to ten times the rate of inflation when operating costs are flat to down demonstrates two things: corporate greed of the highest order and a monopolistic pricing power.

WHILE U.S. SAFETY standards and safety records are the best in the world (four deaths per ten million departures since 1980), they are presently under siege. The FAA's nickname among its critics is the Tombstone Agency, because of its reputation for not ordering corrections to known safety problems until after an air crash has resulted in numerous deaths.

For instance, three of the most recent major air disasters in North America (Valujet 592, TWA 800, and Swissair 111) were caused by uncontrolled in-flight fires or explosions. So far, the FAA has failed to order the use of fire-suppression systems (standard on military aircraft) on commercial airplanes. As a result, commercial passengers lack basic protection against fires and explosions in the air. All large buildings and even restaurant kitchens are required by law to have automatic fire-suppression systems. Not so airliners, where passengers are far more vulnerable.

Although it is true that the FAA has increased inspections to reduce the presence of flammable materials and potential sources of fire, it has supported the industry in dismissing new safety technologies as not "cost effective." The FAA values a human life at $2.7 million, so if a safety improvement costs more than the projected value of lives lost, the agency often refuses to order the necessary improvements. For example, the FAA recommended against requiring technology that would mitigate against center fuel tank explosions because the ten-year cost to the industry of fixing this hazard, believed responsible for the 1996 TWA 800 disaster, would exceed the cost in human lives.

In the mid-1990s, the FAA embarked on an ill-conceived program to bring its safety rules in line with those of Europe, which tend to be far more lax. Take, for example, the program's impact on emergency evacuations. Under U.S. regulations, the distance between seat rows at emergency window exits must be at least 20 inches, just wide enough to allow a passenger to walk normally to the exit in an emergency. However, the FAA has granted waivers permitting most U.S. carriers to reduce the distance between these rows to 14 inches (the absurd European standard is 9 to 10 inches). For comparison, a typical door is 32 to 36 inches wide. Try running in near darkness through a 9- to 14-inch opening. This is what the airline industry expects you to do when your life and that of everyone behind you depends on it.

Just how crucial to safety this is was shown this past June, when ten passengers died and many more were injured after an American Airlines MD Super 80 skidded off a runway in a rainstorm in Little Rock and burst into flames. Many passengers had to exit through a split in the fuselage because the exit doors were inoperable. Over the past fifteen years, about two-thirds of the time, airlines have failed most emergency evacuation tests, in that they were unable to evacuate the projected number of passengers in the allotted ninety seconds.

SERVICE, PARTICULARLY ON U.S. domestic flights, is similarly being degraded. Air travel today takes longer and has more delays. In coach, seats and legroom are cramped as never before. Airline service to smaller communities has been downgraded or discontinued, and passengers traveling to or from smaller cities pay much higher airfares—60 percent higher than their big-city counterparts, according to a 1998 U.S. Department of Transportation study.

About one in every two hundred checked bags is lost or mishandled. The liability limit for lost luggage has not been updated since 1983 (at $1,250 per passenger, it has declined by more than 50 percent in real dollars). In-flight meals have been all but eliminated on most U.S. flights. Carriers have even cut back on oxygen supply, recirculating most cabin air, and refuse to sanitize cabin surfaces between flights. All in order to save money.

THE GOVERNMENT is on the verge of taking action on a so-called pas-sengers' bill of rights. Consumers would be wise to lobby Congress now on the most important provisions (see "Nader's nine").

Whatever the outcome of pending legislation, the need for an airline passengers association that can compete with the aviation industry lobby has never been greater. In 1998, the air transport industry spent more than $16 million on lobbying, primarily to keep the very profitable status quo and to defeat pro-consumer and antitrust measures. Consumers spent practically nothing. Put another way, there are at present approximately two dozen aviation industry political action committees that contribute to the reelection campaigns of members of Congress. Last year, one Senator alone, John McCain (R-Ariz.), chairman of the Senate Commerce Committee and one of the most powerful members of Congress on avia-tion matters, received $1.1 million in airline PAC contributions, largely from industries over which his committee has jurisdiction. Meanwhile, passengers pay more than $15 billion a year in ticket taxes (eight percent, plus assorted other fees and tariffs) to support the FAA, airport con-struction and operations, and various airline industry subsidies, but they are generally unrepresented in the halls of Congress, before administrative agencies, and in the courts that control safety, security, and consumer rights, policies, and decisions.

So what's a consumer to do? You can start by signing a petition to cre-ate an airline passengers association and/or write to your congressional representative, saying, "I support the creation of an airline passengers association to advocate for the rights and interests of air travelers, to be funded with one-tenth of one percent of airline ticket tax and passen-ger facility charge revenues and through voluntary contributions." Sign and print your name and address (telephone number and e-mail address are optional). You can do this on a postcard, in letter form, or by e-mailing me at acap71@erols.com. I will see that it gets to the appropri-ate official.

You can avoid carriers with poor safety records. The problem has been that it's difficult to know which have safety problems unless an accident highlights the issue. The FAA knows but refuses to say: However, it has recently made voluminous safety data available on the Internet, includ-ing fines and safety inspection failures. The Aviation Consumer Action Project (ACAP) is evaluating this data with a panel of experts and, start-ing early next year, plans to rank the top twenty carriers according to their safety records.

You can complain—and complaints, especially in numbers, do matter. You should do so not only to the airline but also to the Aviation Consumer Protection Division (U.S. DOT, C-75, 400 7th St. S.W., Room 4107, Washington, D.C. 20590), the Aviation Consumer Action Project (Box 19029, 589 14th St. N.W., Suite 1265, Washington, D.C. 20036; 202-638-4000; www.acap1971.org/acap.html), as well as your member of Congress (202-225-3121), local and national newspapers, and, of course, this magazine.

You can also send $5 to ACAP for a copy of its "Facts and Advice for Airline Passengers," a 30-page handbook of solutions to the most common problems facing air travelers, including delays, cancellations, overbookings, and lost tickets and baggage, along with tips on health and how to find the best fare.

You can join an aviation consumer organization such as ACAP ($35 per year); the National Air Disaster Alliance, a coalition of more than 50 air-crash-victim organizations (2020 Pennsylvania Ave. N.W., Suite 315, Washington, D.C. 20006; $20 donation requested); or the Fair Airfare Coalition, a consortium of travel-related and civic organizations lobbying for fair competition and lower fares (202-639-7501; no fee).

Finally, if you are over six feet tall, save your and my sore knees by joining my Six Footers Club, to force airlines to provide adequate legroom. For details, write to me care of ACAP or send me an e-mail at the above address. ACAP also has representation on the FAA's many advisory committees dealing with safety and security issues and is looking for volunteers to act as observers and delegates. You can support needed regulatory and legislative action with donations, comments, and testimony relating your personal experiences.

MOST PEOPLE WOULD agree that the American freedom of and right to travel is precious. Air travelers especially must take the necessary steps to protect their rights and interests. Isn't the right to safe, affordable air travel worth preserving and enhancing? If you agree, the next step is up to you.

Nader's Nine

Among the various proposals being bandied about in Washington, the following are the most critical to improving the lot of airline passengers. Let your voice be heard.

+ End the airlines' exemption from state and local consumer protection laws and the common-law rights of passengers. No other industry enjoys such an exemption.

+ Require carriers to quote the lowest fare regardless of the medium of inquiry.

+ Require that frequent fliers be given the option of receiving discounts on regular tickets in lieu of scarce frequent-flier seats and increasingly unavailable upgrades; mandate full disclosure of the number of frequent-flier seats available on all flights.

+ Discourage and break up "fortress hub" airports, where one carrier has a near monopoly, by requiring that most Jetways be shared.

+ Increase compensation for involuntarily bumped passengers from between $200 and $400 to between $400 and $800.

+ Increase the domestic lost/damaged luggage liability limit from $1,250 to $4,000 per passenger, and require carriers to provide excess-value insurance coverage; alternatively, repeal the limit entirely.

+ Prohibit cartel-like airline alliances and code-sharing (one carrier selling tickets for another's flight as though it were its own), which threaten to end price competition and reduce consumer choice.

+ Require that passengers be informed when a flight involves a change of planes and/or airlines, and allow them to decline to fly an aircraft or a carrier with a poor safety or service record.

+ Require that a portion of the revenue from the existing ticket tax and the airport passenger facility charge be allocated to fund an airline passengers association that would advocate for the rights and interests of consumers.

—R.N.

The Consumer Movement Looks Ahead

Originally appeared in Beyond Reagan: Alternatives for the '80s, *1984.*

I N THEIR OWN WAY, the self-styled Republican conservatives and the Democratic liberals have difficulty providing an affirmative role and horizon for consumers. Politically there is a distinction between the comparative sensitivities to consumer rights by these Republicans and Democrats. The former are more averse than the latter to the process of government regulating for greater consumer safety and less consumer abuse. In practice, however, the liberals are not so keen on making a real difference out of that distinction when they come up against determined corporate pressures. This narrowing of the differences between the two parties—especially in a period when recessions paradoxically give corporations more power over government—became deplorably apparent during the last two years of the Carter regime and the present Reagan administration. The transition from one president to another on deregulatory policy was quite smooth due to Carter's paving the way.

But then, how new was all this movement away from using the laws of the democracy to police the marketplace? Historically there had been a moving away during many cycles of the periodic emergence of regulatory agencies designed to defend consumers. Where such a mission is explicit, as with the Food and Drug Administration (1907), the drift is toward industry co-optation, meek leadership appointments and obsolete legal authorities. Where the regulatory mission is less consumer-explicit, as with the Interstate Commerce Commission (1887) and the Civil Aeronautics Board (1938), the agencies become instruments of private cartels who do what they could not otherwise do legally under the antitrust laws.

Conservative and liberal enforcement of the antitrust laws have reflected common tolerances toward obsolescence, as with their inadequacies toward conglomerate mergers and new-technology suppression (product-fixing), their emphasis on behavioral violations (price-fixing) and their neglect of structural market distortions. Some Republican regimes were stronger than Democratic regimes and vice versa during these statutes' ninety-four-year tenure.

Both the regulatory and antitrust approaches to consumer protection were more ministerial than empowering for consumers. The level of activity behind these two mechanisms depended on who was in government office. Apart from Election Day and its often narrow political choices, there was little in these laws that empowered consumers to initiate or challenge any of the numerous economic and safety rules regarding food, drugs, transportation, communications, housing, banking, insurance, energy, health and other services. Consequently, the administration of these laws was subject to instabilities, to ebbs and flows that were not only debilitating to agency staff morale but also invited public cynicism that lowers those public expectation levels that keep agencies on their toes.[1]

The absence of consumer-empowerment laws is, of course, a reflection of the dominant and adversarial power of corporations over both markets and politics. This secular imbalance is more than a predominance of organized economic might; it also is rooted in a predominance of production-side economic theory that embraces the production orientation of both Marx and Ricardo. It is this "cultural bias," which analyzes economic dynamics and criticality as coming from the production side of the market—from capital and labor and selling—that has shaped the historic view of economies by both the Left and the Right.

When the consumption and production functions ceased being lodged in the same family units and began, with the onset of mechanization and specialization, to be more and more separate, it was only natural for scholars to focus on these new agents of change—the capitalist entrepreneur, factory proletariat, capital markets, mass-production systems and the like. The complex exchange economy, replacing barter and consumers producing their own meager food, shelter and clothing, naturally attracted the economic theorists and public philosophers. Then it was only a short step to the widely shared belief that what is most studied is what is most important. Such a belief became a self-fulfilling prophecy that massively excluded empirical acquisitions and imaginative disquisitions regarding neglected social and normative phenomena on the buying side. By contrast, when Marx developed his dialectical materialism and labor theory of value, he set in motion a heightened attention to the labor factor.

Although Adam Smith did write that the end of production is consumption, most economists during the eighteenth and nineteenth centuries focused their observations on the mostly unabated trend from an economy of scarcity to an economy of greater productive abundance. Production was king; production made consumption possible; production put people to work so that they could be more liquid consumers. The measure of economic progress was quantity and those goods and services that could be measured in money terms. There were, to be sure, some successful reform efforts to more equitably distribute income and wealth and to reduce the harshest edges in the workplace and the urban environments. But the preeminent yardstick, as it is to the present, was the monetary and numerical values symbolized by today's gross national product accounts. *It is the number of cars and drugs sold that is the measure, not what the auto and drug industries add and subtract from the transportation usage and health of people.*

In the eighties, both liberals and conservatives believe that production is the engine of consumption (supply-side thinking), although they differ in their commitment of social transfer payments to add extra assurance that poorer consumers will possess some dollars to spend. There are also differences in their concern with health and safety consequences of production—though more in their rhetoric than in their practice. But these distinctions, while important, fall far short of the requisites for a just economy, which a consumer-side economic dynamic and agenda can provide.

The present seller-sovereign economy is quite different from the classical market model where consumer sovereignty is supposed to reign supreme. In this idealized system, "everything" that is sold is, by definition, proof that buyers want that "everything." A seller-sovereign economy includes sellers who are monopolistic or oligopolistic without being confronted by ultimate consumers who are organized in monopsonistic or oligopsonistic modes. It is an economy where enormous skill, artifice and resources are used in getting consumers to buy what the sellers want to sell, notwithstanding the availability of more efficient, safe, economical, durable and effective alternatives, including that of buying nothing at all. Over the past twenty decades, congressional, state, judicial and media inquiries have documented this appraisal. Let a short mnemonic list do for many: widespread price-fixed products and services; product-fixing to thwart innovation; deceptive packaging and false advertisements; wholly ineffective or hazardous drugs; product obsolescence; energy-wasting vehicles, appliances and other products; unsafely designed cars; junk food; serious product side effects such as pollution and poor land use; adulterated products; overselling of credit, insurance and alleged health care.[2]

Allied with this systemic ability to sell such harm and deception are media driven by similar mercantile values and commercial motivation.[3] As a business feeding off other businesses, the media have narrowed the accessibility of consumer-side communications, although when bland, modest consumer messages have been transmitted, reader appeal and viewer/listener ratings have been high. Media that live off advertisements urging people *to buy* are not about to give much time to announcements or programs urging people *not to buy*.

After many years of economic imbalance between sellers and buyers, little-studied corporate practices started putting down roots. Companies began paying more attention to skimming the cream off the top of the market and subjecting the remainder to discriminatory pricing or exclusion. Companies began paying attention more to peoples' wants than to peoples' needs. There are shortages for millions of Americans in housing, food and health care, while there are ample supplies of cosmetics, video games, soft drinks and entertainment.

An expendable subeconomy takes a clearer form. Its millions of members are thrown on the state for sustenance while they are mercilessly exploited by business for their addictions (cigarettes, drugs, alcohol). There appear to be more innovations for wants than there are for needs—perhaps most graphically exemplified over the past generation by the automobile industry. Stagnation for years was the fate of safety, fuel-efficiency and pollution-control needs, in comparison with the creative merchandising of style, power and psychosexual appeals. Increasingly, private capital investment flows from needs to wants and on to speculation such as stock-market-index futures. Forced condominium conversions, empire-building mergers and acquisitions, and other unproductive uses of capital expand, as compared with uses that meet recognized necessities of a population and generate employment. Financial institutions use "other peoples' money" (savings-bank deposits, pension moneys, mutual insurance assets) to service the short-range preferences of economic elites while the economic masses are deprived of the reinvestment benefits from funds that they own but do not control. The separation of ownership from control is a rampant form of centralized manipulation over the economy.

All along the companies perfect the art of flattering consumers while keeping them in the dark about what is being sold. Supermarket chains praise the homemaker as a "human computer" who is "razor-sharp," and then expose her to a stream of supermarket traps. Companies work artfully to induce consumer dependence on them (Texaco was "earning your trust" while fleecing huge sums from consumers during the energy shortfalls of the seventies). Dependence, not critical capability, is what the firms seek from consumers.

Mainstream economic theorists have been legitimizing for decades this conceptualization of corporate behavior. Thorstein Veblen, in his essay titled "Why Is Economics Not an Evolutionary Science," wrote about this consumer stereotype earlier in this century:

> In all the received formulations of economic theory, whether at the hands of English economists or those of the Continent, the human material with which the inquiry is concerned is conceived in hedonistic terms; that is to say, in terms of a passive and substantially inert and immutably given human nature. . . . The hedonistic conception of man is that of a lightning calculator of pleasures and pains, who oscillates like a homogeneous globule of desire of happiness under the impulse of stimuli that shift him about the area, but leave him intact. He has neither antecedent nor consequent. He is an isolated, definitive human datum, in stable equilibrium except for the buffets of the impinging forces that displace him in one direction or another.[4]

With the applied social science known as modern advertising, coupled with electronic media, the large sellers' skill in obscuring, diverting and deceiving adult buyers, while conditioning with shameless persistence the minds of young children, is awesome. When such mercantile bombardment continues daily without countervailing responses, the impact is all the greater. Televised ads, conveying to grown-ups and youngsters alike the lure of false tastiness (chemical additives) over genuine nutrition and flavor, reach into their health as well as into their pocketbooks.

Shaping a widespread consumer perspective among buyers when they go shopping has been the objective of a myriad of books, pamphlets and now videotapes. "How to buy" guides for this and that are legion. Yet they seem little read and less used. The culture is averse. Students grow up being taught by their courses the selling trade, not how to buy—home economics excepted. Schools are filled with free, colorful materials, slide shows and video, compliments of the oil, auto, drug, meat, coal, fashion and other industries.⁵ Nearly a decade ago, a Random House teachers' kit titled "To Buy or Not to Buy," for which we advised, generated unease and controversy. Teachers and curricula were not prepared for its adoption. To some local businesses, such a course was tantamount to teaching subversion. Unlike bland consumer-education courses, this kit encouraged students and their instructors to study or survey, for example, local supermarkets, auto dealers and banks. It was learning by experiencing various buying roles equipped with a refined consumer perspective.

There is a major differential benefit to themselves and to the larger political economy when buyers bring a consumer's perspective instead of a seller's perspective to the market transaction. The energy-consumer value would press for energy efficiency; renewable, self-reliant energy; safer and competitively priced energy. The energy-seller value presses for more centralized energy, supplied by often interlocked sellers whose technologies foster waste, environmental damage, disease and political corruption. If, in the last fifty years, the consumer value had the power to prevail, our nation would be humming along on one-third of the energy now used, with highly advanced passive and active solar energy using direct sunshine, biomass, hydro, wind, solar cells and solarized architecture. We would not be dependent on risky global supply lines; we would not be so indentured to the menace of atomic power, nor the silent violence of acid rain, nor the looming greenhouse effect over our climate, nor the lung-corroding consequences of fossil-fuel combustion. The misallocation of economic resources, unemployment and geopolitical conflict would have been substantially diminished.

The selling of pharmaceutical products and automobiles also reflects the power of the sellers' image rather than the informed preferences of the buyers. An organized consumer perspective on cars long ago would have achieved the safety, efficiency and pollution reductions so ignored by manufacturers who sold stylistic pornography over engineering integrity. That there have been advances in these areas is testimony to a partial reassertion of consumer-perspective power through regulatory programs and sporadic bursts of public exposure. But the interwoven adversities and risks that arise from the vastly expanded influence of global corporations deploying new chemical, computer and genetic technologies can no longer be expected to be contained by the regulatory state of whatever vintage. Public justice in our country is basically nourished from private-sector activities; it cannot be grafted very well onto a private economy concentrated in the hands of the few over the many. This thesis is historically evident. Regions with one-crop economies or company towns have less responsive governmental structures. Regions where workers are organized obtain better treatment from their factories and mines. Where industrial power is less unilateral, elected political representatives tend to be more sensitive to human needs.

The next logical extension of private-sector economic democracy moves to the consumer arena. Unlike workers wanting a greater piece of the economic pie, consumers have it in their interest to reshape the pie and its quality for broader-based well-being for all.

The range of potential consumer demand for any set of products and services is very wide. Buyers can purchase medical services that embody quackery, malpractice, mediocrity or competence. These purchases can sustain fee-for-service medicine or cooperative, prepaid health clinics. These dollars can also lend themselves to understanding the need for greater self-health care (exercise, nutrition, ceasing smoking), which displaces sizable demand for health services. Consumer dues with organizational involvement can generate public policies and law enforcement that take hazardous drugs and devices off the market, prevent waste, reduce disease-producing pollutants in the workplace and community, and facilitate the rights of patients and injured persons in pursuing their individual grievances.

If the documentation of the past quarter-century has taught us anything about consumer abuse, it is that there are readily available ways to dramatically squeeze such waste, fraud, crime, peril and anticompetitiveness out of one industry and commerce line after another. Likewise, there is a popular literature of economic self-reliance, right down to the drawing boards, especially in the areas of housing, food, energy and health care. The large circulations of Rodale publications and *Mother Earth News* are beginning to suggest the emergence of an alternative economy embracing billions of dollars of displaced demand out of the conventional marketplace. Rediscovering old knowledge and applying new do-it-yourself technologies join to expand what consumers are producing and saving for themselves.

The progressive challenge is how to accelerate this process in a more integrated, empirical and conceptional fashion. Since everyone is a consumer, it is difficult to develop a class consciousness; for some consumers see themselves first as workers; other consumers view themselves as part of the poverty class. Moreover, many consumers, when financially strapped, see moonlighting or putting another family member to work as the way out. Few consumers think of broad reductions in their expenditures as a way out, even when they can afford to do so. The supreme ethic is not in that direction. "Thrift is out, growth is in," represents the thrust and ideology of the corporate economy.

However, in the past decade have come warnings of basic shortages and shrinkages—of conventional energy, water, reasonable credit terms—and more scarcities on the way. Sporadic shortages from cartel-prone behavior, such as the natural-gas shortfall in the late seventies, are sending alerts to consumers, who are organizing door-to-door canvasses. Refusal-to-sell shortfalls, as in bank and insurance redlining, are fueling neighborhood solidarity among homeowners and tenants. The compulsory consumption of toxic pollutants and the erosion of the nation's resources are raising serious concerns about seller-sovereign economies, concerns that the Reaganites found they politically could not ignore. Nonetheless, the politicians and media do not view the consumer as a heavyweight economic issue. It would be too tumultuous to do so. Though the recovery and prosperity of an economy rely on consumer confidence and consumer dollars, the players on the primal media stage are still business, government and organized labor. It is not surprising that the burden of many decisions made by these parties is transferred onto the shoulders of consumers. Those most burdened tend to be most ignored.

In one of the more grotesque illustrations of this endemic practice, the federal government, under a 1979 law, is subsidizing high-cost synthetic-fuel production. Then, when that energy moves to market, the government is authorized to subsidize a price-support program. While this corporate welfare program is going on, the Reagan administration has virtually destroyed the Energy Department's conservation programs and standards.

Contempt for consumer justice is seen in many ways, such as legislators' reluctance to back energy-efficiency rules for fear of reducing certain employment or reducing profits; waste here becomes an employment policy as well as a way to increase sales. Or when the Food and Drug Administration proscribes a drug or food product but lets companies sell off their remaining inventory. Or when the Congress and Mr. Reagan enacted a law requiring consumers to bear the full risk of a $40-billion Alaskan pipeline even if it was never finished and no gas flowed to their homes. Or when congressional Democrats and Republicans teamed up in 1982 to pass legislation to pay up to $50 million to manufacturers of tris-treated children's pajamas. It was deemed more advisable to spend this amount of money to save the manufacturers the trouble of taking their chemical suppliers to court than to use such a sum to establish an ongoing program of diagnosis for the children exposed to this carcinogen, or some comparable program of deterrence.

These developments represent the more extreme frontiers of the corporate state's "transfer economy." Using extramarket powers of government, these companies transfer their risks, failures, waste and corruption onto the ultimate consumers with increasing ease. This provocation against the market competition model is driving more conservative and liberal civic groups into active alliances. Such coalitions came forth in the struggles against the Alaska gas pipeline, the breeder-reactor subsidy and the bailout bills for the large banks' foreign loans. It will not be long before more conservatives begin to view the megacorporations as principal subverters of the market enterprise system.

All these currents and crosscurrents are starting to provoke organized consumer response—not simply to demand regulation but to initiate direct private action for negotiating the conditions of buying. These actions revolve around consumers banding together in the following categories:

Banding Together for Group Buying

This format is different from consumer cooperatives, which buy and then resell to their members in an institutionalized context of buildings, inventory, capital investment and other features of an established retailer.

Over the past decade, thousands of informal wholesale buying clubs for fruits and vegetables were organized on a neighborhood basis. Households take turns going to produce wholesalers to purchase, at a discount of 20 percent or so, the pooled order, which then is distributed at a convenient place in the neighborhood. Since 1980, about sixty home fuel-oil cooperatives have started in the Northeast. These co-ops obtain discounts from local fuel dealers, who benefit from larger volume sales. One such co-op, the Citizens Alliance Fuel Buyers Group, with 8,000 members in New York City, saved its members about 20 cents per gallon last year. Individual members place their order directly with the dealers, who provide the fuel under the overall co-op/dealer contract.

On an entirely different scale is the American Association of Retired Persons (AARP), which claims a membership of 14 million composed of anyone age fifty-five or older who pays $5 in annual dues. In 1969, AARP was 1 million strong; now, 100,000 new memberships are coming in each month, according to James Sullivan, director of AARP's member services. AARP's appeal is diverse—members receive a variety of periodicals, support AARP lobbyists on issues before Congress concerning the elderly, and benefit from a variety of other educational and advisory services. But the major attractions are discounts—on prescription medicines and other health-care items, and on group health insurance. Since it broke away from its founder, Colonial Penn. Insurance Company, in 1981, AARP invites bids from insurance companies for its group policy and negotiates the terms for its members.

Banding Together for Group Complaint Handling

With mass production of identical products, like car models and drugs, it was only a matter of time before the victims began to find each other for common action. Class-action litigation and publicity about defective and recalled products helped lay the groundwork for this rise in common consciousness. What follows is refining the instruments for organizing such networks.

Diane Halferty, owner of a GM diesel lemon in Seattle, has organized Consumers Against GM (CAGM) with chapters around the country of similarly indignant GM diesel owners. CAGM has technical, fund-raising, communications and other committees. A newsletter is exchanged. When group negotiations with General Motors, which sent four officials to Seattle, came to naught because GM would not negotiate with its customers *as a group*, lawsuits were filed against the company.

With the coming of two-way, interactive cable TV, there is the likelihood of a quantum leap in such group-complaint associations. Imagine a program that parades a series of such groups across the tube, followed by an address or telephone number for viewers to call if they've been the victims of similar corporate lemons or abuses. Viewers would have to possess certain rights (discussed shortly) for such media freedom to be practiced.

Banding Together for Group Negotiating

Though largely ignored by national media, there is a growing proficiency in neighborhood or community negotiations with banks to reduce their redlining, and with potential cable-company franchisees to provide more access and facilities. Trade-union negotiations for prepaid legal services have reached fruition in some 5,000 plans. The likely next stage of development is for consumer associations to negotiate changes in preprinted contracts covering installment loans, insurance policies, leases and warranties. These contracts are drafted by sellers and are very one-sided—"contracts of adhesion," as the lawyers call them. The unilateral corporate process should become more bilateral with consumers before another decade passes.

The new technologies of home computers, telecommunications and cable (and related methods of transmission) make this projection more than a hope. And the proposed consumer checkoff groups can provide the public policy muscle to make these technologies work for many people and not just for a few corporations. Although there is an abundance of available communications technologies, it will take a public-access drive to make them usable by the American people.

For starters, we have suggested to Congress an idea called "Audience Network."[6] Based on the public airwaves belonging to the public, Congress would charter a viewer and listener group and revert back to this organization (open to membership for $5-per-year dues) one hour of prime or drive time each day on each television and radio station. This audience network, through its full-time producers, programmers and reporters, would use that time both locally and nationally for the vast variety of subjects—scientific, political, cultural, civic, corporate, etc.—that are largely ignored or restrictively treated by contemporary media monopolies. Controlling a little portion of what the audience owns can quickly raise the alert and response levels of citizens to problems and solutions.

The new information technologies will breed a new kind of commercial, consumer-side business: computerized information services that, for a subscription fee, can inform people about the up-to-date best auto-insurance policies in their cities or towns, or the best savings interest rates or loan rates at banks, or the repair services with the best records. Until now computers have been overwhelmingly deployed for sellers and underwhelmingly used by consumers for their market transactions. While it is too early to assess the "community sociology" that widespread home computer use will generate, consumer networking is likely to increase significantly.

In some U.S. and Canadian cities, there are homeowner repair associations whose staffs prepare lists of approved contractors and handle homeowner complaints. Once households band together, the potential for other cooperative activities—from monitoring City Hall to reshaping the cable franchise—is limitless. One of the signal marks of twentieth-century America has been the drastic shift from neighborhoods to the corporate employment site as the all-embracing societal focus. Lately, the tide is turning modestly against this community atomization. Linkages between households on concrete matters within and outside the neighborhood can produce seismic changes in the distribution of power throughout the nation's political economy.

Before that shift occurs, collaborative consumer associations need to be more equal participants in public policy-making with corporations. Decades of legislation have built barrier after barrier and inequity after inequity between consumers and corporations. Most states, for example, prohibit neighbors from joining together to buy group homeowners and auto insurance policies. Also prohibited is bargaining with insurance agents for a reduction of their commission. Long ago, the insurance lobby saw to it that these market-restrictive laws were passed. At the federal level, vast assortments of corporate subsidies, unchallengeable licenses, regulatory abdications and campaign-fund influence serve up large dollops of consumer injustice. Procedural and economic obstacles—such as the lack of standing to sue, or the absence of intervenor funding—present additional hurdles confronting people who wish to petition their government.

Here is where the consumer checkoff insert can revolutionize the consumer movement into voluntary, mass-based policy organizations with professional staff backed at the grass roots by active members.[7] Citizens in Wisconsin find that periodically a small postage-paid envelope comes with their electric, gas and telephone bills. The envelope contains a stimulating headline and several paragraphs explaining why consumers should band together as part of the Citizens Utility Board (CUB) to represent themselves with technical skills, public information and political power before all branches of government on utility matters affecting them. Minimum dues are $3 a year, and about 80,000 residential consumers have chosen to join.

The structure is in place for advocacy in many areas. Similar structures can emerge from similar state or national laws that would simply charter these consumer groups and give them the right to insert their solicitation message in the billing envelopes or on printed contracts (warranties) of legal monopolies (e.g., utilities) or regulated industries (banks, insurance companies, auto companies, etc.). In the future, other mechanisms will be developed to help consumers find one another in order to band together. In the electronic media, for instance, time on the screen can be allocated for both viewer programming and solicitation.

These consumer-empowerment systems have attracted both liberals and conservatives in the states where they have been seriously proposed.

The CUB bill passed four years ago in Wisconsin with a Democrat-controlled legislature and a very conservative governor. The same sequence has just repeated itself in Illinois. In Washington, D.C., the Reagan administration opposed legislation to establish a Postal Service consumer group, based on twice-yearly delivery of solicitations to all household patrons. It is also opposed to pending legislation to create a residential-telephone-customer CUB to cope with the forthcoming, staggering increases in monthly local telephone bills.[8] For all their cries for new ideas, the congressional liberals, with few exceptions, have not responded actively on behalf of these empowerment ideas—none of which either cost the taxpayer anything or create another government agency. The bipartisan sway of corporatism over the U.S. Congress is so profound and PAC-ridden that it will take strenuous popular advocacy to snap many liberals out of their now cozy, industry-indentured status. But then there will be strenuous corporate provocations to fuel such advocacy.

Whether private- and public-sector consumer collaboration will rise to these challenges depends on the perception that there will flow benefits commensurate with this unusual allocation of consumer energy and time. It is necessary for consumers, therefore, to think of their role in broad terms, beyond their pocketbooks and immediate purchases, if they are to be pleased by the consequences for their pocketbooks and purchases. If motorists had thought big and organized together in the twenties to shape the many facets of the automobile economy, motorists today would be getting to their destinations more safely, more healthfully, more economically and more efficiently.

But then, the reader might reply, what about the AAA and its 40 million members? What about the mutual savings and loans associations, and the mutual insurance companies? History does have its lessons. One of them is that any economic organization that presumes to be directed and/or owned by the consumers it is designed to serve will gravitate toward managerial domination and corporatist behavior if consumers are passive owners or members. While the aforementioned institutions did make unique contributions and did engender deterrences of some value in their early years, as they matured they moved toward the corporate model and enfeebled their original purpose of expanding the consumer-sovereign sector of the economy.

A new stage of consumer history is presently unfolding. To succeed, both by the standards of a respectful prosperity and in terms of a sensitivity to reducing the domination of economic concerns over other basic human values, this new movement must be grounded in philosophy and a mass commitment to working at and perfecting the consumption function as a shaper of political economies.

The seller-sovereign economy is delivering less quality and less employment while its failures and greed are implicating our nation in worldwide crises. As long as millions of consumers find themselves, for example, spending hundreds of hours a year to earn enough money to buy food or energy while spending virtually no time learning how to buy food or obtain energy, the deterioration will continue. Banding together as buyers can broaden and metabolize the community quest for economic justice and liberate both political and economic thinkers from their invisible chains of thought.

Notes

1. Morton Mintz and Jerry S. Cohen, *Power, Inc.* (New York, NY: Viking Press, 1976).

2. Mark Green and Robert Massie, *Big Business Day Reader: Essays on Corporate America* (New York, N.Y.: Pilgrim Press, 1980).

3. Ben Bagdikian, *Media Monopoly* (Boston, Mass.: Beacon Press, 1983).

4. Thorstein Veblen, "Why Is Economics an Evolutionary Science," *Quarterly Journal of Economics* 12 (July 1898).

5. Sheila Harty, *Hucksters in the Classroom* (Washington, DC: Center for Study of Responsive Law, 1979).

6. U.S. Congress, House, Committee on Interstate and Foreign Commerce, Subcommittee on Communications, *Hearings on the Communications Act of 1979: H.R. 3333,* 96th Cong., 1st sess., 5 June 1979.

7. Andrew Sharpless and Sarah Gallup, *"Banding Together: How Check-offs Will Revolutionize the Consumer Movement"* (Washington, D.C.: Center for Study of Responsive Law, 1981); and Arthur Best and Bernard L. Brown, "Government Facilitation of Consumerism: A Proposal for Consumer Action Groups" 50 *Temple Law Quarterly* 253 (1977).

8. Joe Waz, *Reverse the Charges: How to Save $$ on Your Phone Bill* (Washington, D.C.: National Citizens Committee for Broadcasting, 1980).

The Burned Children

4000 FATAL FABRIC FIRES

Originally appeared in The New Republic, *July 3, 1971.*

A FIVE-YEAR-OLD BOY was playing in the kitchen while his mother was outside putting wash on the clothesline. The next time his mother saw him, the child was running into the yard and his body was totally black. At first she thought he had been playing with ink or paint. But as she got closer, she realized that his pajamas had burned. All that was left of them were the cuffs burning around his ankles. Later she found bits of charred cloth scattered through the house where the child had run wildly after the pajamas caught fire, apparently on the stove. Four weeks later, the boy died.

This tragic incident occurred just before Christmas last year. It is not an isolated case. Approximately 3000 people die every year after their clothing catches fire. Over 150,000 are injured in the same way. When all fabric fires are included, more than 250,000 people suffer injuries and 4000 die each year. An unusually high proportion are children and elderly people. More children under the age of five die from fires and explosions than from any other kind of injury.

Despite the fact that physicians and public health officials have been pointing out these facts for years, and citing instances as shocking as the case of the five-year-old boy, consumers still have little protection against the hazards of flammable fabrics.

The Flammable Fabrics Act passed in 1953 has long been recognized by safety experts as a sham. William White, former chairman of the National Commission on Product Safety, has noted that the Act "is famous for allowing 99 percent of all fabrics marketed in this country to pass the test. It is well known to the plastic surgeons who repair the burned children who were wearing the clothing made from fabrics that always pass this test."

In 1967, attempts were made to correct this situation. The Flammable Fabrics Act was amended to include home furnishings and wearing apparel such as shoes and hats which were not previously covered, and to provide for new flammability standards to be set by the Department of Commerce. Today, three-and-a-half years later, only one new standard has been set and not a single new standard for clothing. The Secretary of Commerce did not even call a meeting of his advisory committee on flammability standards until May of 1969, nearly one-and-a-half years after the amendments were passed.

All the department has done with regard to clothing is to propose a standard for children's nightwear which is so restricted that by industry's own count it will eliminate only 1 percent of the total clothing-related burns. The standard applies only to sleepwear up to the size of 6X. (Yet even many five-year-olds wear larger sizes.) It is less inclusive than England's regulation, in effect since 1967, that *all* children's sleepwear be flame-retardant and that all adult sleepwear be labeled if it does not pass the tests.

The formal administrative procedures to set a new standard for children's sleepwear began in January, 1970. Department of Commerce officials, after many unwarranted delays, now say that a mandatory standard will be set within a few weeks. However there may be yet another delay; the effective date of the standard may be extended from 1972 to 1973 to allow more time for industry to comply.

The only standard the Department has actually set under the 1967 amendments is a test for rugs and carpets that went into effect April 16, 1971. This test was heartily endorsed by the carpet and rug industry because it is so weak most of their products can already pass it. Even the National Bureau of Standards, not known for its vigorous safety efforts, considers the "pill" test for carpets to be inadequate. This test utilizes an aspirin-sized methanamine tablet as a timed ignition source. The National Bureau of Standards calls it a "first generation test," since it "fails" only those carpets that can be easily ignited by a flame as small as that of a cigarette. It does not measure the reaction of a carpet to a larger fire. The carpet that contributed to the deaths of 32 nursing home patients in Marietta, Ohio, in 1969 would have passed the "pill" test.

Rugs that might have trouble passing the test—small machine-tufted carpets—are virtually exempt. The Commerce Department has ruled that such rugs can still be sold whether or not they pass the pill test. The only "safeguard" for the consumer is a requirement beginning December 8, 1971, that small rugs which fail the test be so labeled. These small rugs, less than 4 x 6 feet, account for 18 percent of the market, with approximately 55 million sold every year. Shag rugs, some of which present the greatest flammability hazard of all rugs, are often made in this size range. According to industry's own statement, 80 to 90 percent of these small rugs are made of cotton or rayon and would fail the pill test.

The final loophole in the standard is that carpets produced before April 16 may be sold without being tested or labeled, so consumers can't tell whether a rug has even undergone the pill test. The Department of Commerce hasn't alerted the public to this fact.

The industry has successfully resisted meaningful flammability standards primarily by persuading the Department of Commerce that consumers should bear the burden of protection. The remarks of George S. Buck, Jr., research director for the National Cotton Council, are typical. Mr. Buck alleged at hearings before the Department of Commerce in January, 1971, that "consumers don't give a damn about inflammable fabrics. . . . They are much more interested in comfort, wear-life, and style than . . . fire-resistance."

Even more blatant was the statement of an industry representative who wrote to the Department of Commerce protesting proposed flammability standards for children's nightwear: "It is impossible for industry or government to completely insulate a child from the hazards caused by careless and negligent parents or guardians that allow a child to become dangerously close to a source of flame. This small minority of parents and guardians who fail in their duty should not force the majority of careful and sensible parents to bear the cost of the hardship."

Passing the burden to the consumer is one of the oldest tricks of the marketplace. In reality, the consumer has almost never been offered a meaningful choice in flammable fabrics. It is virtually impossible to outfit a family and furnish a home in flame-retardant material, even though many fabrics can be made flame-retardant. Nor does the consumer have the information to enable him to make a choice between safe and unsafe fabrics. Few consumers think about flammability when they read advertisements that talk of nothing but style and comfort. How many manufacturers have attempted to sell safety in the way they sell fashion and convenience? The answer is virtually none. Even the Department of Commerce, charged with regulating flammability hazards, devotes an entire page in its textile "consumer guide" to "the exciting world of fibers and fabrics" and another page to wash-and-wear miracles. No page is devoted to warning the consumer about the hazards of flammability.

MOST PEOPLE LEARN about the hazards of flammable fabrics when tragedy strikes their own family. It is almost inevitably a costly lesson. One family in the state of Washington lost two children—a 13-year-old girl and her younger brother—in separate incidents that involved clothing that caught fire.

There are few injuries more traumatic than severe burns—and few burns more serious than those involving clothing ignition. The pain, the scars, the difficult and expensive medical treatment are excruciating burdens for burn victims and their families. The opportunities for fires are all too prevalent in the home, where 80 percent of all burns occur. Another family lost their only child after his pajamas ignited from touching or coming near the burner on an electric stove. The two-year-old child lived for sixty-nine days with third-degree burns over a large part of his body. In most of these cases, it would have been difficult for the parents to protect their children without totally unrealistic precautions.

Such accidents are not restricted to the young. An 86-year-old retired physician sustained burns over nearly half of her body when the sleeve of her nightgown caught on fire after coming in contact with the burner on an electric hot plate. She died after twenty-two days in the hospital.

Even when burns are not fatal, in addition to their anguish, families often have astronomical medical bills. One girl was burned when her jacket caught fire; she sustained second and third degree burns over 45 percent of her body. An HEW report stated that reconstructive surgery for her face, hands, and arms could cost $50,000 or more.

Time after time, physicians have brought in evidence of severe burns that could have been less serious or even avoided if the clothing had been flame-retardant. Two electricians were burned when a flash emitted from the high-voltage fuse panel they were servicing. One suffered a severe 40 percent body burn because his flannel shirt caught fire. He was in the hospital for three months and required several skin graft operations. The second man was wearing a heavy cotton work shirt and suffered only second degree burns to his hands and face. He was in the hospital for twenty-five days and required no grafts. Dr. Abraham Bergman, a Seattle physician, asked at Senate hearings in June 1970: "How many bodies have to be stacked up before effective action is taken to prevent clothing burn injuries?"

EFFORTS TO IMPROVE CONSUMER protection have been hindered by the fact that the magnitude of the fabric-burn problem has been concealed through lack of precise data. Statistics are still collected so haphazardly that current figures on burn injuries may underestimate the real picture. The National Commission on Product Safety took an important step toward correcting the dearth of injury information by instituting a system of hospital reporting, now operated by the Food and Drug Administration. But there are ominous signs that FDA is actually regressing in the investigation of reported burn cases. It has allowed its specialized teams that make in-depth investigations of injuries to deteriorate to the point where both the Boston and Denver Injury Study Units are operating at half their former level. Many injury investigations are now being carried out by FDA field inspectors who have no expertise at all in the area of consumer product safety.

The Department of Health, Education, and Welfare has been woefully inefficient in submitting its reports to Congress on injuries and deaths associated with the use of fabrics. These reports should be made annually under the 1967 amendments to the Flammable Fabrics Act. The first report was due in 1968 and was not delivered until after the second report was due in December 1969.

A chief block to greater safety remains weak government standards, often with loopholes so that manufacturers can avoid meeting even those regulations. The setting of weak standards initially makes it even harder to improve them, a fact recognized by the industry since 1953. The Department of Commerce, one of the least responsive of all government agencies to needs of consumers, has gone along like putty in the hands of manufacturers. Senator Warren G. Magnuson, author of the original Flammable Fabrics Act and Chairman of the Senate Commerce Committee, commented recently on the performance of the Department of Commerce in implementing the Act. He said: "No single bill with which I have been associated has been so bitter a disappointment. . . . A National Commission on Product Safety report last year reached two basic conclusions: the powers contained in the Act are adequate; the Department of Commerce is grossly inadequate."

Regulation has been reduced to an impotent approval of products that are cheapest for industry to make and will yield the highest profits. Low or nonexistent standards have made possible a controlled market where the innovative manufacturer who develops a safer fabric can be undercut by competitors who lower their prices temporarily and drive him off the market. Furthermore, manufacturers have frightened consumers by telling them that prices will go up for flame-retardant clothes (without mentioning that millions of dollars would be saved if burn injuries decreased). The available evidence suggests that the projected price increases are, in large part, either bluff or so much in excess of costs that manufacturers would be able to sus-

234 THE RALPH NADER READER

tain them only by colluding. One garment manufacturer we contacted, for example, anticipates a $1.70 price differential between flame-retardant and regular pajamas. But cost data which he later provided shows that the additional cost of producing flame-retardant pajamas amounts to little more than the extra 55 cents per pair required to buy chemically treated fabric. Instead of intervening on the side of the innovative manufacturer and the consumer, Commerce has been a loyal defender of these textile interests who say they "cannot afford" to provide safety.

Two things are urgently needed if there is to be any change. First, the Department of Health, Education, and Welfare is going to have to provide more vigorous data collection on burn injuries and renew its almost dormant research function. Consumers will have to demand that information collected by HEW be made public and that specific brands be named as market guides, according to their flammability hazards or their safety improvements.

Second, concerted consumer pressure will be required if the Department of Commerce is to be moved to enforce the law. Congressional hearings to inquire into the protracted delays in setting standards is one step. Another step is citizen petitions to the Department to activate administrative procedures to set meaningful standards. The insurance industry could be of key assistance here. It may well be that a legal challenge to the Department's failure to move expeditiously in this area will be required or that the regulatory function should be placed elsewhere. It is Senator Magnuson's firm judgment that "the flammable fabrics program should be taken from the Department of Commerce and merged with the overall product safety program in an agency which is willing and capable to do what must be done."

Many deaths could be prevented and injuries greatly reduced in severity. We know how to make fabric less flammable. We know too that it is more efficient to make clothing safer than to keep children from climbing on stoves or persuade mothers not to buy frills for little girls. In few areas have industry and government been less responsive to consumers.

The Great American Gyp

Originally appeared in The New York Review of Books, *November 21, 1968.*

LAST JANUARY a confidential nationwide survey by the Opinion Research Corporation spread considerable alarm among its corporate subscribers. The poll concluded "that seven Americans in ten think present Federal legislation is inadequate to protect their health and safety. The majority also believe that more Federal laws are needed to give shoppers full value for their money." To many businessmen, this finding merely confirmed what speakers had been telling them at trade gatherings during the previous year—that consumers were beginning to fall prey to "consumerism."

"Consumerism" is a term given vogue recently by business spokesmen to describe what they believe is a concerted, disruptive ideology concocted by self-appointed bleeding hearts and politicians who find that it pays off to attack the corporations. "Consumerism," they say, undermines public confidence in the business system, deprives the consumer of freedom of choice, weakens state and local authority through Federal usurpation, bureaucratizes the marketplace, and stifles innovation. These complaints have all been made in speeches, in the trade press, and in Congressional testimony against such Federal bills as truth-in-lending, truth-in-packaging, gas pipeline safety, radiation protection, auto, tire, drug, and fire safety legislation, and meat and fish inspection.

But what most troubles the corporations is the consumer movement's relentless documentation that consumers are being manipulated, defrauded, and injured not just by marginal businesses or fly-by-night hucksters, but by the US blue-chip business firms whose practices are unchecked by the older regulatory agencies. Since the consumer movement can cite statistics showing that these practices have reduced real income and raised the rates of mortality and disease, it is not difficult to understand the growing corporate concern.

That the systematic disclosure of such malpractice has been so long delayed can be explained by the strength of the myths that the business establishment has used to hide its activities. The first is the myth of the omniscient consumer who is so discerning that he will be a brutal taskmaster for any firm entering the market. This approach was used repeatedly to delay, then weaken, the truth-in-packaging bill. Scott Paper Co. ran an advertising campaign hailing the American housewife as "The Original Computer": "...a strange change comes over a woman in the store. The soft glow in the eye is replaced by a steely financial glint; the graceful walk becomes a panther's stride among the bargains. A woman in a store is a mechanism, a prowling computer.... Jungle-trained, her bargain-hunter senses razor-sharp for the sound of a dropping price...."

However, when companies plan their advertising, they fail to take advantage of the supposed genius of the consumer. Potential car buyers are urged to purchase Pontiacs to experience an unexplained phenomenon called "wide-tracking before you're too old to know what it is all about." Sizable fees are paid to "motivation" experts like Ernest Dichter for such analysis as this: "Soup...is much more than a food. It is a potent magic that satisfies not only the hunger of the body but the yearnings of the soul. People speak of soup as a product of some mysterious alchemy, a symbol of love which satisfies mysterious gnawings.... The term 'pea soup'—mystery and magic— seem to go together with fog. At the same time we can almost say soup is orgiastic. Eating soup is a fulfillment."

A second myth is that most American businesses perform honorably but are subjected to underserved notoriety because of a few small, unscrupulous firms. This notion is peddled by so-called consumer protection agencies as well as by the business-dominated Better Business Bureaus. But the detailed Congressional hearings on drug hazards, unsafe vehicles, vicious credit practices, restraints on medically useful or dollar-saving innovations, auto insurance abuses, cigarette-induced diseases, and price-fixing throughout the economy have made it clear that this argument will not hold up.

Most misleading of all is the myth that irresponsible sellers are adequately policed by local, state, and Federal regulatory agencies. Years ago, corporations learned how to handle these agencies, and they have now become apologists for business instead of protectors of the public. First, the agencies are made to operate on a starvation budget. The combined annual budget of the Federal Trade Commission and the Antitrust Division of the Justice Department in 1968 is $23 million, the highest amount yet appropriated. With this sum, they are supposed to collect data, initiate investigations, and enforce the laws dealing with deceptive and anticompetitive practices of a $850 billion economy.

Secondly, political patronage has undermined local and state consumer protection agencies: it has, for example, helped to make the Federal Trade Commission as ineffectual as it is. Third, business lobbying—including campaign contributions, powerful law firms, trade associations, and public relations—works against vigorous enforcement. Finally, so many regulatory officials resign to go into high-paying jobs in the industries they were once supposed to regulate that these government posts are viewed as on-the-job training by cynical appointees.[1] The Federal Aviation Agency, Interstate Commerce Commission, and Federal Communications Commission all carry on a tradition that inhibits officials from action and attracts appointees who are temperamentally reluctant to act.

The increasing irrelevance of these older agencies was made apparent by the unprecedented consumer legislation enacted under the Johnson Administration. After the dismal spectacle of the cigarette labeling act of 1964—which foreclosed action by the states and the FTC in return for a paltry warning on the package that could serve as a company's defense in liability suits—Congress passed a string of important bills and has other legislation near passage. A shift of responsibilities for consumer protection to the Federal government now seems to be taking place: state and local governments have for years defaulted on these obligations to the consumer.

In no other period of history have the safety and prices of marketed products and services received remotely comparable legislative treatment. Sensing this climate, President Johnson has allowed his consumer adviser, Betty Furness, to speak openly to business groups. In 1964, her predecessor, Esther Peterson, could not get White House clearance even to make a public statement about rigged odometers which misled motorists about the accuracy of mileage traveled, enriched car rental companies to the amount of $4 million a year, and encouraged automobile sales. In 1968 Miss Furness was urging appliance manufacturers to tell their customers how long they can expect their products to last. This spring, President Johnson established the post of Consumer Counsel in the Justice Department—a first small step toward the creation of a Federal office which would have powers to intervene in cases before the courts and regulatory agencies as the representative of consumer interests.[2] In July, Vice-President Humphrey said he favored enlarging the counsel's powers to include making complaints about dangers to public health. He also became the first government official to endorse public disclosure of information about consumer products now in the files of the General Services Administration and the Department of Defense. These agencies test hundreds of consumer products—from light bulbs and bed sheets to washing machines—in order to determine which have the best value. But they have refused thus far to release the data that would rank products by quality—a refusal naturally supported by the business community. The business world, meanwhile, has become increasingly adept in dealing with the rising pressures for consumer legislation. Tutored by their well-connected Washington lawyers, the large corporations and their trade associations can sense the critical moment at which it is wise to stop opposing a bill and begin to cooperate with Congressional committees in order to shape legislation to their liking. For example, after opposing the passage of any auto safety bill whatever, the auto manufacturers relented in the spring of 1966 and hired Lloyd Cutler, an experienced Washington lawyer, who succeeded in weakening the disclosure provisions of the bill and in eliminating all criminal penalties for willful and knowing violations of the law.

Although consumer measures may be weakened in this way, they do at least commit the government to the idea of consumer protection and they lay the groundwork for the stronger legislation that may be feasible should the consumer movement gain more strength. The attack on corporate irresponsibility which produced the recent flurry of legislation in Congress has not, it must be said, been the work of a broad movement but rather of tiny ad hoc coalitions of determined people in and out of government armed with little more than a great many shocking facts. They have gotten important support from Senator Warren Magnuson, Chairman of the Senate Commerce Committee, whose interest in consumer problems set in motion a little-noticed competition with the White House to promote legislation.

What has taken place during the last few years may be seen as an escalating series of disclosures. The charges made by independent Congressmen and people like myself almost always turn out to be understatements of the actual conditions in various industries when those industries are subsequently exposed in Congressional hearings and investigations. As these charges get attention, demands for new legislative action increase. This, at least, has been the case with the exposure of defects in vehicles, industrial and vehicle pollution, gas pipelines, overpriced or dangerous drugs, unfair credit, harmful pesticides, cigarettes, land frauds, electric power reliability, household improvement rackets, exploitation in slums, auto warranties, radiation, high-priced auto insurance, and boating hazards. How many people realized, for example, that faulty heating devices injure 125,000 Americans a year or that poorly designed stoves, power mowers, and washing machines cause substantial injury to 300,000 people annually? Or that, as Rep. Benjamin Rosenthal recently revealed, the food rejected by Federal agencies as contaminated or rotting is often re-routed for sale in the market? These abuses are now starting to be discussed in the press and in Congress.

One result of the detailed Congressional hearings has been a broader definition of legitimate consumer rights and interests. It is becoming clear that consumers must not only be protected from the dangers of voluntary use of a product, such as flammable material, but also from *involuntary* consumption of industrial by-products such as air and water pollutant, excessive pesticide and nitrate residues in foods, and antibiotics in meat. A more concrete idea of a just economy is thus beginning to emerge, while, at the same time, the assortment of groups that comprise the "consumer's movement" is moving in directions that seem to me quite different from the ones that similar groups have followed in the past. Their demands are ethical rather than ideological. Their principles and proposals are being derived from solid documentation of common abuses whose origins are being traced directly to the policies of powerful corporations.

This inquiry is extending beyond the question of legal control of corporations into the failure of business, labor, and voluntary organizations to check one another's abuses through competition and other private pressures. It is becoming apparent that the reform of consumer abuses and the reform of corporate power itself are different sides of the same coin and that new approaches to the enforcement of the rights of consumers are necessary. There are, I would suggest, at least ten major forces or techniques that now exist in some form but greatly need to be strengthened if we are to have a decent consumer society.

1. Rapid disclosure of the facts relating to the quantity, quality, and safety of a product is essential to a just market place. If companies know

their products can quickly be compared with others, the laggard will be goaded to better performance and the innovator will know that buyers can promptly learn about his innovation. On the other hand, buyers must be able to compare products in order to reject the shoddy and reward the superior producer. This process is the great justification for a free market system. Manufacturers try to avoid giving out such information and instead rely on "packaging" or advertising. Auto companies refuse to tell the motorist the safety performances of his car's brakes and tires, and concentrate on brand-names—Cougar, Barracuda, Marauder—and vehicle "personality": "Mustang makes dull people interesting. . . ." From cosmetics to soaps and detergents, the differences emphasized are emotional and frivolous and have no relation to functions. This practice permits the producer with the largest advertising budget to make matters very difficult for a smaller competitor or potential entrant into the market who may have a superior product. The anti-competitive effects of such advertising led Donald F. Turner, the former head of the Antitrust Division of the Justice Department, to suggest that the government subsidize independent sources of consumer information. Senator Philip Hart has gone a step further in proposing a National Consumer Service Foundation to provide product information to consumers at the place of purchase. Computers could help to assemble such information cheaply and quickly. One can, for instance, imagine machines dispensing data on individual products at shopping centers, a plan which Consumer's Union has begun to study.

2. The practices of refunding dollars to consumers who have been bilked and recalling defective products are finally becoming recognized as principles of deterrence and justice. More than six million automobiles have been recalled since September, 1966—the date of the auto safety law. The Food and Drug Administration now requires drug companies to issue "corrective letters" to all physicians if their original advertisements were found to be misleading. Nearly thirty such letters have been sent out by drug companies during the twenty months of FDA action. The threat of liability suits and the willingness of the press and television to mention brand and company names in reporting on defects are causing companies to recall products "voluntarily" even where no law or regulation exists. Earlier this year, for instance, Sears-Roebuck recalled some 6,000 gas heaters after public health officials warned of lethal carbon monoxide leakage. After similar warnings by US Public Health officials and the threat of disclosure by a major newspaper, General Electric made

changes in 150,000 color TV sets which had been found to be emitting excessive radiation. Some insurance companies are beginning to offer "defect recall" insurance.

The duty to refund remains even less well recognized than the duty to recall a product because of defects. Orders to "cease and desist," the usual decree of the Federal Trade Commission after it catches swindlers, at best stop the defrauder but do not require him to pay back the funds. Without this sanction, a major deterrent is lost. The mere order to "go and sin no more," which replaces it, is easily evaded.

The only enforcement action made by the FTC is pertinent here. For thirty years, the Holland Furnace Company used scare tactics and routinely deceived the public. Its salesmen were encouraged to pose as "safety inspectors" and were trained to be merciless: one elderly and ailing woman was sold nine new furnaces in six years, costing a total of $18,000. Following up on complaints beginning in the Thirties, the FTC secured a stipulation from the company that it would stop its misleading advertising. This had little if any effect. A cease and desist order was entered in 1958 but it was not until January, 1965, that the company was fined $100,000 for violating the order and an ex-president was sent to jail. At that point, the Holland Furnace Co. decided to file a petition for bankruptcy. But as Senator Warren Magnuson said: "In the meantime, Holland Furnace at the height of its business cost the American public $30 million a year." The FTC's ponderous procedures and anemic enforcement powers (it has no power of preliminary injunction, no criminal penalties, and no power of its own to fine, assess, or award damages) encourage the unscrupulous businessman to continue his abuses, if he is caught later on, he will merely be told to stop.

Two developments in recent years have strengthened private actions against malpractices by established corporations with large assets. The first is the growing practice of filing treble damage suits against violators of antitrust laws. In the early Sixties, corporate and government customers of G.E., Westinghouse, and other large companies collected about $500 million in out-of-court settlements after these companies and their officers were convicted for carrying on a criminal antitrust price-fixing conspiracy. Although such punitive damage payments are tax-deductible as "ordinary and necessary business expenses," the deterrent is an effective one. Cases brought by both private and government procurement agencies have multiplied in many other industries recently—from drugs to children's books and these will increase, especially with tougher antitrust action by the Justice Department and by the states.

The second development is in the use of "class actions" in which suits are filed on behalf of large numbers of people who have been mistreated in the same way. In modern mass merchandising, fraud naturally takes the form of cheating a great many customers out of a few pennies or dollars: the bigger the store or chain of stores, the greater the gain from gypping tiny amounts from individuals who would not find it worthwhile to take formal action against the seller. Class actions solve this problem by turning the advantage of large volume against the seller that made predatory use of it in the first place. Poverty lawyers, supported by the US Office of Economic Opportunity, are just beginning to use this important technique.

A case of great potential significance for developing broad civil deterrence has been brought in New York City against Coburn Corp., a sales finance company, by two customers who signed its retail installment contracts. They are being assisted by the NAACP Legal Defense and Educational Fund. The plaintiffs charge that Coburn violated Section 402 of the New York personal Property Law by not printing its contracts in large type as specified by law. They are asking recovery of the credit service charge paid under the contracts for themselves and all other consumers similarly involved. If the plaintiffs win, consumers in New York will be able to bring class actions against any violations of law contained in any standard form contracts.

3. Disputes in courts and other judicial forums must be conducted under fairer ground rules and with adequate representation for buyers. Here the recent appearance of neighborhood legal service attorneys is a hopeful sign. These poverty lawyers—now numbering about 2,000 and paid by the Office of Economic Opportunity are representing the poor against finance companies, landlords, auto dealers, and other sellers of goods and services. Because of their work, the law of debtors' remedies and defenses is catching up with the well-honed law of creditors' rights that generations of law students studied so rigorously. These lawyers are bringing test cases to court and winning them. They are gradually exposing the use by slum merchants of the courts as agents to collect from poor people who are uninformed or cannot leave their jobs to show up in court. For the first time, poverty lawyers are challenging the routine contract clauses that strip the buyers of their legal defenses in advance, as well as those involving illegal repossession, unreasonable garnishment, undisclosed credit and financing terms and a great many other victimizing practices.

But even many more poverty lawyers could handle only a few of the cases deserving their services. What is important is that recent cases are documenting a general pattern of abuses and injustices in the legal system itself.

This is beginning to upset influential lawyers; it may prod law schools to more relevant teaching as well as guide legislatures and courts toward much-delayed reform of laws, court procedures, and remedies. At the same time, wholly new and more informed ways of resolving conflicts are being considered—such as neighborhood arbitration units which are open in the evenings when defendants need not be absent from their work. However, if such developments seem promising they must not obscure the persisting venality of the marketplace and the generally hopeless legal position of the consumer who is victimized by it.

4. The practice of setting government safety standards and periodically changing them to reflect new technology and uses is spreading, although it is still ineffective in many ways. Decades after banking and securities services were brought under regulation, products such as automobiles (53,000 dead and 4 1/2 million injured annually), washing machines and power lawn mowers (200,000 injuries annually), many chemicals, and all pipeline systems did not have to adhere to any standards of safety performance other than those set by the companies or industries themselves. With the passage of the auto safety law in 1966, other major products have been brought under Federal safety regulation. To avoid continuing a piece-meal approach, Congress in 1967 passed an act establishing the National Commission on Product Safety to investigate many household and related hazards, from appliances to household chemicals. Moreover, the Commission must recommend by 1970 a more detailed Federal, state, and local policy toward reducing or preventing deaths and injuries from these products.

The commission's recommendations will probably go beyond household products to the problem of a safer man-made environment. So far, most state and Federal efforts to set meaningful safety standards and enforce them have failed miserably. The only organized and effective pressures on the agencies responsible for setting standards have come from the same economic interests that are supposed to be regulated. Two illustrations of this failure have been the Flammable Fabrics Act of 1953 and the oil pipeline safety act of 1965. In both cases, little has happened because the laws have not been administered. It took three-and-a-half years before the Federal government even proposed oil pipeline standards, and these were taken almost verbatim from the pipeline industry's own code. Similarly, when the General Accounting Office recently reviewed the enforcement of the pesticide law by the Department of Agriculture it found that repeated mass violations of the laws between 1955 and 1965 were never reported to the

244   THE RALPH NADER READER

Department for prosecution. This is a typical example of how consumers
are deprived of legal protection in spite of a statute intended to protect
them.

5. If the government is to impose effective standards, it must also be able
to conduct or contract for its own research on both the safety of industrial
products and possible methods of improving them. Without this power, the
agencies will have to rely on what is revealed to them by industry, and their
efforts will be crippled from the start. They will, for example, be unable to
determine whether a better vehicle handling system is required or to detect
promptly the hidden dangers in apparently harmless drugs. The government could also bring strong pressures on business by using its own great
purchasing power and by developing its own prototypes of safer products.
The existing safety laws, however, do not even permit the government to
find out quickly and accurately whether industry is complying with the law.
The National Highway Safety Bureau, for example, has little idea whether
or not the 1968 automobiles meet all the safety standards since no government testing facilities yet exist.

But full enforcement of the law also depends on the existence of effective penalties, and in this respect the recent safety laws are feeble, to say the
least. There are no criminal penalties for willful and knowing violation of
the auto safety and gas pipeline laws; nor have criminal penalties been written into other bills about to be signed into law, such as the radiation control bill. The civil fines are small when considered against the possibility of
violations by huge industries producing millions of the same product. Of
course, the Washington corporation lawyers who lobby to water down the
penalties in these safety laws have no interest in the argument that stronger
sanctions would not only act as a deterrent to industry but make enforcement itself cheaper.

6. In the ideology of American business, free competition and corporate
"responsibility" are supposed to protect the consumer; in practice both have
long been ignored. Price-fixing, either by conspiracy or by mutually understood cues, is rampant throughout the economy. This is partly revealed by
the growing number of government and private antitrust actions. Donald
Turner, the former head of the Antitrust Division, has despaired of effectively enforcing the law against price-fixing with the existing manpower in
the Justice Department. Price-fixing, of course, means higher prices for consumers. For example, the electrical price-fixing conspiracy, broken by the
Justice Department in 1960, involved not only G.E., Westinghouse, Allis
Chalmers, but several small companies as well; the overcharge to the direct

purchasers of generators and other heavy duty equipment was estimated at more than a billion dollars during the ten-year life of the conspiracy that sent several executives to short jail terms.

Even greater dangers arise when the failure of large industry to compete prevents the development of new products that might save or improve the lives of consumers. When such restraint is due to conspiracy or other kinds of collusion, it should be the task of antitrust enforcement to stop the practice of "product-fixing." Traditional antitrust enforcement has been slow to grasp the fact that the restraint of innovation is becoming far more important to big business than the control of prices. New inventions—steam or electric engines,longer lasting light bulbs and paints, and cheaper construction materials—can shake an industry to its most stagnant foundations. For eighteen months the Justice Department presented to a Los Angeles grand jury its charges that the domestic auto companies conspired to restrain the development and marketing of vehicle exhaust control systems. When and if it files its complaint, a pioneering case of antitrust enforcement in a health and safety issue could reveal much about this as yet unused weapon for public protection.

Ideally, one of the most powerful forces for consumer justice would be the exercise of corporate responsibility or private "countervailing" and monitoring forces within the corporate world. Unfortunately for believers in a pluralist economic system, recent decades have shown that the economics of accommodation repeatedly overwhelms the economics of checks and balances.

The casualty insurance industry is a case in point. Logically it should have a strong interest in safer automobiles. In fact it has chosen to raise premiums instead of pressuring the auto industry to adopt safety measures that have been available for a long time. The casualty insurance industry has not demanded legislation to improve the design and inspection of motor vehicles; nor has it encouraged the rating of vehicles according to their safety. It has been equally indifferent to the need to reform methods of fire prevention (where the US is far behind Japan and England) or standards of industrial safety and health. What the industry has done instead is to spend large sums on advertising assuring the public it is concerned about the consumer safety it has declined to pursue in practice.

7. Professional and technical societies may be sleeping giants where the protection of the consumer is concerned. Up to now, such groups as the American Society of Mechanical Engineers, the American Chemical Society, and the American Society of Safety Engineers have been little

more than trade associations for the industries that employ their members. It is shocking, for example, that none of these technical societies has done much to work out public policies to deal with the polluted environment and with such new technological hazards as atomic energy plants and radioactive waste disposal. Except in a few cases, the independent professions of law and medicine have done little to fulfill their professional obligations to protect the public from victimization. They have done less to encourage their colleagues in science and engineering to free themselves from subservience to corporate disciplines. Surely, for example, the supersonic transport program, with its huge government subsidies and intolerable sonic boom, should have been exposed to careful public scrutiny by engineers and scientists long before the government rather secretively allowed it to get under way.

The engineers and scientists, however, had no organization nor procedure for doing this. None of the professions will be able to meet its public responsibilities unless it is willing to undertake new roles and to create special independent organizations willing to gather facts and take action in the public interest. Such small but determined groups as the Committee for Environmental Information in St. Louis, headed by Professor Barry Commoner, and the Physicians for Automotive Safety in New Jersey have shown how people with tiny resources can accomplish much in public education and action. If such efforts are to be enlarged, however, the legal, medical, engineering, and scientific departments of universities must recognize the importance of preparing their graduates for full-time careers in organizations devoted to shaping public policy; for it is clear that professionals serving clients in private practice will not be adequate to this task. Had such organizations existed two or three decades ago, the hazards of the industrial age might have been foreseen, diagnosed, exposed, and to some extent prevented. During the recent controversy over auto safety I often speculated that the same kind of reform might have occurred thirty years ago had a handful of engineers and physicians made a dramatic effort to inform politicians about scandals that even then took more than 30,000 lives a year and caused several million injuries. Instead the doctors were busy treating broken bones and the engineers were following corporate orders, while their technical journals ignored a major challenge to their profession. For all the talk about "preventive medicine" and "remedial engineering," this is what is happening now.

8. During the past two decades, the courts have been making important if little noticed rulings that give injured people fairer chances of recovering

damages. These include the elimination of "privity" or the need to prove a contractual relation with the person sued; the expansion of the "implied warranty" accompanying items purchased to include not only the "reasonable" functioning of those items but also the claims made in deceptive advertising of them; and the imposition of "strict liability" which dispenses with the need to prove negligence if one has been injured through the use of a defective product. At the same time, the laws of evidence have been considerably liberalized.

This reform of the common law of "bodily rights"—far in advance of other common-law nations such as Great Britain and Canada—has been followed by some spectacular jury verdicts and court decisions in favor of the injured. These are routinely cited by insurance companies as a rationale for increasing premiums. The fact is, however, that these victories still are rare exceptions, and for obvious reasons. Winning such cases requires a huge investment in time and money: the plaintiff's lawyers must collect the evidence and survive the long and expensive delays available to the corporation defendant with its far superior resources. But now the rules give the plaintiff at least a decent chance to recover his rights in court or by settlement. It remains for the legal profession to find ways to cut drastically the costs of litigation, especially in cases where a single product, such as a car or drug, has injured many people.

However, the law of torts (personal injuries) still does not protect the consumer against the pollution of the environment which indiscriminately injures everyone exposed to it. Pollution in Los Angeles is a serious health hazard, but how may the citizens of that besmogged metropolis sue? A group of eighty-eight residents of Martinez, California, is suing Shell Oil's petroleum refinery for air pollution and its "roaring noises, recurring vibrations and frightening lights." In an increasingly typical defense, Shell claims that it meets the state's mild pollution-control regulation. But such standards are largely the result of political pressures from corporations whose profits are at stake. Thus, increasingly, justice in the courts must be paralleled by justice in the legislatures. However, there are some signs that the courts are beginning to take account of the right to a decent environment in cases against industrial pollutants. Last year, a lady in Pennsylvania recovered about $70,000 for injuries sustained from living near a beryllium plant which emitted toxic fumes daily. (The case is being appealed.)

9. One of the more promising developments of the last two years is the growing belief that new institutions are needed within the government

whose sole function would be to advocate consumer interests. As I have pointed out, the Johnson Administration has done no more than create earlier this year an Office of Consumer Counsel in the Justice Department—a post that has not yet begun to function. The Executive Branch is hostile to a proposal by Congressman Rosenthal and others for a new Department of Consumer Affairs on the Cabinet level. This proposal has been criticized by Federal officials on the ground that it would duplicate what government agencies are now doing. The fact is, however, that most of the government agencies that are supposed to be concerned with the health and safety of consumers are also promoting the interests of the industries that cause the consumer harm. The US Department of Agriculture represents the farmers and processors first and the consumers second—whether in controversies over the price of milk or over the wholesomeness of meat and poultry. The regulatory agencies themselves at best merely act as referees and at worst represent business interests in government.

Clearly it would be useful if a new bureau within the government itself could both expose these regulatory agencies and challenge them to take more vigorous action. Senator Lee Metcalfe has introduced legislation to create an independent US Office of Utility Consumer's Counsel to represent the public before regulatory agencies and courts. This approach is different from that of Congressman Rosenthal and it remains to be seen which scheme can best avoid the dangers of bureaucratization and atrophy. What is not generally appreciated, however, is that if they are to succeed, such new governmental units will badly need the vigorous support of organizations outside the government which would have similar concern for the consumer and would also be able to carry on their own research and planning.

10. I have already pointed out the need for independent organizations of professionals—engineers, lawyers, doctors, economists, scientists, and others—which could undertake work of this kind. But they do not as yet exist. Still, we can draw some idea of their potential from the example of people like Dr. Commoner and his associates who have managed to stir up strong public opposition to government and private interests while working in their spare time. Similarly, other small groups of professionals have saved natural resources from destruction or pollution; they have stopped unjust increases in auto-insurance rates; they have defeated a plan for an atomic explosion to create a natural gas storage area under public land, showing that excessive safety risks were involved.

Is there reason to hope that the high energy physicists who lobbied successfully for hundreds of millions of dollars in public funds might be emulated by other professionals seeking to improve the quality of life in America? Certainly there is a clear case for setting up professional firms to act in the public interest at Federal and local levels. While thousands of engineers work for private industry, a few hundred should be working out the technical plans for obtaining clean air and water, and demanding that these plans be followed. While many thousands of lawyers serve private clients, several hundred should be working in public interest firms which would pursue legal actions and reforms of the kind I have outlined here. Support for such firms could come from foundations, private gifts, dues paid by consumers and the professions, or from government subsidies. There is already a precedent for the latter in the financing of the Neighborhood Legal Services, not to mention the billions of dollars in subsidies now awarded to commerce and industry. In addition, groups that now make up the consumers' movement badly need the services of professional economists, lawyers, engineers, and others if they are to develop local consumer service institutions that could handle complaints, dispense information, and work out strategies for public action.

Notwithstanding the recent alarm of industry and the surge of publicity about auto safety and other scandals, the consumer movement is still a feeble force in American power politics. The interests of consumers are low on the list of election issues; the government's expenditures to protect those interests are negligible. Some would argue that this situation will inevitably prevail in view of the overwhelming power of American corporations in and out of government. But, as I have tried to show, new approaches to judging and influencing corporate behavior have begun to emerge in the last few years. It seems possible that people may begin to react with greater anger to the enormity of their deprivation. Each year consumers lose half a billion dollars in securities frauds and a billion dollars in home repair frauds, to name only two of thousands of ways in which their income is being milked. The current assault on the health and safety of the public from so many dangerous industrial products, byproducts, and foods has resulted in violence that dwarfs the issue of crime in the streets. (During the last three years, about 260 people have died in riots in American cities, but every two days, 300 people are killed, and 20,000 injured, while driving on the highways.) What the consumer movement is beginning to say and must say much more strongly if it is to grow is that business crime and corporate intransigence are the really urgent menace to law and order in America.

Notes

1. The last two chairmen of the Interstate Commerce Commission are now President of the National Association of Motor Business Carriers and Vice-President of Penn-Central. Both industries are supposedly regulated by the ICC.

2. The first appointee to this job was Mr. Merle McCurdy who died in May. His successor has not been appointed.

Keynote Address
Presented to the Consumer Assembly

Originally delivered November 2, 1967.

I'D LIKE TO DISCUSS very briefly this morning many themes in the hope that they can be elaborated and discussed not only through the remaining time of this Assembly's discussions but also that they will be carried through in the succeeding year and receive perhaps more emphatic treatment at future meetings.

The rhetoric of consumer protection in recent years has been as impressive as the reality of the consumer interest expendability. The thunderous acclaim for such legislation or pending legislation as the Truth-in-lending Bill, the Cigarette-labeling Law, the Truth-in-packaging Bill is not measured commensurately by the forcefulness of the legislation in fact. I sometimes think that industry is perfectly willing to trade off a particular name with a particular legislation such as Truth-in-lending in return for a very effectively gutting of its adequate provisions. The threat is very often not so much whether we have consumer-protection legislation but whether or not we have a law or a no-law law—a no-law law which simply deludes the consumer, deludes the public into thinking it receives a protection when in fact it is the industry which receives the protection by a bizarre, ironic twist.

The Cigarette-labeling Act is a perfect case study here. This act effectively excluded any action for five years by the states and cigarette-

252   THE RALPH NADER READER

protection legislation. It effectively excluded the Federal Trade Commission from any action. It effectively excluded any attendance to the problem of advertising in cigarettes. And it effectively provided a convenient defense in civil liability suits to the cigarette industry by requiring a warning on the package that it may be hazardous to health. This was a bill which the tobacco industry simply could not do without. And yet it was touted as a consumer-protection legislation.

I think that it is important to recognize that even when laws are passed that are adequately drafted the administration of these laws can effectively render them impotent. A good example here in terms of abundant author-ity and not so abundant administration and enforcement affects the Federal Trade Commission, which I think can be called the government's better business bureau with all that implies.

One of the sad by-products of the Federal Trade Commission's pro-nouncements and activites, with some outstanding exceptions, is that the Commission has perpetuated a myth over the years that deceiving the con-sumer or harming the consumer is primarily a fly-by-night phenomenon in terms of the fringe participants of American business that really isn't the mainstream of solid, upstanding businessmen—it is those near-bankrupt firms that are besmirching the reputation of American business in general.

I find this rather difficult to appreciate in the light of the facts. I don't think the packaging problem in this country just affects a few fringe mar-keteers. I don't think the credit practices in this country just affects a few corner pawn shops. I don't believe that the electric price-fixing conspiracy which bills the consumers to the tune of hundreds of millions of dollars over the three decades of the conspiracy ending in 1961 simply was a result of a few fly-by-night electric firms. I don't think the lack of safety in automo-biles is due to a few small garages who hand-make some hazardous auto-mobiles. I don't think the adverse effects of drugs and lack of testing them and the lack of adequate disclosure is due to makeshift pharmaceutical houses in the back of a large pharmacy or two. In effect, the problem of con-sumer protection is very much the problem of American business in gen-eral, very much the problem of the largest industry and the largest company, very much the problem of those who should be able to perform far better and far more responsibly than those fringe businesses who might be up against the wall in terms of their sheer economic survival.

A recent example here is the Greyhound Bus Company which has been routinely until very recently been using balled regrooved tires, regrooving them again and again leading to accidents in which people were killed and injured—leading to accidents whose investigations remain secret within our Department of Transportation because the motor carrier industry wrote that secrecy into legislation years ago—the kind of practices by Greyhound which have never received enforcement. You might be interested to know that the first enforcement process is now underway in New Jersey for a Greyhound accident involving regrooved tires. The maximum penalty on conviction is $500.

Now, are we dealing with a company—a small bus company—whose back is against the wall, and for sheer survival is trying to cut costs on tires? No. We are dealing with the largest bus company in the world—a bus company whose liquid capital is so embarrassingly ample that it owns outright 27 Boeing 707/727 planes which it leases to the airlines.

Another problem of the Federal Trade Commission as an example of the inadequate fulfillment of its authority comes in areas where there is absolutely no doubt, where there is absolutely no shades of judgment possible in terms of the course of action that should be pursued. For years, the odometers have been overregistered—that is they have been designed in a way to make you feel as if you are traveling more than you are. Now there is a far more than a mere psychological consequence to this rigging of a basic measurement device. When an odometer is rigged to the plus side, you tend in the aggregate to trade in your car faster. You think your car is a little older. Your warranty runs out in terms of mileage. You tend to pay more to a rent-car-company which, of course, collects on the mile. You also tend to think you are getting better gas mileage, which is something the auto companies want desperately to convey to their buying public. Yet this problem of odometer deception (which has been going on for years with the knowledge of the Federal Trade Commission) did not achieve attention until about 1964 when the National Bureau of Standards decided to rewrite the standard. Now, even though the standard was rewritten, odometers are still capable of being over-registered and still capable of meeting the new standard. But the important point in the history of the odometer is the statement finally conveyed by an old hand at the Federal Trade Commission, who when confronted with the suggestion that it was the National Bureau of Standards which took the initiative, not the Federal Trade Commission, blurted out, "That is utter nonsense. Why, we have been concerned with odometer problems since the Hoover administration."

Another problem dealing with laws, their adequacy in drafting and their administration and the responsibility of a consumer protection agency or department in government deals with the recent meat inspection contro-

254 THE RALPH NADER READER

versy. Here we have the Department of Agri Business, misnamed the Department of Agriculture, which—since Upton Sinclair wrote the book, "The Jungle" roughly sixty-one years ago, has had the responsibility to inspect meat packaging, meat processing, slaughter houses, the trade in interstate commerce. Unfortunately, over the years there has been a substantial traffic in intra-state meat shipment and at present 25% of all processed meat in this country does not cross state boundaries and therefore escapes the federal inspection service. This is 8 billion pounds a year.

Now, the surveys of the Department of Agriculture in 1962 on a state-by-state basis revealed what everybody in the industry knew all along but revealed it authoritatively—that there were three basic and endemic problems affecting the intra-state meat industry. The first was a kind of Gresham's law: believe it or not, bad meat is good business. And bad meat drives out good meat in some of these local markets. Bad meat meaning the 4-D animals: trafficking in dead, dying, diseased or disabled animals, where, for example, the cancerous portions of the cow are simply cut out and the rest of the carcass sent to market.

The second problem: unsanitary, grossly unsanitary, conditions in the meat-processing plant. The reports here are so nauseating and they are not made by layman, they are made by veterinarians or inspectors—the reports here are so nauseating on a state-by-state basis that nobody, I'd suggest nobody, could ever read them through at one sitting and remain with his equanimity. These descriptions reveal, for example, the prevalence of roaches, flies and rodents having free play of the meat-processing plant and finding their way off into the meat vats. The paint flakings from the ceilings dripping and dropping onto exposed food. There was some indication that some of these inspectors couldn't get close to the plants because of the overwhelming potency of the odor and sometimes they did get close enough but they couldn't talk clearly with the manager because of the flies that screened out his visibility.

The third problem deals with what do you do to make this product—this 4-D product—presentable to the consumer. Of course, here the wonders ingenious of modern chemistry come into play. A seasoning agent, preservatives and coloring agents do the job and the basic natural detection processes of the consumers are masked. He is no longer able to taste, smell or see diseased or contaminated meat. And he pays out his money accordingly. This problem was documented in 1962 and our friendly Department of Agriculture felt it was more important to protect the meat packing industry than to protect the consumer. So for five years they have sat on these reports—for five years they did nothing until there were hearings at the Congressional level and new reports were forthcoming to confirm the 1962 report.

With all of these problems, with all of these disclosures two days ago the House of Representatives by a vote of 140 to 98 passed a weak and meaningless meat inspection act as far as the control of intra-state plants is concerned. The alternative bill called the Smith-Foley Amendment would have brought roughly 98.5 percent of all the meat processing in the country under Federal inspection. That bill was defeated.

Now the interesting aspect presently of the situation is the immediate disclosure after the passage of the legislation that a large meat-packing trade association had recommended in a letter to its members in September that they contribute contributions to the political campaigns of friendly Congressmen—mind you, at the same time, these Congressmen were considering the meat inspection bill and its alternative—the recommendation was that the contributions be from $25 to $99. Ninety-nine dollars so that the individual contributors need not be disclosed. Now this situation was brought to the attention of the Chairman of the House Agriculture Committee who favored the weak bill. He immediately replied to the director of this trade association that it was a terrible thing to have done—it placed the meat industry in a potentially untenable situation, that it jeopardized the meat bill which the meat industry favored—in other words all his concern was directed towards the welfare of the meat industry and being able to escape Federal inspection of its intra-state activity.

Not a word in these letters, mind you, as to the welfare of the consumer. Not a word to the need to publicize this impropriety the moment it was located. In effect, the entire effort of some of these friendly Congressmen at the House Agriculture Committee was to sweep it under the rug, to squash it, to keep it from being disclosed so that nobody learned exactly what is going on.

It's time to look into this situation with a far greater degree of thoroughness. I think the report in today's *Minneapolis Tribune, Des Moines Register* by Nick Cotts, who has been covering this meat problem with great steadfastness and incisiveness, deserves the attention of Congress immediately. A Congressman who is not known to make very flippant and unsubstantiated remarks has said that he has never seen a bill where so much money was involved in the negotiation. I would think a Congressional investigation, particularly in the context of the campaign-financing reform that is now pending in Congress, would be well advised.

There are other aspects of the meat bill which I think give us good lessons to ponder. These are the kinds of lessons, incidentally, which are similar to the battles over here in water pollution, soil contamination, chemical and radiation hazards, inadequately tested and prescribed drugs and so forth. At first it is a misnomer to think that the meat problem is one of tiny, filthy meat-packing plants. Swift and Armour are involved here—they have plants which operate exclusively within state boundaries. Surveys of these plants have shown very substandard conditions and it's quite clear that Swift and Armour, as well as their smaller colleagues, have been engaging in marketing of meats which have no place in being sold to the American consumer.

Now, the role of the administration is interesting here as well. At the last hour the administration finally neutralized the Department of Agriculture, with no small achievement, and came out basically through its consumer office and Miss Furness with a stronger version of legislation. Now that is very encouraging, but obviously that is only the first step in the position which I think the administration should reflect. The administration should not only be on the record for consumer protection; it should be on the ramparts. It should not only give lip service. It should give muscle service. It often intrigues me why the administration is so successfully and powerfully lobbying for the supersonic transport, that great sensational mass alarm clock that is on the horizon, but can be so ineffective, so reticent and so inhibited when it is asked or expected to lobby for meat inspection laws and for auto safety appropriations, to give just two recent examples. It is encouraging that next year will be the first year that the Federal Government will spend more money on traffic safety than the safety of migratory birds. But I don't think it says much for our allocation of our resources in this land. Not when we can spend some $45 million next year for a problem that is killing 53 thousand Americans and injuring over 4 1/2 million at the same time that a nuclear submarine is costing $110 million. That's just one nuclear submarine.

It is time not just to give a serious look at the administration policy on consumer protection but to what extent it is going to really begin to effectively advocate it beyond rhetoric and to effectively reallocate some of our resources to this area. The legislation doesn't mean much if you don't have money to administer it with. For example, it is a reflection of a distorted sense of values when we can spend last year $150 million on highway beautification and about $10 million on highway safety. The presumption here against that kind of allocation of resources is that the best way to get more money for traffic safety is to see that the blood gets on the daisies.

In conclusion, there are two realizations that must be hammered home again and again in the communication process. First, it is necessary to stop concentrating exclusively on the syndromes of the consumer protection phenomena, and penetrate through to the more basic preconditions which give rise to the syndrome. One side of the coin may be consumer protection but the other side of the coin is inescapably corporate reform. It's important to go to the roots of the problem so we don't place ourselves in the situation of running around trying to plug the holes in the dike before it overflows. In catching these problems before they arise, the focus on corporate reform is a must. Corporations now should be required to meet much stiffer disclosure requirements. They should be required to tell specifically the safety performance of their products so that the marketplace can be put to work in a way which it will not perhaps fail.

It is an important distinction to make, that however much lip service corporations give to the free market, they are really more interested in the control market. If they were interested in the free market they would tell you the safety performance of their products, such as automobiles, so the consumer could go to the marketplace and compare make and model and make his choice on the basis of quality. In this way one could generate the feedback mechanism of the marketplace by rewarding good workmanship and penalizing shoddy workmanship. This kind of disclosure requirement really puts the market to work.

Another requirement is to beef up our sanction for corporate violation. We are reaching a point in this country where it is no longer possible to sweep under the rug the tremendously wide double standard operating between the penalties imposed on individual behavior and the penalties imposed on corporate behavior. Corporate behavior, more and more, is being immunized from legal accountability. You see the decline in criminal penalties and in some cases the actual abolition of criminal penalties in safety legislation for knowing and willful violation. Look at the disparity. A driver negligently driving down the highway kills an individual. He can be subjected to manslaughter charges and put in jail for negligence. But a manufacturer can willfully and knowingly leave a defective product on the market place in such a way that it can take human life. Under the new auto safety legislation, there is no criminal penalty whatsoever, only civil penalties—the kinds of penalties that don't penetrate the corporate framework to go to the culpable individuals at the locus of the problem. A perfect and recent example here is the Lake Central Airlines crash in March with thirty-eight people killed in a crash directly attributed to a soft piston problem with the propeller coming off and ripping into the fusselage. It so happens that Allison division of General Motors, which builds the engine and propeller, had known about this defect some time before the crash. Advising all operators to immediately ground this plane and disassemble it is the only conclusion that could be reached once a defect of that seriousness is located. Instead of doing this, they sent a vague advisory saying why don't you have an oil check to see if the oil's contaminated by metal filing. The doomed plane was given an oil check and the result was negative. And thirty-eight people died because the Allison Division was worried about its corporate image and was worried about facing up to this problem. The fine by the Federal Aviation Agency was $8,000.00, about $200.00 a head. Perhaps one must not be too harsh with the FA—they resisted General Motors pressure to reduce the fine to $4,000.00.

Research and development is another area where reform is crucial. It is no longer a luxury on the part of the large corporations, it is an absolute necessity: Simple inaction can bestow immense cruelty on the public welfare and safety. Simple inaction researching ways to clean up the internal combustion engine, or find an alternative, has resulted in a critical air pollution problem in our cities, inaction stemming back many, many years by industry leaders. The problem of research and development, the problem of requiring them to shoulder a responsible portion of this innovative input, is one that is on the first agenda.

A final area deals with standards, and this is probably the most important one. When safety bills are passed, when standards are set for products, they need to be set by government, not by private standards' groups, which have succeeded in insinuating into legislation their particular standards and codes. Government must make these standards, allowing democratic access to the administrative process on the part of both industry and public groups. This is an extremely critical problem. It is one which will be more critical the next year, as the United States Standards Institute of America begins its campaign to receive a congressional charter. They will take on the aura of a quasi-governmental agency and in effect begin to determine the level of standards of safety in products.

I don't want to end without making one comment on competition. I think the Assistant Attorney General, Mr. Turner, will make the point quite clear in a few hours. Competition is not out of date, it is still a very viable principle, however unviably it is enforced. The problem with competition and instilling a competitive flavor, even in the more concentrated industries, is that anti-trust enforcement has not been what it should be. In fact a recent commentator such as Professor Galbraith has begun to erect a theory of the American economy based on the failure of anti-trust. Instead of saying anti-trust hasn't failed *per se,* its enforcement or administration have failed. They are taking the failure as a fact of life—as an enduring fact of life—and building a new theory of oligopoly and concentration.

The recent disclosure that indeed the anti-trust division has done work on the possibilities of applying the Sherman Act to General Motors will have very salutary effects. Anti-trust should no longer be the exclusive province of a few justice department lawyers and a few house counsels for large companies. Anti-trust is intimately related to consumer protection. Anti-trust should be a discussion throughout America. The limitations of anti-trust should be known as well as the potential of anti-trust and the possibility of extending the grasp of the mechanism for competition by additional legislation. It is an eminently reasonable public issue to debate whether or not General Motors should be broken up. I think the concentration of power represented by a company that grosses $2.3 million an hour 24 hours a day, more than any other foreign government except Great Britain and the Soviet Union, that the concentration of economic and political power here is one which may clearly transcend the tolerance of a democratic society. The ability of General Motors for nearly twenty years to delay, thwart, and block efforts in California to develop cleaner internal combustion engines is an impressive example of how a corporation can block democratic process. Even against the second largest and now the largest state of the union, against the unity displayed by California, they have succeeded again and again in delaying reform measures until about two years ago. One of the reasons is the concentration of power here. Another reason is that there is no penalty for delay. There is no penalty for inaction. So I think looking at anti-trust and concentrated industry there should be an important program for any consumer body to consider. A Grand Jury in Los Angeles for the last year has been hearing evidence presented by the Justice Department that the auto industry has restrained the development and marketing of auto exhaust control devices. You see, anti-trust relates to the air we breathe, to the safety of the product we buy, to the quality, to its price. It not only deals with economic efficiency or the lack thereof—it deals with the security of life and limb.

I think a stake here in the whole consumer movement is not just the quality of the goods, not just honest pricing which of course improves our allocation of resources, but also in my judgment the most critical area of all—an area which might be termed as the area of bodily rights. The right of one's physiological integrity from being invaded, assaulted or destroyed by the harmful by-products of industrial products and processing.

We do have something to be encouraged by. Unlike prior eras in history,

we now have a technological period where we can actually program innovation in human welfare and safety. We can invent the technological future
if we will to do so. The vice president of Ford Motor Company, John O'Fry,
said of his industry that basically our engineers can do anything we want
them to do—they "can invent practically on demand." Now with an
increased capability like this, the ethical imperatives to act become all the
more insistent. What we should do proceeds from what we can do. As the
capability increases exponentially, so does our ethical requirement to follow
through.

It is a serious disservice to consumerism, if I may use a recent term
coined in a deprecatory manner by one of our large business executives last
year, to view the consumer movement as a threat to the private enterprise
economy or to big business. It is just the opposite. It is an attempt to preserve the enterprise economy by making the market work better. It is an
attempt to preserve the democratic control of technology by giving government a role in the decision-making process as to how much or how little safety products must contain. It is a new wave of the future, one that will
increase in scope, one that will go to the root of the corporate organization
of our economy, and one that will have a number of spin-offs in terms of
democratic evolution throughout our society. From the dimensions of the
legal profession to the role of professional societies to the role of the communications media, its impact will be felt. The upshot of consumer protection is to hold industry to higher standards of excellence. I can't see why
they should object to that kind of incentive. As it gains momentum, the
consumer movement will begin to narrow the gap between the performance
of American industry and commerce and its bright promise.

We're Still in the Jungle

Originally appeared in The New Republic, *July 15, 1967.*

BEFORE HE WAS ELECTED to the House of Representatives in 1958, farmer Neal Smith (D-Iowa) noticed something curious about the numerous livestock sales he attended. The same buyers seemed to be purchasing all the diseased, sick and maimed cattle and hogs. The destination of this miserable cargo was slaughterhouses not subject to federal inspection because the meat was sold only within the state. These meat-packing houses are outside the federal Meat Inspection Act of 1906. Since they do not have to incur the risk of having meat rejected by a federal inspector, the intrastate packing firms manage to outbid other potential buyers. Once in possession of these animals, they are free, as Rep. Smith points out, to cut the eye out of the cancer-eyed cow and send the rest of the carcass through the stream of commerce on its way to the dinner table.

Since 1961, Smith has been trying vainly to secure passage of strong amendments to the Meat Inspection Act—a law which has not been amended substantively since its enactment 61 years ago following publication of Upton Sinclair's *The Jungle*. The proposed amendments would extend federal jurisdiction to all packing and processing companies operating intrastate but deemed to affect interstate commerce, as well as close glaring gaps which have absolved unscrupulous operators from legal sanctions. Until last month, Smith's bill was not even accorded a subcommittee hearing.

About 15 percent of the commercially slaughtered animals (19 million head) and 25 percent of commercially processed meat products in the US— enough meat for 30 million people a year—are not covered by adequate inspection laws. According to the Department of Agriculture, significant portions of this meat are diseased and are processed in grossly unsanitary conditions, and its true condition is masked by the latest preservatives, additives and coloring agents.

Even in federally inspected plants, management is reluctant to resist the temptation of keeping costs down by keeping revolting meats on the sales shelf. In one year, the Department of Agriculture reported that its inspectors condemned over 22 million pounds of meat as tainted, rancid, moldy, odorous, unclean or contaminated. And consumers of meat sold *intrastate* have not been fortunate enough to have any such screening procedure by public specialists. Contaminated meat, horsemeat and meat from sick animals originally intended for dog and cat food has ended up in hamburger and processed meat. Eyeballs, lungs, hog blood and chopped hides and other indelicate carcass portions are blended skillfully into baloney and hot dogs. Hamburger embalmed with sulfite—a federally banned additive that gives old meat a deceptively bright pink color, abounds. One New York state survey found sulfite in 26 out of 30 hamburger samples.

A New York state official estimated that 90 percent of the uninspected processed meat sold in the state is deceptively labeled. Those big hams that you buy have 10 to 30 percent of their weight in water pumped into their veins at the supermarket's back room, meat is doped with Aureomycin as a substitute for sanitation, and detergents are applied to freshen up unfit meat. So the NY finding is not surprising.

It would be misleading to compare such intrastate operations today with those conditions prevailing at the turn of the century: As far as impact on human health is concerned, the likelihood is that the current situation is worse! The foul spectacle of packing houses in that earlier period has given way to more tolerable working conditions, but the callous misuse of new technology and processes has enabled today's meat handlers to achieve marketing levels beyond the dreams of their predecessors' avarice. It took some doing to cover up meat from tubercular cows, lump-jawed steers and scabby pigs in the old days. Now the wonders of chemistry and quick-freezing techniques provide the cosmetics of camouflaging the product and deceiving the eyes, nostrils and taste buds of the consumer. It takes specialists to detect the deception. What is more, these chemicals themselves introduce new and complicated hazards unheard of 60 years ago.

With conditions worsening year after year, the Department of Agriculture finally moved itself to dispatch a fact-gathering mission on intrastate meat slaughtering and processing operations. (There are 2,500 slaughterhouses and many thousands of meat processors operating solely within state borders.) The report, prepared by Dr. M. R. Clarkson, came in two portions. The public portion was presented in 1963 to a House appropriations subcommittee, while the nonpublic portion—said to be filled with sickening pictures, affidavits and other documentation—remains inaccessible in the department's files. Dr. Clarkson's public findings, however, were jolting enough without the pictorial assists. He criticized packers and processors for:

+ "allowing edible portions of carcasses to come in contact with manure, pus and other sources of contamination during the dressing operations;

+ "allowing meat food products during preparation to become contaminated with filth from improperly cleaned equipment and facilities;

+ "use of chemical additives and preservatives that would not have been permitted under federal meat inspection;

+ "failing to use procedures to detect or control parasites transmitted to man that could lead to diseases such as trichinosis and cysticercosis;

+ "inadequate controls to prevent possible adulteration of meat food products during their preparation with substitutes such as water, gum, cereals or sodium caseinate;

+ "use of false or deceptive labels on packaging;

+ "failure to supervise destruction of obviously diseased tissues and spoiled, putrid and filthy materials."

The Clarkson report fell upon the states with all the force of a helium balloon. Only forty-one states have any form of law at all related to meat inspection. Of these, twenty-six provide for mandatory inspection of animals before and after slaughter; the rest have voluntary programs. Twenty-five states provide for mandatory inspection of processed meat products. The legal authority on paper is weak enough, but its efficacy deteriorates to

near futility because of grossly inadequate enforcement funds, personnel
and laboratory facilities and the omnipresent pressure of local packing and
processing firms. Many of these firms are substantial business operations.
Year after year, attempts to obtain bigger state legislative appropriations are
tabled or defeated.

Probably the most effective restraint working to shield these packers
and processors from inspection and safety standards is their common
interest with both state departments of agriculture and the U.S.
Department of Agriculture in promoting the sale of meat products.
Promotion is the categorical imperative animating these governmental
agencies entrusted with the mission of insuring the safety of meat products. Despite the devastating evidence in its files, the U.S. Department of
Agriculture adheres in its policymaking to the avoidance of unfavorable
publicity about meat products as the first priority. Consequently, years
have passed without congressional hearings when all the department had
to do was to request them.

Finally, late last month, chiefly through Rep. Smith's urgings, the livestock and grains subcommittee of the House Committee on Agriculture
opened hearings on bills to update and strengthen the Meat Inspection Act.
The Administration's bill, HR 6168, is a pathetic response to the needs of
effective regulation. The department's witness, Rodney E. Leonard, took
note of the hazards of "fast-curing processes, artificial tenderizing, artificial
smoking, coloring agents and other additives that are potentially deceptive
or dangerous to one's health." He added that there "are many opportunities
for illegitimate operators to introduce into human food channels meat
derived from dead, dying, disabled and diseased animals—commonly
referred to as '4-D's'." Then he came up with the department's proposal—
federal technical and financial assistance to the states if they desire to
toughen their laws! If a state chooses to remain indifferent to its responsibilities, as there is every indication to believe will occur, the federal government remains powerless. (HR 6168 would eliminate some deficiencies
in federal meat inspection authority but then proceeds to reduce the penalties for knowing violations from the 1906 Act's levels.)

Even such a weak legislative offering is too strong medicine for the states.
The National Association of State Agriculture Departments is scheduled
to appear at the resumption of the House hearings on July 17 with a number of amendments designed to turn the bill into a nullity. If anything
remains of the bill, the Independent Meat Packers Association will tell the
subcommittee how to finish it off.

The administration's position on this entire matter is not being helped by the Department of Agriculture's determination to take over the Food and Drug Administration's powers over unsafe meat, principally seizure authority. The department's conflict of interest between its promotional and safety responsibilities does not merit such presumptuous preemption; nor does the department's record of indifference to the effect of drugs, including antibiotics, in animal and poultry feeds on human health.

The Department of Agriculture's laggard response to the intrastate contaminated poultry problem since enactment of the Poultry Products Inspection Act in 1957 further weakens confidence. A recent study, assisted by the National Institutes of Health, revealed that out of 2,057 samples of poultry taken from two representative plants, 11.2 percent contained the salmonella organisms. (The incidence of salmonellosis has increased sharply in the past 20 years.) The uninspected plant contributed a salmonella rate triple that of the federally inspected plant. The rapid growth of new frozen food products and "ready to serve" dishes that are eaten following short cooking periods are increasing the danger of trichinosis and other bacterial diseases. This trend is alarming scientists at various universities. Yet the department, apart from grudging recognition of the problem, does not rise to the challenge because of an aversion to unfavorable publicity for its clientele.

When Upton Sinclair's book came out on January 25, 1906, it was front-page news from coast to coast. Theodore Roosevelt wired the young author to visit him at the White House to discuss the problem. Now, with many more threats to consumers contained in the combination of old vices with new technology, the great hush-hush is the order of the day. Perhaps, Upton Sinclair, who at age 88 lives just outside of Washington, is needed once again to tell the Congress that the Jungle is still with us.

The *Safe* Car You Can't Buy

Originally appeared in The Nation, *April 11, 1959.*

T HE CORNELL Aeronautical Laboratory has developed an exhibition automobile embodying over sixty new safety concepts which would enable an occupant to withstand a head-on collision at 50 mph with at most only minor scratches. In its design, six basic principles of crash protection were followed:

1. The car body was strengthened to prevent most external blows from distorting it against the passengers.

2. Doors were secured so that crash impacts could not open them, thereby saving passengers from ejection and maintaining the structural strength of the side of the car body.

3. Occupants were secured to prevent them from striking objects inside the car.

4. Interior knobs, projections, sharp edges and hard surfaces have been removed and the ceiling shaped to produce only glancing blows to the head (the most vulnerable part of the body during a crash).

5. The driver's environment was improved to reduce accident risk by

increasing visibility, simplifying controls and instruments, and lowering the carbon monoxide of his breathing atmosphere.

6. For pedestrian safety, dangerous objects like hood ornaments were removed from the exterior.

This experimental car, developed with funds representing only a tiny fraction of the annual advertising budget of, say, Buick, is packed with applications of simple yet effective safety factors. In the wraparound bumper system, for instance, plastic foam material between the front and rear bumpers and the back-up plates absorbs some of the shock energy; the bumpers are smoothly shaped to convert an increased proportion of blows from direct to glancing ones; the side bumpers are firmly attached to the frame, which has been extended and reinforced to provide support. Another feature is the installment of two roll-over bars into the top of the car body as added support.

IT IS CLEAR THAT Detroit today is designing automobiles for style, cost, performance, and calculated obsolescence, but not—despite the 5,000,000 reported accidents, nearly 40,000 fatalities, 110,000 permanent disabilities and 1,500,000 injuries yearly—for safety.

Almost no feature of the interior design of our current cars provides safeguards against injury in the event of collision. Doors that fly open on impact, inadequately secured seats, the sharp-edged rearview mirror, pointed knobs on instrument panel and doors, flying glass, the overhead structure—all illustrate the lethal potential of poor design. A sudden deceleration turns a collapsed steering wheel or a sharp-edged dashboard into a bone- and chest-crushing agent. Penetration of the shatterproof windshield can chisel one's head into fractions. A flying seat cushion can cause a fatal injury. The apparently harmless glove-compartment door has been known to unlatch under impact and guillotine a child. Roof-supporting structure has deteriorated to a point where it provides scarcely more protection to the occupants, in common roll-over accidents, than an open convertible. This is especially true of the so-called "hardtops." Nor is the automobile designed as an efficient force moderator. For example, the bumper does not contribute significantly to reduction of the crash deceleration forces that are transmitted to the motorist; its function has been more to reflect style than absorb shock.

These weaknesses of modern automobile construction have been established by the investigation of several groups, including the Automotive Crash Injury Research of the Cornell University Medical College, the Institute of Transportation and Traffic Engineering of the University of

California and the Motor Vehicle Research of Lee, New Hampshire. Careful coverage of all available reports does not reveal a single dissent from these findings:

1. There are direct causal relationships between automotive design and the frequency, type and severity of injuries.

2. Studies of body tolerances to abrupt deceleration show that the forces in most accidents now fatal are well within the physiological limits of survival under proper conditions.

3. Engineering improvement in safety design and restraining devices would materially reduce the injury and fatality rate (estimates range from twenty to thirty thousand lives saved annually).

4. Redesign of injury-causing automotive components is well within the capabilities of present engineering technique and would require no radical changes in present styling.

5. Many design improvements have already been developed but are not in production.

THE REMARKABLE ADVANCES in crash-protection knowledge achieved by these research organizations at a cost of some $6 million stands in marked contrast to the glacier-like movements of car manufacturers, who spend that much to enrich the sound of a door slam. This is not due to any dearth of skill—the industry possesses many able, frustrated safety engineers whose suggestions over the years invariably have taken a back seat to those of the stylist. In 1938, an expert had this to say in *Safety Engineering*:

> The motor industry must face the fact that accidents occur. It is their duty, therefore, to so design the interiors of automobiles that when the passenger is tossed around, he will get an even break and not suffer a preventable injury in accidents that today are taking a heavy toll.

In 1954, nearly 600,000 fatalities later, a U.C.L.A. engineer could conclude that "There has been no significant automotive-engineering contribution to the safety of motorists since about the beginning of World War II. . . ." In its 1955 annual report, the Cornell crash-research group came to a similar conclusion, adding that "the newer model automobiles [1950–54] are increasing the rate of fatalities in injury-producing accidents."

In 1956, Ford introduced the double-grip safety-door latch, the "dished" steering wheel, and instrument panel-padding; the rest of the industry followed with something less than enthusiasm. Even in these changes, style remained the dominant consideration, and their effectiveness is in doubt. Tests have failed to establish, for example, an advantage for the "deep-dish" steering wheel compared with the conventional wheel; the motorist will still collapse the rim to the hub.

This year, these small concessions to safety design have virtually been discontinued. "A square foot of chrome sells ten times more cars than the best safety-door latch," declared one industry representative. Dashboard padding remains one of a few safety accessories available as optional equipment. This is like saying to the consumer: "Here's a hot car. Now, if you wish to be safe in it, you'll have to pay more."

None of this should be construed as placing the increasingly popular mites from abroad in a more favorable light. Most foreign cars offer far less protection to the motorist than domestic ones.

PREVAILING ANALYSES OF vehicular accidents circulated for popular consumption tend to impede constructive thinking by adherence to some monistic theory of causation. Take one of the more publicized ogres—speed. Cornell's findings, based on data covering 3,203 cars in injury-producing accidents, indicate that 74 percent of the cars were going at a *traveling* speed under 60 mph and about 88 percent involved *impact* speeds under 60 mph. The average impact speed on urban roads was 27 mph; on rural roads, 41 mph. Dangerous or fatal injuries observed in accidents when the traveling speed was less than 60 mph are influenced far more by the shape and structure of interior car components with which the body came into contact than by the speed at which the cars were moving. Many fatalities have been recorded which occurred in panic stops or collisions at a speed under 25 mph. Cornell's concluding statement:

> Statistical tests indicated that even if a top speed limit of 60 mph could be uniformly and absolutely maintained, 73 percent of the dangerous and fatal injuries observed would still be expected to occur. . . . the control of speed alone would have only limited effect on the frequency of dangerous and fatal injuries.

In brief, automobiles are so designed as to be dangerous at any speed.

Our preoccupation has been almost entirely with the cause of accidents seen primarily in terms of the driver and not with the instruments that produce the injuries. Erratic driving will always be characteristic, to some degree, of the traffic scene; exhortation and stricter law enforcement have at best a limited effect. Much more significant for saving life is the application of engineering remedies to minimize the lethal effects of human error by designing the automobile so as to afford maximum protection to occupants in the event of a collision. In a word, the job, in part, is to make accidents safe.

THE TASK OF PUBLICIZING the relation between automotive design and highway casualties is fraught with difficulties. The press, radio and television are not likely to undertake this task in terms of industry responsibility when millions in advertising dollars are being poured into their coffers. Private researchers are reluctant to stray from their scholarly and experimental pursuits, especially when cordial relations with the industry are necessary for the continuation of their projects with the maximum of success. Car manufacturers have thought it best to cooperate with some of these programs and, in one case, when findings became embarrassing, have given financial support. The industry's policy is bearing fruit; most investigators discreetly keep their private disgust with the industry's immobility from seeping into the public limelight. They consider themselves fact-finders and leave the value judgments to others. This adherence to a rigid division of labor provides a convenient rationalization for the widespread amorality among our scholarly elite, who appear insensitive to the increased responsibility as citizens which their superior knowledge should require them to shoulder.

For the past three years, a Special Congressional House Subcommittee on Traffic Safety has been conducting extensive hearings on automobile design. The industry and research organizations have all submitted their testimony and reports. Some revealing facts came out of these hearings, but the press, by and large, has chosen to ignore them. In any case, the subcommittee is proceeding too cautiously for so urgent a matter. It has been too solicitous of recommendations for delay advanced by some academicians who see automotive design from the viewpoint of engineering perfection rather than as a national health emergency requiring immediate, even if not perfect, engineering remedy. Better techniques will be developed, but at least for the present, there will be added protection from remedying known design hazards. This has been the point that many safety engineers and physicians have vainly been urging.

Even if all the facts, laid before the public, did not increase consumer demand for safety design (which is unlikely), the manufacturers should not be relieved of their responsibility. Innumerable precedents show that the consumer must be protected at times from his own indiscretion and vanity. Dangerous drugs cannot be dispensed without a licensed physician's prescription; meat must pass federal inspection before distribution; railroads and other interstate carriers are required to meet safety standards regarding their equipment.

State motor-vehicle codes set minimum standards for certain vehicular equipment. This legislation has not compelled manufacturers to adopt known safety-design features (with the exception of safety glass), but has merely endorsed previous standards long employed by the car producers. Examples: brake requirements, headlight specifications, horns, mufflers, windshield wipers, rear-view mirrors. Thus the impact of these requirements falls primarily on the operator, who has to keep this equipment functioning. The legislative purpose is directed to accident *prevention* and only peripherally to implementing standards that might *prevent injuries*.

But state laws do not begin to cope with design defects of the postwar car which increase the *risk of collision*. Examples: the terrific visual distortion of the wrap-around windshield; leakage of carbon monoxide; rear-end fishtailing in hard turns; undue brake fade and the decreased braking area of the recent fourteen-inch wheel; the tinted windshield condemned as violative of all basic optical principles to the extent that visual loss at night ranges from 15 percent to 45 percent; and the fire hazard of the undercoating and some upholstery.

Motor vehicles have been found to be poorly designed with regard to human capacities and limitations both physical and psychological. For example, there are—especially in truck cabs—unnecessary difficulties in reaching and operating control levers, in reading half-hidden dials and gauges; there are seats that induce poor posture or discomfort, mirrors whose poor placement and size impair vision, visors inadequately shielding eyes from bright light, and uncomfortable temperature, humidity and noise levels. The cumulative effects lead to fatigue, deterioration of driving efficiency and reaction time, and frequently to an accident which cannot be attributed, in the light of such poor design, to the driver.

Recourse to the courts for judgment against a manufacturer by a plaintiff injured by the defective interior design of his car while involved in an accident stands a dim chance of success. While the courts have hung liability on manufacturers for injuries due to defectively designed products, the closest they have come in motor-vehicle cases has been to hold the producer liable for a design defect instrumental in causing the accident, e.g., the braking system. The question of automotive death-traps cannot be dealt with adequately by the limited authority and resources of the judiciary, although a few pertinent decisions would have a salutary effect.

By all relevant criteria, a problem so national in scope and technical in nature can best be handled by the legislative process, on the federal level, with delegation to an appropriate administrative body. It requires uniformity in treatment and central administration, for as an interstate matter, the job cannot be left to the states with their dissimilar laws setting low requirements that are not strictly enforced and that do not strike at the heart of the malady—the blueprint on the Detroit drawing board. The thirty-three-year record of the attempt to introduce state uniformity in establishing the most basic equipment standards for automobiles has been disappointing.

Perhaps the best summation of the whole issue lies in a physician's comment on the car manufacturer's design policy: "Translated into medicine," he writes, "it would be comparable to withholding known methods of life-saving value."

on tort reform

Ralph Nader on Tort Reform

Originally appeared in Legal Times, 1995.

U.S. CORPORATIONS have been duplicitous in their aggressive drive to duck responsibility for dangerous products. The same profitable companies that have told Congress and the media that the product liability "explosion" is driving their business out of business have reported something quite different to investors and the Securities and Exchange Commission. Time after time, the same companies report in their SEC filings that liability exposure poses no material threat to their bottom line.

Executives of the following corporations, for example, have publicly protested the prohibitive cost of product liability, even though the financial reports that their companies file tell another story.

Dow Chemical Co. and Corning Inc.: "Perhaps my biggest frustration is the area of product liability and tort reform," said Frank Popoff, chair and CEO of Dow Chemical, in 1992. "Our uniquely American legal system imposes an annual tax, if I may call it that, of $150 billion to $200 billion on all our industries because of the problem. I think it's a killer for our global competitiveness." (*Chemical Business,* September 1992.)

Apart from the absence of any substantiation for this outlandish estimate, the company's 10-K report to investors for the calendar year 1994 also fails to support its CEO's contention. Liability claims against Dow Chemical for such products as the drug Seldane (produced by subsidiary Marion Merrell Dow Inc.) and silicone breast implants are not seen as significant, according to the SEC filing. "It is the opinion of the company's management that the possibility that litigation of these claims would materially impact the company's consolidated financial statements is remote."

Dow Chemical and Corning are each 50-percent shareholders in the Dow Corning Corp., a leading defendant in the widespread silicone breast implant litigation. Like Dow Chemical, Corning tells investors not to be put off by this and other litigation. "There are no pending legal proceedings to which Corning or any of its subsidiaries is a party or of which any of their property is the subject which are material in relation to the annual consolidated financial statements," says its 10-K filed March 21, 1995.

Monsanto Co.: Out-of-control product liability litigation "clogs our courts, curtails American innovation and creativity, drives up the costs of consumer products, and prevents some valuable products and services from ever coming to market," David S.J. Brown, Monsanto vice president for government affairs, said in a news release. (PR Newswire, Feb. 23, 1995.) "The numbers are in the stratosphere," griped Monsanto CEO Richard Mahoney, referring to jury awards in product liability cases. (*Business Week*, Jan. 9, 1995.)

But if Monsanto's product liability costs are in the "stratosphere," its profits are much further out in orbit. "Because of the size and nature of its business, Monsanto is a party to numerous legal proceedings," the company's 10-K for the period ending Dec. 31, 1993, says. "While the results of litigation cannot be predicted with certainty, Monsanto does not believe these matters or their ultimate disposition will have a material adverse effect on Monsanto's financial position."

Cessna Aircraft Co. and Textron Inc.: Russell Meyer Jr., chair and CEO of Cessna Aircraft, testified before a Senate subcommittee in May 1994 that the general aviation aircraft industry "has been essentially destroyed by the unlimited cost of product liability."

But Cessna's parent company, Textron, reports clear skies ahead for the company in its 10-K filed for the year ending Jan. 1, 1994. "On the basis of information presently available," the report says, "Textron believes that any liability for the suits and proceedings mentioned above, or the impact of the application of relevant government regulations, would not have a material effect on Textron's net income or financial condition."

Pfizer Inc.: Pfizer retained Philip Lacovara of the New York law firm Hughes Hubbard & Reed to draft legislation that could dramatically reduce

Pfizer's liability exposure. "If you assume an American company and a German company are making a similar product that is sold in France, only the U.S. company has to factor in the high cost of liability litigation," Lacovara told *Legal Times* in 1988. ("Lacovara's Risky Cure for Pfizer's Heartburn," April 4, 1988, Page 1.) "As a result, the American firm is at a competitive disadvantage in the foreign market."

Apparently, Lacovara was not reading his client's SEC submissions. As Legal Times observed, Pfizer's SEC filing at the time undercut this argument. "International sales were significantly higher than the year before, whereas U.S. sales remained flat," the article said.

The company's 10-K covering the period ending Dec. 31, 1994, informs investors, "The Company is involved in a number of claims and litigations, including product liability claims." But the reassuring report says that this is "considered normal in the nature of its businesses." The 10-K concludes: "The Company is of the opinion that these actions should not have a material adverse effect on the financial position or the results of operations of the Company."

TRW Inc.: "The current U.S. product liability tort system . . . has imposed a significant burden on manufacturers' ability to design, produce, and market products," said Edsel Dunford, then executive vice president and chief operating officer of TRW. (*Aviation Week and Space Technology*, Aug. 24, 1992.) TRW's annual report covering the calendar year 1994, however, makes no mention of any product liability suits facing the company and assures investors that no litigation against TRW will have an adverse material effect on the company's performance.

Upjohn Co.: Though applauding the United States as "the last bastion of free-market pharmaceutical pricing," Ley Smith, then vice chair and now chair and chief operating officer of Upjohn, said that the United States suffers from "enormous product liability awards." (Chemical Week, March 3, 1993.)

None of these awards, however, seemed to interfere with his company's ability to turn a profit. Although the company cannot predict the outcome of individual lawsuits, Upjohn's most recent 10-K, covering the period ending Dec. 31, 1994, says, "[T]he ultimate liability should not have a material effect on [the company's] consolidated financial position; and unless there is a significant deviation from the historical pattern of resolution of such issues, the ultimate liability should not have a material adverse effect on the company's results of operations or liquidity."

Coleman Co.: The failure to ease U.S. product liability laws "places American companies at a substantial disadvantage," said Larry Sanford, executive vice president of the Coleman Co. unit of MacAndrews & Forbes Holdings Inc. (*Business Week,* Jan. 9, 1995.)

If Sanford was basing his view on his own company's experience, he may possibly have been referring to some very recent development, since Coleman's 10-K for the period ending Dec. 31, 1993, says, "The Company does not believe that the ultimate conclusion of the various pending product liability claims and lawsuits covered under these insurance policies will have a material adverse effect on the financial position or results of operations of the Company."

Cooper Industries Inc.: Alan Riedel, then senior vice president for administration of Cooper Industries, derided what he called "a tort system gone berserk." (*Institutional Investor,* August 1988.) Riedel's company has done its part to bend this tort system to its will. Cooper Industries, which produces heavy equipment and tools, runs a foundation that donated $50,000 to the pro-business Manhattan Institute to make a video promoting industry's anti-tort law agenda. A businessman who recounts his liability horror story on the video runs a Cooper subsidiary, a detail that the video fails to disclose. (*The Washington Post,* Sept. 14, 1992.)

Despite working under a tort system that has "gone berserk," however, Cooper Industries assured investors in its 10-K filed for the 1994 calendar year that "management is of the opinion" that any pending product liability legislation "should not have a material adverse effect on the Company's financial position."

Many of the biggest U.S. corporations work through trade groups, such as the Product Liability Coordinating Committee, to advance their goal of depriving victims of any legal recourse against dangerous products. The PLCC is chaired by David S.J. Brown, the vice president of government affairs at Monsanto.

Another trade group leading the charge to roll back product liability is the Pharmaceutical Research and Manufacturers of America. To hear its spokesperson, Steve Berchem, tell it, there may not be a pharmaceutical industry in the United States soon: "It gets to be so expensive to defend yourself," Berchem said, "that you say, 'Forget it. We'll just get out of the business.' " (*Newsday,* Feb. 26, 1995.)

Despite this bluster, few major players in the pharmaceutical industry are seriously considering abandoning their lucrative business. The industry enjoyed profits of $12.3 billion in 1994, a rise of 29 percent above its high profits of 1993.

These companies and their trade associations grossly exaggerate product liability costs in their presentations to Congress and to the public in order to advance their agenda of rolling back liability for and records disclosure of their dangerous products. Yet their official financial statements filed with the SEC and distributed to investors disclaim any adverse material effects of product liability on the bottom line.

Also disclosed at the SEC and in other reports are data that provide another framework of comparison. The CEO of the giant AIG Inc. insurance company, for example, made $250,000 a week in 1994, while lobbyists for his industry are pushing for a cap of $250,000 for a lifetime of pain and suffering by a victim of major medical malpractice.

What is going on in industry and on Capitol Hill invites serious contemplation. Elected officials have a duty to see through these transparent deceptions and to vote against weakening product liability standards. Experience has shown that this is the best way to minimize the size of the next generation of victims of dangerous and faulty products.

Tort 'Reform' Would Aid Wrongdoers

Originally appeared in the San Francisco Examiner, *April 21, 1995.*

W HEN MEMBERS of Congress return from their spring break, they will begin deliberations on legislation designed to limit the rights of judges and juries to punish corporate and individual wrongdoers.

The attacks on the powers of judges and juries have no foundation. There is no evidence that judges and juries are out of control.

There is no evidence that judges and juries are unjustly punishing wrongdoers and unfairly rewarding people injured by defective products or practices.

And, there is no evidence supporting the notion that Congress should preempt state law. Alas, the debate about civil litigation is not based on facts but is being driven by misleading anecdotes packaged by the wrongdoers' lobby and repeated by a handful of misguided or unscrupulous elected officials.

Unfortunately, if the wrongdoers' lobby prevails, the local control that judges and juries have had over wrongdoers will be severely limited.

Now is the time to contact your U.S. senators and ask them if they are planning to advance the corporate wrongdoers agenda, limit the powers of local judges and juries, and cut off the rights that injured parties have in state courts.

Keep the following points in mind when you contact your senators:

+ There aren't too many lawsuits. According to the Rand Institute, only about 10 percent of those injured by a defective product file a claim for compensation. Moreover, according to the National Center on State Courts, the number of tort cases since 1990 has decreased by 2 percent.

+ Product liability suits are not wrecking the economy. Product liability insurance costs amount to a quarter of a penny on every dollar purchase. All product liability verdicts and settlements, federal and state, average less than $3 billion a year—less than the amount Americans spend on dog food each year.

+ Plaintiffs don't have an easy time winning a suit. Between 1987 and 1993, a plaintiff's chance of winning a product liability lawsuit dropped from 59 percent to 41 percent.

+ Punitive damage awards are not out of control. Between 1965 and 1990, only 355 punitive damage awards were made in state and federal product liability cases. Of this total, ninety-one punitive damage awards involved asbestos cases. This means that on average, there were only about eleven punitive damage awards a year in this time period.

+ "Joint and several liability" is rarely used against deep-pocket corporate defendants unless the corporate defendant is partly responsible for the victim's injury. Joint and several liability can only be applied to a defendant if the defendant's actions caused the entire injury or were an essential factor in causing the injury.

Before your senators vote on tort reform, they should know the facts and know what the impact of changing these laws will be on the victims of the wrongdoer's lobby.

In testimony before the Senate, Professors Nicholas Ashford and Robert Stone of the Massachusetts Institute of Technology said that tort liability promotes safety and health, encourages safer innovation and discourages unsafe innovations.

They also noted that strengthening liability laws would produce safer products and workplaces, and would encourage more socially desirable innovation.

Tell your senators that downgrading the rights of injured consumers to receive fair compensation for injuries caused by dangerous products is bad for our civil justice system, it is bad for consumers and it is bad for taxpayers.

Less deterrence will mean more injuries, more uncompensated victims and greater overall costs to society.

The horrors that countless victims live with as a result of asbestos-related disease, or dangerous products such as the Dalkon Shield, illustrate the need for a stronger, not weaker, civil justice system.

The Assault on Injured Victims' Rights

Originally appeared in the Denver University Law Review:
Tort Reform Symposium Issue, Vol. 64, No. 4, 1988.

Introduction

IT IS DOUBTFUL whether there has been anything like the present attack on injured victims' rights in the two hundred year history of the American civil justice system. During the 1986 state legislative session, forty-one states passed legislation to restrict the rights of innocent victims to sue, and to be fully compensated for their injuries. In a few states, legislatures enacted across-the-board tort law changes overturning state common law which for generations had afforded harmed citizens a means of challenging injustice and negligence.[1]

Insurance industry advertisements suggest that recent tort legislation is the necessary consequence of an unrestrained jury system—"exorbitant awards and unpredictable results"[2] which are not only crippling the insurance industry,[3] but are, in the words of the insurance industry's most powerful ally President Ronald Reagan, "eating away at the fabric of American life."[4]

In almost every state, as well as in Congress, proposals abound to restrict the rights of innocent victims to sue and to recover for their injuries. These restrictions include: arbitrary caps on "pain and suffering" awards;[5] limitations on, or elimination, of punitive damage awards, which often serve as the only effective deterrent against intentionally unsafe practices;[6] mandatory limits on contingency fees for plaintiff lawyers, without corresponding limitations on the fees of defense lawyers;[7] modification or elimination of joint and several liability, which results in penalizing the victim by precluding full recovery in the event a culpable party is unable to pay;[8] restrictions on lump sum payments;[9] repeal of the collateral source rule;[10] and relaxed liability standards, such as elimination of strict liability in product liability actions.[11]

These measures are aimed at weakening the American civil justice system which, for all its embrace of noble concepts of justice, still confronts injured people with the difficult task of prevailing in court before they may recover any compensation. Surveys indicate that these measures are not supported by the American people.[12] Rather, they are part of a legislative package advocated by various special interest groups: the property/casualty insurance industry—seeking to enrich its already large profits at the expense of innocent victims; the business and professional defendants' lobbies—seeking to immunize from suit the manufacturers of hazardous goods and toxic chemicals; and the Reagan administration—pushing to federally regulate downward the decentralized state judicial system that has provided injured victims with access to justice for over 200 years. They call this package "tort reform," but it is one of the most unprincipled public relations scams in the history of American industry.

I. The "Insurance Crisis" Myth

The "insurance crisis" has little to do with lawsuits, but everything to do with a cyclical trend in the insurance industry. This "crisis" is a self-inflicted phenomenon which last occurred in the mid-seventies, and which invariably provokes frenetic talk of a litigation explosion and calls for legislative limits on victims' rights.[13] The last cycle began several years ago when interest rates were relatively high. Capitalizing on higher interest rates, the industry lowered prices and insured poor risks in order to obtain premium dollars which were then invested for maximum return.[14] When interest rates dropped, and investment income decreased accordingly, the industry responded by sharply increasing insurance premiums and reducing the availability of coverage—a repeat of their similarly mismanaged performance of the mid-seventies. In fact, in all the controversy, there is remarkable agreement about the causes of the insurance industry's problems.[15] A January 1987 editorial in *Business Week* may have said it best in concluding that:

> Even while the industry was blaming its troubles on the tort system, many experts pointed out that its problems were largely self-made. In previous years the industry had slashed prices competitively to the point that it incurred enormous losses. That, rather than excessive jury awards, explained most of the industry's financial difficulties.[16]

Even through the most recent downturn the industry continued to make money. Their profits are now soaring.[17] Insurance company stocks are booming on the New York Stock Exchange, and investment analysts and brokers recommend casualty insurance stock for investment.[18]

Coming out of their bottom year of 1984, the insurance industry, in conjunction with their foreign reinsurers,[19] saw a great opportunity to limit their own future payout obligations by exploiting the business community's natural eagerness for additional limitations on liability from lawsuits. So they began dramatically increasing premiums and reducing coverage, and arbitrarily cancelling policies of daycare centers, small businesses, and local governments.[20]

When businesses, professionals and governmental entities protested, the insurers proclaimed, "Don't look at us. It's those courts, those juries, those verdicts, those lawyers." And instead of saying, "Well, can you *prove* that?", these frustrated groups blindly accepted their insurers' rationale, and joined in lockstep with them to forge a powerful new lobby designed to fight for measures which would further limit their own liability for the damage they caused innocent victims.[21]

Aimed in the direction of Congress and the state legislatures, this coalition of insurance companies and corporate defense lobbies has relied on misinformation and anecdotal cases[22] to attack and destroy decades of slow but careful progress made by state court after state court respecting the physical integrity of human beings against harm.[23] The coalition is out to convince lawmakers to view this progressive evolution not as a source of national pride, or as a source of public recognition that the weak and the defenseless sometimes get justice, but rather as a source of shame, as a source of economic destructiveness, as something that should be stopped.

II. The Deterrent Effect of Unpredictability
Keeps Our Tort System Strong

The fundamental message of this special interest coalition is that the jury system is out of control because of the unpredictable nature of the common law and of jury awards.[24] Insurance companies dislike the civil jury system because they dislike a system in which they cannot precisely budget liability as a cost of doing business.

It is this "cost unpredictability", separate from the gradual evolution of liability principles over the generations, which constitutes the very essence of deterrence—a function of the civil justice system which is equally important to compensating the victim, and which cannot be quantified in dollars and cents. The common law of torts reflects and renews ethical and humane traditions which have led to the deterrence of unsafe practices, the disclosure of potential hazards to a wider public, and authoritative expansions of respect for human life which serve to distinguish our country from most other nations.

Our tort system provides several invaluable functions. It is the means of protection for tens of millions of Americans who are less likely to be injured because of the impact of lawsuits brought by prior victims. The prospect of tort liability deters those manufacturers, builders, doctors and other tortfeasors from repeating their negligent behavior; it provides them with a proper economic incentive to curb their damaging practices and to make their endeavors more safe.[25] Tort actions, when reported to millions of people through the mass media, increase public awareness about harmful products, dangerous drugs, toxins and unsafe practices and processes. The system functions to alert citizens to take their own precautions, and to inform regulators and legislators as to the advisability of broader safety laws and stronger safety standards for the prevention of harm.[26]

Finally, the civil justice system provides our society with the moral and ethical fiber that establishes the proper duties and obligations between parties in the marketplace, the workplace, the government and the community. The sources for these basic ethical/legal principles elaborating government and corporate accountability are the trial courts and appellate courts. The decisions of these courts establish limits, duties and rights to protect workers from employers, consumers from sellers, communities from corporations, citizens from governmental entities and future generations from present recklessness. Judicial decisions sow the seed of civilized behavior.

III. A Campaign of Misinformation

Why is the insurance industry so disturbed by this sensitive system? Why do they advocate taking judgment away from the judge and jury who hear the evidence and who have no personal stake in the outcome? Why do they propose to replace judicial determination with a codified system of compensation rates which can be later altered with the corruptive monies of political action committees and the special interest influence-peddling that often reaches the ears and pockets of legislators?[27] The answer must be premised on data. But the insurance industry relies on alarmist, prejudicial, and sometimes unsubstantiated, data and surveys which either belie credulity or are so manipulated and interpreted by the insurance lobby as to more closely resemble fiction than fact. Often the insurance industry ignores reliable compilations of statistics which indicate that the American tort system is *not* out of control.

We know from data around the country that machines break and chemicals burn their victims and that the cost of the casualty count in the workplace and marketplace runs into the millions of dollars annually.[28] We also know that the auto, drug, chemical and other industries which now seek greater protection from liability have been successfully taken to court over and over again for seriously injuring the American public with defective or toxic products, and that as a result of these lawsuits, once dangerous products have been made safer or removed from the marketplace altogether.[29]

However, only a very small fraction of these injured Americans actually reach the courtroom,[30] and only about half of those who obtain jury verdicts receive or collect any compensation. This is the sober reality—even according to figures released by Jury Verdict Research ("JVR"), the legal publishing firm whose figures are widely used by the insurance industry, the United States Justice Department and other supporters of "tort reform" to demonstrate a "lawsuit crisis."[31]

In addition, statistics relied upon by tort reform proponents have often been misused or misstated, and many have been substantially discredited.[32] For example, compilations of data from the federal courts are frequently cited to evidence a United States tort litigation explosion,[33] yet only approximately five percent of all tort filings are in federal court.[34] Increases in these filings largely can be explained by removals from state courts, and by a few epidemic product liability cases involving less than a dozen particularly dangerous products, such as asbestos, which have been the subject of recent litigation by thousands of injured persons.[35] The best available evidence demonstrates that state courts are *not* experiencing a litigation explosion.[36]

Jury verdict data released by JVR is also frequently cited as support for the insurance industry's position.[37] However, according to JVR's recent studies and JVR's chairman, Mr. Philip J. Hermann, this data does not substantiate any claim of recently escalating jury awards.[38] This is, in part, due to JVR's methodology. JVR data, cited by industry, does not reflect inflationary adjustments, and does not factor in settlements, verdicts lowered on appeal, remittiturs, bench verdicts, verdicts for defendants, or verdicts involving no money.[39] Moreover, JVR's "average jury award" figures are misused when cited to represent trends since these averages ignore "zero" verdicts and are heavily influenced by a few large ones.[40] "Median" figures are the correct measurement of typical awards,[41] and the median jury verdict has remained at approximately $8,000 in 1979 dollars since 1959.[42]

JVR figures are also used by tort reform proponents to demonstrate a surge in million-dollar-plus verdicts.[43] According to JVR figures, over the last twenty-five years there have been 2,564 million-dollar verdicts, many of which were settled for lower sums prior to appeal.[44] The claim is made that in the biggest democracy and economy in the world, this is some sort of scandal.

Since JVR figures are not adjusted for inflation, they do not account for the fact that the dollar today buys what thirty-nine cents purchased in 1969. And by JVR's admission, the rate of increase of million-dollar awards is slowing down.[45] Aside from this, in an economy with a $4.2 trillion Gross National Product in 1985, 2,564 million-dollar verdicts over a twenty-five year period is a scandal *in reverse*. Given the horrendous nature and tremendous volume of injuries and illnesses resulting from corporate wrongdoing alone, there should have been more such awards.

While the available evidence indicates that courts are not experiencing a litigation explosion,[46] the debate is bound to continue until insurance companies release information in their possession showing actual payments to injured persons.[47] One suspects that if the insurance industry could substantiate their claims that people are paid too much for their injuries, they would have revealed that data long ago. Until the insurance industry furnishes this information, its allegations of excessive damage payments and its drive to drastically increase premiums must be viewed as a commercial strategy borne out of the industry's cyclical financial mismanagement of recent years.

IV. Specious Hopes: Reduced Premiums, Increased Availability

According to the insurance industry, two of the purported benefits of "tort reform" were to be a reduction in the price of insurance premiums and an expansion in the availability of insurance coverage. These claims were misfounded and misleading. Changing liability laws will *not* reduce premiums. As a matter of fact, leading property/casualty companies have filed rate documents notifying state insurance commissioners that even *extensive* "tort reforms" will not reduce insurance rates.[48] Conversely, a survey of insurance departments by the National Insurance Consumer Organization indicates that access to insurance is increasing in states where tort reform was not enacted.[49]

It also appears doubtful that changing liability laws will increase the availability of insurance. In many jurisdictions the opposite is happening.

In 1978, for example, Pennsylvania enacted a law immunizing all Pennsylvania municipalities from most kinds of liability suits and limiting liability for even catastrophic events to $500,000 per occurrence,[50] yet Pennsylvania cities and towns are still having their insurance policies cancelled.[51]

In Iowa, lawmakers abolished joint and several liability as applied to defendants who were less than fifty percent at fault for all cases tried after July 1, 1984.[52] Still in late 1985, forty-one Iowa counties had their liability insurance cancelled.[53]

In Ontario, Canada, most "tort reform" measures sought by the insurance industry are already law. These measures include caps on awards for pain and suffering, restrictions on the award of punitive damages and prohibition of contingency fees.[54] In addition, Ontario court rules require any unsuccessful plaintiff to pay the defendant's costs. There is no constitutional right to a jury trial in Canada, so most trials are before judges.[55] Yet the insurance industry is raising premiums for many of its customers by 400% or more, cancelling coverage in mid-term and refusing to provide coverage at any price.[56]

Massive premium gouging, arbitrary cancellations and reduced coverage will be the cyclical pattern and industry strategy of the future unless the real causes of this insurance crisis—the cash-flow underwriting practices of the insurance industry—are addressed. Stop the surge and decline in this cycle and the trauma on the economic system will end, and the attack on victims' rights will atrophy.

V. Prescription for Remedy: Some Recommendations
for Insurance Industry Reform

There is no doubt that reform is imperative if this insurance crisis is to be abated. However, it is not the rights of victims which must be evaluated and controlled, it is the unharnessed and grossly unscrutinized insurance industry itself that should be investigated and reformed. The special privileges enjoyed by the insurance industry are largely responsible for the insurance crisis cycle. By virtue of the McCarran-Ferguson Act,[57] the insurance industry is exempt from antitrust laws.[58] It is also exempt from federal regulation and Federal Trade Commission scrutiny.[59] These exemptions should be repealed by Congress.[60]

In addition, Congress should establish a federal office of insurance to monitor the industry and to establish standards for state regulators to follow. A national industry-funded reinsurance program should be established to compete with foreign reinsurers so as to exert downward pressure on reinsurance rates and thus enable insurers to reduce their rates.

At the state level, effective insurance disclosure laws are critical. Insurance companies must be required to routinely disclose in detail and by subline—for day care centers, trucking concerns, municipalities and similar institutions—how much thay take in from premiums and investment income and how much they pay out for verdicts and settlements, reserves and other expenditures. States should also establish joint underwriting authorities to provide insurance at actuarially sound rates to those who cannot get insurance in the open market during insurance cycle bottoms.

State insurance departments must be afforded more authority to regulate rates, and state laws should provide for greater consumer representation before insurance regulatory bodies. This would include establishment of state consumer advocates to directly intervene in rate proceedings as many states now authorize in utility matters.[61] State insurance departments also need greater funding and increased staffing.[62]

Insurance companies should be required to engage in greater loss prevention efforts as well as improvement of health and safety conditions. Presently, some insurance companies are ignoring hazards. When an insurer knows that a claim is legitimate because of a well-known specific hazard, the logical approach is not to cancel coverage, raise rates or limit recovery. The solution is to pay the claim, go back to the insured and make a hazard analysis of the product or unsafe circumstance, and then refuse to continue coverage until all hazards uncovered by the analysis are eliminated or the risk of injury is reduced by specific safeguards and warnings. Instead, the insurer typically ends up defending the hazard so as to shift liability to another party, and as a result, often avoids paying the claim, thereby reducing monetary loss for itself and its insured.

In addition, the absolute immunity enjoyed by employers under worker compensation laws gives employers little incentive for hazard prevention. In many circumstances the absolute immunity granted employers under workers compensation laws allows insured employers to violate recognized hazard prevention measures with disregard for the lives and safety of their employees.[63]

Insurance companies should also participate in experience loss rating,[64] and should be required to disclose evidence of defective products or hazardous conditions to the appropriate law enforcement and regulatory authorities.

Our industrial society produces diverse benefits but it also exposes many people to avoidable injury and disease. Society is not harmed when the rights of injured people are vindicated and when they are compensated—not as chattel—but as respected and dignified human beings. Society and its unafflicted citizens benefit from such justice and from the corresponding deterrence of careless or unsafe behavior.

The insurance industry has looked for scapegoats—victims, lawyers, juries and judges—to cover up its own instability and mismanagement. Giving up basic victims' rights will not stop premium gouging and policy cancellations. Only effective insurance reforms will stop the cyclical insurance crisis which leads to the volcanic eruptions of premiums, and the reduced availability of insurance coverage in the business, professional and non-profit sectors. Increasing the number of obstacles injured or sick citizens must overcome in the already difficult process of prevailing in court is not a solution; it is a degradation of the just norms of the common law which have elevated care, redress, deterrence and knowledge of perils into our nation's consciousness.

Notes

* B.A. Princeton, 1955; LL.B. Harvard, 1958. Mr. Nader is founder and director of the Center for Study of Responsive Law (founded 1969). Attorney Joanne Doroshow provided research assistance for this article.

1. See Proffer, "Coping With A Crisis," *Nat'l Conf. of State Legislatures,* Sept., 1986, at 18.

2. *Ins. Info. Inst., The Lawsuit Crisis* (1986).

3. The insurance industry has undertaken a "massive effort to market the idea that there is something wrong with the civil justice system in the United States." *Nat'l Underwriter,* Dec. 21, 1984, at 2. The goal, in the words of one of the industry's leading spokespersons, GEICO's chairman John J. Byrne, is "to withdraw [from the market] and let the pressure for reform build in the courts and in the state legislatures." *J. Com.,* June 18, 1985, at 10A, col. 1.

    The insurance industry has funded a $6.5 million dollar advertising campaign to convince the public a "lawsuit crisis" is responsible for the scarcity of affordable insurance among certain individuals and businesses. *J. Com.,* Mar. 19, 1986 at 1, col.

2. Magazine and television ads include such captivating headlines as "The Lawsuit Crisis Is Bad for Babies," "Even Clergy Can't Escape the Lawsuit Crisis" and "The Lawsuit Crisis Is Penalizing School Sports."

4. President's Message to the American Tort Reform Association ("ATRA"), 22 *Weekly Comp. of Pres. Doc.* 720 (May 30, 1986) [hereinafter President's Message].

5. Under these provisions, a passenger who became a quadriplegic after a defectively-designed jeep overturned, see Bartels v. City of Williston, 276 N.W.2d 113 (N.D. 1979), and a person burned and permanently disfigured by an exploding Pinto gas tank, see Grimshaw v. Ford Motor Co., 119 Cal. App. 3d 757, 174 Cal. Rptr. 348 (1981), could recover for only a fraction of their actual pain and suffering over a lifetime. Some caps have been held unconstitutional. In striking down Virginia's $1.0 million legislative cap on medical malpractice awards, a Virginia federal district court held:

    > [T]he legislature may not mandate the amount of judgment to be entered in a trial. Such a measure not only infringes upon the right to a jury where that right applies, but, when considered in the light of the proper functioning of the legislature and the judiciary under our system of separation of powers of the respective branches, it also impermissibly interferes with the function of the judicial branch, thereby violating the separation of powers. Viewed in this light, [the cap] is clearly unconstitutional.

    Boyd v. Bulala, 647 F. Supp. 781, 790 (W.D. Va. 1986).

6. Punitive damages are awarded only in the most serious cases where injury was caused by a defendant's "aggravation or outrage, such as spite or 'malice', or a fraudulent or evil motive on the part of the defendant, or such a conscious and deliberate disregard of the interests of others that the conduct may be called wilful or wanton." *W. Prosser & W. Keeton on Torts* § 2, at 9–10 (1984) [hereinafter *Keeton*]. For an example of statutory limits on punitive damages, see *Colo. Rev. Stat.* § 13-21-102(1)(a) (1986) which provides:

    > In all civil actions in which damages are assessed by a jury for a wrong done to the person or to personal or real property, and the injury complained of is attended by circumstances of fraud, malice, or willful and wanton conduct, the jury, in addition to the actual damages sustained by such party, may award him reasonable exemplary damages. The amount of such reasonable exemplary damages shall not exceed an amount which is equal to the amount of the actual damages awarded to the injured party.

7. Defense lawyers, paid by the hour, may be motivated to increase their hours by conducting unnecessary discovery, filing frivolous motions, or refusing to participate in meaningful settlement negotiations until immediately before trial. Plaintiff's attorneys, usually paid on a contingency basis, have no such motivations because they are only compensated upon recovery of a claim. Furthermore, access to legal services on a wide-

spread basis for non-wealthy individuals is made possible through the contingency fee system. See generally Schmidt, "Contingent Fee: Key to the Courthouse," 92 *Case and Comment* 2 (1987).

James L. Gattuso of the conservative Heritage Foundation pointed out that the contingency fee system acts not only to provide injured persons who could not otherwise afford legal representation with access to the legal system, but it helps screen out baseless lawsuits. Gattuso, "Don't Rush to Condemn Contingency Fees," *Wall St. J.*, May 15, 1986, at 28, col. 3.

8. If joint and several liability is eliminated, any one wrongdoer's liability is limited to the "proportion of harm" attributable to that person's misconduct. This would be unfair to the victim in the event that one wrongdoer cannot or will not pay for injuries he helped to cause. The common law of joint and several liability has long recognized that it is more fair to allow an innocent victim to fully and promptly recover for injuries suffered, and to let the wrongdoers decide among themselves, after the victim is compensated, how to apportion the liability. See *Keeton, supra* note 6, at 328, 475. Those arguing to eliminate joint and several liability frequently overlook the fact that in virtually every jurisdiction, a defendant may be held liable in the first place only if the defendant's conduct is a substantial factor in bringing about the harm. See *Restatement (Second) of Torts* § 431 (1965). Moreover, eliminating joint and several liability requires that a legal fiction be introduced into the rules of compensation, by presuming it is possible to define precise percentages of responsibility for an indivisible injury among several wrongdoers.

9. Provisions mandating that damage awards be allocated in periodic payments penalize those victims who are faced with large medical costs immediately after an injury and those who must make adjustments in transportation and housing. Periodic payments allow insurance companies to pocket the interest earned while the funds remain in their possession.

10. The collateral source rule serves to prevent a tortfeasor from reducing its liability by payments that the injured party has received from sources collateral to the tortfeasor. *Restatement (Second) of Torts* § 920A (1965) ("Payments made to or benefits conferred on the injured party from other sources are not credited against the tortfeasor's liability, although they cover all or part of the harm for which the tortfeasor is liable."). See, e.g., Folkestad v. Burlington Northern, Inc., 813 F.2d 1377 (9th Cir. 1987).

    Repeal of the collateral source rule means that payments taken from health insurance, social security and other sources which have already been paid for by the consumer or taxpayers, would be used to reduce a wrongdoer's financial responsibility for injuries to consumers. This system provides a windfall to insurance companies, which have previously received payment of premiums from the victim.

11. The doctrine of strict liability ensures that the one who is responsible for bringing a dangerously defective product into the marketplace or workplace compensates those injured by the product. This approach maximizes incentives for making safer products.

    Strict liability does not mean absolute liability. In a strict liability action an injured victim still carries a heavy burden. He or she must prove: (1) the existence of a defect which renders the product in question unreasonably dangerous; (2) the manufacturer's responsibility for that defect; (3) the nature and extent of plaintiff's injury; and (4) the causal connection between the defect and the injury. See *Restatement (Second) of Torts* § 395 comment b (1965). The additional proof requirements for recovery in product liability actions would increase the costs and evidentiary burdens, and generally make pursuit of legal remedies more difficult for the average victim.

12. A nationwide poll conducted for one "tort reform" group, ATRA, shows that while "[a]t first glance the public appears receptive to a broad range of solutions to the liability

problem . . . focus group discussions reveal that this receptivity is easily reversed when objections to reforms are raised." "The Public Discusses the Liability Crisis," *Burson-Marsteller Res.* at x (June 1986). When pushed to clarify what they really could support, only two solutions could be agreed upon: "1. Educate the public on the proper use of the civil court system; and 2. Impose penalties for frivolous or nuisance suits." *Id.* at xi. The poll was conducted by interviewing a total of 1,002 American adults selected nationwide. In addition, two focus group sessions were conducted involving twenty of the "influential public," defined as heads-of-households with incomes of about $40,000 who voted in 1984. *Id.* at iii, iv.

13. J. Robert Hunter, Federal Insurance Administrator under Presidents Ford and Carter, and now President of the National Insurance Consumer Organization ("NICO"), testified before Congress in 1986:

> On November 3, the *Washington Post* editorialized that liability insurance or the lack of it is becoming a national problem. . . . They went on to say that there must be a limit to all this, that the real beneficiaries of this may be the lawyers, and there has to be a better way of compensating those to whom reparations are due than the clumsy and expensive mechanism that exists today. That editorial was November 3, 1976, and that is my point. We are in a typical cyclical pattern of the insurance industry which is driving prices skyward. This is the insurance cycle. . . . [T]ypical bottoms were in 1965, 1975, and 1984. . . . This . . . has gone on since the early 1900's in fairly consistent patterns.

"Costs and Availability of Liability Insurance: Hearings Before the Subcomm. on Oversight of the House Comm. on Ways and Means," 99th Cong., 2d Sess. 26 (1986) (testimony of J. Robert Hunter, President, National Insurance Consumer Organization) [hereinafter Hunter Testimony]. See also *Michigan House of Representatives, Study of the Profitability of Commercial Liab. Ins.,* (Nov. 10, 1986) ("The property casualty industry is cyclical in nature. Data show that the industry has had profitability cycles at least since the 1920's") [hereinafter *Michigan Report*].

James B. Stradtner, general partner at investment bankers Alex Brown & Son, Inc., described the "boom and bust nature of the industry . . . as predictable as the tide in a three-year swing from flow to ebb." *J. of Com.,* May 15, 1986, at 14A, col. 1. Stradtner was also reported as saying that "the commercial insurance industry has an almost incurable penchant for 'shooting itself in the foot.' " *Id.*

14. See, e.g., Hunter Testimony, *supra* note 13, at 26 ("In the early eighties they were writing the MGM Grand Hotel fire *after* the fire, [which was, in effect] retroactive liability insurance. They lusted after the cash-flow [of] liability policies. When the interest rates dropped, they lost their lust.") (emphasis added).

15. For example, Maurice R. Greenberg, President and Chief Executive Officer of American International Group, Inc., one of this country's leading property/casualty companies, told an insurance audience in Boston that the current industry problems were due to price cuts "to the point of absurdity" in the early 1980's. Had it not been for these cuts, Greenberg said, there would not be "all this hullabaloo" about the tort system. Greenwald, "Insurers Must Share Blame: AIG Head," *Bus. Ins.,* Mar. 31, 1986, at 3.

16. "What Insurance Crisis?," *Bus. Wk.,* Jan. 12, 1987, at 154. See also, e.g., *New Mexico State Legislature, Report of the Interim Legislative Workmen's Compensation Comm. on Liability Insurance and Tort Reform* (Nov. 24, 1986); *Michigan Report, supra* note 13; *Insurance Comm. Pennsylvania House of Representatives, Liability Insurance Crisis In Pennsylvania* (Sept. 29, 1986).

17. The property/casualty insurance industry estimates that its income after taxes for 1986

totalled $11.5 billion. Green, "P/C Insurers Turned a Profit Last Year," *J. of Com.*, Jan. 6, 1987, at 1, col. 2.

Between 1976 and 1985, the property/casualty companies had a net gain of about $81.0 billion on which they paid no federal income tax, according to the General Accounting Office. See "The Liability Insurance Crisis, Hearings Before the Subcomm. on Economic Stabilization, House Comm. on Banking, Finance and Urban Affairs," 99th Cong., 2d Sess. 87 (1986) (statement of William J. Anderson, Director, General Government Division) [hereinafter "Liability Insurance Crisis Hearings"].

18. See, e.g., Curran, "Bargains Beckon in Insurance," *Fortune*, Aug. 4, 1986, at 217; "Analysts Bullish On Insurer Stocks," *Bus. Ins.*, Aug. 4, 1986, at 1.

19. Reinsurance is insurance for insurance companies. The insurer pays the reinsurer a premium, in exchange for which the reinsurer agrees to share the risk with the insurer. Just as primary insurers have been raising the premiums they charge their insureds, reinsurers have been raising the premiums they charge the primary insurers. An independent study for the Michigan House of Representatives found that "reinsurance serves to amplify the [insurance] cycle." *Michigan Report, supra* note 13, at 9.

20. A study based on a questionnaire to insurance companies, released June 9, 1986 by Rep. Peter W. Rodino, chairman of the House Judiciary Committee, demonstrates that the liability insurance industry actually paid out far less in claims than it received in premiums over the past decade, "undermin[ing] the companies' claims of massive losses and rais[ing] the specter of price-gouging and bloated profits." Address by Rep. Peter Rodino, Press Release (June 9, 1986).

21. At a January 17, 1986 press conference, a number of business, professional and insurance trade organizations announced the formation of ATRA whose sole agenda is to change this country's civil justice system.

Former Attorney General Benjamin R. Civiletti resigned as ATRA's general counsel on October 28, 1986, after ATRA made "outrageous and untrue" statements about American lawyers. "ATRA Counsel Quits Over Negative Remarks About Lawyers," *Mealey's Litigation Rep. Nat'l Tort Reform,* Dec. 2, 1986, at 914.

22. Several victims whose stories have been distorted repeatedly in public statements by tort-reform proponents were brought before a congressional committee in an attempt to clear the record regarding their cases. See "Liability Insurance Crisis Hearings," *supra* note 17. For example, Charles Bigbee, whose leg was severed after a car hit a phone booth in which he was trapped (the door jammed after he noticed the car coming towards him), testified:

> I believe it would be very helpful if I could talk briefly about my case and show how it has been distorted not only by the President, but by the media as well. That is probably the best way to show that people who are injured due to the fault of others should be justly compensated for the damages they have to live with the rest of their lives.

Id. at 45.

23. As Prosser noted, in the tort system "change and development have come as social ideas have altered, and they are constantly continuing." *Keeton, supra* note 6, at 19.

24. For example, one industry piece states, "[w]ith no way to gauge the risk of a lawsuit or amount of a potential court award, many businesses, professionals, municipalities, manufacturers, and individuals are exposed to enormous unpredictability that makes it difficult to do business." "The Lawsuit Crisis," *Ins. Info. Inst.* (1986).

25. According to Prosser,

> The "prophylactic" factor of preventing future harm has been quite important in the field of torts. The courts are concerned not only with compensation of the victim, but with admonition of the wrongdoer. When the decisions of the courts become known, and defendants realize that they may be held liable, there is of course a strong incentive to prevent the occurrence of the harm. Not infrequently one reason for imposing liability is the deliberate purpose of providing that incentive.

Keeton, supra note 6, at 25. See also Williams, "The Aims of the Law of Tort," 4 Curr. Leg. Prob. 137 (1951).

26. For example, 20 years ago, United States Senator Gaylord Nelson, relying upon data and sworn testimony from a 1965 lawsuit brought by an injured plaintiff against a major tire manufacturer, sponsored legislation which resulted in the establishment of minimum tire performance safety standards. See 112 Cong. Rec. 9614 (1966) (statement of Sen. Nelson).

27. See generally Note, "Curbing Injurious PAC Support Through 2 U.S.C." ' 441d, 35 Hastings L.J. 869 (1984).

28. D. Bollier & J. Claybrook, Freedom From Harm; The Civilizing Influence of Health, Safety and Environmental Regulation 163 (1986).

29. Among the well-known products which have been removed from the market are: The Dalkon Shield intrauterine device, manufactured by A.H. Robins (see M. Mintz, At Any Cost: Corporate Greed, Women and the Dalkon Shield (1979)); the Ford Pinto exploding gas tank (see Grimshaw v. Ford Motor Co., 119 Cal. App. 3d 757, 174 Cal. Rptr. 348 (1981)); and asbestos (see P. Brodeau, Outrageous Misconduct: The Asbestos Industry On Trial (1985)).

Further, a recent survey of risk managers of 232 major U.S. corporations by the Conference Board, an industry group, found that product liability suits have had a minor impact on revenues, market share, and employee retention. Rather, the study found:

> Where product liability has had a notable impact—where it has most significantly affected management decision making—has been in the quality of the products themselves. Managers say products have become safer, manufacturing procedures have been improved, and labels and use instructions have become more explicit.

"Product Liability, The Corporate Response," Conf. Board (1987). See also, Lambert, "Suing for Safety," Trial, Nov. 1983, at 48 (lawsuits are effective in eliminating defective products).

30. In a recent study, University of Wisconsin Professor Marc Galanter found that only a small portion of troubles and injuries become disputes and only a small portion of these become lawsuits. Of those that do, the vast majority are abandoned, settled or routinely processed without full-blown adjudication. Galanter, "Reading the Landscape of Disputes: What We Know and Don't Know (And Think We Know) About Our Allegedly Contentious and Litigious Society," 31 UCLA L. Rev. 4, 5, 26 (1983). Galanter found that "a sizable minority—probably less than one-fifth—of American adults have sometime in their lives been a party to civil litigation." Id. at 21. Galanter's work in this area has been described as a "masterpiece in the field of social research on law," Wall St. J., May 28, 1986, at 37, col. 3.

31. See, e.g., Department of Justice, Report of the Tort Policy Working Group on the Causes, Extent and Policy Implications of the Current Crisis in Insurance Availability and Affordability (1986) [hereinafter Justice Department Report]. According to JVR, "the plaintiff recovery rate [was] 60%; 26 years ago it

was also 60% . . . the rate is well under 50%." "Liability Insurance Crisis Hearings," *supra* note 17, at 360 (testimony of Philip J. Hermann, Chairman of JVR).

32. A May 1986 report by the Ad Hoc Insurance Committee of the National Association of Attorneys General concluded:

> [T]he major assumptions and conclusions underlying the Justice Department Report . . . are substantially unsupported by the facts. The facts do not bear out the allegations of an "explosion" in litigation or in claim size, nor do they bear out the allegations of a financial disaster suffered by property/casualty insurers today. They finally do not support any correlation between the current crisis in availability and affordability of insurance and such a litigation "explosion." Instead, the available data indicate that the causes of, and therefore the solutions to, the current crisis lie with the insurance industry itself.

Ad Hoc Insurance Comm. *of the National Association of Attorneys General, An Analysis of the Causes of the Current Crisis of Unavailability and Unaffordability of Liability Insurance, at 45 (1986) [here-inafter Attorneys General Report]*. See also, Farrel & Glaberson, "The Explosion In Liability Lawsuits is Nothing But a Myth," *Bus. Wk., Apr.* 21, 1986 at 24.

33. The *Justice Department Report* cites a 758% increase in product liability filings in federal courts between 1974 and 1985 as evidence of a "litigation explosion." *Justice Department Report, supra* note 31, at 45.

Professor Galanter commented on the use of federal court data:

> The only systematic empirical base that played a role in . . . formulations [of a lit-igation explosion] was the statistics on the growth of caseloads in the federal courts, including the growth of appeals. Typically, only gross figures on filings were cited. The fact that little of this was full-blown adjudication was ignored. It was often assumed that what was going on in federal courts was typified by large, highly visible cases. It was further assumed that one could generalize from what was happening in the federal courts to what was happening in courts gen-erally. . . . The literature displays little effort to offset these biases of perspective. But beginning with Barton's 1975 article [Barton, "Behind the Legal Explosion," 27 *Stan. L. Rev.* 567 (1975)], there is a strong admixture of naive speculation and undocumented assertion. Appearing in prominent law reviews, publications in which, notwithstanding their prestige, there is no scrutiny for substantive, as opposed to formal, accuracy, these polemics were quickly taken as authority for what they asserted.

Galanter, *supra* note 30, at 62.

Galanter explained that those who erroneously have cited federal court data as the "scholarly foundation" of a litigation explosion tend to be "a narrow elite of judges (mostly federal), professors and deans at eminent law schools, and practitioners who practice in large firms and deal with big clients about big cases . . . [who] have a limited and spotty grasp of what the bulk of the legal system is really like." Galanter, *supra* note 30, at 61.

34. See, e.g., "Liability Insurance Crisis Hearings," *supra* note 17, at 169 (testimony of Robert T. Roper, Director, Court Statistics and Information Management Project, National Center for State Courts).

35. *Id.* at 301–06.

36. See *National Center for State Courts, A Preliminary Examination of Available Civil and Criminal Trend*

Data in State Trial Courts for 1978, 1981 *and* 1984 (1986). The findings on torts filings are of particular interest. The increase in tort case filings between 1978–81 was only two percent, while the population for those states grew four percent during the same time period. Between 1981 and 1984 the population grew another four percent while tort filings increased seven percent. For the entire period 1978–84 total tort filings increased nine percent. The population increased by eight percent.

> "[T]here is not one shred of evidence to indicate that there is a litigation explosion in the State court system," and "I do not know where Mr. Willard [of the Justice Department] would gather that information, but we do not have it at the National Center for State Courts, and we are the clearing house for all the information."

"Liability Insurance Crisis Hearings," *supra* note 17, at 169 (testimony of Robert T. Roper).

37. See, e.g., *Justice Department Report, supra* note 31.

38. JVR figures demonstrate that the rate of increase of jury awards has declined since 1981. *Jury Verdict Research, Inc., Injury Valuation, Current Award Trends* 6 (1986) [hereinafter *Injury Valuation*]. JVR Chairman Philip Hermann has testified that: "[O]ur studies do not support any claim of recently escalating jury verdict awards. The apparent reason for this erroneous impression is that a number of highly publicized news articles quoting our statistics, have grossly misstated them." "Liability Insurance Crisis Hearings," *supra* note 17, at 346–47.

39. See Localio, "Variations on $962,258: The Misuse of Data on Medical Malpractice," *L., Med. & Health Care,* June 1985, at 126. Localio is the Director of Research at the Risk Management Foundation owned by Harvard University and the hospitals affiliated with Harvard Medical School.

40. "Liability Insurance Crisis Hearings," *supra* note 17, at 594 (statement of A. Russell Localio).

   When questioned about JVR's 1985 $1.8 million average product liability jury verdict figure, repeatedly cited by tort reform proponents (see, e.g., *Justice Department Report, supra* note 31, at 36; President's Message, *supra* note 4), JVR Board Chairman Hermann states that the figure "is the result of a lot of huge verdicts that distort the average, and as a result those are unreliable figures to quote." "Liability Insurance Crisis Hearings," *supra* note 17, at 185 (testimony of Philip J. Hermann).
   Similarly, JVR had reported the 1978 average jury verdict for product liability to be $1.7 million, up from $400,000 the year before and $800,000 the year after. After personally calling JVR to ask them why the jump, I discovered that it was because of a single, $127 million verdict in the case of Grimshaw v. Ford Motor Co., 119 Cal. App. 3d 757, 174 Cal. Rptr. 348 (1981). In that case, the plaintiff was a thirteen-year-old child, who was a passenger in a Ford Pinto which was hit in a rear-end crash and resulted in a gas tank explosion. The plaintiff was burned over 90% of his body. Evidence was introduced at trial which demonstrated that Ford management knew the tanks were defective, yet chose not to recall the cars "based on the cost savings which would inure from omitting or delaying the 'fixes.' " 119 Cal.App. 3d at 777.
   The judge, in denying Ford's post-trial motions, reduced the award to $3.5 million. 119 Cal. App. 3d at 772. The verdict was upheld on appeal. The JVR figure did not take into account this remittitur.

41. Localio, *supra* note 39, at 127.

42. The $8,000 figure was noted by Gustave Shubert in 1986. Address by Gustave Shubert, Director, Rand Corporation Institute for Civil Justice, before the National Conference

of State Legislatures, Denver, Colorado (Jan. 4, 1986); Peterson & Priest, *The Civil Jury: Trends in Trials and Verdicts, Cook County, Illinois,* 1960–1979 (Rand Corporation Institute for Civil Justice 1982).

43. See *Attorneys General Report, supra* note 32, at 36–39.

44. *Injury Valuation, supra* note 38, at 14.

45. *Injury Valuation, supra* note 38, at 29.

46. See *supra* notes 32, 33, 36, and 40.

47. J. Robert Hunter commented that:

> If the insurance companies have data that juries are running wild with their awards, why don't the companies come forward with it? Don't they have the burden of proof if they want to take away our rights? The insurance companies simply refuse to put forth the data to let us analyze it. We've been asking since last September, Where's the data?

Sherrill, "One Paper That Wouldn't Shut Up," *Nation,* May 17, 1986, at 688 (quoting J. Robert Hunter).

48. Two leading property/casualty companies—Aetna Casualty and Surety Co. and St. Paul Marine Insurance Co.—recently filed rate documents notifying Florida's insurance commissioner that even extensive "tort reforms" will not reduce insurance rates. *Nat'l Ins. Consumer Org., "Tort Reform" A Fraud, Insurers Admit* (1986). Filings which calculate the effect of the 1986 Florida tort reform law, were made by 104 insurers licensed in Florida. Out of 277 filings, 175, or 63%, showed no savings from tort reform, while none showed savings of more than 10%; see also *Nat'l Ins. Consumer Org., Tort Reform Will Not Reduce Insurance Rates, Say* 100+ *Florida Insurers* (1986).

State Farm Fire and Casualty Co. notified the Kansas Insurance Department that restricting joint and several liability and limiting punitive damages would have no impact, while capping for pain and suffering would reduce rates by no more than one percent. Great American West, Inc., told the Washington Insurance Department that tort reform could well raise rates. "The Insurance Services Office, the insurance industry group that issues 'advisory' rates, said its advisory rates would not reflect any reduction due to tort reform, and emphasized to its member companies that 'any beneficial effects of tort reform *cannot* be quantified with any degree of accuracy.' "

See also "Tort-reform legislation: Did state get 'suckered'," *The Seattle Times,* July 1, 1986, at 1, col. 1.

49. *Nat'l Ins. Consumer Org., Six Insurance Industry Fibs* (1986).

50. 42 *Pa. Cons. Stat.* §§ 8501–8528 (1978).

51. See *Pennsylvania Local Government Comm., Hearing on Municipal Liability Insurance, September* 24, 1985, *Report, Recommendations and Summary of Testimony* (1985).

52. *Iowa Code Ann.* § 668.4 (West 1986).

53. Statement of Iowa State Sen. Lowell Junkins, before the Florida Senate Commerce Comm. (Jan. 7, 1986).

54. See *Ministry of the Attorney General, Ontario Law Reform Comm., Report on Products Liability* 62, 74–78 (1979).

55. *Id.* at 74, 102–04.

56. See, e.g., "Liability Coverage Crunch May Shut Day-Care Agencies," *Toronto Star,* Aug. 1, 1986, at 1; "Ski Team Can't Get Liability Insurance," *Toronto Globe and Mail,* Jan. 15, 1986, at A1.

57. 15 U.S.C. § 1011–1015 (1982).

58. 15 U.S.C. § 1013 (1982). This section provides that the Robinson-Patman Act "shall not apply to the business of insurance or to acts in the conduct thereof." Accordingly, the matter of regulation is left to state government. 15 U.S.C. § 1012 (1982). This section provides that: "The business of insurance, and every person engaged therein, shall be subject to the laws of the several States which relate to the regulation or taxation of such business." The law does retain, however, a prohibition against boycotts, coercian and intimidation. 15 U.S.C. § 1013(b) (1982). *See* St. Paul Fire & Marine Ins. Co. v. Barry, 438 U.S. 531 (1978) (insurance companies may not boycott their insureds by agreeing to deny them coverage entirely).

59. 15 U.S.C. 1012(b) (1982) provides that: "No act of Congress shall be construed to invalidate, impair, or supercede any law enacted by any State for the purpose of regulating the business of insurance, or which imposes a fee or tax upon such business, unless such Act specifically relates to the business of insurance...."

60. For a discussion on the merits of repealing these exemptions, see Glover, *It's Time to Repeal McCarran-Ferguson*, 1 Antitrust 31 (1987).

61. For example, New Jersey's law authorizes the New Jersey Public Advocate to intervene on consumers' behalf. The cost of intervention is billed back to the insurance company seeking the rate increase. 52 N.J. Stat. Ann. §§ 52:27E-1–52:27E-19 (West 1986).

62. State insurance departments are lacking in investigators, auditors and other professionals and cannot effectively recommend the appropriate levels of insurance rates. United States General Accounting Office, Issues and Needed Improvements in State Regulations of the Insurance Business (1979); *see also* American Academy of Actuaries, 1986 Yearbook (Nov. 1, 1985). There are only 64 actuaries employed by state insurance departments and 26 states have no actuary on staff. Aetna Insurance Company alone employs twice as many actuaries as all the states combined.

63. Bohyer, *The Exclusivity Rule: Dual Capacity and the Reckless Employer*, 47 Mont. L. Rev. 157 (1985).

64. Many professionals and small businesses pay a set rate regardless of their individual claims experience. For example, competent and conscientious doctors are unjustly paying the substantial price of a minority of seriously incompetent, careless, undertrained or disabled physicians.

    A 1985 report to Michigan Governor James Blanchard by former University of Michigan President Robin W. Fleming found that for claims filed between 1976 and 1984, "2.5% of physicians accounted for 19.7% of all claims and 19.3% of physicians accounted for 72.2% of all claims." A study by the *Orlando Sentinel* reported that in Florida, "3 percent of doctors were responsible for 48% of the malpractice claims paid in the state between 1975 and 1984. One doctor had 34 paid claims. Four others had 10 or more paid claims." *Orlando Sentinel*, April 19, 1986 at 1.

"Brown Lung"

THE COTTON-MILL KILLER

Originally appeared in The Nation, *March 15, 1971.*

SEVERAL THOUSAND WORKERS in the nation's textile mills are suffering from the crippling disease—byssinosis—popularly known as brown lung, and many more thousands are exposed daily to the cotton dust that causes the disease. These disclosures, made over the past two years in medical journals, in the press and at Congressional hearings, follow a decade of research by public health officials, carried out in the face of unparalleled obstruction by textile manufacturers who have denied researchers access to their mills and applied political pressure to suppress the results of their studies. When it became evident that byssinosis was not an affliction peculiar to European textile mills, as American textile interests and their company doctors had claimed for years, but a serious threat to the American cotton-mill worker as well, measures were urged to reduce or eliminate it. Specific recommendations were for a significant investment for research on control of cotton dust, medical surveillance in the plants, and financial compensation for victimized workers. Today it is obvious that neither these proposals nor the plight of 250,000 mill workers, who are exposed daily to cotton dust, have made any impression on the directors of the textile industry or on the Nixon administration.

Byssinosis was recognized in British medical literature as early as the 1930s and made compensable as a work-related disease under workmen's compensation laws in 1941. It is not a petty disease. In the first stages, the worker notices a tightness of the chest and has difficulty breathing when he returns to work after a weekend away from cotton dust. This is the well-documented "Monday-morning" syndrome. The symptoms subside during the work week.

As brown lung progresses, the victim is breathless throughout the week, and when the disease reaches a third and final stage, his lungs are permanently damaged. His condition has degenerated into a state resembling emphysema and chronic bronchitis; he is forced to give up all activities that require any physical exertion, including, eventually, his job. In the end, each breath becomes a struggle for life.

According to Dr. Arend Bouhuys, professor of epidemiology at Yale University Medical School, who has led the research on byssinosis in U.S. mills since 1964, at least 17,000 cardroom workers and spinners, those employees exposed to the highest levels of cotton dust, now suffer from brown lung at various stages. Other research substantiates Dr. Bouhuys' findings. Dr. Peter Schrag, formerly a public health officer with the North Carolina Board of Health, has reported that of 509 workers whom he tested, sixty-three or 12 percent were byssinotic, and that 29 percent of the cardroom workers had the disease. In 1969, the North Carolina State Board of Health examined 1,000 cotton textile workers and found an overall prevalence of byssinosis of 6 to 12 percent; the prevalence among cardroom employees was 18 to 28 percent. That same year, Dr. James Merchant of the North Carolina Board reported that 29.6 percent of the carders he tested were byssinotic.

None of these studies exposes the full extent of the disease, particularly since almost no retired workers have been included. (Data collected by the Social Security Administration on relative disability from respiratory diseases show a morbidity ratio for retired textile workers as high as double the "expected" figure.) The North Carolina Board of Health estimates that of the 270,000 textile workers in the state, approximately 125,000 are exposed to cotton dust. What the studies do indicate, therefore, is that brown lung is an occupational disease of serious proportions that potentially threatens nearly half of the industry's labor force.

CONTRARY TO WHAT might be expected, greater mechanization in the industry has increased the danger of brown lung. The mechanical picker, now used in the fields, leaves more trash in the cotton, and the new high-speed cards increase the dust levels in the plants. Modern ventilating systems and air conditioning are deceptive because they remove the larger particles but not the very fine dust that is breathed into the lungs. The use of low-grade cotton in combination with the new synthetic fibers also increases the brown-lung hazard. Dr. Bouhuys says in the *New England Journal of Medicine* (July 27, 1967): "It is sometimes thought that byssinosis is now disappearing because of increased mechanization and better dust control. . . . We suspect that byssinosis may be on the increase rather than on the decline."

In the same article, Dr. Bouhuys reports a case study of a mill worker diagnosed as byssinotic:

> A 46-year-old man started work in the cardroom as a "slubber tenter" at the age of 25. For twenty years he worked in the same mill, which was spinning good-quality cotton yarns. He had no respiratory symptoms during this time. In January 1965, he moved to the same job in another mill, where conditions were bad. This mill was spinning low-quality cottons. The cardroom was provided with a dust exhaust ventilation system, but according to the patient, the ducts were insufficiently cleaned and therefore usually clogged. "At times you could not see ten feet in front of you because of the dust." Symptoms of tightness in the chest and breathlessness soon developed and were worse on Mondays and Tuesdays than on other days. In April 1966, he had to stay away from work because of severe symptoms. He consulted one of us, who diagnosed byssinosis and wrote to the mill suggesting that the patient be transferred to a non-dusty job. However, the personnel manager told the patient, "I have never heard of such a disease," and discharged him from his job. The patient said that many other cardroom workers were similarly affected. On clinical examination he was emaciated.

Other physicians have said that they are reluctant to notify the mill that a patient is byssinotic, for fear that the bosses will simply discharge him. Then the mill worker not only receives no compensation for the loss of his health—byssinosis is not specified under workmen's compensation in any state—but is jobless as well. In most cases he has no union to back him up (only 18 percent of textile workers are unionized) and no government authority making any effort to reduce the hazard to his health. The North Carolina Commissioner of Labor, Frank Crane, says that his department does not inspect textile mills for dustiness, and until recently the state's health department has not had right of entry to the mills. South Carolina, with the second largest population of textile workers, does not even have an occupational health and safety unit in its health department. The federal government, whose failure to enforce Walsh-Healey job health and safety standards is notorious, has provided no safeguards for the mill worker whose plant sells to the government.

THE REACTION OF THE industry to warnings of brown lung has been to deny existence of the disease and to block attempts to study it. On July 10, 1969, one of the industry's extremist trade papers, the *Textile Reporter,* referred to byssinosis as "a thing thought up by venal doctors who attended last year's ILO meetings in Africa where inferior races are bound to be afflicted by new diseases more superior people defeated years ago."

Other industry spokesmen have used tactics hardly less crude. In 1964, when the U.S. Public Health Service gave Dr. Bouhuys a grant for a five-year study of brown lung, the industry's lobby in Georgia attempted to discredit him and to halt the study by applying pressure on the president of Emory University, where Bouhuys was then teaching. T. M. Forbes, excutive vice president of the Georgia Textile Manufacturers Association, wrote President Sanford S. Atwood of Emory that the study was a waste of taxpayers' money. "If this disease were prevalent among cotton textile employees," Forbes wrote, "it would seem to me that at some time during my thirty-seven years in this industry that fact would have come to my attention during the hundreds of meetings and conferences of textile manufacturing employers which I have attended."

Forbes then sent a secret memorandum to the members of the GTMA, suggesting that they tell any Emory alumni or trustees whom they knew "what your company has done to provide safe, healthful and comfortable working conditions in your plants." In the event that this did not stop the study, Forbes urged manufacturers to keep Bouhuys out of their mills. "Your participation would be purely voluntary on your part. There will be no legal or governmental compulsion involved in the survey." Dr. Bouhuys was not admitted to a single textile plant in Georgia. He conducted his study in the mill at the U.S. penitentiary in Atlanta from which he could not be barred.

In 1966, Dr. Schrag attempted to survey textile workers in North Carolina, but was at first denied entrance at every mill he approached. Finally, one mill admitted him, on condition that he keep his findings secret. As Dr. Schrag put it later, "I had to reassure them that they would be commended rather than criticized for having so many sick people." Schrag managed to publish his findings, but shortly thereafter lost his job with the North Carolina Board of Health. (He is now with Columbia University's Harlem Hospital Center in New York.)

In 1969, the industry announced that it was making its own study. The American Textile Manufacturers' Institute had contracted with the Industrial Hygiene Foundation of Pittsburgh to find out, first, whether byssinosis existed and, second, its prevalence. The results of the study are not yet known, but this is the foundation that defended the coal mine industry during the recent struggle to make black lung disease compensable. Meanwhile, the fact that Industrial Hygiene is at work has been used to discourage other inquiries.

In October 1969, state Rep. Troy Hyatt of South Carolina tried to open an investigation in that state. John K. Cauthen, executive vice president of the State Textile Manufacturers' Association, wrote to the Governor and every member of the legislature, reminding them of the study in progress and saying that Hyatt's study would only "fragment" research efforts and "might result in a variety of findings which conceivably would confuse the situation rather than finding answers to whatever problems may exist." The textile lobby did not succeed in stopping the study outright, but the legislature limited expenditures to $1,500, thus assuring an inadequate inquiry into a problem affecting more than 150,400 South Carolinians.

STATE INVESTIGATIONS HAVE been stifled in other ways. One Georgia public health official has admitted: "We have done no studies in connection with byssinosis, but have been advised of its existence by industrial physicians in an unofficial manner. Such a study would involve the cooperation of several managements. Some are agreeable to such a study when contacted singularly [sic], but as a group this has not been the case."

Such reactions from industry and from the major textile states make the federal government's responsibility to take action against brown lung the more urgent. In August 1969, I wrote the then Secretary of HEW, Robert Finch, asking that he initiate a federal campaign to reduce this occupational hazard by making more money available for research, by alerting workers to the danger, and by setting standards of dust control and medical care in the mills that sell to the government. In his reply, dated September 19, 1969—almost a year and a half ago—Secretary Finch noted that "it appears that thousands of workers may be adversely affected by cotton dust." He went on to say, "I strongly agree that effective action must be taken to curb this occupational hazard."

We have yet to see the "effective action" the Secretary promised. In 1970, the U.S. Public Health Service gave Dr. Bouhuys another grant of $68,390 for research and spent about $40,000 for a conference on occupational health and safety in the textile industry. Appropriations of that size do not begin to support the kind of research that can lead to prompt and effective elimination of a disease that has crippled tens of thousands of workers, and right now is disabling a known 17,000 and almost certainly thousands more. Almost no study is being made of technological control, such as removing cotton trash at the gin. The U.S. Department of Agriculture has resources for that kind of research, and money could be given to textile schools that undertook to develop a safe technology. But USDA is doing nothing. The National Cotton Council gets $1 for every bale of cotton sold (close to $10 million a year) for promotion and research. It spends not one cent to solve the brown-lung problem.

THE TEXTILE INDUSTRY WILL probably continue to do nothing until it is threatened with large expenditures to compensate its workers for loss of their health—expenditures considerably larger even than the present cost of early retirements, sick leaves and loss of efficiency among its injured employees. Therefore if the federal government would make brown lung a compensable occupational disease, that one step would both encourage preventive measures and assist those victims for whom prevention is now too late. Rep. Phillip Burton (D., Calif.) has introduced a bill to provide such compensation. By supporting the measure the Administration could take a first step toward redeeming its promise of "effective action," made a year and a half ago. With state governments in the grip of their powerful textile lobbies, and with the industry itself displaying an unprecedented callousness to the suffering of thousands of its employees, protective steps can come only at the national level.

They're Still Breathing

Originally appeared in The New Republic, *February 3, 1968.*

IT STARTS WITH breathlessness and ends with death. Along the way, the victim can experience bronchitis, emphysema, an enlarged heart and progressive massive fibrosis leading to severe respiratory disability. The disease is coal pneumoconiosis. In 1963, a U.S. Public Health Service study concluded that, at the very least, about one of every ten active, bituminous coal miners and one in five inactive miners have it.

Five years ago was a little late in discovering this widespread prevalence of the disease. Coal miners have been depleting themselves for an energy-hungry society for over a century. However, even more unsettling has been the inaction during the years after the PHS study.

Far more attention and expense is being devoted to the aesthetic costs of strip coal mining than to preventing the human wreckage which continues to stumble out of the mines after years of working in quietly miserable conditions. These are the coal mines which are bringing their owners record profits. This is the industry which is subject to coal mine safety laws that have been deprived of both their nourishment and inspiration by inert administrators who are surrounded by indifference.

Reports on coal mine safety emanating from the Department of Interior have never fully reflected the health hazards endemic to this occupation. Recommendations for action, particularly those not dealing with mine operating safety, have been cut out of final revisions so as not to discomfort coal operators. Both the operators and officials of the United Mine Workers are more concerned about the problems of competing energy sources and anti-air pollution drives than the slow death in the mines. UMW hospitals are available for the sick worker but the UMW seems far less interested in the toxic environment of the mines.

If the dimensions of this occupational hazard are not revealed by the Interior Department, which is responsible for coal mine safety, then most certainly the resources to develop methods of disease recognition and treatment, engineering techniques for dust control and safer working standards, will not be forthcoming. And, despite the very vague rhetoric, they have not been forthcoming.

In 1952, there were 335,217 coal miners employed. A little over a decade later, the number of miners dropped to 128,698. These figures give some indication of the number of inactive and active miners exposed to coal dust. Coal is far from a dying industry, however. Its star has been rising since 1961, and now coal accounts for about 27 percent of U.S. energy output, with a dollar value at the mines exceeding $2.3-billion. The larger coal companies are so profitable that they have become prime acquisition targets of oil, copper and other industrial giants. But growing concentration, efficiency and profit have not brought a more healthful mine environment. On the contrary, government specialists believe that mechanization may have increased the miner's exposure to coal dust.

Workman's compensation costs run $27 million annually in Pennsylvania alone—a state which accounts for just 20 percent of total coal mining employment. Yet when Congress finally appropriated $100,000 in 1963 for a PHS study of the incidence of coal workers' pneumoconiosis, the European Coal and Steel Community was spending $9 million annually researching this disease from coal mine to laboratory. Environmental controls in the mines, such as water spraying for dust suppression during blasting and on automatic equipment, have resulted from the findings.

The PHS study concluded that death rates for coal miners were twice that of the general working male population, while death rates for diseases of the respiratory system were about five times that for the general working male population. British soft coal miners were reported to have a considerably longer life expectancy than American coal miners.

The Public Health Service, which has contracted for a number of small studies on coal workers' pneumoconiosis in recent years, is preparing a major report on health hazards of coal mining. Its contents will certainly provide a basis for serious concern. But like the rasping voice of the wasting coal miner, the report alone will be unlikely to move the U.S. Bureau of Mines, the coal industry or even the United Mine Workers toward sustained action. Like the recent hearings on radiation exposure in the uranium mines, that is dooming large numbers of these workers to early death from lung cancer, a congressional inquiry is necessary to supply the necessary metabolism for dealing with the insidious ravages of coal dust. A Congress, which has displayed such staunch efforts to preserve tax depletion allowances for companies engaged in extractive industries, should have little difficulty persuading itself of the need for preventive measures to diminish the bodily depletion of their employees.

on citizen action
and social change

Making a Difference

Originally appeared as a special advertisement in the Washington Post *May 1–7, 1995.*

As A GROWING PERCENTAGE of our population moves across the 65-year-old threshold toward long life, the political and civic activity of seniors will increase. Already, senior citizens are the most prolific generators of civic groups and organized political action. The influence of these groups is more feared in Congress than organized labor, in part because of their higher voter turnout and focus on several specific issues, including social security.

Because its leaders and activities are rarely on national television news or talk shows, the ferment of community involvement often goes unnoticed by the wider population. AARP, the National Council of Senior Citizens, UAW retirees, and the Gray Panthers are more active in their chapters back home than they are given credit for by a media obsessed with crime, violence, sex and addiction.

Our book, *Spices of Life: The Well-Being Handbook for Older Americans,* designed to provide retired people with a broad menu of opportunities for improving their economic, health and safety conditions and contributing to their community's civic culture, chronicles the activities of some older American groups.

Older citizens, for example, are crucial to the spread of the Time Dollar-Service Credit movement that is now operating in more than one hundred communities. This program essentially turns time into a currency of exchange by "depositing" volunteer hours in computer time banks run by civic, health, college or neighborhood associations. These time dollar hour credits can then be drawn on by volunteers whenever they need help. Elderly participants, for example, might tutor teenagers. In exchange, they will receive a time "payment" that will help them meet their own needs. The Time Dollar movement appears about to take off.

Alumni classes of colleges and universities, usually after their 35th or 40th reunions, are beginning to put together similar programs in which class members, liberated by early retirement, apply their experience and talent to more than service projects. My Princeton class of 1955, for example, has established a National Center for Civic Leadership in Princeton that places nearly 10 percent of Princeton undergraduates in civic groups that are systemically dedicated to social problem-solving. The classmates network their own projects in elementary education and other pursuits.

My Harvard Law School class of 1958 has opened an Appleseed Foundation to organize state centers for law and justice—again focusing on systemic approaches to entrenched failures in society. These alumni efforts—and there are more across the nation—may begin to redefine "retirement" to mean a civic career undeterred by the invisible chain of previous employment or affiliation.

My classmates are holding for results, not rhetoric. As John Gardner, former Secretary of Health, Education and Welfare put it, they are ". . . saying something that is profoundly relevant to American life at this moment . . . that commitment matters . . . that self-adsorption is not enough . . . that we do have shared causes worth of commitment, even sacrifice . . . and that to solve our problems is not a hopeless venture."

Following the decision to create a full-time, operating institution which would train future leaders and work on many of the serious problems affecting society, our classmates have learned that they are not alone in their erupting need to make a fundamental difference to their country.

A generational stirring is rumbling among those who grew up in the fifties when America was number one in just about everything and who now find their land in deep trouble on almost all domestic fronts. With their children raised and some financial security achieved, more of them are looking outward to help solve the country's problems.

There is an increasing intergenerational dimension to these civic efforts. The Gray Panthers are now explicitly dedicated to working with young people. Enormous human resources among older people need to be translated from potential to performance in order to create what a Japanese civic leader called "ageless living." Intergenerational conflicts need to be replaced by intergenerational alliances and that objective requires more muscular foundations for our society.

In the context of budgetary restrictions, there has been speculation about a coming collision of interests between older Americans and corporate power over competing entitlements. The elderly community is beginning to show early signs of disapproval of large corporate welfare programs and the way public funds go toward gouging health care industries without adequate auditing. As the federal dollar tightens, this conflict is likely to intensify.

Why, one octogenarian asked me, should the Congressional politicians talk about reducing benefits under Medicare instead of cracking down on Medicare fraud by practitioners and hospitals who also massively overbill?

All in all, the last fourth of life is likely to be much more exciting, unpredictable and politically consequential for our country than past predictions by gerontologists.

Princeton's Class of '55's Gift
Is for the Students and the World

Originally appeared in The Philadelphia Inquirer, *June 4, 1994.*

NEARLY SEVENTY YEARS of alumni classes were part of the traditional "P-rade" at Princeton University yesterday where the "old grads" marched under their banners through the campus until they reached the 1,100 members of the class of 1994.

One class in the P-rade had gathered to do more than share nostalgic memories and perhaps write another check to the alma mater. The class of 1955, of which I am a member, has devised Project 55—a pioneering redefinition of an alumni class that is reaching out to help students find civic action careers and reaching inward among classmates to work together on long "suppressed crusades" to improve our society.

Project 55 was born in 1989 just before the class of 1955's 35th reunion. Meeting in Washington that spring for a mini-reunion, around seventy classmates, using their own money, established a National Center for Civic Leadership in Princeton, N.J. to work for social change and encourage a new generation of leadership among Princeton students.

This summer, the center will place more than one hundred Princeton students and new graduates in summer internships and full-time fellowships in dozens of citizen groups around the country. These groups are working not in charitable service activities but in advancing systemic approaches to entrenched problems in such areas as housing, labor, environment, mass transit, youth needs, municipal government, health deficiencies and education.

These student placements are meant to be career-shaping opportunities for strengthening the civic culture of the nation. Class members are concerned that our country is losing the charity race, important as these ministrations are from day to day.

Other 1955 class members are developing mentoring and school oversight projects in Trenton and Norwalk, Conn., advancing effective character-education programs in elementary schools throughout the country, and laying the basis for a renewable energy initiative involving top corporate executives.

The alumni class is an ideal but long, neglected community for civic efforts. How many organizations do we belong to whose members we met when we were seventeen or eighteen years old? Between classmates, candor is not scarce, nor are the diverse talents and skills that can facilitate action through a background of long experience and contacts. Add to these assets the unwritten code that special interest hats are left at home and a modestly ideal community for civic achievement emerges among the thousands of such alumni classes from coast to coast.

Something more is also at work—a generational stirring among alumni in their fifties and sixties who grew up in the 1950s when America was number one in just about everything but is now in deep trouble on many domestic fronts. They want to give back. With their children grown, many are not ready to retire in a few years and play shuffleboard or golf at some age-segregated community.

Dozens of alumni classes and alumni organizations at colleges are engaged in service activities or sponsor a scholarship or two. Notre Dame alumni are notable in this respect.

But there are indications among classes at other schools—Yale, Dartmouth, Harvard—that a more rigorous and fundamental effort at rebuilding our democracy and our communities is needed.

All these assets, feelings and bondings came together at the 35th reunion of the Harvard Law School Class of 1958 last year to establish the Appleseed Foundation. Its purpose is to help organize public interest law centers at the state level that will work to connect law and justice in improving the lives of people. Already, Harvard Law School and George Washington University Law School are developing special clinical programs for law students.

It was not agreement on many policy issues that drew together classmates who are corporate lawyers, labor lawyers, law professors and business executives. Rather it was a shared concern that respect for the law and the legal profession is to be earned by actions and engagements, not image-building and rhetoric. The Appleseed law centers around the country will help liberate human energies for systemic problem-solving that involve other citizens and professions.

Young Princetonians and recent Harvard Law graduates have responded with an enthusiasm that started even the more optimistic alumni working in these two projects. The delight is cross-generational. Chet Safian, the president of Project 55, told a recent gathering of students and alumni, "I don't know who gets more out of this effort, me or the students."

Rather than being an object of coddling by university administrations, the alumni class can generate multiple intelligences to awaken the social consciousness of their educational institutions and help build a democracy that applies knowledge to human betterment.

Children: Toward Their Civic Skills
and Civic Involvement

Originally appeared in Social Education, *April/May 1992.*

THE UNITED NATIONS Convention on the Rights of the Child is far-reaching in its call for protection of basic human rights such as adequate shelter, nutrition, and health care for children. The convention also addresses the right of children to participate in society, including the right to education, the right to diverse sources of information, and the freedoms to associate, to assemble, and to express opinions.

Article 29 of the CRC states that "the education of the child shall be directed to: . . . (d) [t]he preparation of the child for responsible life in a free society." Civic education, which prepares students for such a responsibility, therefore, is a right as defined in the convention. Civic participation, however, can be seen as more than protection of the right to participate. Civic participation is a formula for human happiness—both private and public. It is more than a duty to be self-imposed; it is a delight to be savored.

Children as Activists

Throughout U.S. history, citizens, including many children, have inspired significant social change. Children working in the mills in Paterson, New

---

Jersey, went on strike to protest their working conditions in the 1840s and were soon joined by adults demanding a ten-hour workday. Children led marches in Birmingham, Alabama, during the struggle for civil rights. And students led the protests against the Vietnam War. The lives of the young people who participated in these events were changed forever. Every child is entitled to opportunities to participate in making their world a better place to live.

Every school in the country has a duty to teach students about their responsibilities as public citizens and to provide them with inspiring examples that elaborate the adage that "one person can make a difference." Unfortunately, traditional civics courses and many textbooks define citizenship narrowly. Citizen responsibilities most often mentioned in these books are those required by law: paying taxes, obeying the law, serving in the armed forces if necessary, performing jury duty, and attending school. In addition, voting and some type of volunteer activity are listed as obligations not binding by law. These books focus on citizen rights and pay little, if any, attention to the responsibility of citizens to ensure and protect their rights and the rights of others.

Who is Educating Our Children?

Our schools and our teachers must enable students to realize both the duty and the opportunity of participation. Too often, however, corporations educate our children—from the five hours daily that the average child spends watching television to the flood of corporate materials in the classroom, including Whittle Communication's Channel One (twelve minutes of news including two minutes of mandatory commercials) now used in nine thousand schools across the country.[1]

In 1979, the Center for Study of Responsive Law published *Hucksters in the Classroom: A Review of Industry Propaganda in Schools,* written by Sheila Harty, which documented the pervasiveness of corporate influence on classroom teaching materials. For example, a widely promoted 1972 booklet, available free from General Motors, featured colorful cartoon characters "Charlie Carbon Monoxide" and "Harry Hydrocarbon" who dispelled fears of the health hazards caused by air pollution and assured students that air pollution will "no longer be a problem" in "the near future" (12). Twenty years later, of course, auto emissions are choking our cities.[2]

A 1990 report from Consumers Union, *Selling America's Kids: Commercial Pressures on Kids of the 90's,* finds that the corporate presence in schools continues unabated. Consumers Union found that corporate-sponsored teaching materials reach more than 20 million students every year. *Selling America's Kids* recommends the following:

1. Make schools "ad-free zones," where students can pursue learning free of commercial influences and pressures, by adopting and enforcing guidelines restricting the use of such crass, business-sponsored materials.

2. Insist that promotions targeting children meet higher standards of disclosure than those aimed at adults.

3. Educate children about the nature of commercial messages directed at them and develop their ability to resist high-pressure or seductive sales promotions; teach them how to "analyze ads, demythologize products and clarify alternatives" in the marketplace (Consumers Union 1990, 23).

The Consumers Union report also details out-of-school commercial pressures on young people, including celebrity sponsorship of popular and expensive products such as sports shoes, the pervasiveness of licensed products from movies and television shows, and product placement of advertisements in movies. Given the unrelenting pressure to buy, schools have an important role to play in alerting students to their exploitation.

In 1975, the Center for Study of Responsive Law, in conjunction with Random House Publishers, developed a consumer skills curriculum called *To Buy or Not to Buy.* The mini-course, written by Melinda Blau, teaches students basic consumer skills including how to shop astutely and how to pursue complaints. Students then practice their new skills in the community by, for example, surveying their supermarkets for compliance with open-dating laws or learning how to use small claims court.

Although all one thousand sets of the curriculum were sold, Random House decided not to publish a second edition, in my opinion, for three reasons: (1) teachers could not fit the materials—a filmstrip, readings on various consumer issues, and fifty activity cards considering various aspects of purchasing decisions—into the established curriculum; (2) often teachers themselves did not know enough to teach the unit; and (3) schools were receiving complaints from the business community. Corporate influence, therefore, contributed in this case to self-censorship. Principals and teachers frequently hesitate to teach their students to think critically out of concern that it will invite controversy.[3]

The Community "Laboratory"

In addition to the corporate atmosphere, civics courses often teach only dry, abstract theories about rights and responsibilities, failing to translate the abstractions into concrete training for action. Our schools do not teach chemistry without a laboratory nor cooking without a kitchen; schools must also teach citizenship using the community as a natural laboratory. Experimenting with their knowledge and skills in the community, students will experience firsthand and internalize the various methods and techniques necessary for effective civic participation. Students need to learn how to communicate effectively through the media, how to conduct investigative research to advocate their cause, and how to petition their government to bring about change.

To this end, the Center for Study of Responsive Law in 1992 published a civics book providing students and teachers with inspiring examples of citizen action and participation from U.S. history, including the struggles for civil rights and women's rights, and the movements for peace and environmental protection. This book teaches teachers and students about tools of change including getting messages to the media, lobbying, and using the courts. It also outlines activities to involve students in investigating and solving community problems—e.g., how to improve voter participation rates, conduct an energy waste hunt in the school, and profile members of Congress.

Taking Responsibility

Fortunately, we continue to hear about inspiring examples of teachers who are willing to take the risk and have equipped their students to make positive changes in their communities. Following are three examples.

1. When students of elementary school teacher Barbara Lewis expressed their concern over a hazardous waste dump near their school in Salt Lake City, Utah, Lewis encouraged them to tackle its cleanup. The students investigated the problem and possible solu-

tions and then rallied community and government support for their cause. When they discovered that the state legally could not accept the money they raised to clean up the dump site, they successfully lobbied the state legislature to change the law. Lewis then wrote a book, detailing her experiences, hoping to provide the means for other teachers to involve their students with action civics.[4]

2. New Jersey teacher Karl Stehle taught his high school students about Tom Paine's role in the American Revolution by having them launch their own campaign on a current issue of importance to them. Student Tanja Vogt's concern over the use of environmentally harmful polystyrene cafeteria trays soon spread throughout the school and, eventually, across the state. Students lobbied the school board to replace the polystyrene with reusable trays by conducting surveys to demonstrate that students were willing to pay more for lunch to support the change. Successful in their own school district, the students wrote letters to more than seven hundred schools in New Jersey, challenging them to follow their example. The students formed an environmental club and are now lobbying the state legislature for a bottle deposit bill to encourage recycling.[5]

3. In southern Florida, teacher Charles Deveney's students took on developers who were threatening the last stand of cypress trees in their county. The students collected thirty-five hundred signatures on a petition calling for the city council to protect the trees and spoke at city council meetings. Eventually, the issue was placed on the ballot and the voters backed the students, preserving several sites around the county. The students have since turned the area into an outdoor classroom to teach environmental awareness. The club they started, called Save What's Left, has spread to schools in five other states and overseas.[6]

Conclusion

The teachers mentioned above take seriously the responsibility and participatory aspects of citizenship embodied in Article 29 of the UN Convention on the Rights of the Child. In all cases, the teachers encouraged their students to take responsibility for community problems, to come up with solutions, and to follow through on changes. Moreover, these teachers shared the pleasure of solving problems with their students.

Why are these examples so few and far between? Certainly a lack of access to interesting, alternative classroom materials and fear of upsetting the principal, school board, and community are contributing factors. What then enabled the three teachers cited above to overcome these obstacles? An open discussion is needed to address these questions. We welcome teachers to send us their thoughts on what they see as obstacles to engaging their students actively in critical thinking and in training for both effective citizen skills and participation. Write to: Center for Study of Responsive Law, P.O. Box 19367, Washington, DC 20036.

Notes

1. See Christopher Power, et al., "Getting 'Em While They're Young," *Business Week*, 9 September 1991, 94.

2 See Philip Shabecoff, "In Washington, It's the Year for Clear Air," *New York Times*, 21 January 1990; and "EPA Announces 96 Areas Failing to Meet Smog Standards, 41 Areas Violating Carbon Monoxide Standards," EPA News Release, 16 August 1990.

3. See Stewart M. Lee, "Business Pressure on Consumer Educators," *Journal of Home Economics* 75 (Winter 1983), pp. 11–13.

4. See Barbara Lewis, *The Kid's Guide to Social Action: How to Solve the Problems You Choose And Turn Creative Thinking into Positive Social Action* (Minneapolis, Minn.: Free Spirit Publishing, 1991).

5. See George James, "Student Starts Revolution of Her Own," *New York Times*, 28 April 1989.

6. See Chuck Clark, "The Fourth 'R': Recycling Finds Niche in School Curriculums as Their Teen Activists Rally behind the Environment," *Fort Lauderdale Sun-Sentinel*, 20 January 1991.

Reference

Consumers Union. *Selling America's Kids: Commercial Pressure on Kids of the 90's.* Mount Vernon, N.Y.: Consumers Union Education Services, 1990.

Additional Readings

Blau, Melinda. *To Buy or Not to Buy.* New York: Random House, 1975.

Harty, Sheila. *Hucksters in the Classroom: A Review of Industry Propaganda in Schools.* Washington, D.C.: Center for Study of Responsive Law, 1979.

Introduction to *More Action for a Change*

Originally appeared as the Introduction to
More Action for a Change *by Kelley Griffin, 1987.*

THE STUDENT MOVEMENT of the 1960s showed that students have the potential for providing the direction, person-power, and ideals to have an impact on society. Young people of that era were concerned with problems that tended to be visible and readily susceptible to direct action—the Vietnam War was raging and blatant racial discrimination was under challenge. In the 1960s and early 1970s, in part due to student protests, policy makers changed positions on both the war and civil rights. But newspaper and television commentators viewed the student movement as dead or dying—"Gone is the movement of the 1960s," they would tell us with a touch of sadness or glee, depending on their politics. Sit-ins are out, toga parties are in—or so the media said.

While the media highlighted one student fad or another, some major interests persisted. Students were still concerned about the quality of life around them, and many were still doing something about it. They were not as demonstrative as their counterparts in the sixties, but their ability to be effective was undiminished. The complex issues of the 1970s demanded more diverse approaches than the direct protests typical of the sixties. The draft was gone, the Vietnam War was scaled down, and civil rights legislation had been passed. Many abuses were perceived as less obvious, and knowledge of law, economics, science, and engineering were frequently required to uncover problems and propose solutions.

As activists spoke on campuses, they began to observe that students wanted to do "good works" but lacked the organizational structure to translate idealism into longer-term constructive action. From the outset, students were attracted to the public interest research group (PIRG) model. First organized seventeen years ago, PIRGs now operate in twenty-five states and Canada. PIRGs are student-run, student-funded nonpartisan organizations that conduct research, advocacy, organizing, lobbying, and educational and media campaigns on a wide range of issues such as consumer rights, social justice, environmental protection, political reform, energy policy, and government responsibility. PIRGs were formed to convince students and other consumers that "you can fight City Hall!"

PIRGs provide student growth and education through direct experience that will develop both a commitment to a lifetime of citizen action and the skills necessary to be effective as activists. PIRGs also act as a counterforce to the organized economic and political power that can abuse American society. PIRGs represent the underrepresented—the broader "public interest"—as opposed to the many powerful and well-represented private or special interests.

These objectives are fulfilled primarily through research and education; students document a particular social problem and then attempt to marshall public opinion behind efforts to achieve reform.

PIRG reforms are seen as a means of improving society under our framework of constitutional rights and through society's major institutions. PIRGs work within the rules of the system—and with society's major institutions. As a result, many PIRG projects benefit from cooperation with policy makers at the local, state, and federal levels.

In a PIRG, the student board of directors, elected by their fellow students, hire professional organizers, researchers, and lobbyists to support their efforts and to provide continuity and a permanent base to the PIRG's work. At every juncture, however, students have the opportunity to learn by doing. Students not only select the projects PIRGs work on, they also determine the tactics and strategies that will be used. They combine knowledge with action in working on PIRG projects; the experience and skills they gain are invaluable assets for whatever they choose to do in the future, and can even earn them academic credits. Because of the structure and organization of PIRGs, three unique features have become the legacy of the movement: longevity, constant renewal as an institution, and proof that scholarship by students should be taken seriously.

The one underlying principle behind all PIRGs is that students are citizens, and that therefore their education should include experience in recognizing and solving society's shortfalls. Beyond that basic premise of students as citizens, PIRGs do not cling to any dogmatic ideology; they are simply democratic in operation and philosophy. College or university students vote democratically to form a PIRG on campus and to tax themselves to support it, student members then democratically elect PIRG leaders, and those leaders democratically choose the issues the PIRG will work on. The goal of PIRGs, then, is to give students and others the information and skills needed to function effectively in a democratic society—a goal that is often overlooked by high schools, colleges, and universities.

In PIRGs, students plan, implement, and follow up on sophisticated projects. These projects can be two-day surveys that call attention to a problem, or books that take two years to complete. After the research is done, students get the word out to the public and to appropriate officials or lawmakers. In addition to the usual publicity and media channels, several PIRGs use campus radio station facilities to produce syndicated radio shows on issues of student and community interest; others, like CALPIRG in San Diego, have had their own cable TV shows. Because of the volume of material they produce, some PIRGs have their own printing and graphics equipment for creating brochures, flyers, booklets, reports, and posters. Most PIRGs produce regular newsletters that go to students, community people, news media, and elected officials.

Most PIRGs offer some kind of hotline or action centers, with assistance on everything from consumer complaints to income and property tax matters. Sometimes the problems under study require legislative solutions. Here the prior PIRG work on an issue is invaluable; the most effective PIRG advocates (often student interns, supervised by a staff lawyer) approach their work as lobbyists armed with extensive research on a problem, backed up with real-life stories or experience gained through an ongoing action center. In this way, PIRGs have successfully defended product liability laws and obtained improvements in small claims systems, better regulation of auto-repair shops, stronger protection for the elderly against fraud, and fairer property tax laws, among many others.

Part of successful advocacy is being able to demonstrate to politicians that there is a powerful constituency behind a certain proposal. Since PIRGs are based on the notion that students belong to the larger community, not just to the campus, it is natural that PIRGs reach out to the community to build up support for their initiatives.

PIRG community organizing takes on many forms. Sometimes simple petition-gathering or letter-writing drives grow out of a consumer action center or out of a PIRG-sponsored radio show. Other times, well-planned, multistaged campaigns involve door-to-door leafletting, rallies, and community meetings. PIRGs with established door-to-door outreach programs have access to a network of tens of thousands of citizens who can be called on to do intensive grass-roots lobbying when necessary (an approach that worked well for the Massachusetts PIRG during the victorious 1981 fight to pass the state's bottle bill). Other PIRGs have done community organizing among low-income people—the New York PIRG in low- or moderate-income urban communities, for instance, and New Mexico and California PIRGs among Chicano farm workers.

Sometimes the courts are the best forum for addressing problems. PIRG lawyers have sued successfully in a number of instances—to stop improper expenditures of government funds, to protect constitutional rights, and to prevent government or private action that would endanger the environment, among others.

PIRGs also intervene in regulatory hearings—for instance, by representing residential consumers in utility rate-setting proceedings, or fighting environmentally unsound proposals.

Today there are more than 350 professional staff people employed by the PIRGs to help them carry on their work.

Over the past seventeen years students have been building a movement by combining solid research with organized action. Indeed PIRGs have accomplishments that are as diverse as they are impressive:

+ Massachusetts PIRG published the report "Hazardous Waste in Our Drinking Water" in April 1986 and successfully obtained voter passage of the Hazardous Waste Cleanup Initiative in November 1986 after collecting one hundred twenty-nine thousand petition signatures to place the measure on the ballot.

+ Legislation written by MOPIRG, signed into law in early May 1986, will force at least 70 percent of Missouri's banks to shorten their check-clearing periods.

+ Ontario PIRG and New York PIRG sponsored an educational "acid rain caravan" in New England and Canada in the summer of 1982.

✛ Several PIRGs joined in a nationwide student effort in 1982 to oppose federal budget cuts in financial aid for higher education.

✛ Minnesota PIRG litigated successfully in 1982 to gain major energy-conservation and antipollution-program concessions from a utility applying to construct a new coal-fired power plant north of Minneapolis.

✛ New York PIRG advocated successfully in 1979 for the nation's first truth-in-testing law regarding multiple-choice standardized testing.

✛ A California PIRG inquiry into fraudulent beef grading and price fixing was featured on a *60 Minutes* report in 1977, and led to fairer beef retailing practices in San Diego grocery chains.

✛ Vermont PIRG won legislation in 1973 establishing the country's first public dental health program for children.

✛ Indiana PIRG has conducted the country's longest-running grocery price survey, since 1972.

✛ New Jersey PIRG has sponsored the very successful "streamwalkers project," which monitors water pollution and industrial discharges in New Jersey; New York PIRG has produced several major reports on toxic chemical contamination in New York State, and its work has been featured on two 60 Minutes reports.

In addition, PIRGs have worked to eliminate discrimination against students by auto insurance companies and banks; they have established food cooperatives, consumer hotlines, and small-claims-court advisory services, and they have published a variety of useful reports—such as New Jersey PIRG's manual on solar energy and others on financial aid, property tax, banking services, toxic wastes, and auto repair.

A national PIRG movement is active and growing. The state PIRGs have established a national office, which helps students to organize new PIRGs and provides support services to the individual state PIRGs. Organizing drives to establish new PIRGs are continuing across the country.

The PIRG movement has been endorsed by national leaders over the years. In a special message in 1978, President Carter called on "faculty, university administrators, and all concerned students . . . to provide the support necessary to PIRGs so they may further expand their valuable work in solving some of the pressing political and social problems of our country."

Despite all that PIRGs have done they still face some obstacles. Though there are still plenty of serious problems today to be worked on by PIRGs, it is more difficult to link the idealism of students to the more complex and more diffuse problems of today. We are faced with a seller-sovereign economy that includes sellers who are monopolistic or oligopolistic. Less ethical business executives use significant resources trying to persuade consumers to buy what the sellers want to sell, notwithstanding the availability of more efficient, safe, economical, durable, and effective alternatives. This economy results in widespread price-fixed products and services; product fixing to thwart innovation; deceptive packaging and false advertisements; wholly ineffective or hazardous drugs; product obsolescence; energy-wasting vehicles, appliances, and other products; unsafely designed cars; junk food; serious product side effects such as pollution and poor land use; adulterated products; overselling of credit, insurance, and alleged health care—all complex problems to solve. We are reaching the point where the more default there is by citizens toward major pressing problems, the bigger the penalty. Fifty years ago if citizens did not do much about their electric utility, they paid a few dollars more on their monthly bill. Now if we do not do something we end up with a nuclear plant a few miles away and trucks and railway cars carrying radioactive waste. Different responses, and different consequences, result from citizen inactivity or indifference. Whether it is the arms race, asbestos, pesticide contamination, or acid rain and the greenhouse effect of carbon dioxide build up, there is an inescapable impact on the quality of community life. Now, because of the interdependence of society and the velocity of technology's impact, many perils know fewer boundaries.

The biggest immediate hurdle, however, is that most students do not adequately know the historic role of earlier students in American history and their contemporary role. First of all, they do not look at themselves enough as a unique class. In the United States there are thirteen million college students: community college, undergraduate, and graduate.

Students who are thirteen-million strong do not even have one weekly national television program that addresses what they are doing and thinking about outside the athletic arena. There is little self-realization that students need, deserve, and can demand such a program because they do not look at themselves as a class in the population, engaged in very interesting activities on campus. There are engineering students who are further developing solar energy and new kinds of automotive engines. Students are artists, poets, activists. They deserve the kind of attention now paid to the foolishness and the rites of spring that get most of the publicity.

Second, students underestimate their own power. If intimidated by university trustees who deny their democratic or educational rights, they must look for ways to challenge the trustees, uncover their conflicts of interest, and appeal for alumni and community support. They should realize that they can become the statewide experts on an issue, and that collectively they can put together a successful information or legislative campaign. It takes time, planning, and skill, but it can be done. Some people forget that students have been key organizers or backers of the major American social movements of the past two decades: the civil rights movement, the antiwar movement, the cultural movements of the 1960s, the women's movement, the welfare rights movement, and the environmental and antinuclear movements. And still today they have the time, energy, idealism, and resources at their disposal to act on the movements of today and the future.

Students today do not lack the basic generic idealism or desire for a better society. They do not lack the analytical ability to get the facts and the truth out about issues. Indeed, they can use the experience of past students' movements to build upon. But absent are street demonstrations, the draft, a disdained war, and other provocations and motivations that stir the young to action; instead, students face larger debts and a tighter job market than in the sixties. Nevertheless, in essence students are the same today as they were in the 1950s, the 1960s, and the 1970s.

So students need to look at their present assets. Students today are in different ways as important a source for citizen action as workers, homemakers, retired people, farmers, or other such groups of people in the United States. As a class, they measure up quite well both in terms of visibility and impact.

Students have four important assets that always should be remembered. They are near the peak of their idealism. They have access to technical information that is highly desirable in any kind of public policy struggle, to libraries, laboratories, and faculty.

Third, students can double-track their scholarly or academic work with their civic action. For instance, in political science courses, students can profile members of Congress or agency heads and disseminate what they learn through the media. In chemistry and biology courses, students can test drinking water, air samples, and food contamination and apply the knowledge to action.

A steel worker is going to have trouble going to the steel mill, putting in a day's work, and fighting pollution at the same time. The worker might be fired for being an advocate. Students are much freer, which is another asset. They are at an age and in a situation more conducive to assuming bold steps, to going out to protest and to demonstrate. The invisible chains are not so tight.

Fourth, students have their own media—newspapers and radio stations—and their gathering halls in which to meet and rally for their causes. Most citizens do not have these ready facilities where they are every day. What remains to develop is a frame of reference and sound directions for student energies. Students need to compare their rights with the rights, for example, of peasants in dictatorships—who cannot speak out, cannot protest, cannot demand better working conditions, cannot stop police brutality, cannot have democratic elections. The peasants feel they do not count, and they are alienated and they are blocked from participating in their own society.

The United States is different from many other nations because, in a thousand little ways over two hundred years, enough few people have at crucial times reversed the slide toward authoritarianism and brutality and cruelty. Today, students in other countries are on the ramparts risking their lives to get a fraction of the rights students in the United States have and do not use.

In our schools and universities, there is inadequate emphasis on learning the civic skills needed to study, evaluate, and improve society. Students are not encouraged to develop citizen skills. This results in a shameful waste of human potential and in millions of students who lack civic self-confidence. Given the opportunity, many students could become effective advocates for democratic solutions to our society's problems.

Our educational institutions are in large part neglecting an important mission. Students rarely have the opportunity to study the phenomenon known as corporate crime even though it is widespread in the United States. Engineering or physics courses do not provide students with an opportunity to apply what they have learned to a particular issue in the community that invites the merging of theory and practice. A pollution exposure or a sewage-system problem could provide a clinical opportunity for students to contribute to their community.

Students are citizens, they are buyers, they are or will be taxpayers—yet they are not taught enough about the ways citizenship skills can improve their performance in these roles.

Most students do not know how to shop wisely for credit, insurance, or a car. In the aggregate, this means that we will continue to have a seller-sovereign economy, not a consumer-sovereign economy.

Many students are not involved in civic activity because they have too many personal anxieties and concerns and problems. Different commitments and different priorities for more important civic purposes such as environmental health, a just government, or minority rights can help dissolve or reduce these personal perplexities.

Thousands of students have found it quite fulfilling to work with their own student public interest research groups. Students can learn and grow and start to be judged by what they do—rather than by their looks or their socioeconomic status. PIRGs allow students to learn how to manage an organization, affect their surroundings, and make their society a better one in which to live.

PIRGs are fine adjuncts to classroom education because practical civic education meshes well with the humanities, social sciences, and physical sciences. Students never forget PIRG experiences. They know that they can be effective citizens. They know how to take on the legislature. They know how to prod a mayor, run referenda, build coalitions, get their views across to the public.

The role of a citizen, the role of an advocate, the role of a consumer are rarely evaluated. These evaluations are relevant to the pain and pleasure of students. These roles are intellectually stimulating and challenging—and necessary. We cannot simply inherit what we inherit and ride along like a toboggan sliding down a slope. We have got to carve out new paths. The hard fact is that each of us is both a private citizen and a public citizen. Most students want a good station in life, a good income, a home, a car, and a vacation cottage. That's being a private citizen. Usually people are adequately motivated in that area. What we need is a special effort in the public citizen area. That effort can be endlessly rewarding. It is a pleasure for students to fulfill themselves by applying the principles of justice in a community in a democratic forum—complete with debate, dialogue, advocacy, assertion, and implementation. You lose some, you win some. You keep going. You create positive benefits out of losing and adversity by becoming more strategically astute and more determined.

The commonly accepted definitions of worthy and remunerative work in any society need periodic expansion. In a nation characterized by a progression of humane values, what starts out as a sensitive effort by a few volunteers often matures into more deeply rooted structures defending and implementing these values on a daily basis. Fire fighting, libraries, soil conservation programs, women's right to vote, worker safety, civil rights, consumer rights, legal services for the poor, feeding programs for the hungry, laws protecting the many against the few, educational institutions and services—these are a small sample of social improvements stimulated into being by people who had a broader definition of human values or citizen work than their contemporary cultures recognized.

Today, as our society comes under even greater pressures and risks, people should have the opportunity to raise their sights and expand their horizons well beyond the vocational training that comprises so much of what is called their formal education. They should see that there are careers whose essence includes the right, if not the duty, to take their conscience to work every day. There are careers that encourage people to be primary human beings, not secondary persons who have to prostrate themselves before the imperatives of corporate or governmental managers in order to make a living.

Taking one's conscience to work opens more doors to the wedding of analytic skills and developed values for a better society. More creativity, initiative, and idealism result. Psychological satisfaction and other forms of job enrichment flow from such good works. Certainly the demand for such work is increasing. Citizens groups all over the country are redoubling their efforts to defend the fundamental rights of Americans and to strive for safe products, healthy environments and work places, civil liberties and civil rights. New civic efforts, on matters as disparate as the nuclear arms race and utility rates, are in need of a wide spread of talented people to consolidate their energies into permanent organization. Consumer-buying groups—from heating fuel to insurance—can use business administration and marketing skills along with suitable computer applications. The growing number of statewide citizen utility boards (CUBs)—which began in Wisconsin in 1979 when a state law required telephone, electric, and gas utilities to carry periodically in their monthly billing envelope a notice soliciting residential ratepayers to join the CUB—are in need of economists, mass-mailing specialists, organizers, engineers, and other skilled staff members. The expansion of telecommunications into cable, video, and other outlets does not have to be restricted to Madison Avenue definitions of content. A whole new set of people, values, and needs can find expression if the citizen-entrepreneurs are at work to help people know or find out more about their world.

With so much of our economy afflicted by trivial jobs chasing manipulated wants, with so many of our public institutions replete with dronelike sinecures, there are serious unmet needs—shelter, food, education, health, justice, peace, safety—that go begging for enduring, imaginative, and problem-solving attention. There are openings for people who want to work the frontiers of a just society, who want to be such a society's pioneers in foreseeing and forestalling abuses while inventing a future in pursuit of genuine happiness.

Nourishing the taproots of an ever deeper democratic society can be considered one of life's great joys. Fulfilling one's talents and dreams in such a quest is the antithesis of a job that, however well-paying, makes you feel that you are just putting your time in, that life begins after the nine-to-five drudgery is over.

The wonderful aspect of social change work is the multiple exercise of your abilities that is involved. This work is not like the narrow-gauged responses on multiple-choice standardized tests. This work invites the application and development of multiple intelligences through the elaboration of one's mind, heart, and personality. No tunnel vision here.

The flow from knowledge to action draws upon the complete person with his or her catalytic and synergistic potential. Almost every skill and academic discipline can find a ready use in the complex drive for social change and in the protection and advancement of people and environmental rights in our society. Commitment, a reasonable self-confidence, a resiliency to overcome recurring adversities, a zest for work, and the ability to focus on larger goals without neglecting the daily details are some obvious traits of such a primordial advantage. A sense of humor for perspective and self-control also comes in handy.

And in good stead is an appreciation that there are not that many countries in the world where civic work can be carried forward as it can be in the United States under the blessing of our Constitution and the active citizens who give its words both foundation and life.

Many of America's students are among these active citizens. Thousands have joined together in public interest research groups, learning to combine their energy, academic knowledge, and organizational skills with their dedication to the community around them. They are preparing themselves for life and for work as citizen/activists—the true legacy of a democratic society.

Introduction to *A Public Citizen's Action Manual*

Originally appeared as an Introduction to
A Public Citizen's Action Manual, *by Donald K. Ross, 1973.*

IN THE EARLY DAYS of the Republic, the federal government did little beyond run the post office, collect tariffs, and provide for the common defense. And the state governments did even less. Instead, the symbol of American democracy was the New England town meeting, where citizens would gather by the village green to discuss and decide public affairs for their local government. Town meeting self-government should not be overidealized. There were the power elites and the poor in each little town. Yet it did, in an age far simpler than today's, operate on a premise that regular participation in government, beyond merely voting at election time, was an obligation of every citizen. The very format of the town meeting helped assure that that obligation would be fulfilled. The voters were the local legislature.

A pundit of 150 years ago might have reasonably predicted that citizen-oriented governmental formats would continue and that citizen efforts would expand as the nation's economic, legal, and technological structures expanded, as growth made people interdependent with one another and with institutions near and far. Such a logical development did not occur; in fact, something closer to the opposite happened. City political machines and city councils replaced the town meetings. Institutions of government and business became bigger and more distant from the people they were supposed to assist or to serve. The power of citizens was delegated to secretive legislatures and executive bureaucracies surrounded and dominated by well-organized special-interest groups that in turn learned that their best investment was the financing or buying of elections. Although increasingly shielded by institutional corruption, complexity, and secrecy from being regularly accountable to the public, government institutions fed the propaganda that elections were enough of a mandate and that such elections were adequately democratic. Especially during the past thirty years, corporations and other special interests have become only bigger and more astute in using governmental power and tax revenues to support their goals and subsidize their treasuries. This interlock between government and business has further complicated the task of citizen effort. For no longer can citizens start with the assumption that government is uncommitted to a special-interest group.

The people's loss of the power to govern themselves has deepened as the need for such self-government has risen. Certainly, the costs of citizen powerlessness are accelerating, if only because more people are being affected more ways by more events beyond their control. The American Revolution rang with the declaration that "the price of liberty is eternal vigilance." That is also true for "justice" and "peace"—and for "clean water" and "clean air" and "safe cars" and "healthy work places." But these good things, the blessings of liberty, will not come to pass until we cease viewing citizen involvement as just a privilege and begin defining our daily work to include citizenship toward public problems as an obligation.

This process starts with the individual's use of his or her time and energy. Most people think they are good citizens if they obey the laws and vote at election time. First of all, this is not enough by its own measure because too many people and powerful groups do not obey the laws and almost half the people over eighteen do not vote. But by a broader measure, voting can never be enough simply because decisions affecting people are made by government between elections. It is what citizens do *between* elections that decides whether elections are to be meaningful exercises of debate and decision or whether they are to remain expensive contests between tweedledees and tweedledums. It is not difficult to describe the citizenship gap. How many decisions in Washington, in the state capital, or in the city council involve even modest citizen participation? Why, at all levels of government, does the bureaucracy of executive branch agencies and departments decide matters without the legislature's knowledge or restraint?

The average worker spends about a quarter of his time on the job earning money to pay his taxes but spends virtually no time overseeing the spenders of those taxes. In the marketplace the same disparity between expenditure and involvement prevails. A consumer will spend thousands of hours driving a new automobile or eating food from a supermarket, but can find no way to spend any time to correct the overpricing, fraud, and hazards associated with these products. This is also the case with consumers taking out a loan or purchasing an insurance policy. It is no wonder that in the marketplace or in the halls of government, those who are organized and knowledgeable obtain their way. And those people who abdicate, delegate, or vegetate are taken.

Look at the United States today. Can anyone deny that this country has more problems than it deserves and more solutions than it uses? Its massive wealth, skills, and diversity should never have tolerated, much less endured, the problems and perils that seem to worsen despite a continuing aggregate economic growth. There seems to be less and less relationship between the country's total wealth and its willingness to solve the ills and injustices that beset it. The spirit of pioneering and problem-solving is weak. National, state, and local political leadership is vague at best, manipulative at worst. Facing the world, the United States stands as an uncertain giant with uncertain purposes toward a world in great need of its help and encouragement.

The reversal of these trends requires different leadership, to be sure, but it also requires a new kind of citizenship—public citizenship, part-time-on-the-job, and full-time—that engages in more exercise and less delegation of citizen power. The impulse to become a public citizen can spring from many sources—for example, a fundamental compassion for people and a sense of how inextricably interdependent a society we have. But in a practical, animating way, the spark is learning by doing, developing the techniques and strategies for citizen organization and action. If it can be shown that civic action can solve problems, then more people will shuck their indifference or resignation and want to join the effort.

How much work there is to do can be gauged by how little has been done. Every week, thousands of government agencies are making decisions which will affect the environment, utility rates, food prices and quality, land use, taxes, transportation, health care, employment, job safety, rent, schools, crime, prisons, peace, civil liberties and rights, and many other conditions of social coexistence now and into the future. Surrounding these agencies are lobbyists and advocates for special economic interests, some of whom take jobs for a few years within these agencies to make themselves more useful to their private employers later. Using numerous combinations of the carrot and stick, these pressure groups more often than not get exactly what they want. On rare occasions, a few full-time public interest advocates are present at the scene of the action.

Greatly outnumbered and equipped with only the justice and knowledge of their cause, these full-time citizens have achieved remarkable successes in the courts and before regulatory agencies and legislatures. The national citizens' struggles against the Supersonic Transport (SST), cyclamates, and the laxness of the Atomic Energy Commission neglect of adequate safety standards in nuclear power plants can be paralleled by hundreds of smaller victories at the state and local levels by an aroused citizenry. These Americans have learned that practice makes perfect and the more experience they accumulate, the more effective they become.

Given what a few citizens have done, it is a source of optimism to ask what many, many more like them could do in the future. A look at the past can make future projections of citizen impact more credible. Imagine that twenty-five years ago, citizens concerned about the future quality of life in America—say one out of ten adults—had gotten together to do something about it. Our urban centers would not be choked with cars, or laced with concrete belts that strangle the polluted cities in ever-increasing slums, corruption, crime, noise, and public waste. Our rivers, lakes, and oceans would still be producing untainted fish and would be safe for swimming. Drinking water would not be increasingly imperiled by pollution. The air would not be as filled with vile and violent contaminants, and the land not ravaged by insensitive corporate and government forces wasting our resources faster than they are replenished. Consumers would not be exploited by shoddy goods and services, deceptive practices, and price-fixing that (according to Senator Philip Hart's studies) take at least 25 percent of every consumer dollar.

Thousands of American workers would not be dying or sickened each year because of the toxic chemicals, gases, and dust that pervade so many factories, foundries, and mines. Equal opportunity in education and employment and adequate medical care would have avoided the misery that cruelly affects many Americans. Nor would hunger and poverty have been belatedly "discovered" in the sixties to be affecting some thirty million Americans. Factory and office workers would not be federally taxed 20 percent of their wages while countless men of great wealth are assessed 4 percent or less and many corporations with enormous incomes pay nothing or next to nothing. Small businessmen and homeowners could not be squeezed by powerful corporations whose predatory practices, underpayment of property taxes, and other abuses serve to further concentrate their powers and plunders.

Our Congress and state legislatures would not have continued to be underequipped and indentured to pressure groups instead of monitoring the executive branches and responding to the real needs of all the people. The power and expenditures of the military establishment and their civilian superiors would have been scrutinized, and perhaps curtailed, many painful, costly years ago. Above all, our political system would have reverberated with higher quality and dedication as the momentum of expert citizen movements increased.

A small number of citizens throughout our country's history have kept the flame of citizenship burning brightly to the benefit of millions of their less engaged neighbors. These true patriots have known that democracy comes hard and goes easy. To make democracy work, it takes work—citizen work. Many practical lessons can be learned from their experiences. Today, citizen groups are flowering all over the country, but they need to be better organized, better funded, and staffed with skilled, dedicated, full-time people. New citizen organizations such as Action for Children's Television in Boston (to stop television exploitation of children), Consumer Action Now in New York and Citizen's Action Program in Chicago (getting large industries to stop underpaying their property taxes), and GASP in Pittsburgh (fighting air pollution) are showing what can be done with minimum funds and maximum civic spirit. Courageous public citizens, such as education advocate Julius Hobson in Washington, D.C., are the true unsung heroes of American democracy. They have weathered community pressure to fight for a more just society in cities, towns, and villages around the country.

Many more citizens work to correct small abuses or deficiencies in the community once or twice and then retire to their former state of inaction. Such withdrawal does little to encourage others to engage in similar activities and does nothing to push initial drives beyond symptoms and treadmills to more fundamental reform that lasts. Easy disillusionment, the inability to rebound from difficulties, and lack of stamina must be candidly assessed and overcome through modest amounts of self-discipline. This is done in athletics and games all the time; it should also become the practice in the citizenship arena.

Citizen effort is everybody's business and everybody can engage in such effort. Who, for example, is better equipped to fight for women's rights or conduct consumer surveys than women, all too many of whom may be wasting much of their time daily watching soap operas, gossiping on the telephone, or "keeping in their place"? Who is better situated to further the job safety laws than workers exposed to occupational hazards and capable of organizing themselves or invigorating their unions to humanize the workplace? Who could be better motivated to reform the motor clubs than the disenfranchised members of these clubs—the millions of motorists? Who should be more inclined to expose the gross underpayment of property taxes by large companies than homeowners, small businessmen, and taxpayers generally? These are not wholly rhetorical questions. There are people who have indeed done all these things with some success. Had they been joined by some of the 99 percent of their neighbors, co-workers, or co-members who were inactive, truly enduring progress would have taken place. Sometimes one or two individuals are enough; over two million Chevrolets were recalled for defects because of one inspector in a GM plant speaking out; cyclamates were taken off the market because of two outspoken scientists in the Food and Drug Administration. For the most part, however, there is need for organization around public issues particularly when the hurdles are high and the facts are not yet available to the public.

Citizenship is not an endeavor reserved only for the most talented; anybody can do it and everybody should do it.

The exercise by citizens of their rights and responsibilities is what makes a working democracy ever sensitive to the just needs of its people. Such citizen effort is a learning process which can be increasingly advanced with practice. For increasing numbers of Americans, citizenship should become a full-time career role, supported by other citizens, to work on major institutions of government and business for a better society. It is this fundamental role of the *public citizen* in a democracy that must attract more adherents and supporters from across America.

Toward an Initiatory Democracy

Originally appeared in Action for a Change, *Grossman Publishers, New York, 1972.*

THIS COUNTRY HAS more problems than it should tolerate and more solutions than it uses. Few societies in the course of human history have faced such a situation: most are in the fires without the water to squelch them. Our society has the resources and the skills to keep injustice at bay and to elevate the human condition to a state of enduring compassion and creative fulfillment. How we go about using the resources and skills has consequences which extend well beyond our national borders to all the earth's people.

How do we go about this? The question has been asked and answered in many ways throughout the centuries. Somehow, the answers, even the more lasting ones, whether conforming or defiant, affect the reality of living far less than the intensity of their acceptance would seem to indicate. Take the conventional democratic creeds, for example. Many nations have adopted them, and their principles have wide popular reception. But the theories are widely separated from practice. Power and wealth remain concentrated, decisions continue to be made by the few, victims have little representation in thousands of forums which affect their rights, livelihoods, and futures. And societies like ours, which have produced much that is good, are developing new perils, stresses, and deprivations of unprecedented scope and increasing risk. As the technologies of war and economics become more powerful and pervasive, the future, to many people, becomes more uncertain and fraught with fear. Past achievements are discounted or depreciated as the quality of life drifts downward in numerous ways. General economic growth produces costs which register, like the silent violence of poverty and pollution, with quiet desperation, ignored by entrenched powers, except in their rhetoric.

But the large institutions' contrived nonaccountability, complex technologies, and blameworthy indifference have not gone unchallenged, especially by the young. The very magnitude of our problems has reminded them of old verities and taught them new values. The generation gap between parents and children is in part a difference in awareness and expectation levels. Parents remember the Depression and are thankful for jobs. The beneficiaries—their children—look for more meaningful work and wonder about those who still do not have jobs in an economy of plenty because of rebuffs beyond their control. Parents remember World War II and what the enemy could have done to America; children look on the Vietnam War and other similar wars and wonder what America has done to other people and what, consequently, she is doing to herself. To parents, the noxious plume from factory smokestacks was the smell of the payroll; children view such sights as symbols of our domestic chemical warfare that is contaminating the air, water, and soil now and for many years hence. Parents have a more narrow concept of neighborhood; children view Earth as a shaky ship requiring us all to be our brother's keeper, regardless of political boundaries.

In a sense, these themes, or many like them, have distinguished the split between fathers and sons for generations; very often the resolution is that the sons become like the fathers. The important point is not that such differences involve a statistically small number of the young—historic changes, including the American Revolution, have always come through minorities—but that conditions are indeed serious, and a new definition of work is needed to deal with them.

That new kind of work is a new kind of citizenship. The word "citizenship" has a dull connotation—which is not surprising, given its treatment by civics books and the way it has been neglected. But the role of the citizen is obviously central to democracy, and it is time to face up to the burdens and liberations of citizenship.

Democratic systems are based on the principle that all power comes from the people. The administration of governmental power begins to erode this principle in practice immediately. The inequality of wealth, talent, ambition, and fortune in the society works its way into the governmental process which is supposed to be distributing evenhanded justice, resources, and opportunities. Can the governmental process resist such pressures as the chief trustee of structured democratic power given it by the consent of the governed? Only to the degree to which the governed develop ways to apply their generic power in meticulous and practical ways on a continual basis. A citizenship of wholesale delegation and abdication to public and private power systems, such as prevails now, makes such periodic checks as elections little more than rituals. It permits tweedledum and tweedledee choices that put mostly indistinguishable candidates above meaningful issues and programs. It facilitates the overwhelming dominance of the pursuit of private or special interests, to the detriment of actions bringing the greatest good to the greatest number. It breeds despair, discouragement, resignation, cynicism, and all that is involved in the "You-can't-fight-City-Hall" syndrome. It constructs a society which has thousands of full-time manicurists and pastry-makers but less than a dozen citizen-specialists fighting full-time against corporate water contamination or to get the government to provide food (from bulging warehouses) for millions of undernourished Americans. Building a new way of life around citizenship action must be the program of the immediate future. The ethos that looks upon citizenship as an avocation or opportunity must be replaced with the commitment to citizenship as an obligation, a continual receiver of our time, energy, and skill. And that commitment must be transformed into a strategy of action that develops instruments of change while it focuses on what needs to be done. This is a critical point. Too often, people who are properly outraged over injustice concentrate so much on decrying the abuses and demanding the desired reforms that they never build the instruments to accomplish their objectives in a lasting manner.

There are three distinct roles through which effective citizenship activity can be channeled. First is the full-time professional citizen, who makes his career by applying his skills to a wide range of public problems. These citizens are not part of any governmental, corporate, or union institutions. Rather they are independently based, working *on* institutions to improve and reshape them or replace them with improved ways of achieving just missions. With their full-time base, they are able to mobilize and encourage part-time citizen activity.

With shorter workweeks heading toward the four-day week, part-time involvement can become an integral part of the good life for blue- and white-collar workers. Certainly many Americans desire to find the answers to two very recurrent questions: "What can I do to improve my community?" and "How do I go about doing it?" The development of the mechanics of taking a serious abuse, laying it bare before the public, proposing solutions, and generating the necessary coalitions to see these solutions through—these steps metabolize the latent will of people to contribute to their community and count as individuals rather than as cogs in large organizational wheels.

The emergence of capabilities and outlets for citizenship expression has profound application to the third form of citizenship activity—on-the-job citizenship. Consider the immense knowledge of waste, fraud, negligence, and other misdeeds which employees of corporations, governmental agencies, and other bureaucracies possess. Most of this country's abuses are secrets known to thousands of insiders, at times right down to the lowest paid worker. A list of Congressional exposures in the poverty, defense, consumer fraud, environmental, job safety, and regulatory areas over the past five years would substantiate that observation again and again. The complicity of silence, of getting along by going along, of just taking orders, of "mum's the word" has been a prime target of student activism and a prime factor leading students to exercise their moral concern. When large organizations dictate to their employees, and when their employees, in turn, put ethical standards aside and perform their work like minions—that is a classic prescription for institutional irresponsibility. The individual must have an opportunity and a right to blow the whistle on his organization—to make higher appeals to outside authorities, to professional societies, to citizen groups—rather than be forced to condone illegality, consumer hazards, oppression of the disadvantaged, seizure of public resources, and the like. The ethical whistle-blower may be guided by the Golden Rule, a refusal to aid and abet crimes, occupational standards of ethics, or a genuine sense of patriotism. To deny him or her the protections of the law and supportive groups is to permit the institutionalization of organizational tyranny throughout the society at the grass roots where it matters.

On-the-job citizenship, then, is a critical source of information, ideas, and suggestions for change. Everybody who has a job knows of some abuses which pertain to that industry, commerce, or agency. Many would like to do something about these abuses, and their numbers will grow to the extent that they believe their assistance will improve conditions and not just expose them to being called troublemakers or threaten them with losing their jobs. They must believe that if they are right there will be someone to defend them and protect their right to speak out. A GM Fisher Body inspector went public on defectively welded Chevrolets that allowed exhaust gases, including carbon monoxide, to seep into passenger compartments. He had previously reported the defects repeatedly to plant managers without avail. In 1969 GM recalled over two million such Chevrolets for correction. The inspector still works at the plant, because union and outside supporters made it difficult for GM to reward such job citizenship with dismissal.

The conventional theory—that change by an institution in the public interest requires external pressure—should not displace the potential for change when that pressure forges an alliance with people of conscience *within* the institution. When the managerial elite knows that it cannot command its employees' complete allegiance to its unsavory practices, it will be far less likely to engage in such actions. This is a built-in check against the manager's disloyalty to the institution. Here is seen the significant nexus between full-time and part-time citizens with on-the-job citizens. It is a remarkable reflection on the underdevelopment of citizenship strategies that virtually no effort has been directed toward ending these divisions with a unison of action. But then, every occupation has been given expertise and full-time practitioners except the most important occupation of all—citizenship. Until unstructured citizen power is given the tools for impact, structured power, no matter how democratic in form, will tend toward abuse, indifference, or sloth. Such deterioration has occurred not only in supposedly democratic governments but in unions, cooperatives, motor clubs, and other membership groups. For organizations such as corporations, which are admittedly undemocratic (even toward their shareholders), the necessity for a professional citizenship is even more compelling.

How, then, can full-time, part-time, and on-the-job citizens work together on a wide, permanent, and effective scale? A number of models around the country, where young lawyers and other specialists have formed public interest firms to promote or defend citizen-consumer rights vis-à-vis government and corporate behavior, show the way. Given their tiny numbers and resources, their early impact has been tremendous. There are now a few dozen such people, but there need to be thousands, from all walks and experiences in life. What is demanded is a major redeployment of skilled manpower to make the commanding institutions in our society respond to needs which they have repudiated or neglected. This is a life's work for many Americans, and there is no reason why students cannot begin understanding precisely what is involved and how to bring it about.

It may be asked why the burden of such pioneering has to be borne by the young. The short answer is to say that this is the way it has always been.

But there is a more functional reason: no other group is possessed of such flexibility, freedom, imagination, and willingness to experiment. Moreover, many students truly desire to be of service to humanity in practical, effective ways. The focused idealism of thousands of students in recent years brings a stronger realism to the instruments of student action outlined in this book. Indeed, this action program could not have been written in the fifties or early sixties. The world—especially the student world—has changed since those years.

Basic to the change is that victims of injustice are rising to a level of recurrent visibility. They are saying in many ways that a just system would allow, if not encourage, victims to attain the power of alleviating their present suffering or future concerns. No longer is it possible to ignore completely the "Other America" of poverty, hunger, discrimination, and abject slums. Nor can the economic exploitation of the consumer be camouflaged by pompous references to the accumulation of goods and services in the American household. For the lines of responsibility between unsafe automobiles, shoddy merchandise, adulterated or denutritionized foods, and rigged prices with corporate behavior and governmental abdication have become far too clear. Similarly, environmental breakdowns have reached critical masses of destruction, despoliation, ugliness, and, above all, mounting health hazards through contaminated water, soil, and air. Growing protests by the most aggrieved have made more situations visible and have increased student perception of what was observed. Observation has led to participation which in turn has led to engagement. This sequence has most expressly been true for minorities and women. The aridity and seeming irrelevance of student course work has provided a backdrop for even more forceful rebounds into analyzing the way things are. Parallel with civil rights, anti-war efforts, ecology, and other campus causes, which have ebbed and flowed, the role of students within universities has become a stressful controversy which has matured many students and some faculty in a serious assessment of their relation to these institutions and to society at large.

This assessment illuminates two conditions. First, it takes too long to grow up in our culture. Extended adolescence, however it services commercial and political interests, deprives young people of their own fulfillment as citizens and of the chance to make valuable contributions to society. Second, contrary to the old edict that students should stay within their ivory tower before they go into the cold, cold world, there is every congruence between the roles of student and citizen. The old distinction will become even more artificial with the exercise and imaginative use of the eighteen-to twenty-year-old vote throughout the country.

For the first time, students will have decisive voting power in many local governments. One does not have to be a political science major to appreciate the depth of resourceful experience and responsibility afforded by such a role. The quality of electoral politics could be vastly improved, with direct impact on economic power blocs, if students use the vote intelligently and creatively around the country.

Such a happening is not a foregone conclusion, as those who fought successfully in the past for enfranchisement of other groups learned to their disappointment; but there are important reasons why this enfranchisement of the eighteen- to twenty-year-old could be different. Over a third of the eleven and a half million people in this group are college students with a sense of identity and a geographical concentration for canvassing and voting leverage. Certainly, problems of communication are minimized, and a resurgent educational curriculum can be an intellectually demanding forum for treating the facts and programs which grow into issue-oriented politics in the students' voting capacities.

Full use of voting rights will induce a higher regard for students by older citizens, and elected and appointed officials. It is unlikely that legislators will rise on the floor of the legislature and utter the verbose ridicules wrapped in a smug authoritarian condescension that students are accustomed to hearing. From now on, legislators will pay serious attention to students. Therefore the student vote and the student citizen are intimately connected. Student Public Interest Research Groups (PIRGs) composed of full-time professional advocates and able organizers recruited by and representing students as citizens can have an enormous, constructive impact on society. It could be a new ball game, if the student players avoid the temptations of despair, dropping out, and cynicism.

There are other obstacles which students put in their own way that deserve candid appraisal by all those involved in establishing and directing student PIRGs. These are the shoals of personal piques, ego problems, envy, megalomania, resentment, deception, and other frailties which are distributed among students as they are among other people. On such shoals the best plan and the highest enthusiasm can run aground, or be worn to exhaustion by the attrition of pettiness. Even after the PIRGs are established, these frictions can continue to frustrate and weaken their missions. They will surface at every step—from recruitment to choice of subject matters to the relations with the PIRG professionals. They must be averted at every step with candor, firmness, anticipatory procedures, and a goal-oriented adhesion that reduces such interferences to nuisances. Such nuisances will serve to remind all how important are character, stamina, self-discipline, and consistency of behavior with the values espoused to the success of the PIRG idea and its repercussive impact.

Self-discipline must be emphasized in this student age of free-think and free-do. Many kinds of cop-outs come in the garb of various liberated styles which sweep over campuses. Clearly, there has to be, for the purposes discussed in this volume, a reversal of the dictum "If you desire to do it, you should do it" to "If you should do it, you should desire to do it." Such an attitude makes for persistence and incisiveness. It forces the asking of the important questions and the pursuit of the pertinent inquiries. It develops an inner reserve that refuses to give up and that thinks of ways for causes to be continually strengthened for sustained breakthroughs. The drive for a firmly rooted *initiatory* democracy is basic to all democratic participations and institutions, but initiatory democracy does not rest on the firmaments of wealth or bureaucratic power. It rests on conviction, work, intellect, values, and a willingness to sacrifice normal indulgences for the opportunity to come to grips as never before with the requisites of a just society. It also rests on a communion with the people for whom this effort is directed.

More and more students today are realistic about power, and they reject merely nominal democratic forms which shield or legitimize abuses. The great debates of the past over where power should be placed—in private or public hands—appear sterile to them. Students are suspicious of power wherever it resides because they know how such power can corrode and corrupt regardless of what crucible—corporate, governmental, or union—contains it. Moreover, the systematic use of public power by private interests against the citizenry, including the crude manipulation of the law as an instrument of oppression, has soured many of the brightest students against the efficacy of both government and law. At the same time, however, most concerned students are averse to rigid ideological views which freeze intellects and narrow the choices of action away from adaptability and resiliency.

Such skepticism can become overextended in a form of self-paralysis. I have seen too many students downplay what other students have already accomplished in the past decade with little organization, less funds, and no support. Who began the sit-in movement in civil rights, a little over a decade ago, which led to rapid developments in the law? Four black engineering students. Who dramatized for the nation the facts and issues regarding the relentless environmental contamination in cities and rural

America? Students. Who helped mobilize popular opposition to the continuance of the war in Vietnam and, at least, turned official policy toward withdrawal? Who focused attention on the need for change in university policies and obtained many of these changes? Who is enlarging the investigative tradition of the old muckrakers in the Progressive-Populist days at the turn of the century other than student teams of inquiry? Who is calling for and shaping a more relevant and empirical education that understands problems, considers solutions, and connects with people? Who poured on the pressure to get the eighteen- to twenty-year-old vote? A tiny minority of students.

Still the vast majority of their colleagues are languishing in colossal wastes of time, developing only a fraction of their potential, and woefully underpreparing themselves for the world they are entering in earnest. Student PIRGs can inspire with a large array of projects which demand the development of analytic and value training for and by students. These projects will show that knowledge and its uses are seamless webs which draw from all disciplines at a university and enrich each in a way that arranged interdisciplinary work can never do. The artificial isolations and ennui which embrace so many students will likely dissolve before the opportunity to relate education to life's quests, problems, and realities. The one imperative is for students to avoid a psychology of prejudgment in this period of their lives when most are as free to choose and act as they will ever be, given the constraints of careers and family responsibilities after graduation. The most astonishing aspect of what has to be done in this country by citizens is that it has never been tried. What students must do, in effect, is create their own careers in these undertakings.

The problems of the present and the risks of the future are deep and plain. But let it not be said that this generation refused to give up so little in order to achieve so much.

We Need a New Kind of Patriotism

Originally appeared in Life *magazine, July 9, 1971.*

A T A RECENT MEETING of the national PTA, the idealism and commitment of many young people to environmental and civil rights causes
were being discussed. A middle-aged woman, who was listening closely stood
up and asked "But what can we do to make young people today patriotic?"

In a very direct way, she illuminated the tensions contained in the idea
of patriotism. These tensions, which peak at moments of public contempt
or respect for patriotic symbols such as the flag, have in the past few years
divided the generations and pitted children against parents. Highly charged
exchanges take place between those who believe that patriotism is automatically possessed by those in authority and those who assert that patriotism is not a pattern imposed but a condition earned by the quality of an
individual's or a people's behavior. The struggle over symbols, epithets and
generalities impedes a clearer understanding of the meaning and value of
patriotism. It is time to talk of patriotism not as an abstraction steeped in
nostalgia, but as behavior that can be judged by the standard of "liberty and
justice for all."

Patriotism can be a great asset for any organized society, but it can also
be a tool manipulated by unscrupulous or cowardly leaders and elites. The

development of a sense of patriotism was a strong unifying force during our Revolution and its insecure aftermath. Defined then and now as "love of country," patriotism was an extremely important motivating force with which to confront foreign threats to the young nation. It was no happenstance that *The Star Spangled Banner* was composed during the War of 1812 when the Redcoats were not only coming but already here. For a weak frontier country beset by the competitions and aggressions of European powers in the New World, the martial virtues were those of sheer survival. America produced patriots who never moved beyond the borders of their country. They were literally defenders of their home.

As the United States moved into the 20th century and became a world power, far-flung alliances and wars fought thousands of miles away stretched the boundaries of patriotism. "Making the world safe for democracy" was the grandiose way Woodrow Wilson put it. At other times and places (such as Latin America) it became distorted into "jingoism." World War II was the last war that all Americans fought with conviction. Thereafter, when "bombs bursting in air" would be atomic bombs, world war became a suicidal risk. Wars that could be so final and swift lost their glamour even for the most militaristically minded. When we became the most powerful nation on earth, the old insecurity that made patriotism into a conditioned reflex of "my country right or wrong" should have given way to a thinking process; as expressed by Carl Schurz: "Our country . . . when right, to be kept right. When wrong, to be put right." It was not until the Indochina war that we began the search for a new kind of patriotism.

If we are to find true and concrete meaning in patriotism, I suggest these starting points. First, in order that a free and just consensus be formed, patriotism must once again be rooted in the individual's own conscience and beliefs. Love is conceived by the giver (citizens) when merited by the receiver (the governmental authorities). If "consent of the governed" is to have any meaning, the abstract ideal of country has to be separated from those who direct it; otherwise the government cannot be evaluated by its citizens. The authorities in the State Department, the Pentagon, or the White House are not infallible: they have been and often are wrong, vain, misleading, shortsighted or authoritarian. When they are, leaders like these are shortchanging, not representing America. To identify America with them is to abandon hope and settle for tragedy. Americans who consider themselves patriotic in the traditional sense do not usually hesitate to heap criticism in domestic matters over what they believe is oppressive or wasteful or unresponsive government handling of their rights and dignity. They should be just as vigilant in weighing similar government action which harnesses domestic resources for foreign involvements. Citizenship has an obligation to cleanse patriotism of the misdeeds done in its name abroad.

The flag, as the Pledge of Allegiance makes clear, takes its meaning from that "for which it stands": it should not and cannot stand for shame, injustice and tyranny. It must not be used as a bandanna or a fig leaf by those unworthy of this country's leadership.

Second, patriotism begins at home. Love of country in fact is inseparable from citizen action to make the country more lovable. This means working to end poverty, discrimination, corruption, greed and other conditions that weaken the promise and potential of America.

Third, if it is unpatriotic to tear down the flag (which is a symbol of the country), why isn't it more unpatriotic to desecrate the country itself—to pollute, despoil and ravage the air, land and water? Such environmental degradation makes the "pursuit of happiness" ragged indeed. Why isn't it unpatriotic to engage in the colossal waste that characterizes so many defense contracts? Why isn't it unpatriotic to draw our country into a mistaken war and then keep extending the involvement, with untold casualties to soldiers and innocents, while not telling Americans the truth? Why isn't the deplorable treatment of returning veterans by government and industry evaluated by the same standards as is their dispatch to war? Why isn't the systematic contravention of the U.S. Constitution and the Declaration of Independence in our treatment of minority groups, the poor, the young, the old and other disadvantaged or helpless people crassly unpatriotic? Isn't all such behavior contradicting the innate worth and the dignity of the individual in America? Is it not time to end the tragic twisting of patriotism whereby those who work to expose and correct deep injustices, and who take intolerable risks while doing it, are accused of running down America by the very forces doing just that? Our country and its ideals are something for us to uphold as individuals and together, not something to drape, as a deceptive cloak, around activities that mar or destroy these ideals.

Fourth, there is no reason why patriotism has to be so heavily associated, in the minds of the young as well as adults, with military exploits, jets and missiles. Citizenship must include the duty to advance our ideals actively into practice for a better community, country and world, if peace is to prevail over war. And this obligation stems not just from a secular concern for humanity but from a belief in the brotherhood of man—"I am my brother's keeper" that is common to all major religions. It is the classic confrontation—barbarism vs. the holy ones. If patriotism has no room for deliberation, for acknowledging an individual's sense of justice and his religious principles, it will continue to close minds, stifle the dissent that has made us strong, and deter the participation of Americans who challenge in order to correct, and who question in order to answer. We need only to recall recent history in other countries where patriotism was converted into an epidemic of collective madness and destruction. A patriotism manipulated by the government asks only for a servile nod from its subjects. A new patriotism requires a thinking assent from its citizens. If patriotism is to have any "manifest destiny," it is in building a world where all mankind is our bond in peace.

on practicing law

Opinion

From Student Lawyer, *December 1997.*

THREE THINGS every law student should remember:

1. You can make a difference to society as a lawyer.

2. You can make a difference to society today as a law student.

3. Nearly everything and everyone you encounter in law school and the legal profession will tempt you away from making a difference and toward making more money.

The law school brochures and commencement addresses show little evidence of the dominant influence on law school culture, particularly at the largest and most selective schools: the big law firms that service major corporations. For first-year students, it is not long before talk of Carbolic Smoke Balls and Blackacre gives way to the corporate recruiting season, with discussion of flybacks, hotels and summer associate perquisites like Circle Line cruises around Manhattan.

The ways and means of big-firm practice become part of a massive grapevine. From friends ensconced as corporate associates, from the legal newspapers and from summer jobs and numerous big-firm interviews, law students learn about what it takes to succeed in those richly decorated office suites. The acculturation process is dramatically pervasive.

Sociologist Robert Granfield published in 1992 an insightful book, *Making Elite Lawyers*, about what happens to Harvard Law School students between their acceptance and graduation. Granfield says that law school often turns idealists into amoral pragmatists. "The first-year students see the second- and third-year students interviewing with corporations and corporate firms," Granfield says. "They hear about the big money that can be made and the perks, the six-figure income down the road. Even the most 'socially progressive' students begin to rationalize working for the large corporate firms. They think that is the way to power and that they will be able to reform perceived wrongs from the top down. The only problem is that by the time they get there, they don't push for change because they have become part of the very power system they once disdained."

When the recruiters post their sign-up sheets, there is little time to deliberate. It can't hurt to sign up for the interviews, it can't hurt to try it for the summer, it can't hurt to do it for a few years after graduation. . . .

It *can* hurt you and it *can* hurt society. For a new book I have co-authored, we encouraged corporate lawyers to share their experiences with us. Here is a typical response from young lawyers at large firms: "Whatever happened to the belief that being a lawyer is a public service? On some days, I wonder why I went to law school. Many of us who have gone through the big-firm experience are sick of the hypocrisy, the overbilling and the ethical violations."

Young corporate lawyers wrote to us about endless hours, stifling specialization, unconscionable litigation tactics and shocking cynicism. Indeed, as power has shifted in recent years away from mega-law firms and toward increasingly demanding multinational clients, conditions look darker inside the corporate law factories.

But at the same time, things are looking up a bit in the law schools—at least as compared to when I attended Harvard Law School in the 1950s. More than today, the curriculum was shaped by the job market and business interests. We studied the estate of a wealthy person but never the legal problems of the poor. Motor vehicle tort cases involved negligent drivers, but never negligent automobile design. In criminal law, we learned about a teller stealing from a bank, but never about a bank defrauding customers. Basic questions about justice—the justice of the legal rules and the justice of the allocation of legal firepower—were rarely even asked.

Today, there are not many law professors who attempt to instill idealism in their students. Many come from corporate law backgrounds and, indeed, maintain lucrative corporate law practices on the side. An aggressive school of thought on the law school campus is the empirically starved, narrow ideology of "law and economics," which provides business with convenient formulae—ones that downplay hard-to-quantify human costs—to block health and safety regulations and antitrust enforcement.

But the law school of today at least does offer courses on topics like consumer law, environmental law and civil rights. You have more clinical programs that give students a chance to discover how the law can assist, or thwart, people of modest means. And corporate law firm interviewers sometimes will trumpet their authentic pro bono activities. Other times pro bono boasts are window-dressing, and lawyers who pursue them are unable to credit their efforts toward the billable-hours race.

These changes did not come out of nowhere. Nor did they spring from the self-enlightenment of law school deans. Your predecessors—students in the 1960s and early 1970s—made them happen. Law students organized civil rights work and even went to jail for their beliefs, illuminating the conscience of cloistered law professors. Law students insisted that poverty law and environmental law be added to the curriculum. They also demanded that corporate firms report their pro bono efforts to them.

Times are quieter now. The great injustices of today—embodied by the dominance of large corporations on our economics, politics and democratic procedures—are no less insidious but are more subtle. But that does not mean law students cannot use their new skills and status to improve society. A glimmer of how law students can still inspire their elders is seen every year at the annual meeting and dinner of the nonprofit National Association for Public Interest Law (NAPIL) in Washington, D.C. There the efforts of NAPIL in expanding its summer and year-long public interest fellowships and nudging law schools to establish loan forgiveness programs draw almost wistful admiration from the corporate lawyers who choose to attend. (You can reach NAPIL at 1118 22nd St. N.W., Washington, DC 20037; 202/466-3686.)

Finding a public cause or two—on campus or off—and devoting energy and passion to it can keep your legal education empirically rooted and normatively fired up. This is important because you need a sense of injustice in order to have a sense of justice.

The doors opened by your predecessors give you opportunity. There are not only a range of clinics—serving clients with legal problems in areas like housing, disabilities, welfare, immigration and consumer protection—but also, in some schools, programs to assist students who want to pursue good works after graduation. There are summer stipends, loan forgiveness policies and public interest coordinators in placement offices.

But it still isn't easy. Many schools lack such programs. And notwithstanding the growth of nonprofit public interest organizations since the 1960s, there are still a relatively small number of positions. Congress has cut, and threatens to destroy, the federal legal services program for the poor. So, for many, especially the less well-connected, it is a choice between a high-paying job and a low-paying job that lets you take your conscience to work.

The intrepid will find the rewards of a public-spirited career well worth the deprivations. Compare the world described above by disenchanted corporate lawyers to a recent letter to *The New York Times* from a legal aid lawyer: "My salary will never reach the stratospheric levels enjoyed by those in corporate law firms, but there are other compensations. I deal with clients personally, and try the most serious cases myself. Therefore, I get the satisfaction of seeing direct results from my efforts. Before I turned 30, I even argued an appeal before the U.S. Supreme Court. Equally important, I have time for other pursuits, like outdoor recreation, community affairs and a family life."

Public interest work is available, and new opportunities loom. In 1993, I joined with my classmates from the Harvard Law School class of 1958 to create the Appleseed Foundation, whose chief purpose is to establish, with young lawyer organizers, Centers for Law and Justice in state after state throughout the country. Appleseed (733 15th St. N.W., Suite 700, Washington, DC 20005; 202/393-1223), which has already started six centers, focuses on producing systemic solutions to pervasive problems, rather than on individual legal aid.

Appleseed offers one public-spirited alternative to a life of corporate law drudgery, but there are others. (See *Good Works, A Guide to Careers in Social Change*, edited by Donna Colvin, Barricade Books.) The choice is yours, and it's coming fast. Do you want to serve 40 or 50 years solely as an *attorney*, an agent representing zealously the commercial clients who hire you—or do you want to partake also of the world of the *lawyer*, a professional serving the higher goals of society and the justice system?

Daniel Webster said that the greatest work of human beings on earth is justice. You have an opportunity, beginning immediately, to advance this work.

Leadership and the Law

Originally published in Hofstra Law Review, *Spring 1991, from an address delivered at the Hofstra University School of Law on March 5, 1991.*

I WANT TO ASK a couple of questions so that I can get an idea of where you are on the spectrum of futility or grandeur. How many of you are determined, after you have finished your education and passed the bar, to be leaders in the advancement of justice in our society? Not very many. How many have decided to be followers? That leaves about seventy-five percent of you who have not expressed a preference for such an important career choice. Does that mean you still have the subject under contemplation? Or have never thought about it? Unfortunately, leadership and the law are not the subjects of a seminar, or even, very often, a topic of discussion of future leaders of the American legal system as they walk down the street. And yet, if you do not pivot around that sort of vector in terms of your future, you are going to get caught in a pattern of drudgery that has its own momentum. Although it is generally hard to find drudgery that has its own momentum, in our profession it is relatively easy.

For those of you who do very well, you will just repeat year after year and become partner. And you will get on some Bar Association committees, and maybe make a statement once in a while as a distinguished member of the Bar. And even those of you who do not do quite as well financially will be part of a process of legal representation that ignores most of the serious problems in our society and represents very few people in need.

But you will have status. People will refer to you as "counsel." And you will be able to walk with your head high at Bar Association meetings. The expectation level of the public, vis-a-vis the legal profession, is now lower than it is for George Bush. And when you have a profession that is confronted with such a level of cynicism or low expectation on the part of the lay people, that does not give you much of a push. You can begin to internalize your own status symbols, your own success, and live happily ever after as part of the core of five hundred thousand people in our country who, for the most part, represent about ten percent of the people who retain lawyers. The rest do not know, or are afraid, or cannot afford to use your services. This is not a very optimistic scenario, but it is something of which you ought to be aware. You have about fourteen thousand days left before you turn sixty-five, if you are about twenty-three or twenty-four. Some of you I see are a little further along. So you have about two thousand weeks, unless you want to make your imprint when you are in your seventies. Two thousand weeks. What is two thousand weeks? Look how fast last week went. . . . how fast yesterday went. . . . There is not much time.

Of course, it will last longer if you achieve less. It will feel longer, anyway. I recall a cartoon from the fifties. We used to have cartoons on morons, moron jokes. And one moron was demanding that he live a boring life so he would live longer. So if you do lead sluggish, routine-ridden, repetitive lives, where you keep saying, "I'm getting experience; I don't like what I'm doing at the firm, but I'm getting experience," forty years later you will have one year's experience, multiplied forty times, and life will have gone slowly for you. So that's a consideration. If you want time to slow down, engage in very tedious, repetitive work. On the other hand, if you look around and ask what the function of the law is in a society like ours, well there are a lot of possible functions. One of them is to defraud; to give people a sense that there is justice out there, but that they simply have not been lucky enough to find it; to give people a sense that there is some kind of ongoing structure, staffed by educated people who are able to foresee and forestall problems, to anticipate them, and to engage in preventative medicine, broadly defined, in society. And there are people who feel comfortable with this. There are people throughout history who live in hovels, who lose nine of their fourteen kids, but who feel comfortable because they can look at the King and Queen and feel part of the regal focus by way of osmosis or some sort of political empathy. They do not ask, "What are the King and Queen doing for us, with all of those jewels, all of that money, all of that power to change things?" Theirs becomes an observer society.

There are other functions of the law, one of which is to create jobs. The law does that very productively. It is an employment agency. Just imagine the number of jobs created by the lawyers who wrote the Internal Revenue Code and the Regulations. If you piled the Code and Regulations up here for the U.S., and then you did it for Canada, the pile for the U.S. would be about three times higher. Both are industrial societies; Canada would presumably come up with all kinds of similar legal problems. But their way is just not as good at creating jobs for bookkeepers, lawyers, accountants and congressional staff. So, the law is a job producer—a tremendous job producer. As a matter of fact, the more our society fails, the more jobs are produced. For example, street crime produces an enormous number of jobs—people designing alarm systems and closed circuit TV, policing neighborhoods. And now we have a corporate crime epidemic in our country, which, of course, we never study in law school.

When I was in law school, we had Criminal Law I, and it was street crime all the way until about May, when we stumbled upon a few larcenists—devils who stole something from banks. It was all crime in the streets, no crime in the suites. Besides, there were no job opportunities. You did not come out of Harvard Law School and, in being interviewed by a senior partner from Cravath, Swaine or Ropes, Gray, inform him that you had majored in corporate crime. And the curriculum just reflected the job market. By and large, it is the rare law school that will teach a course that does not have its counterpart in the job market, which includes law school teaching. And law schools have gotten better than they used to be. They used to be really the complete mirror image of the commercial job market. So if you had a lot of jobs available for estate planning, you had Estate Planning I, Estate Planning II, and a seminar on Estate Planning. If there were no jobs available for environmental lawyers, you had no courses on environmental law. At our law school, we had several courses planning for the dead, but none planning for the living. And it goes right down the line. Now you have some seminars in Poverty Law, where you may not be able to get a job right away, but by and large the curriculum reflects that prospect. And that is a tremendous depreciation of the potential of the law, because the principal function of the law ideally should be to curb the abuses of raw power and to clear the way for the fulfillment of the human potential.

And what if we asked ourselves, "What if the law were entirely abolished today . . . all laws were abolished, were repealed . . . would there be more street crime? would there be more corporate crime? would there be fewer or more opportunities?" Obviously, people do a lot of things in society irrespective of the law. They do not kill their neighbors, or refrain from killing their neighbors, because there are statutes on the books. You can have a situation in which you have a tyrant in charge of a society, and even the tyrant could not kill anybody that he wanted to kill. He would not kill just anybody; he would kill somebody, but not anybody. Why? What is it that curbs the discretion of even a totalitarian tyrant? There is obviously something at work—custom, a certain reciprocity, certain desires for tranquility, certain fears of vigilantism or revenge, and so on, that operate quite outside the law. But if you say that the law's function is to curb the abuses of power and to allow for the fulfillment—the courage and fulfillment—of the human potential, then what has happened to our society in the last fifty years? Can you develop some sort of index? Is there more power and less law operating? There's a lot more law on the books, but is there more power or less law?

Well, let's look at the decline of the ability of non-law to curb raw power—the schools for instance are a good example. Elementary schools: More and more of them are scenes for mayhem. There are all kinds of laws that prohibit kids from beating up each other, and beating up teachers, and so forth, but the mayhem keeps increasing. In 1939, in California, the principal student-related problems that were cited by the superintendent of the schools were as follows: talking out of line; sassing the teacher; chewing gum; and running in the aisles and the walkways. Now, according to a list made in 1989, these have been replaced by knives, guns, drugs, rape, arson, assault on teachers, and all kinds of mayhem. The laws have not changed; something else has changed. That is, we have gone beyond the effective limits of legal action or enforcement.

Take Washington for example. You have the breakdown of some very critical countervailing forces, which has resulted in hegemony between corporations and the White House, which usually is their business agent, certainly in recent years. The Congress has weakened vis-a-vis the Executive Branch; the Executive Branch is into so many things now that many judges say, "Well, that's a political question" or "That question is not subject to legal standing for challenge." You have the Democratic Party losing its status as an opposition party, through a lot of its own fault. So you no longer have a countervailing political force against the Republicans, who have been in charge of the White House and Judiciary for so long. The labor unions have declined seriously in terms of their countervailing force. So this pluralism that we all read about, which began building up early in this century, in the thirties and the forties, now has declined to a point where the multinational corporation has an ability to socialize its losses and privatize its profits; an ability to shape elections, to shape the agenda of elections; an ability to threaten domestic controls by saying it will just go overseas—close down the plants and go overseas—and export back into the U.S. to evade certain tax requirements, or environmental requirements, or whatever; an ability to merge with the media and not just to *influence* the media, but to *become* the media. GE owns RCA, which owns NBC, and the media is becoming more and more a conglomerate concentration from year to year. So, after law school, you will enter the midst of a fifty-year period characterized by the greatest corporate power ever in our history, except possibly that of the post-Civil War nineteenth century.

What does this mean for you? Well, first of all there is the great ability of some people not even to think about what it means. For example, if someone asks you, "How did you grow up?" you say to him, "Well, I grew up in Garden City . . . or Brooklyn." "And what was the main influence on your life?" "Well, I had a couple of parents, . . . or an uncle, . . . or a neighbor, . . . or whatever." Do you know how we grew up? We grew up corporate; the household is corporate. Right down to residential patterns, commuting patterns, housing adequacy, all the way down to what is placed in our minds. Let me give you some examples. Just ask yourself if you have ever spent five minutes of your life thinking about who owns the media, and who owns the airwaves. And why do the landlords—who are the public, which owns the airwaves—lease the spectrum to radio and TV networks, who are the tenants, for no rent, and the tenants decide, after paying the landlords no rent vis-a-vis the FCC, who says what on TV and radio. We have no access to our own property. We do not even have the models of Britain, or Canada—CBC or BBC—not to mention Holland. We do not have any assigned time for an audience network. We are shut out of our own property. Has anybody thought about this for five minutes? Well, here is where it ends. They say, "Well, if you don't like a program on TV in the United States of America, land of the free and home of the brave, you are free to. . . ." To do what? Switch it off. That is the beginning and the end of it—an absolutely devastating rejection of "I Love Lucy" reruns. Now, to think of it in terms of who owns property, who controls property: We own it; they control it; the FCC does not even charge rent for it. The end of the fairness doctrine has been decreed by the FCC. We do not even have the ascertainment requirements of community news needs incumbent upon radio and TV stations. The FCC is about to get rid of the cross-ownership laws. This only deals with the biggest operating media, which, poll after poll says, produces most of the news for most Americans. And have we talked about ownership and control for five minutes in our lives? No, because we grow up corporate.

There are millions of people who grow up and never distinguish the strategies employed by food companies for selling food. They attract you with one or more of the following criteria: tasty; easy to chew; pretty to look at; easy to prepare. You can meet all the criteria, and buy all the food with those criteria, and end up with low nutrition, unsanitary food, and harmful ingredients. How many people discuss that? How many people are aware of it? How many people are doing anything to fight against it? Not many. In a country that has enormous foodstocks and enormous malnutrition and adverse effects to the wrong kinds of food. We grow up corporate.

Standardized testing. We have all taken it, haven't we? The PSAT and the SAT and the LSAT. And we take these tests, and we get our scores, and we internalize the scores as a measure of our self-esteem and self-worth, providing the testing industry with a free police corps, mainly its victims. We decide whether we can do this or that in life depending on how we perform for three hours one April or one October. And the system is very administratively convenient for academia, and it has a pseudo-objectivity based on some very subjective assumptions, and the gates are opened or closed depending, to a far more significant degree than it should, on how you do on the standardized test. How much time have we spent challenging this kind of sorting out, this focusing on a very narrow brand of analytic skill, if you want to call it that? Some people would not even want to go that far. By the use of these tests, we ignore all kinds of other multiple intelligences that people develop in one form or the other, and we make our career choices based upon our performance on a multiple choice exam. Your bar exam is multiple choice, as you know, and I do not know how many people would go to a multiple choice lawyer, but the bar exam has it. So it's as if somebody is saying, "I'm going to test your athletic ability," and they test only your ability to play basketball. You say, "That's not a full test of my athletic ability. I can play soccer, and baseball, and tennis, and have a go at archery," and so on. But they say, "I'm sorry; we're just testing for basketball."

Well, that is what the multiple choice tests are. They are an insult to the diverse and multiple intelligences that people have, all of which are in great demand in our society. Take organizational skills, for example. What if you were the best social organizer ever to come to Hofstra? Would that have helped you with one question on the LSAT? It would not. Now, the LSAT does not purport to be that broad, and law schools claim not to give it an exaggerated significance. I love it when Harvard says that it does not give major weight to the LSAT. Whom are they kidding? How come so many of my classmates got C+s out of CCNY and a 98 on the LSAT, and got into Harvard Law School? Because Harvard loved CCNY? It is very easy to assume that you are going to be bright because you can answer, very quickly and under totally unrealistic time pressures, these kinds of foolish, fraudulent questions that allow for no human intellectual nuance, not to mention ingenuity or creativity. So we go through all of this while these tests do not test the most important features of our personalities; those that will spell success in our lives. Nor do they purport to. They do not test our judgment, experience, wisdom, creativity, imagination, idealism, stamina or determination. Otherwise, they test everything.

Now, until NYPIRG started questioning, until we put out a report on the ETS, it was not even a subject of debate. We grew up corporate. Defining human intelligence and then measuring you up against that narrow definition are pretty powerful tools in the hands of a couple of corporations called ETS and the College Board. We grew up corporate. We not only did not question it; we willingly became its victims, and we went through life moping or with our heads held arrogantly high, depending on how we scored on those tests.

We grew up corporate in many other ways as well. For example, we rarely question whether there can be equal justice under the law if corporations, as artificial entities, are given the same set of constitutional protections as individual flesh and blood human beings are. Now, there are certain things that corporations can do that we cannot do, no matter how ambitious we are. First of all, we cannot create our own parents, and corporations create their own holding companies. Ask Chase Manhattan Bank and Citicorp. They, a number of years ago, created their own bank holding companies, chartered them in Delaware, and knocked out some interesting provisions in federal law dealing with cumulative voting. They can create their own parents. They can also commit a crime and then disappear. People often try to do that, but they are called fugitives. Corporations are just called Chapter II. They have immunities and privileges and insularities and an ability to transfer costs that human beings do not have. When General Electric and Westinghouse were convicted of a price-fixing conspiracy around 1960, in a rare criminal prosecution of the antitrust laws that ended with jail terms, hundreds of millions of dollars were involved, and the longest sentence was six weeks. They did not like rubbing elbows with somebody who was in for five years for forging a two hundred dollar check. Before it was over and the fines were imposed, a lawyer representing them in Washington got the IRS to issue a regulation allowing these payments to their victims (these were treble damage settlements to the electric utilities and so on) to be deducted as ordinary and necessary business expenses. Next time you get a traffic violation ticket, see if you can deduct the fine as an ordinary and necessary business expense. So we grow up corporate, and law students and lawyers are no exception.

We have got to face up to the citizens' movement in terms of what the roles of lawyers are going to be. First of all, a most important point to recognize is how little of what you do and get paid for as a lawyer is done to advance the quality of our democracy. Rather, it is to represent power and to make it more powerful; or it is to represent power and to preserve it from being tamed by an assault from some legal process or regulation. What are the challenges that you are going to be facing and do you care? Well, one is that violence is now becoming environmental on a big scale and the law is not catching up. You have got the greenhouse effect, the warming of the planet, acid rain, ozone depletion. For those of you who think big, those are going to be real challenges to the international rules of law: treaties, multinational, international type commissions, dealing with the predations of multinational corporations vis-a-vis the ocean, the tropical forest and other natural resources. That is a major new chapter of world violence that will occur, and it will rebound in terms of famine and soil erosion, and more human "emotion pictures" that we see on television when we are asked to help Africa or Asia or some other area.

Violence then will come in some other forms as well. For example, the misuse of genetic engineering. The day will come when there will be more talk of the adverse effects of changing the genetic codes of flora, fauna, and eventually human beings. That is going to be a very, very serious ethical challenge—probably the most serious ever in the history of the law. There are also some of the more traditional problems: hunger; no housing; police brutality; discrimination; and others that present their own forms of violence, of course. Where are the institutions to deal with this? Where are they? We can count them on the fingers of two or three hands. The NAACP, the ACLU—they are starving for funds to begin with. We have a few more environmental groups. We have roughly a thousand full-time public interest lawyers in the country. We have four thousand legal service attorneys. They are under very strong pressure not to bring law reform lawsuits, but rather just to represent clients in the run-of-the-mill landlord-tenant cases, or domestic relations cases. Heaven forbid that you bring class actions; that you bring suits dealing with wholesale justice. That is one of the legacies of the Reagan-Bush regime, which spent so much of its time building a government in Washington, of the Exxon, by the General Motors, for the DuPonts. And that, of course, limits the desirability of entering public service law since there is no longer a strong law reform component to it.

Now, as lawyers you are growing up in a society in which you are very lucky to grow up. For better or for worse, lawyers have a tremendous role in society. They become secretaries of state. They are heads of corporations. I was in Japan last year and I talked to a group of Japanese lawyers. One lawyer came up to me and said, "Did you know that you just addressed ten percent of the entire bar of Japan?" I said, "What do you mean?" He said, "Well, there are fifteen thousand lawyers in Japan and you addressed fifteen hundred of them. And I asked him, "Why are there so few lawyers?" And he said, "Because in Japan things are worked out." What does that mean, "things are worked out?" I'll leave that to your imagination. But lawyers have a lot of leverage in our society. They are not as circumscribed as they are in Western Europe, not to mention China. There is a much broader leeway.

So what do you want to do with yourself as a lawyer? Let's look at some scenarios. First, let us eliminate the factor of salary and bonus, okay? Let us assume that money is no object, no object whatsoever. How many of you would choose to become public interest lawyers rather than corporate lawyers? [An overwhelming majority of the audience members raise their hands.] Alright, keep your hands up. Okay, now let's say that the most you could make as a public interest lawyer was fifty thousand dollars. How many hands would stay up? [Less than one third of the raised hands remain raised.] That's worse than I thought. I was ready to go to twenty thousand. Alright. So you are being deterred by debt load and other things.

Now you have to ask yourself, how many of you are first stage pioneers? First stage pioneers are the following: Edgar and Jean Cahn, out of Yale Law School in 1964, who wrote an article in the *Yale Law Journal* that led to the development and establishment of legal services—four thousand jobs. They went to Washington, they got the Bar Association and the ABA behind them, and they lobbied it through Congress. First stage pioneers: four law students out of Northeastern area law schools—1970—wanted to do environmental law, but could not find any jobs. They started the Natural Resource Defense Council—budget last year: fifteen million dollars. Dozens and dozens of lawyers working all over the country and other parts of the world on arms control, water purification, pollution control, radiation lobbying, research. Those are first stage pioneers. They came out with nothing and they built institutions that have developed many, many public interest jobs.

How many of you think you could handle being first stage pioneers? Two? Alright, second stage pioneers. Second stage pioneers—lower risk. What they can do is, they say, "Look, I worked for a summer with some canvassing organization, so I'm a little familiar with canvassing. What I'm going to do is, I'm going to set up my own canvass, delineate my own issue, my own geography where I'm going to work, and I'm going to raise my own funds for my public interest law office." Let us say that you want to focus on migrant worker mistreatment here on Long Island. I am not sure that there is any agricultural land left. Or you want to deal with subterranean water contamination. And you want to start your own program. And you have had experience canvassing with NYPIRG or some other group. And you know that it is largely a matter of two things: organizational expertise and a good issue that appeals to people at the door. So that is the second stage pioneer. You go with relatively low risk. You are able to marshall your own support. How many of you are interested in doing something like that? More.

Okay, let us go to the third stage pioneers. The third stage is where you work two jobs. You work by day to pay your debts and your rent and so on, and you have a part-time job in the area of your belief. So, for one job you leave your conscience at home for your client involvement, and the other part-time job is what you really want to do in life, but you are inching in as a practitioner, and you cannot afford to do it full-time. Now, there are a lot of groups that need to be pushed forward in the civic arena in new and bold ways. They need fresh blood. They need new ideas. You can attach yourself to one of the ongoing groups: a homeless action group or any number of groups all over the place. So you can basically work by day the regular job, and during weekends and a few hours at night you can begin to establish the kind of career pattern you really want to pursue. How many would be interested in that one? Even more.

Now, the fourth stage is where you say, "Look, I've got to earn a good amount of money, and I'm going to go and take a government job that's a good government job. I'm going to go work for the Civil Rights Division, the Justice Department or the dwindling Solar Energy Unit of the Department of Energy, or any other unit, state or local. And I want to do it because, first of all, it pays a living, a salary, and second, it develops an understanding of why things do not work in government, so that when I'm on the outside, battering away against some powerful interest group, to get a safety standard issued, or a subsidy stopped, I'll know how to do it. But,

I'm not going to stay forever in this civil service job. I'm going to stay, pay my debts, learn the techniques, and then go out and do the kind of work I want to do." How many? Government? [Almost no one raises a hand.] Wow, it really is bad, isn't it? See, that's where many of us wanted to work when we were in law school. And now, I guess the denigration of government service—people thinking that government cannot accomplish anything—has lowered it in many people's esteem. Remember, there is a lot of good whistle-blowing that can be done in the government, to the press, if you do not want to do anything else. And there is a lot of good work that still can be done if you go in as a group and develop a network among agencies.

For instance, why did the Federal Trade Commission, three weeks ago, bring an antitrust suit against baby formula manufacturers? For price-fixing; enormous overcharging, especially to government agencies that had to buy the formula for feeding programs for poor infants. Why did they bring it? This is the Reagan-appointed Federal Trade Commission, long de-fanged, the leading pretense of protecting consumers. Well, first of all, there is an organization called the Council on Budget Priorities, which was started by Bob Greenstein, who used to work for us. And he puts out reports on all kinds of government services and how the budget is allocated: so little is going to human beings and so much is going to armaments, etc. And in doing that, he started studying the infant feeding program, the WIC program. And he was being told that they do not have enough money in the budget to get enough infant formula for all the infants who need it, who have been abandoned. And he asked, "Well, how much are you paying for the formula?" And they said, "We're paying so-and-so." And he said, "This is ridiculous! There must be price-fixing going on. There are only two or three companies manufacturing infant formula." And he had lunch with a former Federal Trade Commission Chairman, Mike Pertschuk. And Pertschuk studied this problem, and he went over to the Federal Trade Commission and he said, "You know, you ought to do one thing this year with your budget. Why don't you bring an antitrust suit?" So now they are bringing an antitrust suit. Suddenly, some young lawyers in the Federal Trade Commission have a reason for being. They are beginning to enjoy what they are doing.

See how it works? You have a citizens' group; someone who left government who heads another citizens' group. Pertschuk heads the Advocacy Institute in Washington, which trains citizen lobbyists and develops strategies to go after the tobacco industry, for example. Very creative strategies are developing in the anti-tobacco drive in this country. And, going to the government agencies with a lot of data in order to get something like this done is a good strategy.

Now, there are other opportunities too. If you want to go into the cooperative movement, a consumer cooperative bank has opportunities in Washington. Most students have never heard of it. Turns out they have got more money to lend than they have co-ops filing loan applications. But they have a development unit that is supposed to encourage development of co-ops in poorer urban and rural areas around the country. Again, you do not know about it, and if you do not know about it, you are not going to aspire to an alternative form of economic delivery, which is the consumer cooperative form.

Now, this continues in many modes. The point is, you have got to give yourself a chance. Do not immediately prejudge the absence of the kind of work you would like to do but cannot find. You know, the S & L bailouts are producing enormous work for lawyers. The RTC just paid a half a billion dollars to outside law firms. And that sum is to deal with the wreckage of the S & L bailout, which proceeded from speculation or criminal business activity, and a heavy dose of mismanagement affecting about one third of the S & Ls in the country. Now, that is very parasitic work. That is clean-up work for something that never should have happened in the first place. Now, how do you work as a lawyer and anticipate those kinds of problems? Whether it's insurance, banking, utilities, nuclear power, or whatever. Here is where you get down to something that should be a seminar at every law school, and that is "Institution Building."

How do you, as lawyers, put yourself in a position where you are able to develop mechanisms that facilitate the banding together of like-minded citizens around certain goals and certain missions to improve the society? Now, you have millions of ratepayers of electric, gas and telephone services. You probably have one to two percent of them who will pay to join a national and state ratepayers' organization. But how are you ever going to reach them? You do not have money to put ads in the paper or on television. How are you going to reach them? So you think—you've got a seminar exam here—of a mechanism to organize, inexpensively and repeatedly, residential ratepayers, so they can have their own lawyers, economists, organizers, canvassing, to shape TV and energy policy in the United States and to be the important players with the utilities on the other side of the table. How would you do it? You've got an exam. The clock is ticking. How would you do it?

Governor Cuomo, about a month and a half ago, had a news conference adopting our proposal to develop a solicitation envelope and to allow it to be put in any state government mailing to more than fifty thousand New Yorkers, inviting them to join the Citizens' Utility Board, where they would elect their council of directors, who would provide them with full-time consumer advocacy. We proposed this in Wisconsin, which adopted it; in Illinois, which adopted it. And just like that in Wisconsin, over one hundred thousand people joined. Minimum dues were five dollars, but people averaged twelve or fifteen. And, in a state like Wisconsin, which is not much bigger than Long Island in population, to have a ratepayers' group with one hundred thousand members, and a full time staff, and an ability to reach more people through their newsletter and the media, is quite impressive. One hundred eighty thousand people joined during the first twenty months in Illinois. All it was, was that when they opened their electric or gas bill, out fell a little postage paid envelope that said, "Are you fed up with high utility rates?" They said, "What's this doing in my bill?" So you would reach them at their peak point of interest. And the result, this is what it looks like, in your bill, just a little insert like this, "Dear friend," and a little coupon. Look at this carefully. It is going to be the silicon chip of the citizens' movement once it gets under way.

Now, the beauty of it is that it does not cost the taxpayers a cent and is voluntary to the consumer to join. And it does not cost the utilities anything, because they do not exceed the weight for first-class postage. So it is very ideologically invulnerable to the right wing yahoos who do not want to give the people any voice vis-a-vis their own corporate vehicle. Now, look what happened—I will show you how ideology and power affect Constitutional law. Now, here you have monopoly utility companies. You cannot say that you are going to go across the street to a competitor. Gas, telephone, electric. Monopoly. Guaranteed rate of return. And they hire lawyers, advertisers, public relations people and consultants to beat you in rate proceedings, and then hand you the bill, and that is permitted! Now, these are three very powerful privileges, are they not? Monopoly, guaranteed rate of return, and the power to force you to pay for your own defeat.

To counteract this, a California regulation says that the utility company has to put this in their envelope so that people can band together and protect themselves. And it does not cost the utility company anything! It then goes up to the Supreme Court of the United States, after having been dismissed by the California Supreme Court—a lawsuit by the utility claiming that this insert requirement is a violation of the monopoly utilities' freedom of speech right to remain silent. The utility claimed that the polemic in this insert was so provocative that they had an irresistible impulse to rebut, and that this constituted an impermissible violation of their first amendment right to remain silent. The opinion, by Lewis Powell, a five to three decision—Powell was a former utilities lawyer from Richmond, Virginia—said that the companies'—the monopoly utilities'—First Amendment rights were being violated. And this California requirement was no longer constitutional. Rehnquist dissented, with heaps of scholarship and ridicule, but he lost, five to three.

So, now it is done on a state mailing basis because the utility companies cannot complain if the Motor Vehicle registration envelope reaches you with this insert. This is what Governor Cuomo is in the process of instituting. Now, you just look for a moment at the opportunities for full-time legal work in these kinds of organizations. We hope to overturn the decision, Powell's decision; there are grounds to believe that it could be overturned if we get a proper case. Utility companies, banks, insurance companies, all over the country, would have these groups noticed in their billing envelopes or bank statements. Your 1040 tax return could have a notice saying, "Are you fed up with the way your taxes are used?" You could join the taxpayers' group. Television could open an audience network where one hour of prime time would revert back to a Congressionally chartered non-profit audience network, open to any viewer who wanted to join for minimal annual dues. And they could establish their own reporters, producers, studios, for professional use of that one-hour period. That would open up opportunities.

Now, building institutions like these—and this is just a glimmer of the possibilities—is something you should give yourself a chance to imagine and to dream about, and perhaps to work with as interns, and as part-time jobs to go along with your conventional work. The law schools have fellowships, student-funded fellowships—I think you have such programs here—loan forgiveness programs. Twenty-five law schools now have loan forgiveness programs, so that if you get a job with a non-profit group or in public interest law, and you make under thirty thousand dollars, or whatever, your loan, principal and interest, are forgiven for every year you have that job and meet the criteria. I am told that at many law schools these programs are undersubscribed. That is, there are more opportunities than law students are taking. This is a rather sad situation, and it goes to what the problem is: you have got to free your imagination; you have got to value yourself more; you have got to have a higher estimate of your own significance and ability to change this world. You have to avoid the deadening hand of routine induced by lucrative bonuses and salaries. You cannot simply plod through law school, a pseudo-Socratic method of memorization, regurgitation and veg-etation. You have got to look at yourself as relatively unique and fortunate human beings, compared to people your age around the world who live under dictatorships, or in places where there are no civil juries, contingent fees, and roles for lawyers; where almost everything done has to be accomplished through formal political parties, such as in Western Europe, for instance, rather than also through civic action organizations. There are not many people like you around the world, people who can breed justice, build institutions, and begin to have the law be more far-seeing and preventative. I do not know how to convey the quality of life you would lead if you chose that, other than to urge those of you who have experience in these lines of work to do some clinical work for some group, or to intern for some group, or simply to read. Yes, read. There is a school in Dallas, a junior high school, that put disks in place of books for science, and the kids love it. They said, "We don't have to read. We only have to watch." Watch the screen.

This is a book called *The Other Government: The Unseen Power of Washington Lawyers,* by Mark Green who, as many of you know, is New York City Commissioner of Consumer Protection. Two thirds of the book is a case study of Covington & Burling, the biggest then—law firm in Washington; how they represent the drug industry and the tobacco industry; how all these lawyers go home and tell their spouses and children the wonderful things that they have done. And the other third is on Wilmer, Cutler, Pickering. There has never really been a book quite like this. It gives you an idea of what corporate practice is like; what you have to do in terms of your conscience, and sense of justice, in return for a large retainer. So it is quite important to read this book. It has gotten worse since this book came out, and this is before the whole merger & acquisition racket, before Finley Kumbel's collapse. And you should read one of the two books on Finley Kumbel's collapse. There is also a book called *Verdicts on Lawyers,* written by lawyers and a couple of judges. You can imagine what the answer was. It opens up a critique of the profession that you may not be getting in your courses. And you read a book like *Taking Ideals Seriously,* and you say "Oh yeah, I should have thought of that." And of course that's right, which indicates some sort of a deficiency in your formal curriculum, and how narrow it might be. There is a lawyers' public interest movement called Equal Justice Foundation, which itself is now merged into a group called NAPIL—National Association of Public Interest Lawyers—which is fostering and pushing for more loan forgiveness programs, student-funded fellowships, and trying to get the corporate bar to pay for some of these, shall we say, public interest chairs.

Professor Harry First at NYU was an early summer intern for us, and he wrote a law review article on Delaware Corporate Law, and he has never been the same since. He put out the first casebook on business crime—not white collar, not individual, but basic organizational corporate crime—with the hope that there would be more seminars and courses in this area. And his experience in Delaware was that, as you know, Delaware is the corporate Reno for chartering—and they have used it as a revenue source all these years, since 1900, when they beat out New Jersey, which wanted to be the number one corporate Reno; but they could never match Delaware's race to the bottom. The corporate charters and constitutions are very biased against the shareholders and consumers, and very much out of date. And we still do not have federal charters for major industrial or other corporations; they are all chartered at the state level. Four hundred fifty of twelve hundred New York Stock Exchange companies are chartered in Delaware. Their franchise fees at one time represented twenty-five percent of Delaware's revenues, but are presently down to about ten percent. Now, Delaware has no interest whatsoever in using the corporate charter as a mechanism for corporate accountability. It is a very permissive jurisdiction: a permissive judiciary and an even more permissive legislature. GM could buy Delaware. It is a very small jurisdiction. GM could buy it in a weekend if Dupont was willing to sell it.

Now, I want to end with some more quick job opportunities. There are four thousand attorney's fees statutes at the state level that are grossly under-utilized. There are one hundred twenty federal attorney's fees statutes that are also grossly under-utilized. There must have been some gnome on Capitol Hill who slipped these provisions into the amendments of statute after statute. We had to have a seminar for lawyers in Washington ten years ago to teach them about the Moss-Magnuson Act, which provides that attorneys who represent car owners against dealers and manufacturers for breaches of implied warranties can be awarded attorney's fees if they win. The use of the Odometer Disclosure Act is almost zero.

There are environmental statutes that award attorney's fees—not just civil rights statutes—and it would behoove you to consider, in your own practice, whether you want to supplement your income using more of these attorney's fees statutes. Now, Duke's journal, *Law and Contemporary Problems,* has collected these four thousand state attorney's fees statutes, and we have a list of the federal attorney's fees statutes. And it is remarkable how these market-oriented attorney's fees statutes are not catching a market response, in large part because of lack of knowledge about them, and in large part because when you are in a typical law firm, they do not want to mess around with this sort of stuff. They are after bigger fish and larger corporate clients against whom many of these attorney's fees statutes are directed.

And finally, there are group buying organizations. We are going to see more group buying. Up and down the east coast there are heating oil group buying associations comprising many thousands of households that are negotiating discount heating oil contracts. Now that, with two-way cable and computer networks, can spread all over the country, so that maybe ten or fifteen years from now there will be, on one side of the table, lawyers for four million dues-paying consumers, across from the lawyers from Sears Roebuck or Citicorp, to redraft the loan contract so that it is not so much a contract of adhesion and so that it reflects consumers' rights. Or in the negotiations of warranties with the auto companies. Or developing, through negotiations with testing laboratories, specifications for products to ensure environmental or consumer health and safety. This will be the biggest consumer lawyers' job producer of all. And it will lead to the development of the concept of the giant organized consumer negotiating with the giant multi-national corporation, as larger and larger portions of the corporate market devolve into fewer and fewer corporate hands.

NYPIRG started the fuel buyers' group, which has about fifteen thousand members, and they are thinking of moving into other areas. Home repair costs, based on the Triple A model, for example, is a very attractive opportunity for any legal entrepreneurs in this audience. You can go into counteracting privacy invasion databases. You can begin developing information systems for discerning the cheapest auto insurance, life insurance or other insurance policies, through a subscribed, computerized system. Through telecommunications technology, the sky is literally the limit.

I hope that I have succeeded in conveying some of the opportunities and horizons open to you. Those who come after you will have an easier time than you did if you are the pioneers. But nothing can happen in this area without your developing a heady sense of injustice about situations that you are not going to tolerate in this society or in this world. And that is something very few people can help you with (other than to give you experiences in which you are up against injustice) unless you are able to evolve your intellect and develop the motivation as to what you want to do with your time and your skills. As Professor Cahn at NYU once said, "You'll never have an adequate sense of justice unless you have an adequate sense of injustice as a frame of reference." And to do that, you have got to light a fire inside yourself, so that your heart works in tandem with your mind, and you begin to . question the assumptions of a society that raises its children corporate.

I must add that this is not just a matter of perceiving a duty, or of recognizing the canon of ethics of your profession. Rather, you should see it as a key to human happiness. The application of your conscience to the implementation of your talents should be seen as a way of enhancing not only your pursuit of a more just society, but also your pursuit of your own personal satisfaction. You will be teaching people that they do not have to go through life feeling as though they do not count; that they can take on City Hall or Exxon; that they do not have to swallow their grievances. You will be teaching them that they do not have to submit to the destruction of their primary identities as functioning members of this society. All of those feelings produce a lot of anxiety, frustration, introversion, taking it out on family and friends, and unhappiness, broadly and deeply. Just go to some third world countries where people are brutalized, starved, homeless; where there is a huge rate of infant mortality; and see what happens when people go through life with the feeling that they cannot do anything about their deeply entrenched misery and self-destructiveness. See how people turn the violence that society inflicts on them against others weaker than they, or fall into lifelong pits of violent addiction or mayhem.

So I speak of a pursuit of happiness; something about which you should think very definitively. You must resolve to make a mark on this law school before you leave, so that those who come after you will have a better law school. Do not simply coast and take what those who have gone before you have given you. Try to change and improve, or expand, or enliven, the atmosphere, the environment, the courses, the curriculum, so that you can get a sense of built-in legacy that will be very valuable to you throughout your life. And since a legacy means that you may not benefit from what you are working on, but the ones who come after you will, you maintain your motivation in a way that transcends one generation, or one period of time, and gives you a longer view. When I was in law school, we had five hundred fifty students, two blacks and thirteen women among us. And the professors at Harvard Law School were some of the brightest people in the United States. If you did not believe it, you just had to ask them. So we asked them, "Why are there so few black or female law students?" And they said to us, almost without exception, that they would love to have more black and female law students, and that Harvard Law School was open to any qualified student, and that there were no barriers. There you have it from the best and the brightest: professors at Harvard Law School from 1955 to 1958. Watch out for the best and the brightest. They can be more wrong than people who do not attempt to aspire to their intellects.

Ralph Nader Asks Law Students to Change

Originally delivered as a Forum speech at Harvard Law School, February 26, 1972.

IT'S MUCH MORE difficult to discuss the present scene than it was three years ago, when I was here last. Then a great deal of attention was given to portraying the realities of the legal system and the injustices committed by it. A few years ago, and when I was at law school, we were full of innocence, even though what was going on was intolerable, insupportable, and often inscrutable. We don't have that innocence now.

Let's flash back to 1958. Say this room, the Ames Courtroom, is the same as it was—pure white—and there is a speaker standing where I am. The following questions are asked. "Why aren't more women admitted to the Law School?" The speaker responds, "We will admit qualified women, but we don't think it's fair to prospective male law students, because of the attrition in the occupation that women have reflected after they have graduated." Second question: "Why were there only three black students in the class?" "We simply cannot find enough qualified blacks." Third question: "What are the Law School graduates in '58 going to do?" "Well, some will teach, more will practice law, a few will become judges, and some will go into government service." Period.

Today those kinds of answers (except perhaps the last) would be treated with incredulity, and rightly so. Because the old arguments don't hold water, and one wonders how a group with insight and a relatively stable level of intellectual acuity and technical skills could accept an argument in 1958 and completely refuse to accept it in 1972.

A degree of the intellectual arrogance at the Law School is based on technical competence. Some of the brightest minds in the country go through *Harvard Law Review.* They are not only bright, but they are self-disciplined in study and are confident about their futures.

I've looked into the way the Law Review editors and officers of the class of '58 have deployed themselves. The latest figures are that out of 33, four are in business, one is in government-foreign service, fifteen are in law firms, nine are law professors, one is in solo practice, one is writing a book in Maine, and two are not accounted for. Is that a set of statistics subject to normative evaluation? It can be assumed that these people are doing honest work, applying their integrity, trying to improve what is being done in their organizations and firms. And we can still evaluate them the same way that we would evaluate, for example, all doctors who decide to practice in a place like Gross Pointe and who do a very good job by all their patients— while the rest of the country, where the people of lesser means are, do not have doctors.

In short, the evaluation of a professional role is not only internal, based on day-to-day activities; it must also take into account the far broader context—namely, how it is deployed to meet the legitimate claims upon the profession. The deployment is of course the key issue. Evaluation is no longer a description of all the grievances, evils, and injustices. The question now is not even what kind of society we must grope toward. The question is even more basic than that. It is, are we up to it? Are we cowards, purely biological beings, who have to have two cars, split-level homes, money in the bank, and the comfort of a steady job—the kind of life whose trajectory is well known if we follow the tried steps of getting along by going along.

In many areas we know where we should go and what the problems are. We know that the Uniform Commercial Code (UCC) is not all honey and milk. We know that the tax system is not all equity. We know that housing is not all in good shape. We know that the courts are among the most demonically inefficient and inaccessible as well as forbidding institutions in the country. We know the state of our mental retardation and mental institutions, of our schools for criminal behavior, called prisons. We know the bureaucratic paralysis that comes under the mantle of government administration, the enormously varied forms of silent violence that the law has yet to recognize, especially from corporate pollution, product and job hazards, and the impact of poverty and disease. We know there is widespread hunger in this country and terrible discrimination—not just by race and sex, but by age and attractiveness, as those two value-standards are manipulated by industry, particularly Madison Avenue. We know there is discrimination against youth, that the discrimination has become institutionalized and is called adolescence. (We have the most prolonged adolescence in the history of mankind. There is no other society that requires so many years to pass before people are grown up, although finally we are allowing 18 year olds to vote. Adolescence is nurtured and prolonged by educational processes and by industry that has found a bonanza in embracing the adolescent population and in fortifying "adolescent values." This prolongation of adolescence robs the country of the population group having the most risktakers and the highest ideals.)

It is very tempting to talk about how administrative law is taught, what it leaves out. What the situations in Washington and state capitals are. We could probably even agree that the injustice, incompetence, and lack of foresight that pervade are challenges to intellectual endeavor. It is also very tempting to talk about the "solutions" that we have that we are not using—institutional and technical solutions, and legal solutions used as a catalyst for the foregoing two.

It's exciting to talk about case studies, vigorous defense, vigorous offense. How some people have prevailed over overwhelming odds, primarily because they brought to a set of facts values backed by stamina, a sense of strategy and the willingness to see it through. We do have models of exceptional performance. It would be nice to talk about them, because we might ask ourselves, why aren't they replicated?

Why does the hoola hoop sweep across the country, but not such models? Why don't we have models for dealing with the challenges to the law, old and new, that do not proceed through a market system or a retainer system? If there is one sweeping change over the last fifty years, it is that the legal challenges and injustices are increasingly outside even the best intentioned commercial practices' ability to resolve. They don't come with retainers. They come as a plea to the broader ethical missions of this profession. And that must be responded to not by a few pro bono organizations, but by the creation of new and supportable roles that will heed these pleas on a systematic day-by-day, month-by-month, year-by-year basis. Legal aid, public defender, neighborhood legal services are only a tiny part of the solution. It's part of what a few people using the leverage of the law can do on some social conditions.

These days we are told that many people deployed on a case-by-case tax law situation don't take advantage of the leverage that is possible. But is it possible for free lawyers to overthrow the corrupt administration of a major city? That would be a nice soap opera, a nice fiction, a nice challenge to the imagination. As a matter of fact, it would also make a nice Law School examination. The problem is that we live in a very intricately-meshed society, which means that we can develop a much more repercussive impact with creative litigation, lawmaking, and coalition support for such strategies than we could with less communication, transportation, and technology.

One of the most difficult things to discern is that the most boring subject at a given time can be crucial. Ten or fifteen years ago the subject of food regulation was considered a very boring subject. And it was very low on the academic totem pole. One didn't specialize in it at law school. Auto safety probably produced more yawns than any six subjects; it wasn't considered much of a challenge. (The challenge, I was told as a first-year student riding out to Logan Airport with a Washington attorney, interviewing him for the *Harvard Law Record,* was taxes. I saw a light come into his eyes when I asked him what he thought students should specialize in during the fall of 1955, and he replied, "Tax." He said, "A fabulous intellectual challenge, exquisite permutations, exquisite loopholes and basically," he added knowingly, "the coming thing.")

Why are the most important problems so often treated in such a boring way, or so often believed to lack intellectual challenge? If you look, for example, at the written work done at the Law School a dozen years ago, you will see that the concentration was not in the areas where most people can be afflicted, affected or helped by the legal system—areas like torts, urban development, housing, pollution, and industrial health and safety.

When you study labor law, exactly what do you study? Look at the textbooks and case books. What determines what gets into a case book? What you see is basically what gets appealed. Now and then there are snatches of documentary material, excerpts from articles. And so the question is: what determines what gets appealed? The answer is: what gets tried, or what gets heard. The next question is: what determines what gets tried and who gets heard? And then you start talking about power and its distribution, wealth and its distribution, access and its distribution, lawyers and their distribution. As you can see, from textbooks you get exposure to a narrow spectrum of legal material, and raw material, compared with the rest of the legal society. If you consider all the complaints (consumer, tenant, citizen complaints, etc.) of Americans that are subject to legal resolution, you find that most

ON PRACTICING LAW   383

Americans are shut out of the legal system. That can be statistically shown, even with very sloppy sampling methods like your memory.

Our legal system has been priced out of the reach, delayed out of the reach, politicized out of the reach and mystified out of the reach of most Americans. (And of course the last is especially true in the administrative law area, where so much of the action is at the local, state, and federal agency levels.)

Now it would seem that one of the principal subjects to be studied in law school is who uses the legal system. Who can use the legal system, who wants to use the legal system, and who does not want to use the legal system. All very distinct and self-supporting studies. And I doubt whether that is being given, even in a preliminary way, any integrated attention.

If you review the history of law students' attitudes, evolution or devolution, you see that the first was basically the conveyor belt attitude—get on it and it will reward. You should have seen the eyes of the students coming into some of the courses in the fifties known as bread-and-butter courses. These were students on the material make. They made no bones about it. Would this course get them the kind of job that would make them the most money? As Dean Griswold said to us in 1955, "There are no glee clubs at the Harvard Law School." That was a very telling metaphor, and we all knew what it meant.

The attrition of idealism is not a function, as we once thought, of technical professionalism, of getting down to the business at hand. It is basically a function of a more serious cultural problem with legal education. Students get on a conveyer belt, and the most pernicious aspect of this conveyer belt is the *Law Review*. If there had been a plot to pull in students' talents and expectations and direct them into paths predetermined by a systematically structured and coordinated subeconomy, called the commercial practice of law, those responsible would have created the *Law Review*. Now let me briefly explain that, because it involves a recommendation I'd like to make. The *Law Review* can be considered, in legal terms, an irresistible impulse to many students. It is not compulsory—you can turn it down. (We have a student working with us in Washington who has declined to serve twice, because he is working on the water pollution situation—the only public interest lawyer paying attention to that complicated legislation full-time, or even part-time, as it is winding its way through to Congress.) It's just that the goals and horizons nurtured by law schools depend for their achievement on the *Law Review* or how close you get to it. If you want to join Cahill Gordon, you aspire to it, because it increases your chances. If you want to maximize your options, you still usually aspire to it, because it does maximize your options.

It gives you a lot of invitations to turn down. And because it has that magnetism, a lot of behavior, choice, and risktaking at law school begin to be shaped because of and by the *Law Review*. If indeed the acme of achievement by a law student is considered the *Law Review*, then it is quite clear that, both as an integrator of curriculum priorities and as a shaper of what is considered real legal scholarship, it is going to have that kind of radiating impact on the range of permissible intellect, norms, and imagination.

The *Law Review* is not just the editors and officers. In important ways, the *Law Review* is the Law School, the *Law Review* is the alumni, the *Law Review* is the faculty. If you were to ask yourself the question, "What should be done with the 2500 hours a week spent by some of the brightest students at the Law School?" would you have them working in Gannett House? I couldn't think of a more useless appropriation of that kind of time and talent. All of us could think of dozens of activities that would be less demeaning, routine, redundant, and hierarchical, and much more productive, enduring, and advancing of the law. Not just temporary contributions to an awareness level, a perception level, a manning-of-the-ramparts level in terms of extracurricular activies, but in terms of assuming the role that needs to be created and expanded for a legal system which responds to or anticipates present and future crises of the community and the world. Taste it now, because you may never have another chance; the personal, conventional sacrifice in taking that opportunity becomes greater and greater as the years unfold after law school.

It boils down to how students are going to use their time in trying to understand, create and experience these roles. Even if they have to shake the profession to its foundations or develop a completely new paralegal dimension. Now there is one problem that you have to face—that is, some of the things that need to be done are not considered to require high technical ability or experience. For instance, there are some law students on campus right now trying to develop a students' public interest research group for eastern Massachusetts, based on a student assessment or contribution, which would hire lawyers, scientists, and other professionals to work full-time for students in the social arena and be directed and controlled by students. This is an attempt to create new opportunities and could open the way for hundreds or thousands of similar jobs across the country, wherever students similarly organize. They are already organized in Oregon and Minnesota, and probably more states will come in with over a million students by next year.

That is something good happening in terms of extracurricular activities at the Law School. This kind of thing is no longer as off limits as it was. But it does suffer, because it doesn't get the status recognition that it is marketable, and so many students don't gravitate towards it. In short, there is a very sensitive weighing of how students use their time in law school, in terms of what will pay off and what won't. I suppose that one of the most difficult problems to face is what people are willing to sacrifice, what totems to question and what taboos to jettison. I use the word *sacrifice,* but not in its historical sense. Historically, *sacrifice* had a more critical meaning—people died, were injured, thrown out of their professions, jailed, exiled, etc.

Sacrifice today is that of time, and, quite frankly, fewer people are willing to engage in it. In fact, the changes in recent years which have stimulated students about public interest work are the following. Civil rights; the draft; riots (most law students are not unlike most members of the bar—they are luminated by student fires rather than by the light of their own intellect); the Vietnam war, not only because of the draft, which affected many students, but also because it is a form of violence that law students, like many other people, understand—that is, raw physical violence, not hunger, brain damage, lead poisoning, pollution—not the silent forms of violence that take so long to prevent.

Why does the Law School graduate go into one field and not another? The questions he might ask are: is it an intellectual challenge? Does it pay? Is it a normative challenge? Does it provide creative outlet, independence of action? And the answers for the public interest area are all yes with the exception of pay. And what does that boil down to? The materialism syndrome, and that's what it is all about. To what small degree are law graduates willing to sacrifice their material standard of living? The model and year of car, the type of apartment or house, clothes and food, the conspicuous consumption. Ah, the debts, the Law School debts, the strongest argument yet. (The way the projections are now, it seems that students will get out of law school with such enormous debts that their risktaking ability will be crippled even further.)

One response to that is that you have to begin generating political and other persuasive power so that millions of dollars will start flowing into public interest law work. It is one step to develop student groups, and it *is* a step, but as long as the oil industry gets billions a year out of the government's tax and quota policies and the defense industry many times as much in its inimitable way, as long as subsidies and loopholes flow out into the billions for support of commercial activities, it hardly strains reason to demand a very significant diversion into this area—far, far greater than the OEO budget and neighborhood legal services. If 150 million dollars goes into just one nuclear sub, what is the response to deep poverty children, that there is only money to defend their misery? Where is their legal right to counsel that will obtain food, health, safety, and a future?

And we have to provide them, and the best way to start on this long road is a small step. The disillusionment, disappointment, and dropping out on the part of some students today is often because of their eagerness to take big fast steps and being told that they can only take small ones. So they don't take any steps. If you can't take big steps you have to take small steps. There is now a necessary modesty to horizons in the public interest area that lays the groundwork for more expansive justice in the future.

I would suggest that the Law School and the students ask themselves whether they couldn't split themselves into two groups, those who want to go down to State St., LaSalle St., and Wall St., and those who want to go another direction. Start the distinction right from the first day of school. Start with the distinction that rests on the foundation that there cannot be expert analysis based on empirical starvation or malnutrition.

There is great merit in breaking down the homogeneity of law students and faculty, not just by encouraging diverse backgrounds, but also by having other people participate who have nothing to do with law. It would be broadening and prodding for law students if the labor unions sent fifty or sixty on-the-line workers to spend a semester at the Law School, and if that kind of residence were established, a host of other occupations could be included. I suspect that if fifteen or twenty farmers had spent a semester at the Law School 15 years ago, something quite different would be reflected in textbooks and scholarship today. Because very often we can't empathize, we can't project and we can't reduce the agony and the pain to classroom recognition. We can only remotely observe or hear about them, and coming from a law school that used to consider going down to Harvard Square as a trip abroad, coming from a law school that has tunnels linking its buildings underground so that you never have to see the sky, this isolation is a very, very serious and myopic deprivation of the mind.

One doesn't have to want to operate a lathe, serve in a hospital or a restaurant, go down in a coal mine, work deep in the bowels of the federal bureaucracy, or in corporate management, to appreciate that that is where the problems for the law come from. You should never mistake desire with relevance. We can refuse to have anything to do with these kinds of experiences, but that doesn't mean that they are not relevant to us, that they shouldn't provide the wellspring, the insight, the motivation for our chosen profession in redirecting itself in the great catalytic role that it is so important for it to play.

We don't have to be egocentric about the law to believe that it is the primordial profession in the country. There is no other profession where it is acceptable to be a generalist, to deal with a wide range of facts, institutions, and roles, and where it is acceptable to go into other occupations. There is no other profession that deals so intimately with the accumulation, distribution, and defense of power, that draws in the other professions in the formation of public policy, conflict resolution, planning, etc. This is a very important profession, not to be demeaned by styles, rigorous trivia, semantic diversions, lack of courage, or lack of sacrifice.

I ask you to look at the official heroes in the Harvard Law School pantheon. How many of them sacrificed? How many of them endured the abrasions and the assaults of an unforgiving or an un-understanding society? How many of them were offensive attorneys for justice? How many of them developed institutions that lasted and that filled brave new roles and needs? How many of them were really pioneers (including the best of them, with their exquisite analytic minds and their great judicial decisions)? Those who tried or those who did pioneer are likely to be forgotten.

There is a real world out there starving, starving for this kind of lawyer redeployment. In many ways there is no way to complete these observations; it has to become self-analysis. It really is a personal decision.

But I leave you with this one concluding thought. If there were no market determinants—if, no matter what you chose to work on at Law School and afterwards, there were only one salary level, what would you do? How would you design a new law school? How would you design your own career? How would you change your thinking and your habits? If you will just go through that exercise and develop this hypothetical model, then you can step back from it and begin asking the questions why, where, and how you should and can redefine your careers. There are too many capable youths who preceded you here who should have been what they might have been if they could have been. Your resolve can avoid that duplication of comparatively wasted human resources.

Crumbling of the Old Order
Law Schools and Law Firms

Originally appeared in The New Republic, October 11, 1969.

IT WAS A SIMILAR ritual every year. About 550 new law students would file into venerable Austin Hall at Harvard Law School on a September day and hear the no-nonsense dean, Erwin N. Griswold, orient them. The good dean had the speech down to a practiced spontaneity. He advised them that at that instant they had become members of the legal profession, that law firms were the backbone of the profession, that there were no glee clubs at the Harvard Law School and that the law was a jealous mistress. Thus was launched a process of engineering the law student into corridor thinking and largely non-normative evaluation. It was a three-year excursus through legal minutiae, embraced by wooden logic and impervious to what Oliver Wendell Holmes once called the "felt necessities of our times." It is not easy to take the very bright young minds of a nation, envelop them in conceptual cocoons and condition their expectations of practice to the demands of the corporate law firm. But this is what Harvard Law School did for over a half century to all but a resistant few of the forty thousand graduates.

The Harvard Law pattern—honed to a perfection of brilliant myopia and superfluous rigor—became early in the century the Olympian object of mimicry for law schools throughout the country. Harvard also did everything it could to replicate its educational system through its production of law school teachers, casebooks, and an almost proselytizing zeal. This system faithfully nourished and fundamentally upheld a developing legal order which has become more aristocratic and less responsive to the needs and strains of a complex society. In turn, the established legal order controlled the terms of entry into the profession in ways that fettered imagination, inhibited reform and made alienation the price of questioning its assumptions and proposing radical surgery.

Unreal as it may appear, the connection between the legal establishment and the spectacular increase in the breakdown of the legal system has rarely been made outside the fraternity. This is due to the functional modesty of the profession, its reluctance to parade itself as the shaper, staffer and broker for the operating legal framework in this country. What is not claimed is not attributed. This escape from responsibility for the quality and quantity of justice in the relationships of men and institutions has been a touchstone of the legal profession.

Anyone who wishes to understand the legal crises that envelop the contemporary scene in the cities, in the environment, in the courts, in the marketplace, in public services, in the corporate-government arenas and in Washington—should come to grips with this legal flow chart that begins with the law schools and ends with the law firms, particularly the large corporate law firms of New York and Washington.

Harvard Law's most enduring contribution to legal education was the mixing of the case method of study with the Socratic method of teaching. Developed late in the nineteenth century under Dean Christopher Columbus Langdell, these techniques were tailor-made to transform intellectual arrogance into pedagogical systems that humbled the student into accepting its premises, levels of abstractions and choice of subjects. Law professors take delight in crushing egos in order to acculturate the students to what they called "legal reasoning" or "thinking like a lawyer." The process is a highly sophisticated form of mind control that trades off breadth of vision and factual inquiry for freedom to roam in an intellectual cage.

The study of actual law cases—almost always at the appellate court level—combines with the Socratic questioning sequence in class to keep students continually on the defensive, while giving them the feeling that they are learning hard law. Inasmuch as the Socratic method is a game at which only one (the professor) can play, the students are conditioned to react to questions and issues which they have no role in forming or stimulating. Such teaching *forms* have been crucial in perpetuating the status quo in teaching *content.* For decades, the law school curriculum reflected with remarkable fidelity the commercial demands of law firm practice. Law firm determinants of the content of courses nurtured a colossal distortion in priorities both as to the type of subject matter and the dimension of its treatment. What determined the curriculum was the legal interest that came with retainers. Thus, the curriculum pecking order was predictable—tax, corporate, securities and property law at the top and torts (personal injury) and criminal law, among others, at the bottom. Although in terms of the seriousness of the legal interest and the numbers of people affected, torts and criminal law would command the heights, the reverse was true, for the retainers were not as certain nor as handsome. Courses on estate planning proliferated, there were none for environmental planning until a few years ago. Other courses dealt with collapsible corporations, but the cupboard was bare for any student interested in collapsing tenements. Creditors' rights were studied deeply; debtors' remedies were passed by shallowly. Courses tracking the lucre and the prevailing ethos did not embrace any concept of professional sacrifice and service to the unrepresented poor or to public interests being crushed by private power. Such service was considered a proper concern of legal charity, to be dispensed by starved legal aid societies.

The generations of lawyers shaped by these law schools in turn shaped the direction and quality of the legal system. They came to this task severely unequipped except for the furtherance of their acquisitive drives. Rare was the law graduate who had the faintest knowledge of the institutionalized illegality of the cities in such areas as building and health code violations, the endemic bribing of officialdom, the illegalities in the marketplace, from moneylending to food. Fewer still were the graduates who knew anything of the institutions that should have been bathed in legal insight and compassion—hospitals, schools, probate and other courts, juvenile and mental institutions and prisons. Racialism, the gap between rich and poor, the seething slums—these conditions were brought to the attention of law firms by the illumination of city riots rather than the illumination of concerned intellects.

Even the techniques of analysis—the ultimate pride of the law schools—were seriously deficient. Techniques which concede to vested interests a parochial role for the law and which permit empirical starvation of portions of their subject matter become techniques of paralysis. This was the case in the relation of tort courses and motor vehicle injuries. Law as prevention, law as incorporator of highway and vehicle engineering facts and feasibilities was almost totally ignored. The emphasis was on legal impact after crashes occurred, so as to assign liabilities and determine damages between drivers. Another failure in analysis was thematic of the entire curriculum. Normative thinking—the "shoulds" and the "oughts"—was not recognized as part and parcel of rigorous analytic skills. Although the greatest forays in past legal scholarship, from the works of Roscoe Pound to those of Judge Jerome Frank, proceeded from a cultivated sense of injustice, the nation's law schools downplayed the normative inquiry as something of an intellectual pariah. Thus the great legal challenges of access to large governmental and corporate institutions, the control of environmental pollution, the requisites of international justice suffered from the inattention of mechanized minds. There was little appreciation of how highly demanding an intellectual task it was to develop constructs of justice and injustice within Holmes' wise dictum that "the life of the law is not logic, it is experience." Great questions went unasked, and therefore unanswered.

POSSIBLY THE GREATEST failure of the law schools—a failure of the faculty—was not to articulate a theory and practice of a just deployment of legal manpower. With massive public interests deprived of effective legal representation, the law schools continued to encourage recruits for law firms whose practice militated against any such representation even on a sideline, *pro bono* basis. Lawyers labored for polluters, not antipolluters, for sellers, not consumers, for corporations, not citizens, for labor leaders, not rank and file, for, not against, rate increases or weak standards before government agencies, for highway builders, not displaced residents, for, not against, judicial and administrative delay, for preferential business access to government and against equal citizen access to the same government, for agricultural subsidies to the rich but not food stamps for the poor, for tax and quota privileges, not for equity and free trade. None of this and much more seemed to trouble the law schools. Indeed, law firms were not even considered appropriate subjects of discussion and study in the curriculum. The legal profession—its organization, priorities and responsibilities—were taken as given. As the one institution most suited for a critical evaluation of the profession, the law school never assumed this unique role. Rather, it serviced and supplied the firms with fresh manpower selected through an archaic hierarchy of narrow worthiness topped by the editors of the school's law review. In essence it was a trade school.

The strains on this established legal order began to be felt with *Brown vs. Board of Education* in 1954. *Brown* rubbed the raw nerves of the established order in public. The mounting conflict began to shake a legal order built on

392   THE RALPH NADER READER

deception and occult oppression. The ugly scars of the land burned red. Law students began to sense, to feel, to participate, and to earn scars of their own. Then came the Kennedy era with its verbal eloquence, its Peace Corps—overseas and later here. Then came Vietnam and Watts, Newark and the perturbation became a big-league jolt. Law students began to turn away from private practice, especially at the Ivy League law schools. Those who went directly to the firms were less than enthusiastic. The big corporate firms in New York and Washington began to detect early signs that their boot camps were not responding to the customary Loreleis of the metropolitan canyons. Starting salaries began to reflect the emergence of a seller's market. Almost two years ago, the big New York Cravath firm set a starting salary of $15,000 a year and many firms followed. Still the law graduate detour continued. The big firms began to promise more free time to engage in *pro bono* work—the phrase used to describe work in the public interest such as representing indigents. The young graduates were still dissatisfied—first over the contraction of the promises and second over the narrow interpretation given to pro bono work.

At the same time, more new or alternative career roles in public service began to emerge. Neighborhood Legal Services, funded by OEO, was manned by 1,800 young lawyers around the country at last count. The draft is driving many graduates into VISTA programs. There are more federal court clerkships available. And the growth of private, public-service law institutions such as Edgar Cahn's Citizen's Advocate Center and the Urban Law Institute headed by his wife, Jean Cahn, are not only providing such career roles but articulating their need throughout the country.

Meanwhile back at the law schools, student activism has arrived. Advocacy of admission, curriculum and grading reform is occurring at Harvard and Yale. Similar currents are appearing at other law schools. New courses in environmental, consumer and poverty law are being added to the lists. The first few weeks of the present school year indicate that the activists' attention is turning to the law firms that are now coming on campus to recruit. In an unprecedented move, a number of detailed questionnaires, signed by large numbers of students, are going out to these firms. The questions range far beyond the expected areas of the firms' policies on minority and women lawyers, and pro bono work. They include inquires about the firms' policies on containing their clients' ambitions, on participation in law-reform work, on conflict of interest issues, on involvement in corporate client and political activity, and on subsidizing public-interest legal activity. Such questionnaires are preliminary to the developmental courses on law-firm activities, and to more studies on specific law firms, which began this past summer with a study of the largest Washington, D.C. firm, Covington and Burling.

The responses which the firms give to these questionnaires, and whatever planned response the students envisage for those firms who choose not to reply, will further sharpen the issues and the confrontations. The students have considerable leverage. They know it's a seller's market. They know how vulnerable the very private firms are to effective public criticism. Status is crucial to these firms. Status is also a prime attraction for competent law school graduates.

IN RECENT MONTHS, there has been much soul-searching among the larger firms. Memos suggesting various opportunities for *pro bono* work by younger associates have been circulating between partners. A few decisions have been made. Some New York and San Francisco firms are considering or have instituted time off allowances ranging from a few weeks a year to a sabbatical. Piper & Marbury, a large Baltimore firm, has announced its intention to establish a branch office in the slums to service the needs of poor people, without charging fees if there is an inability to pay anything. Arnold and Porter, the second largest Washington, D.C. firm, has appointed a full time *pro bono* lawyer and is permitting all firm members to spend, if they wish, an average of 15 percent of their working hours on public service activities. Hogan and Hartson, the third largest D.C. firm, is setting up a "Community Services Department" to "take on public interest representation on a non-chargeable or, where appropriate, a discounted fee basis," according to the firm's memorandum on the subject.

The Hogan and Hartson memorandum is a fairly candid document. Like other firm memorandums on *pro bono* ventures, there is the acknowledgment that such a move "may have a favorable impact upon recruitment." The executive committee of Hogan and Hartson concedes that "there is a tendency among younger lawyers, particularly those with the highest academic qualifications, to seek out public-service oriented legal careers as an alternative to practice in the larger metropolitan law firms." In its internal firm statement, the committee notes that it "regards the relative disfavor into which the major law firms have fallen to be attributable, at least in part, to the feeling among recent law school graduates *that these firms have failed to respond to the larger problems of contemporary society.*" (Their emphasis.) Some statistics impressed the senior partners: the University of Michigan Law School reports that 26 of its 1969 graduates entered Wall Street law firms as compared with an average of 75 in preceding years. Harvard Law School reported that the percentage of its graduates entering private law practice declined from 54 percent in 1964 to 41 percent in 1968, and an even more significant decline is expected in the next few years.

It is too early to appraise these programs because they have not yet gotten underway. The likelihood that serious or abrasive conflict of interest situations will arise depends on the kind of *pro bono* work selected. If this work deals with "band-aid law" in the slums on a case basis, few conflict of interest problems should arise. On the other hand, should the *pro bono* lawyers grapple with the financial institutions who fund the slum moneylenders for example, or strive toward structural reform of a legal institution, then the probability of conflict is increased.

Because of the enormously greater cost-benefit which attached to the more basic *pro bono* efforts, the external and internal pressures on the firm's leaders will be in that direction. This could lead to more profound clashes between the firm's allegiance to its paying clients and its recognition of public service responsibilities. With additional law student and younger lawyer demands for cash contributions for scholarships to minority law students, for admission of more minority lawyers to firm membership, and for senior partners to pay "reparations" out of their own salaries to assist the legally deprived—all demands made or in the process of being made—the pressure may soon exceed the firms' threshold of tolerance. At that point the experiment in pro bono may terminate.

WHATEVER THE OUTCOME, the big firms will never be the same again. They will either have to dedicate substantial manpower and resources to public service, and somehow resolve the conflict of interest problem, or they will decline in status to the level of corporate house counsel or public relations firms. The polarization of the legal profession seems a more likely development. Before he left Harvard almost two years ago to become U.S. Solicitor General, Dean Griswold wrote of his belief that there would be a "decline in the relative importance of private law practice as we have known it in the past." This trend is in fact occurring as far as the younger lawyers' concept of importance is concerned. However, the immense power of these firms and their tailored capacity to apply know-how, know-who and other influences remains undiminished.

Recent evidence of the resourcefulness of large corporate law firms in overwhelming the opposition on behalf of its clients comes from the firm

ON PRACTICING LAW   395

of Wilmer, Cutler and Pickering. A firm team, headed by Lloyd Cutler, obtained last month on behalf of the domestic auto companies a feeble consent decree in return for the Justice Department's dropping its civil antitrust case charging the domestic auto companies with conspiracy to restrain the development and marketing of pollution control systems since 1953. Earlier Mr. Cutler succeeded in having the Antitrust Division heed his representations that the original policy to initiate criminal proceedings, after an 18-month grand jury strongly wanted to return an indictment, be dropped. The terms of the consent decree are being challenged by a number of cities in federal district court at Los Angeles. The petitioners allege that there are inadequate provisions for disclosure of the conspiracy information and for long-term compliance, and that the great deterrent effect of a public trial was lost. Without going into further detail, it is sufficient to state that many law students and younger lawyers see a divergence in such a case between the lawyer's commitment to the public interest and his commitment to the auto industry.

Professor Charles A. Reich of Yale Law School expressed one form of this heightened expectation of the lawyer's role as follows: "It is important to recognize explicitly that whether he is engaged publicly or privately, the lawyer will no longer be serving merely as the spokesman for others. As the law becomes more and more a determinative force in public and private affairs, the lawyer must carry the responsibility of his specialized knowledge, and formulate ideas as well as advocate them. In a society where law is a primary force, the lawyer must be a primary, not a secondary, being."

The struggle of the established law firms to portray themselves as merely legal counselors affording their corporate clients their right to legal representation is losing ground. So too is their practice of hiding behind their responsibility to those clients, and not taking the burden of their advocacy as the canons of ethics advise them to do wherever the public interest is importantly involved. Either they are technical minions or they bear the responsibility attendant upon their status as independent professionals.

Clearly, there is need for a new dimension to the legal profession. This need does not simply extend to those groups or individuals who cannot afford a lawyer. It extends to the immense proliferation of procedural and substantive interests which go to the essence of the kind of society we will have in the future, but which have no legal representation. The absence of remedy is tantamount to an absence of right. The engineer of remedies for exercising rights is the lawyer.

The yearning of more and more young lawyers and law students is to find careers as public-interest lawyers who, independent of government and industry, will work on these two major institutions to further the creative rule of law. The law, suffering recurrent and deepening breakdowns, paralysis and obsolescence, should no longer tolerate a retainer astigmatism which allocates brilliant minds to trivial or harmful interests.

on the information age

Supersonic Brain Shredder

Originally appeared in Forbes *magazine, November 30, 1998.*

TO PARAPHRASE Abraham Lincoln, time is society's stock-in-trade. Over several millennia, humans have measured time in ways that reflect their development and technology. What began with the sun and seasons moved onto a yearly calendar and its days, then clocks with hours, minutes, seconds, and now nanoseconds. The ever more microscopic cultures of time imprint themselves on human and social behavior in more insistent and pressured ways.

Take the timescale for measuring performance. An excess of instant gratification can lead a person down self-destructive paths. Narcissistic societies that ignore future consequences and avoid thinking ahead sow the seeds of their own demise. Corporations have been criticized for judging their progress on too short a time period (quarterly profits and losses). A longer time yardstick would make company leaders think and plan ahead, engage in more research and development, and be more concerned with longer-range issues such as the global environment, natural resources, worldwide diseases, poverty, and illiteracy.

Time pressures lead people to apply ever briefer timescapes to their rewards, sanctions and joys, and to the ratio between spending and saving. Consider, for example, what the frenzy of "microtime" and a higher density of "micro-advertisements" do to television—a veritable blizzard of screens clamoring for the attention of people who still possess only 24 hours a day.

News programs are now down to 8.2-second sound bites when covering elections, compared with forty-two seconds in the late 1960s. At this rate, the sound bite will be replaced by a sound bark in a couple of decades— essentially a human grunt or shrug. Microtime becomes a brain shredder that rewards the banal supersonic speech so often heard on the Sunday morning talk shows.

Overdosing on the frenzy of the video screen, viewers' attention spans and patience for sequential thought shrink. Teachers have long told us this is happening to school-children: Children become more susceptible to manipulation by TV marketers who cynically target 2-year-olds or younger. Microtime fosters low-grade sensuality in children's cartoons, filling them with unceasing violent actions separated from any enduring meaning or social context.

For both children and adults, microtime means spending more time in virtual reality than concrete reality, day after day. The results are social and personal estrangements we have hardly begun to understand.

The information age is similarly afflicted by the nano-second addiction—and feeds it. With information overload inundating users, there is less time to digest data into knowledge, judgment, and wisdom before more information pours inward. Workers are receiving so many inputs that, to diminish or divert calls, voice mail becomes the barrier of choice. In 1988, the *Wall Street Journal* reported that "only one in six business callers gets through on the telephone to the intended party on the first try." It is now much worse, due to technologies that shield callees from callers. Billions of hours yearly are spent trying to use modern telecommunications and software to contact one another through the "press one, two, three" economy. Meanwhile, even newer technologies, such as email and faxes, are also becoming snarled in information traffic jams. They pile up as secretaries spend nearly half a day processing the avalanches.

Are we fooling ourselves in thinking that timesaving office automation actually saves net time and improves productivity? Some thoughtful books and articles have been written by computer processing specialists who think we are. A computerized office is open to floods of indiscriminate information, bloated software, and poorly designed systems that glitch and crash. After a while, even the will to distinguish between what is happening and what seems to be happening fades.

Technology's unintended consequences have done this to us again and again. Traffic is down to 5.4 mph in midtown Manhattan during work hours, not much different from the horse and buggy one hundred years ago. But then there is the open highway, and we forget the time we spend commuting.

Automation in the office is supposed to increase net output per time unit. Yet, apart from so much office talk directed to software—its changes, complexities, viruses, and failures—what opportunity remains for people to engage in broader, longer-range, more creative labor? Is "timesaving" automation automating the behavior of workers themselves?

Some adjustments are desperately funny. Young stockbrokers wear telephone headsets while their hands send emails. Beepers, cell phones, and air phones open new time frontiers. But the InfoLords are exponential in their demands. The industry of timesaving techniques and tranquilizers keeps growing precisely because we are losing the race.

I've stopped counting the number of legislators, programmed to the minute by Congress, who have told me they do not "have the time to read or to think." The same lament was voiced by corporate executives we interviewed for our book *The Big Boys*. Given the weighty responsibilities of these leaders, this neglect of time for such purposes is disturbing. Loss of control over one's time amounts to a loss of self-control, devoured by ever greater separation of means from ends.

"I just don't have the time" is the standard response when busy Americans are asked whether they comparison shop or write formal complaints to companies. Such a plight has not gone unnoticed by the business community. With more complex products and services and often without much difference between brands, vendors take advantage of the hubbub and confusion. With 99 percent of all contracts not negotiated—e.g., insurance policies, credit card conditions, mortgage instruments, shrink-wrap licenses, and installment loan agreements—sellers demand that consumers sign on the dotted line and give up rights, remedies, and bargaining power ab initio in the fine print.

Even if you have the time to read these contracts, to question their terms, or to demand changes, time compression makes any reasonable negotiation an anathema to the car dealer, the insurance agent, or the large retail chain. Vendors have been known to "fire" their customers for taking too much time.

By contrast, consider how vendors save on their labor expenses by shifting the time burden onto potential customers by forcing them to spend hours waiting on the phone or to perform their own delivery. After consumers finally reach a human being to register a complaint, auto dealers or landlords threaten to damage their credit rating should they persist in the grievance. Vendor-forced consumption of consumer time is a strategic way of getting rid of "troublesome" customers. Experienced customers say to themselves that it is not worth the time to complain—so, for example, inscrutable bills and then computerized billing fraud grow.

What would Henry Thoreau, Ralph Waldo Emerson, and Walt Whitman think of one-minute managers, fast food, fast TV, radio talk, fast-blinking MTV, higher speed limits, summaries of classical novels for students, disposable products, virtual this and virtual that replacing the slower reality of nature?

The march of time has been replaced by the blitz of time, and no one, short of a hermit, can escape the pace without some sort of defensive personal philosophy. But that too is part of the problem. Without quality of time becoming a subject of public discourse, the necessary civic consensus will not emerge to enable us to change our accelerating high-speed, wayward culture.

A civic consensus usually flows from an aggregate of personal conceptions of time. I have my own: Jettison needless complexity. Leapfrog redundant and diversionary means to the objectives one has in mind. Discern patterns that cut through the seemingly unrelated information that clutters time. Develop a balance between input and output so that the former serves the latter and does not become an end unto itself. Contribute to a society that foresees and forestalls, where prevention precludes endless torments that burden people's time. A just society not only saves time, it greatly improves the product of its use.

Digital Democracy in Action

Originally appeared in Forbes, *December 2, 1996.*

INFORMATION IS the currency of democracy, and information age technologies can make information current, accurate, and inexpensive for people to use to create a more just and prosperous society. But technology does not have its own imperative. It reflects the distribution and the concentration of power and wealth that shape its quality, quantity, and accessibility. Right after World War II, two high technologies were touted by their boosters to the point of euphoria. One was television and the other was atomic power.

I recall my seventh-grade schoolteacher regaling us with the coming benefits of atomic power—oh, so cheap ("too cheap to meter," said one of its prominent promoters), so safe, and so adaptable. Why, just a little atomic power gadget installed in our cars, she said, would replace gasoline for the lifetime of the car. She was citing the leading scientific projections at that time. What a difference reality makes! Troubled and risky, nuclear power is in a de facto moratorium in this country—not a single reactor has been ordered by the cost-conscious utilities for more than two decades. And gasoline stations are still flourishing.

Then there was television. My first-year high school teachers told us that an age of enlightenment was awaiting us. Whole new worlds of information, geography, debate, and mobilization would come from this living room technology. What was now controlled by the few would soon be accessible by the many. The parochial world of youngsters, they forecast, would disappear and be replaced by a young generation that would be aware and have an understanding of worldwide events. This was before Tony the Tiger, Chester Cheetah, and Mortal Kombat.

To be sure, the information age has produced much information. We are inundated with data and information, less so with knowledge, even less with judgment, and almost not at all with wisdom. Millions of information specialists never get past the information stage, and the few who deal with the next stages of knowledge and judgment are called gurus. Wisdom, alas, is left for philosophers who probably use manual Underwood typewriters.

Also, there's this sense of incompleteness about the development and application of computers. Used mostly by businesses and government, computers still seem exotic to most consumers, who usually limit their personal computer use to entertainment and modest record-keeping purposes. Computers, however, could usher in an age of consumer information that would drive competitors to offer products with higher levels of health, safety, and quality for shoppers. But, except for consumers' push to compare auto insurance premiums online, the future is not here.

Even on the business side, computers have not fulfilled their promise of greater productivity in the service sector, other than in the telecommunications industry. Computer design pioneer Thomas K. Landauer in his new book, *The Trouble with Computers: Usefulness, Usability, and Productivity* (MIT Press), explains why, despite enormous investments in computers over the last twenty years, productivity in the very service industries they were built for has virtually stagnated everywhere in the world.

Because of their speed and productivity, however, when technology is driven by fundamental values of democracy and justice, these same machines can produce highly useful knowledge to change conditions for the better. Our current project on banks and mortgage redlining is a case in point.

The project demonstrates that the rapid advances in computer technology have provided a valuable and powerful tool to fight lending discrimination. To the chagrin of banks and other financial corporations, public interest groups and community activists are using the new technology to plow through mountains of aggregate data, in order to detect, with great precision, who gets mortgage loans and who gets shut out.

For the first time, the new technology has put some truly sharp teeth in the long-standing, but often futile, effort to prevent banks from adopting lending practices that deprive minority and low- and moderate-income neighborhoods of credit—a practice commonly referred to as "redlining."

These efforts have led to significant improvements. Aware that many community activists have computer-generated data, compiled from government reports, quite a few banks have cleaned up their act rather than risk public exposure. In the process, they have discovered that there is profit to be made in lending to the residents in underserved neighborhoods.

The information age is young. It has an opportunity to mature into a responsible, contributing force in our democratic society. But it requires civic engagement by many Americans for this prospect to be realized.

The Dossier Invades the Home

Originally appeared in The Saturday Review *as one of a three-pronged investigation on the assault on privacy, April 17, 1971. It was adapted from a report commissioned by the American Civil Liberties Union as a part of the ACLU's 50th Anniversary program.*

INVASION OF PRIVACY used to carry an almost luxurious connotation, a concept reserved for special public figures whose private lives were invaded by scandalmongers or seekers of vicarious thrills. It is no longer an elitist term. Hundreds of bits of information filed in dossiers on millions of individual Americans today constitute a massive assault on privacy whose ramifications are just beginning to be realized.

Most adults have at some time sought credit (or a credit card) and bought insurance. If you have done these things, there are probably at least two dossiers with your name on them.

When you seek to borrow money, your creditor receives a file from the credit bureau to establish your "credit rating." This dossier contains all the personal facts the credit bureau can assemble—your job, salary, length of time on the present job, marital status, a list of present and past debts and their payment history, any criminal record, any lawsuits of any kind, and any real estate you may own. The dossier may include your employer's opinion of your job performance or even your IQ rating from a high school test. By the time the creditor has finished talking to the credit bureau, he is likely to know more about your personal life than your mother-in-law does.

When you try to buy life insurance, a file of even more intimate information about you is compiled by the "inspection agency." The insurance company finds out not only about your health but also about your drinking habits (how often, how much, with others or alone, and even what beverage), your net worth, salary, debts, domestic troubles, reputation, associates, manner of living, and standing in the community. The investigator is also asked to inquire of your neighbors and associates whether there is "any criticism of character or morals," and he must state whether he recommends that the insurance be declined.

Credit bureaus and inspection agencies are the major sources of information about individuals. But government, schools, employers, and banks are also collectors, and sometimes suppliers, of information. Employers frequently make information on their employees available to a credit bureau or inspection agency. They may also exchange information among themselves. *The Wall Street Journal* has reported that department stores in many cities have formed "mutual protection associations" that trade the names of former workers who were fired for suspected theft. This information-trading means that an individual may be denied a job on the basis of a former employer's untested—and unrefuted—suspicions.

Anyone possessing an individual's bank records—now extensively recorded on computers—can reconstruct his associations, movements, habits, and life-style. The recently enacted Foreign Bank Secrecy Act can be used to require every FDIC-insured bank to make a reproduction of each check you draw on it and keep those reproductions for up to six years. The purpose is to ensure records of large quantities of money going out of the country so as to prevent tax evasions through use of secret Swiss bank accounts. But the act contains no protection for the depositor by limiting in any way the banks' use of these records. Conceivably, a bank could sell them to a credit bureau or investigation agency.

IT IS THE RARE American who does not live in the shadow of his dossier. The "dossier industry" is a huge and growing business. There are 105 million files kept by the Association of Credit Bureaus of America (ACBA). Retail Credit Company of Atlanta, Georgia, the giant of the industry, has forty-five million files and makes thirty-five million reports each year. Credit Data Corporation, the second largest firm, has twenty-seven million files and adds seven million new dossiers each year.

These economic interests have almost total control over the information they collect and sell. They are not accountable to anyone except those who seek to purchase information. Further, for reasons of profit, these companies place a premium on the derogatory information they assemble. Except in three states, citizens do not have the right even to see these dossiers in order to correct inaccuracies. They will have that right for the first time when a federal law, the Fair Credit Reporting Act, goes into effect April 25, 1971. But they still will not have the right to control access to the information, on which there are in effect no legal restrictions, or the right to control the kinds of information that can go into their dossiers.

Until there are adequate protective measures—an "information bill of rights" that protects him against invasion of privacy through information dissemination—the citizen's major recourse is to understand how these agencies operate and what are his limited rights under present and pending law.

The first problem of the dossier is accuracy. There is no doubt that inaccurate information comes into the files of credit bureaus and insurance inspection agencies. In fact, credit bureaus disclaim accuracy in their forms, because most of the material is obtained from others (merchants, employers) and not verified by them. The information "has been obtained from sources deemed reliable, the accuracy of which [the credit bureau] does not guarantee."

Illustrations of errors are legion. New York State Assemblyman Chester P. Straub was refused a credit card because his dossier revealed an outstanding judgment. The judgment actually was against another person with a similar name, but the bureau had erroneously put it against Straub's name. Testimony before a U.S. Senate committee has accused credit bureaus of using a "shotgun" approach to recording judgments against consumers—entering any judgment on all the records bearing the same name as the defendant's, or a similar name, without checking to see which individual was actually involved.

In addition to errors of identification, there are errors due to incomplete information. A woman ordered a rug, but the seller delivered one of the wrong color. He refused to take it back and sued for payment. Although his case was thrown out of court, her credit record showed only that she had been sued for non-payment, and she was unable to get credit elsewhere thereafter. Arrests and the filing of lawsuits are systematically collected by credit bureaus and rushed into dossiers, but the dismissal of charges or a suit is not reported in the newspaper and so the credit bureau never learns of, or records, the affirmative data.

Also, there is the problem of obsolescence of information, as shown by the man whose bureau dossier in the sixties listed a lawsuit from the thirties. It was a $5 scare suit for a magazine subscription he had never ordered, and "nothing had come of it"—except in regard to his credit rating.

The introduction of computers can create its own set of problems. Although mechanical errors in the handling of information by people may be reduced, the probability of machine error is increased. In addition, credit data are taken directly from a creditor's computer to a credit bureau's computer without discretion. Your payments may have been excused for two months, due to illness, but the computer does not know this, and it will only report that you missed two payments. Storage problems alone will prevent the explanation from being made. Your rating with that creditor may not be affected, but with all others it will be.

These credit bureau inaccuracies generally relate to "hard data," which are subject to verification or contradiction. The insurance inspection agency, on the other hand, reports "soft data," or gossip, and they are not subject to verification at all. This creates new sources of inaccuracies. Where the information is inherently uncheckable, the biased employee or the biased informant can easily introduce inaccuracies. Even where bias is not present, innuendo or misunderstanding can create error, while a vindictive inspector can abuse his power for personal reasons.

Why don't inspectors check the accusations made by informants with the accused? One reason is they don't have the time. If they must make ten or fifteen reports a day, they can spend only forty minutes on an average report, including transportation and typing it up. This allows no time for checking accusations, or even facts.

A more vicious reason is the agency's penchant for derogatory information and the fact that it records on both a weekly and a monthly basis the percentage of cases in which an inspector recommends declines. He must file a certain percentage of derogatory reports (at one time 8 per cent for life and 10 per cent for auto reports) if he is to be known as a "good digger." If he has not met his "quota," the temptation to use any rumor, without confirmation, may be overwhelming. These quotas may be regarded by the agency as a necessary control device to prevent inspectors from filing fake reports without investigation, but they show a reckless disregard for the safety of the investigated public.

Gossip-mongering with a quota on unfavorable comments can lead the harried inspector to rely on innuendo. A vivid illustration of the problems in insurance reporting is the case of two successful young businesswomen who applied for a life insurance policy required for a particular business transaction. On completion of a routine report, Retail Credit Company advised the insurance company not to issue the policy. It reported "severe criticism of the morals of both women, particularly regarding habits, and

Lesbian activities." The investigator's information came from neighbors. None of these neighbors actually stated they had seen any illicit activity, but innuendo accomplished the same result. "Informants [unidentified] will not come out and state that applicant is Lesbian, but hint and hedge around and do everything but state it." The insurance company followed Retail Credit's advice and denied the policy.

Until passage of the Fair Credit Reporting Act, the law offered no protection against an inaccurate report, except in three states. There was no way one could even see a report to correct it. However, this new act offers some solutions to problems of accuracy.

1. It requires users of reports to notify consumers of the name and address of the consumer reporting agency whenever the user (e.g., creditor, insurer, or employer) takes adverse action on the basis of the agency's report.

2. It gives the consumer the right to know the "nature and substance of all information" on him in the agency's files, except medical information and the sources of "investigative information" (i.e., gossip). The limitation on sources of gossip is a serious weakness. Such sources can be discovered in litigation, however, and a suit is made easy to bring. Thus, *the agency can no longer guarantee the confidentiality of its sources.*

3. If a dispute arises between the consumer and the agency about the accuracy of an item, the agency must reinvestigate and *reverify* or delete the information. This will usually mean going back to the same neighbors and obtaining the same gossip. If the dispute is not settled by reinvestigation, the item must be noted as disputed. This leaves the user free to believe the agency.

These provisions are the strongest in the bill. They are weak from the consumer's point of view in two areas: The consumer should be allowed to learn the sources of gossip before litigation so that he can effectively rebut inaccurate gossip; further, he should be provided a quick, simple procedure for obtaining a declaratory judgment on the truth of any item.

4. The act also provides for enforcement through private actions if the agency is negligent. Negligence is easy to allege, but may be difficult to prove. Only time will tell what standards the courts will set.

Even though the agency's secrecy is now partially broken, relief may still not be available because most agencies are granted immunity for agency libel. Under the law of most states; the agencies are given a "conditional privilege" to publish false statements, so the libel action will not succeed. The privilege is granted on the grounds that they are fulfilling a private duty by providing businessmen with information they need in the conduct of their affairs. Georgia and Idaho (and England) do not grant the agencies such a privilege on the grounds that the privilege itself does not benefit the general public, but only a profit-oriented enterprise, and that individual rights take precedence over the self-interest of the enterprise.

IN THE STATES GRANTING the privilege, it is conditioned on the agency's 1) disclosing the information only to those with the requisite commercial interest, and 2) acting in good faith and without malice. However, proof of malice requires more than just the falsity of the report. In the past this has conferred an effective immunity on false reports. Malice, however, may be shown by the quota systems of the agencies or by their secrecy. Arguably, these company policies show a "wanton and reckless disregard of the rights of another, as is an ill will equivalent." Such theories, however, have not yet been tested in court.

There is no regulation on sale of the extensive personal information collected by credit bureaus, insurance agencies, and employers. The dossiers are considered their "property," and they may do what they wish with it. The only influence to limit availability is an economic one, arising from the condition on the privilege for publishing libel—the report can be given only to subscribers of the service or others claiming a legitimate interest in its subject matter. However, claims of interest are easy to make and are not often scrutinized.

Furthermore, the citizen never knows when these dossiers are opened to someone. His consent is not sought before release of the information. He is not warned when someone new obtains the information, or told who they are—unless, under the new law, they take adverse action. There are no pressures on the information agencies to account to the subject of the dossier, nor have these agencies shown any willingness to assume such responsibility.

Credit bureaus may follow the Associated Credit Bureau guidelines and release information only to those who certify that they will use it in a "legitimate business transaction." This, of course, includes not only credit granters but also employers, landlords, insurers, and dozens of others. But even these weak guidelines are unenforceable by the association, and a CBS study found that half the bureaus they contacted furnished information to

CBS without checking the legitimacy of their business purpose. Announced policies of inspection agencies also require a showing of a business purpose. But this includes anyone who has $5 and announces himself as a "prospective employer."

In April, the Fair Credit Reporting Act will impose a restriction on the release of information, but it is no better than those presently available. An agency will be able to sell information to anyone having "a legitimate business need" for the information. There are no economic or legal restrictions preventing any credit bureau or inspection agency from giving out their dossiers indiscriminately to anyone who can pay.

The consequences of making highly personal information easily available have only begun to be recognized. Credit reporting agencies may serve as private detectives for corporations that want to intimidate a critic. Recently the press reported that American Home Products, a drug manufacturer with more than $1-billion in sales, hired Retail Credit Company to investigate the personal affairs of Jay B. Constantine, an aide to the Senate Finance Committee who had helped draft legislation opposed by the drug industry. The investigation was stopped only "after their stupidity was uncovered," according to Senator Russell Long, Finance Committee chairman, who also said that the company had tendered "a complete letter of apology."

The introduction of computers furnishes other possibilities for use and misuse of personal information. Arthur R. Miller, in his new book, *The Assault on Privacy,* reports that MIT students in Project MAC (Machine Aided Cognition) were able to tap into computers handling classified Strategic Air Command data. If they can do this, any time-sharing user can tap into a computer data bank. There is no way at present that computer people can guarantee their control over access. They cannot even guarantee that they can prevent rewriting of the information in the computer by outsiders.

What can be done to control the availability of these dossiers? Primarily, anyone obtaining information on you should be required to obtain your express consent to the release before receiving the information. This would recognize your interest in preserving the privacy of your own personality. It would allow you to decide whether any particular transaction was worth the invasion of your privacy by the other party.

Even if the information in the dossier is completely accurate and available only to creditors, insurers, and employers, there may be personal or private details—perhaps irrelevant to the demands of the credit-insurance industries—that people want kept to themselves. Some kinds of information may be so personal that their storage and sale are offensive. For example, it is possible to assemble a list of the books a person reads by observing his bookshelves, talking to his neighbors, or obtaining the records of the public library. An employer or insurer could manufacture a "business purpose" for obtaining such information—to determine the subject's knowledge or intelligence, generally, or in a specific field. There is little doubt that such an effort would be offensive to most people, violating their privilege of private thoughts and opinions. It would be offensive even if accurate.

Currently, the information gathered in most dossiers includes a subject's past educational, marital, employment, and bill-paying record. His "club life," drinking habits, and associates are recorded. Also included are an employer's opinion of his work habits and his neighbors' opinion of his reputation, character, and morals, which probably includes gossip about old neighborhood feuds.

Insurance company underwriters indicate that many do not use some questions (e.g., "What social clubs does he belong to?"). Some questions are overdrafted (e.g., the query "Who are his associates?" is useful to them only as "Does he have any criminal associates?"—a quite different version). The reason for asking what *kind* of alcoholic beverage an applicant drank was incomprehensible to at least two underwriters.

When asked whether they ever sought to have unnecessary questions struck from the form, the response was "Why should we? It's just as easy to skip over them when reading." There was no indication that they had any scruples about, or even any understanding of, the problem as an invasion of privacy.

Credit bureaus and investigation agencies do not generally gather such information as test scores or personality traits. Nor are lists of books assembled—yet. But there is nothing to prevent these investigators from adding this information to the standard items in their dossiers. The FBI has tried a similar form of investigation. Common law doctrines seem not to cover these problems, and, until recently, legislatures and relevant administrative bodies have shown no interest. Most information agencies have no announced policies that would preclude them from including any type of question. Thus, the only reason such information is not gathered is an economic one: No one is sufficiently interested to request and pay for it.

New technology is also tipping the balance against the individual's right of privacy as far as kinds of information are concerned. With problems of storage and transmittal solved, the technological tendency is to collect more data on individuals, inevitably more sensitive data.

The way information is gathered also has ominous implications for the individual's privacy. Credit bureaus gather their information from employers, newspapers, and credit-granters who are members of the bureau. They also collect data from the "welcome wagon" woman who visits homes and notes what buying "needs" you have so that you can be dunned by the right merchant. American Airlines' computer can give anyone information about what trips you have taken in the last two or three months. Further, it can give your seat number and be used to determine who sat next to you, perhaps inferentially describing your associates. In addition, it can tell your telephone contact number and, from this, determine where you stayed or your associates in each city of departure. Credit card accounts can do much the same thing, telling what you have bought recently (to establish standard of living and life-style) and where you shop.

Each of these methods of inquiry constitutes a serious invasion of privacy, but the most serious invasion is the neighborhood investigation by the inspection agency. Here information is gathered by questioning your neighbors, building superintendent, grocer, or postmaster about what you do while you are in your own home. There is the threat not only of gossip-mongering and slander, but of the creation of a kind of surveillance on your home. For most people, the only available private place is "home." Here, even though observed by neighbors perhaps, the individual can feel free to discard his social role and be more expressive of his own personality. It is here that the "neighborhood check" of the inspection agency is most frightening.

How does an inspector go about obtaining information from your neighbors? Frederick King of Hooper-Holmes candidly described the procedures used when a married man is suspected of an extramarital affair. "You go to a neighbor and establish rapport. Then you ask, 'What's your opinion of him as a family man?' This will usually elicit some hint—through the expression on his face or the way he answers. Then you start digging. You press him as far as he will go, and if he becomes recalcitrant you go somewhere else. If you go to enough people, you get it."

Do present laws give you any protection from these invasions of your privacy in regard to either the types of information stored and sold or the manner in which they are gathered? Probably not.

There is a tort cause of action for invasion of privacy, but instead of furnishing a broad protection device, the courts have established four subcategories of the right. Two of these subcategories related to the gathering and publication of personal material are "public disclosures of private facts" and "intrusion."

Public disclosure of private facts has not been actionable without a finding of "unreasonable publication," and publication to a "small group" would include the subscribers of a credit bureau or investigation agency, in much the same way that publication of defamation to such groups has been held privileged. The exemption is based on the same reasoning that sustains the conditional privilege to defamation and has the same dangers to the subject, who may not be able to correct falsehoods or defend himself against the consequences of having intimate details of his life revealed to the business community in his town.

Intrusion has been found most often in cases involving physical intrusion. Peering through windows, wiretapping, and eavesdropping seem to strike a more responsive chord in courts than does interviewing your neighbors or acquaintances. This tort is usually held to require an "extreme" or "shocking" violation of your privacy, and physical trespasses are most easily perceived as shocking.

In a New York Court of Appeals decision involving the author and General Motors, the court went beyond physical intrusions to include surveillance for an unreasonable time. However, even this decision makes actionable only those intrusions that are for the purpose of gathering confidential information. The question whether this doctrine covers investigations seeking to discover marital relationships, sexual habits, or housekeeping abilities has not been presented to the courts since the New York decision. However, three of the court's judges specifically stated that the four recognized subcategories of the right to privacy are neither frozen nor exhaustive.

If judicial protection against the collection and sale of overly personal information is limited, legislative protection is still nonexistent, even after passage of the Fair Credit Reporting Act. That statute may provide accuracy protection, but the Senate conferees refused to accept any provisions that would limit the types of data about you that can be gathered and sold.

The invasion of privacy should more accurately be called the invasion of self. The right to protect himself against an informational assault is basic to the inviolability of the individual. On the one hand, we recognize that an arrest record may haunt an individual, and there is precedent for a wrong arrest that is thrown out of court to be expunged from the record. But we have not yet recognized that the bits of information contained in dossiers kept on 105 million Americans may be just as decisive and just as damaging to their lives.

The individual's right to privacy of self is crucial to the functioning of our society. Suppose you walked into a courtroom and picked up a pamphlet relating everything the judge had ever done in his personal life. What would that information do to your interaction with that court? To some extent it is absolutely necessary to preserve barriers of privacy and protection about people's lives in order to permit ordinary interaction between people, an interaction that is to a significant degree based on trust.

Our Founding Fathers developed Constitutional safeguards in the Bill of Rights against the arbitrary authority of government. The rights against unreasonable search and seizure and against self-incrimination were examples of basic rights of privacy deemed critical for a free people. Generations passed and the country developed private organizations possessed of a potential for arbitrary authority not foreseen by the early Constitutional draftsmen. Most pervasive and embracing of these organizations is the modern corporation. Aggressive by its motivational nature, the corporation, in a credit-insurance economy spurred by computer gathering and retrieval efficiency, has created new dimensions to information as the currency of power over individuals. The secret gathering and use of such true or false information by any bank, finance company, insurance firm, other business concern, or employer place the individual in a world of unknowns. He is inhibited, has less power to speak out, is less free, and develops his own elaborate self-censorship.

What this costs in individual freedom and social justice cannot be measured. It can only be felt by the daily contacts with human beings in invisible chains reluctant to challenge or question what they believe to be wrong since, from some secret corporate dossier, irrelevant but damaging information may be brought to bear on them. The law and technology have provided the "dossier industry" with powerful tools to obtain and use information against people in an unjust way—whether knowingly or negligently. The defenseless citizen now requires specific rights to defend against and deter such invasions of privacy.

The Fair Credit Reporting Act will take steps toward solving some of the problems of accuracy in individual dossiers. For the first time, people may find out what credit bureaus and inspection agencies are saying about them, and they now have some means of correcting inaccuracies. But there are still no restraints on availability of this information or on the kinds of information gathered. Unless citizens are provided with an "information bill of rights" enabling them to see, correct, and know the uses of these dossiers, and to impose liability on wrongdoers, they can be reduced to a new form of computer-indentured slavery. The law must begin to teach the corporation about the inviolability of the individual as it has striven to teach the state.

What You Can Do

What can you do to protect yourself from your dossiers? The Fair Credit Reporting Act—when it becomes effective this month—allows you to protect yourself, but only if you take action. Let me use, as an example, the ordinary purchase of a life insurance policy. After you have decided to purchase some life insurance, you should first consider how much of an invasion of privacy you are willing to suffer in order to get it.

If a character investigation will be made, you are entitled under the act to be told automatically only that it will be made, and you are told that fact three days after the investigation has been ordered. Once you have been informed, it is up to you to take any further initiative. You must request in writing additional information. Once you have made that request, the insurer must reveal "the nature and scope" of the investigation. According to Representative Leonor K. Sullivan of Missouri, the House manager of the bill, this means they must tell you "all the items of questions which the investigation will cover. The best method of meeting this criterion is for the agency to give the consumer [you] a blank copy of any standardized form used." Unfortunately, all of this happens at least three days after you have signed the contract.

However, you can still insist on receiving this information before you sign the contract. Nothing in the law prevents you from obtaining this information earlier. The agent and the insurer are both anxious to sell you insurance. If you don't like too much snooping, demand that the scope of the investigation be revealed before you buy. If you think it is overzealous, complain to both the agent and the insurer and be specific about what you think is too intrusive. If the company will not listen to your complaints, find another one—or consider using group insurance. It is an interesting fact that group insurance does not usually require an investigation, and its use has been growing.

Once the privacy problems have been settled between you and the insurer, you must also worry about the accuracy of the report. If you are turned down or high-rated by the insurer, due in part to an investigation and report, the insurer must tell you that it was due to a report and give you the name and address of the agency making the report.

This entitles you to go to the agency and demand that it disclose "the nature and substance of all the information (except medical information) in its files." According to the House manager of the bill, this means disclosure of "all information in the file relevant to a prudent businessman's judgment" in reviewing an insurance application. If you have demanded a blank copy of the agency's standard form, you will know whether you have been told all that you are entitled to know.

If you disagree with any information in your file, tell the agency. The agency is then required to reinvestigate and reverify or delete the information. If they do not claim reverification, make certain that they delete the information, and then personally notify all prior recipients that it has been deleted. If they do claim reverification, ask how they reverified, from whom, and exactly what was said. Don't be satisfied with general answers because you cannot refute specific accusations with generalities. Although the act does not give you access on request to the names of those who lied about you, it does give you access to those names if you file suit under the act. Thus, the names cannot be protected forever. Many reputable agencies should see this and be willing to attempt to settle disputes with you without litigation. Even if the agency claims reverification, you can still have the item listed as disputed if it is in error, and file a brief statement outlining your side of the story.

A second common example is the credit card company that charges you improperly and will not answer your letter of complaint, but continues to bill you and threatens to ruin your credit rating if you don't pay. You can follow the procedure discussed earlier and wait until some other creditor turns you down, then go and get the file corrected. It may be better, however, to go and check your file at the local credit bureau periodically, so that you can correct errors before they are reported and you are turned down.

Remarks before the Public Affairs Symposium on "The Invasion of Privacy in Our Computerized Society."

Originally delivered February 7, 1971 Dickinson College, Carlisle, Pennsylvania.

I N A PERIOD of our history when rotting cities, hardened bureaucracies, racial tension, the Indochina War, pollution and consumer abuse form major lines of front-rank concerns, a Symposium on the invasions of privacy may appear to some to be an exercise in the leisure of the theory class. Not so. Such an impression misses a key set of preconditions for a more rational, democratic society; namely, that individuals must be protected against the uncontrolled accumulation of unverified information about their lives which is used often secretly as an extension of an uncheckable power against their basic rights.

Unfortunately, "invasion of privacy" is a poor choice of words inasmuch as it popularly connotes the fragile affectation of a cinema star under media coverage. What the phrase legally connotes, however, is an "invasion of the individual." Our Bill of Rights treats some of the protections against such invasion with clear gravity. The rights against unreasonable search and seizure and against self-incrimination, for example, were considered basic rights of privacy necessary for a freer people nearly two centuries ago. The worry of the founding fathers at that time was the need to protect citizens from government's arbitrary power. The recent memory of King George III helped give them this focus.

With the passage of generations, new institutions of arbitrary or oppressive power emerged called corporations. These institutions were not envisioned by the authors of our Constitution and consequently The Bill of Rights was directed only against "state action."

The complexity and velocity of the economy and its markets grew along with the large corporation. With this growth came an expotential increase in the points of vulnerability to privacy invasions of individual citizens. From the self-reliant, isolated farmer to the inter-dependent citizen-consumer in an urban, credit, bureaucratic, employed society reflects in one simplified spectrum this transition to the "dossier society."

It is hardly necessary to emphasize that governmental intrusions are still enjoying a bullish growth, as witnessed by the current disclosures of the Army's spying on thousands of civilian Americans in and out of politics. Although much needs to be done about government dossier collecting and its uses, there is a deep cultural resentment and anger against such activity. Such is not nearly the case with corporate invasions of privacy, partly because of an effective business camouflaging of its scope and abuse, partly because the resistance against it produces more immediate and personal consequences for many more millions of Americans, and partly due to an absence of adequate laws to make any resistance or deterrence possible. The widespread deployment of computers to cheaply store and retrieve personal information has revolutionized this invasion into much larger orders of magnitude.

The "dossier industry" is booming as a result. There are 45 million files on Americans in the storage rooms of Retail Credit Company in Atlanta—the largest credit investigative bureau in the United States—not far beyond is Credit Data Corporation, the second largest, with 27 million files. These files contain information that covers an individual's job, associations, marital situation, personal habits and background gossip drawn from neighbors or anyone willing to talk to the credit bureau's investigator. Banks and insurance companies, particularly life and health insurance companies, collect intimate details themselves and obtain such files from the credit bureaus. Government agencies routinely reach into credit bureau's for information about individuals they are investigating. In fact, anyone posing as a "prospective employer" and willing to pay the $5 or $10 price can obtain one or more of these reports.

All institutions justify the need for such information to make accurate judgments about people they hire or sell services to in their business. Government has its own expandable rationales for needing similar information. Who and what checks the abuse of such information so as to deny individuals jobs, insurance, credit, and to inhibit the exercise of free speech, dissent and the other right of democratic citizens? Structurally, the potential for abuse is enormous—whether the abuse is in using the information for illegal or oppressive purposes or for prejudicially denying someone a service or employment. The millions of individuals on whom files are kept by the credit bureaus have had, with few exceptions, no right of access to their file to check its accuracy or include their rebuttals to gossips, slanders and plain lies. They have no power to learn of or control the use or transfer of such information to other business firms and government agencies. There is also no right to control what kinds of information can be placed into their dossiers.

Consider the case of Charles Green (a pseudonym), related to the Senate Banking and Currency Committee. Green was turned down for many jobs during a four-year period due to an "insurance inspection agency" report which (1) detailed how he had spit at a neighbor, (2) stated that his landlord at the same location disliked him, and (3) included the statement "Said to have been dishonorably discharged from the Army." Mr. Green's story was quite to the contrary. The "abused" neighbor was an elderly crank who complained about many young couples and even demanded that Charlie take off his shoes in his apartment to be quiet; further he never spat at her. The landlord wrote that Mr. Green was a "perfectly satisfactory tenant." He had been honorably discharged from the Army and had the papers to prove it.

Congressional hearing records are full of evidence of many inaccuracies, in dossiers, both investigative and machine error. Beyond this state of affairs is the pressure and even the premium placed on finding derogatory information. If inspectors have to make ten or fifteen reports a day, they have little time for checking accusations or hearsay information. Many inspection agencies and credit bureaus also hold their inspectors to a quota, or a certain percentage of derogatory reports, to remain in good standing. The existing law in most states provides a shield, called a conditional privilege, for credit bureaus and other commercial dossier collectors against suit by citizens for such slanderous information dispersal. Indeed, until the new Fair Credit Reporting Act, passed by Congress last year, goes into effect on April 25, 1971, the citizen is just about without any realistic defenses against such abuses. The FCRA is only the beginning of a citizen's remedy, however. It gives people the right to see their files (except medical information and sources of investigative information) in credit bureaus and inspection agencies and some ways to dispute or correct inaccuracies. But there are still no general or invokable controls over what is gathered, how it is used, to whom it is given or sold. The notorious "conditional privilege" still prevails in forty-seven states which protects the commercial firm from a liability action.

The weakness of available legal rights and remedies is more clearly illustrated by direct corporate snooping into employees or other people's personal lives without any color of commercial service. These corporate forays—and they occur with a far higher frequency than commonly believed—are most difficult to document, or even be aware of where pretexts are used. Legions of private and in-house detectives perform this work regularly for management. Except by personal observation, persuasive oral narrations, and some public cases, there is no body of evidence that details this practice. Our legal system doesn't look for it and the absence of effective discovery and substantive rights keeps down the number of court cases. Recently, some corporate invasions of privacy have been described in Congressional documents.

The cost of such company meddling is, in my judgment, devastating to the society. How many engineers, lawyers or scientists in industry choose to remain silent concerning unsafe products and practices, fraud on the consumer, corruption of regulatory actions or electoral politics, because of their concern that some personal or intimate information entirely irrelevant to these issues may be used against them. My experience with such employed professionals suggests that conditions are worsened or progress prevented owing to such concerns. I have been told by reliable corporate sources that personnel departments or higher management often collects such information on employees in order to deter employee expressions about workplace conditions or product safety. An elaborate personal set of antennae builds up a self-censorship by individuals enmeshed in invisible chains that stifle their initiatives and obligations as citizens. As the interdependence of peoples' lives with the political and economic system increases, the power of those who can engage in privacy invasion increases. For example, consumers are complaining more frequently about how an automobile dealer or other retailer threatens to "ruin their credit" if they don't stop complaining or defying him concerning an auto lemon or other defective product. Anyone with a modest knowledge of the efficiency of the dossier industry to widely transmit such information as the retailer wants to report knows that the retailer knows of what he speaks.

Clearly, the erosions of democratic rights come in many, daily, subtle forms without dramatic or historic upheavals. Such is the case in corporate invasions of privacy, now equipped with the computer. No one is more sensitive to the fact that information is the currency of power than the large corporation.

Because of corporate lobbying and power, elaborate laws exist to prevent the disclosure of company information under an umbrella of proprietary information or trade secrets. Corporations have developed shields against disclosure of far more than proprietary information. They have claimed privacy for the lethal pollutants dumped into the environment, thereby blocking federal government questionnaires from being issued to them to discover the amount, time and place of their pollution. Price-fixing, product design fixing (eg. the internal combustion engine) and other antitrust violations are elaborately screened from public view. So too is the funnelling of corporate funds into campaign coffers—a federal crime. So also are such diverse informations as the amount of fat and water added to processed meats or the substantiation, if any, of the advertising claims, or the way pesticides are oversold and alternative methods suppressed or research discouraged.

There is a very severe imbalance between individuals and organizations—both private and governmental. And when corporate and governmental power merges or converges into a corporate state or corporate socialism, the appeal for relief, for a preventive strategy against privacy invasions, becomes more urgent.

Basic to any change for the better is the development of legal rights which are self-executing on demand by an aggrieved citizen vis-a-vis the credit bureau, inspection agency or other company harboring or misusing such personal files. These rights can go toward access to, correction of, and some restrictions on use of such information. Additional rights would ease the ability of a citizen to sue for damages against a company misusing or abusing his dossier. The Fair Credit Reporting Act is likely to be in for a series of strengthening amendments as consumers and legislators react to the wider usage of the new though limited access rights provided for in the law. The Fair Credit Reporting Act requires users of reports to notify consumers of the name and address of the consumer reporting agency whenever the creditor, insuror or employer takes adverse action on the basis of the agency's report. Further, we must begin to develop the computer and its applications into an information utility that will serve or defend consumer and citizen interests. Such a utility, accessible to citizens, much as the telephone or electronic light outlet is today, would begin to redress the imbalance created by the one-sided use of the computers by business organizations on the other side of the market or employment aisle. The efficiency and safety of marketed products and services and the rights of employees in large organizations would be strongly advanced in this fusion of legal and computer reform.

There is no way a complex society as a whole or in its constituent parts can intelligently plan for a just society without detailed information. What is needed are greater rights of participation, initiative and control by citizens so that more can be beneficiaries and not victims of such information.

If people would pause once in a while and ask themselves why they condone or why they do not speak out, when to do the opposite would save lives, avoid injuries and disease and prevent the unjust taking of people's rights, perhaps they would develop a more sensitive appreciation for greater safeguards against the mounting privacy invasion.

on the media

A Response to Robert W. McChesney's Proposals for Media Reform

Originally appeared in Boston Review, *Summer 1998.*

I F WE ARE TO reconfigure the media so that it expands, deepens, enlightens, and enriches democracy, we have to think big thoughts. Consider our current media: corporate-concentrated, saturated with trivialization and entertainment. To get from this status quo to a deliberative information sector that enlivens as well as engages will require both bold proposals for structural reform and a mobilized constituency. Robert McChesney is right: we cannot slip into defeatist realism, deluding ourselves about the potential importance of modest initiatives that do not fundamentally restructure the media industry.

In addressing the issue of media concentration, it is natural to turn to antitrust policy, despite the inadequacy of existing statutes. Consider several examples. For antitrust regulators, the fact that cable consumers have 50 or 60 channels from which to choose may in itself be evidence that there is sufficient broadcasting competition. Likewise with the concepts of "potential competition" and "barriers to entry." In antitrust law and practice, a merger that will highly concentrate a market may be permitted if it is determined that new competitors can easily enter the market. The "potential competition," it is typically held, will be enough incentive for dominant market players to keep prices low. This logic is frequently used to rational-ize mergers that should be prevented, but in reality "potential competi-tion" does little to encourage existing broadcasters to air more diverse viewpoints.

The problem goes beyond the horrendous antitrust case law of the last two decades, however: antitrust asks the wrong questions to promote truly democratic media. Concentrated media markets could be more easily bro-ken up through direct statute and regulation by the Federal Communications Commission, as was the case until recently with the tight limits on how many television and radio outlets could be owned by a single entity. This is not to deny a role for antitrust in democratizing the media. Digital broadcasting satellite (DBS) technologies offer the possibility of new conduit competitors, but TCI and Rupert Murdoch are racing to gob-ble up the new satellites. Antitrust policy and enforcement can help in this area.

Perhaps the most important role for antitrust, though, is in enabling the Internet and digital technologies to achieve their democratic promise. In a host of ways, Microsoft is seeking to leverage its control over computer operating systems to gain control over Internet content and transactions. Similarly, Microsoft and the Baby Bells in different ways hope to control the technologies that physically connect homes and businesses to the Internet. Antitrust enforcement should be able to stop these companies from exert-ing a chokehold on the Internet, and at the same time help ensure that the guiding concepts for digital technologies are interoperability and open architecture.

McChesney is right to tweak utopians who think the promise of freedom is an inherent feature of the Internet, but he is too quick to dismiss its importance. We need to prevent the corporate capture of the Internet, and doing so will require us to focus our attention on the structure of digital industries. Ensuring broad access to the Internet is not enough; we cannot assume that the democratization of traditional media will automatically have good results. And we need to take advantage of the opportunities afforded by the Internet.[1] While it may not be salvation, it offers new tele-casting opportunities, for example, at minimal cost. It also provides inter-active possibilities unlike any afforded by traditional broadcasting.

Still, for the foreseeable future, at least, it will be important to have diverse, noncommercial alternatives in the traditional broadcasting media. Between McChesney's two categories of noncommercial programming—private, independent non-profits and public television—both of which

merit strong support—there is space for public, nongovernmental broadcasting: programs and networks produced and operated by government-
chartered, citizen membership organizations.

The public owns the airwaves. We lease it, 24 hours a day, 365 days a year,
to broadcasters who pay no rent. The government could take back an hour
a day of prime-time television and drive-time radio from each broadcaster,
and grant it to a government-chartered, nonprofit citizen membership
organization. The organization, Audience Network, governed by a board of
directors elected from members who pay small dues, could sell some of the
television and radio time back to broadcasters to raise funds, and use the
proceeds to produce programming.[2] With digital technologies making possible the airing of five or six times the number of existing over-the-air
channels, the government could take back whole channels and allocate them
to the Audience Network.

Similarly, when cities negotiate monopoly contracts with cable companies, they could demand the companies include billing inserts that invite
consumers to join a local Cable Action Group that would operate a local
Audience Channel, well-funded and equipped by the cable company. Such
a group would serve a dual purpose: operating the local channel and organizing consumers into a mobilized interest group to advocate for pro-consumer and pro-democracy media policy. Cable Action Groups must be just
part of a much broader strategy to develop a permanently mobilized constituency for fundamental media reform.

In the absence of a mobilized constituency, even structural reforms will
inevitably fall short of achieving their democratic purposes. Corporate
interests will reassert themselves (or new corporate interests will arise) to
corrupt even a decentralized media, and eventually chip away at the structural limitations on media concentration.

Notes

1   See www.essential.org for some early innovations in using the Internet to advance civic
     debate.

2   For a fuller discussion of Audience Network, see Ralph Nader and C. Riley, "Oh, Say
     Can You See: A Broadcast Network for the Audience," Journal of Law and Politics 5,
     no. 1 (1988).

Microradio: Opening the
Airwaves for More Democracy

Originally appeared in The *(Albany)* Times Union, *July 17, 1999.*

EVER WONDER WHY radio has become so canned, flat and insipid, bereft of local news, stuffed with commercials, mercantile values and the same old, tired junk, not to mention the downright offensiveness of Howard Stern and the other shock jocks?

First, for years, more than 90 percent of all radio time has been composed of entertainment (music) and advertisements. In addition, in the last three years, diversity in radio station ownership has been decreasing. The Telecommunications Act of 1996 raised the number of radio outlets that any single corporation may own in any market, which loosed a flood of radio company mergers.

So, station ownership is not only concentrated in fewer corporate hands, but formulaic programming takes the few reporters left and local coverage to the back seat. Two conglomerates—Chancellor Media Corp. and Clear Channel Communications Inc.—own more than 400 radio stations each, all over the country. One woman complained about the sameness of Cleveland radio, following two huge radio company mergers: "It's as though McDonald's bought every restaurant in town and all you could get was a Big Mac."

The purpose of these corporate radio mega-conglomerates is to maximize profits by reducing costs of reporters and editors, and not to enrich public discourse or cover the news in their areas. Market forces have led to anything but vigorous radio culture, or thoughtful programming that gives voice to the community.

In their quest for larger audiences, more advertising and greater profits, commercial broadcasters cater to the basest standards, with ever more blatant effusions of crassness, sex talk and nihilism. Commercial rewards drive the creation, production and marketing of ever more Howard Sterns, Greasemans and other deplorable shows.

Inevitably, this leads to a coarsening of our culture, which has particularly harmful effects on children.

Even "public" radio is becoming commercialized. National Public Radio now carries many ever longer "underwriting messages"—which are a form of advertisement.

Meanwhile, the public is mostly silent on the airwaves that we legally own.

Radio is supposed to serve the ends and purposes of the First Amendment; to protect public discourse, which is essential to our form of democratic self-government.

But the current regulatory regime for radio thwarts the First Amendment rights and interests of most Americans. We speak little, if at all, on our own airwaves, while the wealthy may speak through radio by controlling who uses their stations and for what purposes.

What good is freedom of speech if nobody can afford it? Is speech truly free if only the wealthy can buy it?

Here's the good news: At last, the Federal Communications Commission may come to the rescue. Right now, the FCC is considering whether to set up noncommercial low-power FM (LPFM) radio stations of up to 100 watts, with a range of a few miles. That's a big deal. Imagine the new voices that could flourish on these micro-stations—service and advocacy groups, universities, community and civic organizations, ethnic groups, arts organizations, seniors groups and others.

They could really liven up the radio dial. They could give us some choices.

But authorizing LPFM service is not enough. The FCC should allocate more spectrum for low-power radio broadcasting and introduce it when radio switches from analog to digital signals. These small stations could enrich the public's understanding of civic issues and social problems. They could be a modest but important step toward more cohesive communities, a renewed public discourse and a richer and more realistic culture. It is not often that a federal agency could achieve so much with so little.

Americans are drowning in a sea of commercialism. Americans are immersed in advertisements, junk mail, junk faxes, TV and radio ads, telemarketing, billboards and more. There are ads in schools, airport lounges, doctors offices, hospitals, convenience stores, toilet stalls, on the Internet, beach sand, floors of supermarkets, and countless other places.

Advertisers even tried, unsuccessfully, to put ads in space and on postage stamps. Tom Vanderbilt, author of *The Sneaker Book*, writes of advertisers' effort to "hang a jingle in front of America's every waking moment."

Three cheers for the Microradio Empowerment Coalition, a coalition of microradio stations, community and civic groups, organizations and individuals, which is working to make noncommercial LPFM radio a reality.

There is a profound need for public spaces in which people can talk to one another. We don't need more advertising talking at us. Can't we have just a few commercial-free sanctuaries? Is that too much to ask?

The FCC ought to use its authority to establish noncommercial LPFM stations to build a stronger democracy in America, and thus serve a vision grander than the profit-driven trivialization of most of the broadcasting and advertising industries. The FCC was not intended merely to protect the speech rights of broadcasters, advertisers and the wealthy. It ought to uphold and protect the public's First Amendment interests in radio, to rededicate this medium to the service of American democracy. Non-commercial LPFM radio is one modest step toward that goal.

Public is Not Served by Media's Refusal to Ask Specific Questions

Originally appeared on Knight Ridder/Tribune News Service, February 1, 2000.

THE MAJOR PRESIDENTIAL candidates are grinding through the various TV and radio press interviews and the town meetings with their three-minute daily, redundant speeches and highly predictable replies to mostly predictable questions. That is what their advance people are supposed to accomplish.

But what is remarkable is that both the national and the local TV questioners give them this predictability without the candidates even asking. Every four years, campaigns revolve around a half-dozen issues that are drably questioned and drearily answered. This year, some of the main issues are education, taxes, Social Security, Medicare and health insurance.

Under education the sub issues are class size, teacher salaries, computer linkups and vouchers. Notice the gap that envelopes what kind of education the children deserve. Wouldn't a question about the need for civic education to develop both the civic skills and motivation to participate in a democratic civil society advance the election year enlightenment? Never asked.

Under taxes the sub issues are reducing tax rates and returning alleged surpluses back to the taxpayers. Wouldn't questions about a different kind of tax system, such as a wealth tax or a pollution tax be useful? And how about asking about the candidates' take on taxpayer assets such as the public lands, government giveaways to big drug companies of taxpayer funded and developed medicines, or the massive bonanzas known as corporate welfare?

Then there are the questions that could lead to some action. For example, the leaders of both parties in Congress have declined to place the voting records of each member of the House and the Senate on the Internet in clearly retrievable fashion. Asking whether the candidates favor this important voter access to their representatives' actual performance in Congress, in contrast to their propaganda and sugary slogans, might quickly get these votes online to invigorate and make concrete election-year evaluations. Never asked.

Even the questions from the town meetings, apart from those that are planted, often reflect the narrow covey of "issues" that the candidates and the ditto media trumpet. There is some reluctance among citizens not to stray from the familiar subjects in the news, when they stand to ask.

Yet there are numerous polls that show people want all kinds of changes from the existing status quo; for example, they want much stronger enforcement against environmental, consumer and workplace crimes and frauds by corporations. In a phrase, people want the fairness that comes from basic corporate reform.

The media are supposed to be able to ask these fundamental questions about the concentration of power and wealth and its effect on peoples' everyday lives. But these "power questions" are never asked. Nor are questions offered about ways to give people more leverage in their roles as voters, workers, taxpayers, consumers and small saver-investors.

Too much power in the hands of the few has further weakened our democracy in the last 20 years. People need stronger civic tools to band together, learn together and act together to make the Big Boys behave.

One group, the Florence Fund, is trying to do something about raising fundamental issues about corporate power. It is placing notices in newspapers that replace myths with facts and pose actual questions for the candidates.

One set of questions came from prize-winning, veteran reporter, Morton Mintz who spent many years at the *Washington Post*. Mr. Mintz's sample questions and compelling observations by others about this year's campaigns and candidates can be accessed on the Internet at TomPaine.com: Money and Politics, Environment, Media Criticism, History.

At the least, the Florence Fund's efforts should make this election year more interesting and keep fewer citizens from sending the message, "Wake us up when it's over."

TV News Failing in Its Mission

Originally appeared in The Charleston Gazette, *August 23, 1996.*

CAN THE LATE EVENING television news get any worse? I put this question recently to some TV news reporters who rolled their eyes and together said, "not much." Three national consulting firms have convinced most local television executives that the formula of pursuing tragedy (street crime and natural disasters) and trivia (chitchat, fluff and tidbits) produces profits.

These late news programs are profitable, but are they "news?" Once you subtract the time for commercials, sports, weather and chitchat, there is not much time left for news.

And what dominates the news night after night? Almost typical was the news broadcast on the night of Sept. 20, 1995, when WRC-TV in Washington devoted 69 percent of its late-night newscast to street crime, violence, disasters and "fluff." Fluff, defined as anchor chatter, teasers, celebrity stories or "factoids" such as "Cat stuck in a septic tank" amounted to about 30 percent of the newscast.

Between April 1995 and February 1996, my associate, Hayden Roberts, watched at random 30 Washington local television news shows shown either at 11 p.m. or 10 p.m. He found that 75 percent of the stories on the four network affiliates were either about violent crimes or disasters. Over half the newscasts surveyed led with stories involving assault, robbery or homicide.

A visiting Martian watching these newscasts would think that little else happens in Washington except street crimes, disasters, movies, weather and sports. This, after all, is the nation's capital where events in the business, government, educational, labor and civic arenas occur regularly. Yet, night after night, the newscasts open with the police blotter and grisly scenes and sirens which meet part of the consulting firms' formula: "If it bleeds, it leads." Stories about violence, sex, addiction and distant storms provide the action that the camera thrives on.

On the other hand, the negative side of the consultants' formula—"If it thinks, it stinks"—leaves out a great deal of what used to be considered news.

The best investigative segments are reserved for the ratings sweeps to get the largest audience for advertisers. If solid investigative pieces are good for ratings periods, why not run them throughout the year? The stations prefer not to spend the money on the camera crews, reporters and other related expenses, that's why.

Max Frankel, former editor and now columnist for the *New York Times*, has devoted three full columns in the past year alone to poor local news coverage. In one article, he wrote: "I think that too few of the owners look up from the bottom line to actually watch what is offered the community in their name. They should be challenged to defend their newscasts and prove their respect for the community." Well said. Now, let the stations hear more from the viewers.

Let's Put the Audience on the Air

Originally appeared in Chicago Tribune, May 27, 1987.

THE HOUSE SUBCOMMITTEE on Telecommunications and Finance recently held hearings on the impact of mergers, acquisitions and changes of management on the national television networks' news operations.

This subcommittee effort was urgently needed. By gathering such information, Congress will be better prepared to assume responsibility for the much-neglected "public interest standard" in the 1934 Communications Act upon which the system of broadcast regulation is supposed to rest. The 100th Congress is aware that the Federal Communications Commission's misplaced faith in undefined "market forces" has made the flow of information in this country totally dependent on the drive by a few companies to maximize profits. Further congressional efforts, however, should focus on how best to defend the public's 1st Amendment right to a wide variety of information from diverse and opposing sources. The drive to pursue policies which, in effect, limit what little public voice exists in the use of the public's airwaves must be halted.

The 1st Amendment recognizes communication among citizens as the cornerstone of our democratic form of government. Yet under the current system, ordinary citizens can speak to their neighbors but not to millions of their fellow Americans through the electronic media without paying a giant toll and obtaining the permission of large corporations. On the other hand, the powerful few—Capital Cities/ABC, CBS, General Electric (NBC), Westinghouse, Post-Newsweek—can use their licenses to command national audiences and decide the price, frequency and use of communications systems with a global reach.

This gross inequality of electronic access through the workings of exclusive license authorities forces the public to rely on a few corporations' perceptions of society, politics, the arts and the public itself. A democracy does not thrive when information sources, values and access remain so limited. Congress is justifiably concerned about the impact of merger mania on the electronic press.

While broadcasters have the opportunity to assert their 1st Amendment right to shield them from government interference, over the last six years little time or attention has been given to furthering a comprehensive definition of the public interest 1st Amendment right.

Congress must oversee the broadcast system by delicately balancing the twin dangers of government censorship and government abdication that might result in irresponsible corporate control of public airwaves. Unfortunately, for 50 years the scales have been tipped in the broadcasters' favor; the minimal obligations imposed on broadcasters have never been equal to the ever-increasing value, in terms of money and influence, that a broadcast license generates. It is time for the public to receive a more reciprocal benefit from the lucrative use of the airwaves licenses without fee to broadcasting companies.

With access to the airwaves and the ability to act as an organized community, the public could finally exercise its 1st Amendment rights. To organize and mobilize the audience, Congress could create the framework for a national membership institution of viewers and listeners—let us call this institution the Audience Network. Any citizen over 16 who paid a minimum amount, say $10 a year, could be a member of the nonprofit Audience Network. The group wouldn't cost the taxpayers a dime. Through local and national chapters, Audience Network would be run democratically, with members electing a board of directors who would see that appropriate studios with skilled producers and reports would be operating.

The group's primary access asset would be airtime granted by Congress: a prime-time hour a day on each commercial radio and television station. During its time slot, the Audience Network could air a variety of cultural, political, entertainment, scientific or other programs that it produced or obtained. It could also provide central production facilities and act as a time broker for other nonprofit groups that wished to produce and air programs.

Audience Network would represent the interests of its members before the FCC, the courts and Congress itself—wherever broadcasting policy is made. With a full-time staff, Audience Network could, for example, advocate broadcast reform measures or evaluate children's programming on local stations.

The Audience Network, in short, could serve as a self-funded, independent, ongoing communications link between viewers and listeners. Returning a modest portion of the public's airwaves to the public would allow the audience—not the government or private business—to give itself what it wants and needs.

Must Candidates Avoid Free TV?

Originally appeared in The New York Times, *October 8, 1984.*

T HE REAGAN-BUSH and Mondale-Ferraro campaigns are pouring millions of dollars into paid radio and television spots while ignoring broadcasters' invitations to expound their views for free. This is a foolishly cautious attitude, self-defeating for the candidates and bad for the quality of our national campaigns.

The three morning network shows—*Good Morning America, Today* and CBS *Morning News*—have offered standing invitations to all four candidates. None of them have appeared on *Good Morning America*. Walter F. Mondale and Geraldine A. Ferraro have appeared on *Today* but have not responded to return invitations. Only George Bush has been on the CBS *Morning News,* although all four could have. On the Sunday news-interview shows, only Mrs. Ferraro appeared on ABC's *This Week With David Brinkley* though all four have standing invitations. Mr. Bush appeared on *Meet the Press,* but Mr. Mondale and Mrs. Ferraro have declined to do so. All four have been invited on *Face the Nation;* only Mr. Bush accepted. Cable News Network says all four have "pretty much" open invitations with little response. The weekday *Phil Donahue* show, which has ten million viewers and no equal time requirement, invited all four candidates to appear separately after the party conventions. None have accepted. The *MacNeil/Lehrer Newshour* has also offered invitations to all four candidates, with no acceptances. None has appeared on *ABC News Nightline*. The nightly network news shows want interviews with the candidates but have had difficulty in finding takers. *60 Minutes* wanted to tape four-hour interviews with each pair of candidates. Transcripts of the taped interviews would be made public and an edited one-hour selection would be aired. Mr. Mondale accepted, according to the producer of *60 Minutes*, Don Hewitt, but snarled communications with the Mondale press office aborted negotiations with the White House. Mr. Hewitt also said that he offered Geraldine Ferraro the large part of one Sunday show shortly after she was nominated, but the Mondale campaign declined.

What is going on here? Campaign strategists are more comfortable with controlled media, such as paid advertisements and photo opportunities. They have found it easier to campaign on image, symbol and personality than on the issues or their records. They also worry about making gaffes, about insufficient preparation time and about upsetting questions by interviewers and audience participants. Sometimes there are logistical reasons to decline, but television technology is rapidly overcoming those obstacles. In some cases, these reasons cannot be entirely dismissed. But as a rationale for wholesale avoidance of free national media, they have the ring of shoddy excuses. As incumbents who are leading by a sizeable margin, President Reagan and Vice President Bush are understandably pursuing a tactic of minimal risk. But Mr. Mondale has little to risk, if he believes his standing in the polls. Further, his principal liability is that many Americans do not know him. It's not surprising: he generally appears for half a minute on the nightly news, often reading from a statement. His national advertising campaign does not feature him but focuses instead on specific failures of the Reagan Administration. Were he to respond to offers of free media, the blur that is Walter Mondale in the minds of millions of Americans, particularly the younger generation, might well be replaced with an experienced, witty candidate with a solid record and appealing message. Were he to accept these invitations, his campaign could give the green light for Mrs. Ferraro to do the same. If Mr. Mondale and Mrs. Ferraro were to appear on Phil Donahue's program, for example, ten million viewers could see a kind of town meeting on the air—without scripts, teleprompters, editing and thirty-second time limits. A better use of free media would help slow the deteriorating quality of presidential campaigning and meet the voters' need for information. The candidates can hardly afford to refuse.

RALPH NADER is a consumer advocate, a lawyer, and an author.

Born in Winsted, Connecticut on February 27, 1934, Nader received an AB magna cum laude from Princeton University in 1955, and in 1958 he received a LLB with distinction from Harvard University.

His career began as a lawyer in Hartford, Connecticut in 1959 and from 1961-63 he lectured on history and government at the University of Hartford. In 1965-66 he received the Nieman Fellows award and was named one of ten Outstanding Young Men of Year by the U.S. Junior Chamber of Commerce in 1967. He later returned to Princeton as a lecturer, and he continues to speak at colleges and universities across the United States.

As a consumer advocate he has founded many organizations including the Center for Study of Responsive Law, the Public Interest Research Groups (PIRGs), the Center for Auto Safety, Public Citizen, Clean Water Action Project, the Disability Rights Center, the Pension Rights Center, the Project for Corporate Responsibility and *The Multinational Monitor* (a monthly magazine).

BARBARA EHRENREICH is the author of many books, including *Blood Rites: Origins and History of the Passions of War* and *Fear of Falling: The Inner Life of the Middle Class.*